Archaeology of Domestic Landscapes of the Enslaved in the Caribbean

Florida Museum of Natural History: Ripley P. Bullen Series

FLORIDA MUSEUM

ARCHAEOLOGY OF DOMESTIC LANDSCAPES OF THE ENSLAVED IN THE CARIBBEAN

Edited by
James A. Delle and Elizabeth C. Clay

University of Florida Press
Gainesville

Publication of this paperback edition made possible by a Sustaining the Humanities through the American Rescue Plan grant from the National Endowment for the Humanities.

First cloth printing, 2019
First paperback printing, 2022

27 26 25 24 23 22   6 5 4 3 2 1

Library of Congress Cataloging-in-Publication Data
Names: Delle, James A., editor. | Clay, Elizabeth C., editor.
Title: Archaeology of domestic landscapes of the enslaved in the Caribbean /
    edited by James A. Delle and Elizabeth C. Clay.
Other titles: Ripley P. Bullen series.
Description: Gainesville : University of Florida Press, 2019. | Series:
    Florida Museum of Natural History: Ripley P. Bullen series | Includes
    bibliographical references and index.
Identifiers: LCCN 2018061105 | ISBN 9781683400912 (cloth) | ISBN 9781683402695 (pbk.)
Subjects: LCSH: Slavery—Caribbean Area—History. | Archaeology and
    history—Caribbean Area. | Excavations (Archaeology)—Caribbean Area. |
    Caribbean Area—History.
Classification: LCC HT1071 .A735 2019 | DDC 306.3/6209729—dc23
LC record available at https://lccn.loc.gov/2018061105

UF PRESS
UNIVERSITY
OF FLORIDA

University of Florida Press
2046 NE Waldo Road
Suite 2100
Gainesville, FL 32609
http://upress.ufl.edu

Contents

List of Figures   vii
List of Tables   xi

1. Household, Village, and Landscape: The Built Environments of
   Slavery in the Caribbean   1
   Elizabeth C. Clay and James A. Delle

2. An Examination of Housing for Enslaved and Free Blacks on Sugar
   and Cotton Plantations on the Southeast Peninsula of St. Kitts   19
   Todd M. Ahlman

3. The Present Past: The Design Legacy of Laborers' Housing in the
   Landscape of Vernacular Architecture on Nevis   42
   Marco Meniketti

4. Building a Better Village? Transformations in French West Indian
   Slave Village Architecture from the Ancien Régime to
   Emancipation   66
   Kenneth G. Kelly

5. Asymmetric Architectures of Enslaved People in Jamaica: An
   Archaeological Study of Household Variation at Good Hope
   Estate   87
   Hayden F. Bassett

6. Variation within the Village: Housing Enslaved Laborers on Coffee
   Plantations in Jamaica   116
   James A. Delle and Kristen R. Fellows

7. Humanitarian Reform, Model Cottages, and the Habitational
   Landscape of Slavery on a Bahama Island   141
   Allan D. Meyers

8. Landscape and Labor on the Periphery: Built Environments of Slavery in Nineteenth-Century French Guiana 166
Elizabeth C. Clay

9. Royal Enslaved Afro-Caribbeans in Christiansted: Exploring the Archaeology of Enslavement in a Caribbean City 188
Alicia Odewale and Meredith D. Hardy

10. Households and Dwelling Practices at the Cabrits Garrison Laborer Village 217
Zachary J. M. Beier

11. Built Environments: Slavery, Materiality, and Usable Pasts 238
Mark W. Hauser

References 249
List of Contributors 275
Index 277

Figures

2.1. Location of St. Kitts and sites mentioned in the chapter   20

2.2. An 1846 painting of Brimstone Hill Fortress by Lt. William Mason Inglis   26

2.3. Early twentieth-century postcards of Kittitian housing by A. Moure Losada   27

2.4. Images of early twentieth-century Kittitian housing   28

2.5. Plan view map of a small cotton plantation   31

2.6. Plan view map of a large sugar plantation   33

2.7. Plan view map of a sugar plantation   35

3.1. Hypothetical reconstruction of a laborer's house   51

3.2. Closeup image from the Clarke Estate map   51

3.3. House platforms and terrace walls at the Morgan's Village site on Nevis   57

3.4. A modern image of the manner in which stones are still used to support small houses without foundations   62

4.1. Map of Guadeloupe and Martinique   69

4.2. Plan of Grande Pointe   71

4.3. Plan of La Mahaudière   72

4.4. Plan of Crève Coeur   76

4.5. Masonry houses at Anse Latouche   79

4.6. Morne Patate   80

4.7. House on pilings   82

4.8. Detail of pilings   83

4.9. "Improved" housing at Trois Ilets   85

5.1. Location of Good Hope Estate in Trelawny Parish, Jamaica 89

5.2. Section of 1794 Schroeter plat depicting the Good Hope slave village 90

5.3. Map of the Good Hope Great House and domestic servants' village 91

5.4. Archaeological site plan of Village 1 at Good Hope 94

5.5. Reconstruction of Good Hope slave village site plan based on geostatistical analysis of shovel test pit survey data and stratigraphic sampling 95

5.6. Archaeological site plan of Village 2 96

5.7. Site plan of rear yard of the Tharp town house 98

5.8. Scatterplot of length and width for slave housing excavated in plantation contexts in Jamaica 102

5.9. Spatial distribution of average ceramic sherd size in Village 1 at Good Hope and interpretation of geostatistical results 105

5.10. Spatial distribution of average ceramic sherd size in the Tharp House rear yard 109

5.11. Ceramic scaling at the multi-dwelling household in Village 1 and solitary household of domestic servants in Village 2 at Good Hope 111

5.12. Functional analysis of domestic artifact assemblages from Villages 1 and 2 at Good Hope 112

6.1. Plan view of the village of Marshall's Pen 121

6.2. Negro House Hill as it appeared in 1999 129

6.3. House Area 6 under excavation 132

6.4. A selection of nails recovered from House Area 6 133

6.5. A board house in Porus 133

6.6. House Area 1 under excavation 135

6.7. A fragment of Spanish wall in situ in House Area 1 135

6.8. A Spanish wall house in Porus 136

6.9. Construction detail of a Spanish wall house in Porus 136

6.10. House Area 2 under excavation 137

7.1. Location of Newfield Plantation archaeological sites at southeastern end of Cat Island   149

7.2. Main complex at Newfield Plantation with inset showing details of a duplex structure   151

7.3. Plans of John Wood's second-class cottages compared to plans of hall-and-parlor dwellings   154

7.4. Plan of the Gambier Bluff site based on a 2016 field survey   156

7.5. A single-room cabin at the Gambier Bluff site   157

7.6. Relationship between house size and proximity to the main house at the Newfield estate   159

7.7. Recording the north exterior doorway of Structure 1 at the Gambier Bluff site   161

8.1. The circum-Caribbean location of French Guiana   167

8.2. The port of Cayenne in the nineteenth century   168

8.3. Postcard showing a clove plantation in Zanzibar, East Africa   171

8.4. Roura, the center of the clove industry in the nineteenth century and the site of Habitations la Grande Marée and la Caroline   175

8.5. Elevated platform, slave quarter, paths, and waterway at Habitation la Grande Marée   176

8.6. House 2 at Habitation la Grande Marée   177

8.7. Coins dated 1818 and 1846 recovered at House 2 at Habitation la Grande Marée   178

8.8. Monumental stone staircase at Habitation la Caroline   180

8.9. Elevated platform and roadway, slave quarter, paths, and canal at Habitation la Caroline   181

8.10. Corner of stone house foundation visible on surface at Habitation la Caroline   181

8.11. Nineteenth-century illustration of housing for the enslaved at a plantation in Cayenne   185

9.1. Map of six historic structures included in Christiansted National Historic Site, St. Croix   192

9.2. A 1779 map of the Danish West India and Guinea Company Warehouse   193

9.3. Circa 1803 plan of the Danish West India and Guinea Company warehouse 195

9.4. Drawing by Frederik von Scholten entitled "Bitling near West-End, Santa Cruz Women," St. Croix, ca. 1844 199

9.5. Bar graph of frequency of natural disasters in the Danish West Indies 1720–1871 202

9.6. Map of 2015–2016 excavation units and shovel tests 208

9.7. Bar graph showing artifact frequency by excavation unit 209

9.8. Metal artifacts recovered from Units C and F 210

9.9. Possible base of a baking oven in Unit F that is filled with and surrounded by gray ash 211

10.1. View looking north along the coastline of Portsmouth and Prince Rupert's Bay in Dominica 218

10.2. Map of Dominica and its location in the eastern Caribbean 222

10.3. Maps featuring the Cabrits Garrison laborer village, 1791, 1792, 1799, and 1812 225

10.4. Survey map of the Cabrits Garrison laborer village highlighting location of excavated domestic contexts and types of settlement features 227

10.5. Plan map of Structure 1 in the Cabrits Garrison laborer village and Structure 1 in the village 231

10.6. Plan map of Structure 2 in the Cabrits Garrison laborer village and view looking south over the platform for Structure 2 234

Tables

3.1. Dimensions of house platforms at Morgan's Village   56

5.1. Dimensions of published slave housing excavated in plantation contexts in Jamaica to date   101

9.1. Total artifact inventory for 2015–2016 excavations   209

9.2. Count and weight of artifact categories by excavation unit (percent)   210

1

Household, Village, and Landscape

The Built Environments of Slavery in the Caribbean

ELIZABETH C. CLAY AND JAMES A. DELLE

Over the course of the past generation, an increasing number of archaeological studies have focused on the material world of enslaved people in the Caribbean. That world was dominated for several centuries by plantation agriculture, a pursuit that created vast wealth through the forced migration and coerced labor of enslaved African people. Building on the pioneering work of Lydia Pulsipher (1994), Mac Goodwin (Pulsipher and Goodwin 1982), Douglas Armstrong (1985, 1990), Barry Higman (1974), and Michael Craton (1978) and influenced by early work conducted on plantation sites in the American South (e.g., Fairbanks 1974; Singleton 1980, 1985a, 1985b; Moore 1985), Caribbean historical archaeology has largely focused on the excavation and analysis of the domestic sites of the enslaved, the people who constituted the vast majority of the population of the Caribbean world and yet profited least—and suffered most—from a deeply insidious economic system based on a racialized social order.

The landscapes and built environments of enslaved laborers in the Caribbean are rightly an important focus of archaeological study in the region. Significant work has been done on the analysis of the "small finds" material culture recovered from enslaved habitation sites (e.g., Hauser 2007, 2011; Galle 2011; Bates 2016) and on evidence of foodways (e.g., Wilkie and Farnsworth 2005; Wallman 2014) and burial practices (e.g., Handler and Lange 1978; Delle and Fellows 2014). However, with a few notable exceptions that focused on the construction and use of houses (e.g., Higman 1998; Pulsipher and Goodwin 2001), the studies that have dealt with the built environment of the plantation system have tended to

2 · Elizabeth C. Clay and James A. Delle

emphasize the macro scale, examining landscapes from a plantationwide or even islandwide perspective (e.g., Delle 1994, 1998; Armstrong and Kelly 2000; Hicks 2007b).

This volume focuses on the structures and other constructed features that made up the living quarters and villages that housed enslaved Africans and their descendants in a number of Caribbean contexts, including on plantations, in urban areas, and on military installations. Our archaeological approach to domestic landscapes builds on the definition of the built environment Suzanne Spencer-Wood (2010, 507) has proposed: "structures constructed on and into land, including buildings, roads, bridges, and patios." However, we broaden this definition to include spaces that may or may not have been constructed with durable materials but were created through daily practices that can be identified archaeologically. Exterior domestic spaces, including yards and gardens, were equally if not more important to daily life in enslaved communities. In many of the settings described herein, these areas were in fact built through the daily sweeping of dirt yards and the use of stone to construct animal pens and gardens or walls that demarcated kinship groups or other boundaries in the broader slave village. These spaces certainly fall within our classification of the built environments of enslaved people.

Through the analysis of archaeological evidence collected from a wide range of sites across the Caribbean region, this volume examines the diversity of living environments that enslaved people inhabited in the Caribbean in the eighteenth and nineteenth centuries. Archaeological investigation of domestic architecture and artifacts illuminates the nature of household organization, fundamental changes in settlement patterns, and the ways that power was invariably linked with the material arrangements of space among the enslaved people who lived and worked throughout the region. While the term "built environments of slavery" could be applied broadly to the entirety of contexts under study in this volume (e.g., plantation complexes, urban port cities, military fortifications), we are interested primarily in living environments because this is the realm where enslaved peoples were able to exercise the most self-determination, regardless of whether or not they played a direct role in designing or constructing the built features that framed their lives. For the enslaved, domestic areas inevitably meant living spaces planters created to impose labor discipline upon enslaved workers and to define familial and social relations and areas that were internal to the slave community such as spaces for growing supplemental crops and gathering informally. This relationship between social control and autonomy is one of the particularities of the built environments of slavery that the authors in this volume discuss.

Although research in the region has provided a considerable amount of data at the household level, much of this work is biased toward artifact analyses. This has resulted in a lack of understanding regarding the considerations that went into constructing and inhabiting households, although some notable exceptions do directly address architectural description (Armstrong 1990; Armstrong and Kelly 2000; Farnsworth 2001). Therefore, this volume brings together case studies from across the Caribbean region to highlight architectural variability among enslaved laborers in the hopes that this will provide a baseline understanding of the diversity of architectural forms and elicit further study in this direction. Despite the volume's focus on describing architecture, the overall goal is to understand what was involved in building residential structures and how enslaved people lived in these spaces.

While artifact classes recovered archaeologically on colonial Caribbean plantations are generally analogous, housing for the enslaved was in no way a uniform practice, either in or between individual Caribbean societies. Instead, as the authors here highlight, living environments were influenced by a wide variety of interrelated factors that include global historical trends, local realities, and labor regimes. The chapters in this book provide detailed reconstructions of the living environments of the enslaved, taking into account the cultural behaviors and social arrangements that shaped these spaces.

Housing Enslaved Laborers in the Caribbean

While architectural detail and variety have not traditionally been the central focus of many recent archaeological studies, a few key exceptions have shed considerable light on the built environment of enslaved people, including the scale and dimensions of house-yard compounds, the methods used to build houses, and the sizes and forms of houses. Barry Higman (1998) offers one of the most thorough accounts of housing for enslaved laborers in his study of Montpelier, a sugar estate in western Jamaica in operation from the eighteenth century until the early twentieth century.

Early in his chapter on village architecture, Higman (1998) makes a statement that is perhaps a given for archaeologists today but is nonetheless at the core of the discussion:

> A simple but crucial characteristic of the architecture of the villages of Montpelier during slavery is that the slaves lived in individual, free standing houses rather than in barracks or the row houses typical of industrializing Europe and North America. This was true of Jamaica generally. . . . This changed after emancipation, when barracks became the typical accommodation of indentured plantation laborers. (Higman 1998, 147)

Perhaps because freestanding houses were such a ubiquitous mode of housing, much archaeological research on slavery-period Jamaican plantation villages has occurred at the scale of the individual household represented by a house surrounded by a yard and perhaps a small compound of outbuildings (Armstrong 2011). Although there was a rise in the use of barracks-style housing on Jamaican plantations in the later phases of slavery (Nelson 2016), this seems to have been focused on sugar plantations where owners attempted to minimize costs as the world markets for sugar began to change around the turn of the nineteenth century. In addition, in places like Cuba where the sugar plantation complex dominated later in the colonial period, prisonlike barracks were a more standard housing situation for enslaved laborers (e.g., Singleton 2001). However, the archaeology of enslaved people throughout the Caribbean has largely focused on villages composed of freestanding structures, which seem to have been the most common form of plantation housing before emancipation throughout the region.

Paul Farnsworth's (2001) analysis of the architecture of "negroe houses" in the Bahamas is one of the few studies to explicitly deal with architecture and offers an interesting point of comparison to the examples from Jamaica. Farnsworth looks at the documentary and the archaeological records to examine the presence of a particular Bahamian tradition of stone construction. Local knowledge places the origins of this architectural style with the quarters enslaved laborers inhabited on plantations. According to Farnsworth's documentary research, before around 1802, most enslaved people lived in housing with thatched roofs. Some of these structures would have been built of wattle and plaster while others would have been frame houses with stone chimneys; very few would have been made entirely of stone. However, Farnsworth notes that the documents generally offer few details or even baseline descriptions of such quarters (Farnsworth 2001).

Analyzing data from multiple sites and excavations, Farnsworth turns his attention to the archaeological record. According to Farnsworth, "The overall picture of slave housing painted by archaeological studies is predominantly one of stone-built cabins, mostly with only one room, some with chimneys, and probably with thatched roofs" (Farnsworth 2001, 260). He points out that the excavated structures seem to date after 1800 and that there is evidence on some sites for earlier wattle-and-plaster houses. This leads him to acknowledge the biases inherent in the archaeological record, namely the more ephemeral nature of wattle-and-daub construction and the need for more subsurface testing for signatures of this housing style. Based on his research, Farnsworth seems relatively confident that in earlier phases of Bahamian plantations, one-room wattle-and-plaster housing would have dominated the village landscape until stone houses began to appear after 1800 due to the influence of the British. Of course, more testing on the ground is needed, but it appears that housing for enslaved laborers in the Bahamas changed in material, albeit not in form, over time. He also argues that the wattle-and-plaster precursors to the stone houses represent the cultural traditions of West African and creole peoples. Thus, the form of Bahamian stone houses and the materials used to build them reveal a blending of architectural knowledge and execution.

Plantation owners and managers increasingly used architectural planning from the beginning of the nineteenth century, particularly after the African slave trade was suppressed in the opening decade of the century. The central importance of the African slave trade is often overlooked in discussions of Caribbean slavery. Those who shipped and brokered human cargo to supply plantations with labor made vast fortunes. Mortality rates among those who were enslaved were astronomically high. Death was a common visitor and hard-hearted planters often cared little about the overall health and well-being of the people they enslaved, who were easily replaced with fresh bodies captured and transported from Africa. After the slave trade ended, planters faced the reality that they would have to invest in maintaining the enslaved population. This included investing in changes in the design and construction of housing. Numerous treatises on plantation management were published in the opening decades of the nineteenth century, each designed to instruct planters on how best to organize the management of their estates. Most of these authors provided advice on how to construct efficient and hygienic houses and villages in the hope that implementing such reforms would help planters maintain the profitability of their plantations. These treatises are a remarkable source of information on how some planters intended to design and build housing, but like all such documents they must be treated critically as plans rather than as executed designs. The great variability in the archaeological record indicates that not all planters paid heed to the advice of plantation theorists: what archaeologists find in the ground does not always correspond with the best-laid plans of designers. Similarly, the period drawings and maps that depict slave housing are sometimes romanticized visions of what housing should be rather than what actually existed. Contemporary descriptions of slave housing can provide clues to how structures may have appeared, but they also provide insights into the racialized social order that shaped these accounts of space, place, and people.

While plans, descriptions, and drawings must be considered with a critical eye, one thing is certain: all of the scholars in this volume use as many types of data as possible, including documents, drawings, standing ruins and foundations, in situ architectural features, and associated artifacts.

Landscape and Household Approaches to Caribbean Historical Archaeology

The chapters in this volume blend perspectives and methods from landscape and household archaeology in their efforts to define the built environments of slavery. Landscape archaeology arose in response to an archaeological practice that privileged individual sites in isolation. In contrast to this approach, landscape archaeology regards the landscape itself as a form of material culture (Dunnell 1992; Deetz 1990). Historical archaeologists who work in the Caribbean have most recently employed landscape methods in order to appreciate the multiple scales of landscapes that were experienced in the past (Delle 1998, 1999; Hauser and Hicks 2007; Bates 2016; Opitz et al. 2015). Landscape perspectives are especially useful in the Caribbean because plantation complexes, port cities, and fortifications were more than just individual sites: they were each connected through the broader Atlantic systems that linked these Caribbean spaces and the vast numbers of enslaved people who labored in them with distant European markets. The landscape changes European colonizers wrought in the Caribbean region "were quite drastic and had a distinctly European flavor" (Pulsipher 1994, 202). These interactions with the landscape contrasted with how indigenous groups had used the spaces of the Caribbean. The introduction of the plantation system quickly destabilized whatever environmental stability may have been present before colonization. Colonists cleared forests; demarcated land holdings; built houses connected by paths; bounded fields and properties with fences; and built roads that connected estates to each other and to planned towns on major harbors protected by forts. Because individual estates were intended to represent the interests of colonial empires in the New World, generate profit through intensive crop production, and signify the power and status of the individual planter to his enslaved laborers and social peers, they required significant modification and investment in land. The ideal plantation and urban landscapes were clearly recognizable in contrast to the "natural" forested environment on the edges of estates. However, forests were also actively managed sites: plantation owners extracted wood for fuel and for building structures and furniture (Britt 2010).

The enslaved population, which greatly outnumbered Europeans in the Caribbean, also made an impact on the landscape, although they did so on steep slopes, in ravines, and in mountainous interiors, all areas that were difficult to reach and/or unsuitable for cultivating the export crops that drove this sector of the global economy (Pulsipher 1994). The spatial domain of enslaved people included the slave quarter or village, house-yard gardens, provision grounds, and (by extension) local market towns. Some plantation owners provided ground to enslaved workers where they could produce their own food in lieu of weekly food rations; the enslaved producers could sell or exchange any surplus provisions. To that end, plantation owners usually gave slaves one day per week to cultivate their gardens and to prepare for weekly markets, where they were able to exchange goods and information with enslaved people laboring in port cities. House-yard gardens were smaller plots outside house structures that were used to raise animals and plant crops, medicinal and kitchen herbs, ornamental plants, and fruit trees. The built environment of the Caribbean was thus one fraught with tension: in many contexts, planters simultaneously demanded complete subservience to the labor demands of the plantation economy and complete autonomy in producing a means of subsistence that extended to the development of an independent market economy where the enslaved could sell produce for a profit and purchase goods that they needed or wanted (Hauser 2007; Delle 2014). The fact that enslaved people were allowed and encouraged to grow their own food for subsistence and for sale in local markets—and therefore were provided time to cultivate their own small plots and gardens and free movement to travel off the plantation to sell what they produced—is a major contradiction of Caribbean plantation slavery and points to the importance of not limiting our analyses to a single plantation (Mintz and Hall 1960; Mintz 1978, 1984; Hauser 2008; Bates 2016). How enslaved people responded to and moved within structured environments in their daily lives, thus creating creolized identities in the restrictive space of the plantation, is of major interest for Caribbean historical archaeologists (Pulsipher 1994; Heath and Bennett 2000; Wilkie 2000; Wilkie and Farnsworth 2005; Gibson 2007, 2009; Hauser 2008; Wallman 2014; Bates 2016). These scholars emphasize the movement of enslaved people and the islandwide connections they formed at markets that enabled them to move across boundaries, interact with others, and experience their world in ways that challenge the ostensibly ordered and bounded nature of an individual plantation (Hauser 2009).

Given the interconnected nature of Caribbean economies, landscape perspectives offer fruitful ways to investigate boundaries and community as expressed through space (Crumley and Marquardt 1990; Yaeger and Canuto 2000), to consider how social actors experienced and moved within the same constructed spaces at different scales (Upton 1984; Ingold 1993; Hauser and Hicks 2007), and to explore how power, class, and social relationships were negotiated and reinforced through space (Orser 1988; Delle 1998, 1999). Enslaved people constructed and interacted with built environments of slavery that stretched far beyond individual residential spaces.

In contrast to landscape studies, which focus on settlement patterns, household archaeology explores how social organization is reflected in human behavior at the microscale, where the social, economic, and political intersect (Wilk and Rathje 1982; Ashmore and Wilk 1988; Hirth 1993; Nash 2009). While households are basic units of social organization in any given society, dwelling structures may or may not have housed easily identifiable social groups (Wilk and Netting 1984; Allison 1999). In other words, dwelling structures can house both kin-based and/or non-kin-based groups. While understanding what households "do" and identifying distinct activity areas across dwelling spaces, as Ashmore and Wilk (1988) first proposed, remains important to household scholars (e.g., Douglass and Gonlin 2012), such a functionalist analysis of households places less emphasis on the people who lived in structures and their relationships to one another, gendered labor in the household, and the daily practices that took place in residential areas (Hendon 2006, 2008; Beaudry 2015). Despite the recent emphasis on a broadly comparative perspective in household studies that ties an individual household to its global context (Pluckhahn 2010; Reeves 2015), an archaeology centered on one or several houses still offers the most direct evidence of daily life, including how people constructed and lived in a domestic structure, what types of inter-actions they had with international markets, and the impact of broader societal conditions on how people built spaces to suit their needs and in response to the world outside the house.

The fact that individuals could belong to and participate in activities across multiple household groups is especially important to consider in the context of Caribbean slavery, since shared residence may or may not have derived from biological relatedness. Furthermore, studies of households occupied by enslaved laborers must take into account the fact that dwelling structures were not the only spaces that made up a household: outside communal areas were equally as important (if not more important) than the house. These exterior spaces include the house yard and (on the plantation) the provision grounds. Scholars who have examined the functioning of houses and house-yard areas and their variation have made essential contributions to understanding how households were formed and how they functioned in the confines of forced labor (e.g., Thomas 1998; Anderson 2004; Fesler 2004; Franklin 2004; Battle-Baptiste 2007; Gibson 2007; Reeves 2011). Studies of variation in housing and social organization across diverse settings will inform how we approach social relations in spaces that were likely heterarchical or in some way organized around overlapping forms of social organization within the strictly hierarchical organization of colonial labor regimes (Crumley 1987; Hendon et al. 2009).

The chapters in this volume highlight the fluid boundary between landscape and household studies. The interest in the architecture and built environments of dwelling areas for the enslaved naturally concerns landscape archaeology because these built forms were part of coherent landscapes that cannot be analyzed in isolation from other landscape features, larger social networks, and the global economic circumstances that propelled slave labor in its many forms. At the same time, deeply analyzing architectural features, identifying activity areas in houses and in associated yard spaces, and comparing the use of space within and between slave habitation areas requires a situated household approach in order to consider what went into building and living in a house. This deeply situated study must precede analysis of the meaning of the household and the community for the specific context under study, what differences in construction might say about social organization, and how individual houses were shaped in response to the broader empires in which they were enmeshed.

House, Yard, Garden, Ground: Owning Space in the Colonial Caribbean

Unsurprisingly, power dynamics have been central to scholarly discussions of colonial settings where enslaved people consistently and considerably outnumbered the free population and the white population. To date, most of the discussion about the construction of villages for enslaved laborers has focused on issues of control and resistance. But what more can these sites reveal? The skills and knowledge sets that were present within the population? The limits placed on materials and time during construction? Shifts within the village as different materials became available? Cultural variations? Responses to local landscapes and environmental threats? Furthermore, what can local architectural features and spatial relationships tell us about social relations on a given site? Considerations of self-determination within an enslaved population in the Caribbean often rely on analyzing the overall spatial organization within the residential quarter as a way of assessing levels of control or autonomy in building and living within social space. To take an example from Jamaica, Armstrong and Kelly (2000) found that the plantation slave village layout at Seville shifted from ordered rows to a more organic plan just before emancipation. They argue that at that historical moment, slaves were allowed to follow their own spatial logic of organization, which included a greater focus on the yard and communal social areas. However, Delle (2014) observes the opposite at Marshall's Pen; there, planter oversight increased as abolition grew near. These two examples point to the variation present within one colony and raise questions about what factors drove differences in the use of space.

It is well to remember that in many contexts, housing for enslaved workers was constructed by enslaved people themselves, using building materials that may have been provisioned, purchased, or created locally. Through self-defined manipulations, the enslaved designed and constructed elements of the built environment for their own use, often on their own terms. Enslaved carpenters, sawyers, and masons built—and often conceptualized—the buildings and landscapes they and their fellow enslaved laborers inhabited. These landscapes include not only dwelling structures but also yard compounds. The yard space has been widely recognized as an area of autonomy for the enslaved. Yards were important economically but also had social and ideological value as areas where the enslaved practiced self-representation through social and spiritual gatherings and through the activities of preparing food, gardening, and caring for animals (Mintz 1960; Pulsipher 1994; Heath and Bennett 2000; Armstrong and Fleischman 2003). Communities of enslaved people made these dwelling areas their own and gained a sense of proprietorship over their living spaces. Archaeological evidence of yard sweeping (Heath and Bennett 2000; Bon-Harper 2009, 2010), activities that took place in yards outside the view of the planter (Armstrong and Kelly 2000), house-yard burials (Armstrong and Fleischman 2003), and communal cooking (Battle-Baptiste 2007) support the importance of yard areas. Studies of land tenure practices after emancipation and the legacies of houses and grounds in defining working-class rural economies have stressed how "family land" remains a symbol and a resource that intersects with community, gender, the state, and migration (Olwig 1993; Besson and Momsen 2007; Chivallon 2007). People were clearly tied to their family houses and gardens, and these connections persisted long after emancipation (Armstrong and Fleischman 2003; Delle and Fellows 2014).

While many analyses of social space in the Caribbean emphasize domination or resistance as key elements of the daily experience of enslaved people, feminist perspectives of space and power argue that power in the landscape was relational and was not limited to strict dichotomies of domination and resistance or structure and agency (Spencer-Wood 2010). This approach may be better suited to understanding the nuances of the social interactions that unfolded in the spaces of the Caribbean.

While domination and resistance certainly played a part in the construction of the built environment in the colonial Caribbean and in how the enslaved were permitted to move within that environment, the construction of space was the result of a number of factors internal and external to the enslaved community. The authors in this volume emphasize the multiple and overlapping influences on both planters and the enslaved that led to differences in housing construction and residential organization, including a response to local environmental constraints, the need to mitigate environmental conditions or prepare for future threats, a desire to establish an economically efficient landscape or an ideal landscape that met the expectations or exigencies of empire, a means to express status or occupational differences within the community, or a determination to construct space in a way that best suited the needs of kinship and/or community networks. The variation present within and between housing speaks to the need to evaluate each context of slavery on its own terms.

Contributions to the Volume

The chapters in this volume highlight the diversity of living environments slaves in the colonial Caribbean experienced. Differences can be attributed to the specific context of slavery (plantation, fortification, urban setting), the European colonial power that oversaw the slave system, and the historical circumstances particular to the individual site under study, among other factors. Each of the authors focuses on themes related to the study of the vernacular architecture enslaved people inhabited and how enslaved people used the landscape. They highlight the attempts at social manipulation on the part of architectural planners, the social meaning of the spaces enslaved people built and used, and the methodological difficulties scholars face who conduct research on the built environment of enslaved people in the Caribbean.

The first set of chapters, which includes contributions by Todd Ahlman, Marco Meniketti, and Kenneth Kelly, focuses on the built environment of plantation contexts in what are collectively known as the Lesser Antilles, the archipelago of small islands that arc southeast from Puerto Rico to the South American mainland. In the first chapter, Ahlman contextualizes work conducted on the island of St. Kitts by reviewing what is known about the architectural variation of plantation housing across the British Lesser Antilles. In this review, Ahlman explores the difficulty scholars have in using documentary sources, which are generally either silent or unclear about the nature of slave housing. Through his investigation of village layout and house design, Ahlman turns a critical eye on contemporary paintings and other renderings of slave housing and villages, noting that contemporary depictions of the same village literally paint different pictures of the placement of villages on the landscape, how houses were situated within a village, and the types of construction of houses. Ahlman looks at spatial distinctions between slave villages and yards at three plantations on St. Kitts, one cotton plantation and two sugar estates, attributing differences in use of space on the three sites to environmental concerns and local conditions at each individual site. He also compares archaeological evidence to historical representations of slave housing. His careful analysis of the material culture recovered during excavations allows him to conclude that there was a visible shift in architectural styles around the time of emancipation from houses made generally out of inexpensive, impermanent materials like wattle and daub and thatch to more substantial structures built of more durable and expensive materials, including boards and shingles.

Meniketti explores plantation housing for enslaved people on the island of Nevis, a former British colony in the Lesser Antilles. Meniketti observes that since no examples of housing for enslaved workers are known to exist on Nevis, a multidisciplinary approach to understanding the built environment of slavery must be deployed. Like Ahlman, Meniketti considers multiple data sources, including an analysis of later vernacular houses on the island, which he reasonably theorizes were constructed similarly to the plantation houses that preceded them. He supplements documentary and architectural analysis with archaeological data recovered from three plantation sites on Nevis and evidence from two houses for slaves that appear to have been isolates. The evidence suggests that plantation houses were constructed of ephemeral materials, including perishable wattles woven around earthfast posts. The dearth of nails recovered from house sites suggests that the houses were not sided with boards and were not shingled but roofed with thatch. Slave quarters were situated on rocky and hilly terrain; houses were sometimes precariously sited near ravines. Houses on Nevis were typically built on stone platforms and thus house areas can be archaeologically identified by arrangements of stones of similar sizes and shapes and by the presence of terracing and animal pens made of stone. Meniketti notes that whereas a discourse of efficiency in production circulated in Britain at the time, on Nevis, houses were not built in orderly rows. Instead, they were situated on whatever land was not suitable for cultivation.

Kelly examines variation in housing on sugar plantations in the French West Indies to show changes through time and space both within and between different island contexts. He shows a shift in architecture in Guadeloupe during the period following the French Revolution, when earth-fast slave housing was replaced by houses built on masonry foundations and laid out in orderly rows. He also notes the presence of a stone wall around one village site. Kelly argues that the new form of organization after the Revolution was meant to improve surveillance during the forced reenslavement of the population in Guadeloupe after an eight-year period of emancipation during the Revolution. Whereas stone foundations could also be tied to efforts of the movement to improve conditions of slavery, on Martinique, where slavery continued without the revolutionary upheavals of Saint-Domingue, Guadeloupe, and French Guiana, this architectural transition is not evident and dispersed houses made of wattle continued to be built on hillsides.

The second set of chapters focuses on Jamaica, the largest and most profitable of the British sugar islands. In his chapter on Good Hope Estate, one of Jamaica's largest sugar plantations, Hayden Bassett examines variation in architecture and social organization. He analyzes three separate laborers' habitation areas associated with Good Hope Estate: the primary village that housed over 400 enslaved laborers, a much smaller settlement closer to the great house that he defines as the domestic servants' village, and an urban house lot associated with the planter's town house near the plantation's wharf. He finds a wide variety of differences in architectural forms within the primary village (boarded houses, Spanish wall, and wattle). He also finds that the stone foundations in the domestic slave village suggest different construction methods there from those in the primary village. The main laborers' village was composed of shared swept yard spaces and gardens that were eventually separated by stone fencing. Bassett argues that different forms of labor and their attendant differences in experiences of enslaved people in terms of market participation, autonomy, time outside labor requirements, and so forth led to differences in the size and composition of households. He argues that household composition was influenced more by kinship than by higher or lower status positions on the estate.

James Delle and Kristen Fellows examine house-yard settlements at Marshall's Pen, a coffee plantation in central Jamaica. Of particular note in this study is the diversity of architectural forms present in a single village. Slave laborers constructed the slave village at Marshall's Pen at some distance from the estate on elevated sloping ground. The plantation came about during the dual crises in sugar production and labor that followed the Haitian Revolution and the abolition of the African slave trade, respectively. The concomitant disruption of the centuries-old plantation mode of production on Jamaica made space in the export economy for coffee production. However, this shift required a sustainable natural increase within the enslaved population. Enslaved builders used the ample limestone available locally to terrace hillsides, build house platforms, demarcate house areas with stone walls, and construct animal pens and gardens. Houses clad in shingles and cut boards and built using Spanish wall construction have been identified in the village, as have differences in house size, yard organization, and variations in flooring and roofing. In addition, the fact that distinct activity areas are discernible in separate house areas in the village points to differences in construction and social organization.

The third set of chapters examines the built environment for enslaved people on the geographical periphery of the world of Caribbean sugar production, in places where sugar was not the dominant crop. The first of these, by Allan Meyers, examines housing for enslaved people in the Bahamas, located on the northern fringe of the circum-Caribbean. Meyers explores the impact the antislavery British reform movement had on Bahamian plantation architecture and finds distinct parallels between housing standards recommended in published guides and architectural evidence at Newfield Plantation on Cat Island. He provides an update to slave housing in the Bahamas by revealing variations in house forms that were previously undocumented in the archipelago, including single-room, hall-and-parlor, and duplex row housing constructed of stone. Meyers argues that more durable architecture was meant to improve living standards: building on stone foundations raised houses off the ground, reduced humidity and decay beneath the building, and protected inhabitants from storms, fires, and insect infestations. Meyers argues that the planter at Newfield did not implement these architectural shifts simply to improve the welfare of enslaved peoples but that he intended them to create an outward perception of benevolence and paternalism toward the enslaved. Thus, this architecture served an ideological purpose.

Elizabeth Clay explores the plantation landscape in French Guiana, on the southern periphery of the sugar complex. Her examination of the built environments of slavery focuses on two nineteenth-century plantations that produced clove and annatto. Despite the typically smaller size of French Guianese plantations and the task-based labor system associated with clove and annatto, the slave village at each plantation Clay studied follows a classic structural layout: two rows of equally spaced and similarly sized house foundations and a central roadway leading to the slave owner's domestic quarter. Clay argues that this organized spatial layout was tied to the reestablishment of slavery in the French colonies after the Revolution and the need to reimpose order on the landscape and control the population. While very few studies of plantation slave quarters have been undertaken in this region, there is some evidence that during the ancien régime, post-in-ground housing was more common.

The final set of chapters examines the built environment in contexts beyond the plantation. Alicia Odewale and Meredith Hardy explore the built environment of slave housing in an urban context in the town of Christiansted on St. Croix. In addition to looking at the urban forms of labor that included heavy work in warehouses and at the docks, their investigation focuses on an enslaved community owned by the Danish Crown. As royal property, these men and women would have been in direct contact with centers of government power. This may have influenced the structure of their daily lives. The authors document shifts in architecture that came with the end of the slave trade and the crisis in sugar production, concluding that these crises resulted in improved living conditions for workers, including new housing options.

Zachary Beier looks at the slave village attached to a military installation, the Cabrits Garrison on Dominica, offering a unique take on slave housing at military sites. His chapter explores the connection between military and domestic life evident in the built environment at the fort, including terraces, dwelling and workshop foundations, and water management infrastructure. The variability in household forms at the fort highlights the complicated relationship between life and labor in a military setting of enslavement. This final set of chapters is followed by a commentary on the volume as a whole by Mark Hauser.

Conclusion

Despite the diversity of settings and sites discussed in this volume, some interesting parallels and themes connect the various contributions. Among these is the visible shift in architectural forms that followed the end of the slave trade and the decline of Caribbean sugar hegemony around the turn of the nineteenth century. The post-1800 shifts in architecture can be seen in a transformation from post-in-ground or earthfast construction to stone buildings or wooden houses built on stone foundations. This change is evidently tied to several concurrent historical events, including the end of the slave trade, which required planters to pay closer attention to the living conditions and livelihoods of their slaves, not necessarily through a sense of increased altruism but as a cold economic calculation intended to prolong the useful lives of enslaved laborers. These changes came at a time when there was an expansion of the abolition and humanitarian reform movements that called for improved living conditions for laborers in England and enslaved workers in the Caribbean. In the case of the French Caribbean, this shift may also be tied to the post-Revolution reenslavement of the workforce that occurred in Guadeloupe and French Guiana in 1802 and 1803, respectively.

Given the dearth of surviving structures and the lack of definitive archival descriptions of enslaved housing across the Caribbean, many of the authors relied on representations of housing on historic maps and illustrations, twentieth-century postcards, and present-day vernacular architecture. When these sources are compared to archaeological remains, they can provide illuminating information about the makeup of individual houses. However, another thread between several of the chapters is the fact that historical representations of housing are often idealized according to the colonial imaginary and/or are simplified, not accurately reflecting the precise number of structures, their layout, or the techniques used to build structures.

Finally, as evinced by the contributions in this volume, different forms of labor—associated with plantations, the military, urban contexts, specific types of crop, or individual European powers or planters—had a discernable impact on the social and spatial organization in slave villages and the construction methods and materials people used to build domestic structures.

We hope that, taken together, the collection of studies presented in this volume will expand our collective understanding of the spatial frameworks in which people lived and toiled under the harsh regime of Caribbean slavery.

2

An Examination of Housing for Enslaved and Free Blacks on Sugar and Cotton Plantations on the Southeast Peninsula of St. Kitts

TODD M. AHLMAN

The island of St. Christopher (Figure 2.1), more popularly known as St. Kitts, was the first permanent British settlement in the Caribbean. During the mid- to late eighteenth century, it was one of the most important sugar islands in the British empire. Historical maps show that at the height of the sugar industry on St. Kitts in the mid-eighteenth century, over 200 sugar plantations dotted the island's landscape. William McMahon's 1828 map of St. Kitts reflects the declining fortunes of the sugar industry, showing only around 100 sugar plantations across the island (Higman 1995). McMahon's is the only map that depicts slave villages across the island; it shows 121 slave villages where over 20,000 enslaved Africans resided. These villages, which ranged in size from 0.69 acres to around 30 acres and had an average size of 4.27 acres, were home to from fewer than 50 people to over 200 people; an average village housed around 160 individuals. Higman (1995, 223) notes that three to six enslaved people lived in a house, suggesting that there were ten to forty houses per village on St. Kitts (assuming an average of five people per house). Following Higman, I estimate that in the 1820s, enslaved people occupied somewhere in the range of 2,000 to 4,000 houses on the island. McMahon's map uses squares to represent houses in the slave villages. However, since he uses a fairly common number of squares per village across the map, it probably does not depict the true number of houses.

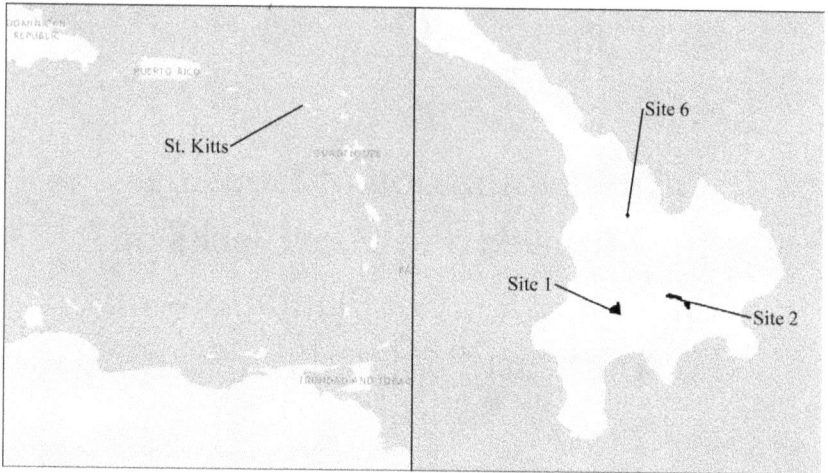

Figure 2.1. Location of St. Kitts and sites mentioned in the chapter. Map created by Todd M. Ahlman.

Often relegated to marginal land on hill slopes, along ghuts, and in some cases the ocean beach, enslaved Afro-Kittitians were given little space for their communities, gardens, and animal pens. Slave village organization changed following the enactment of laws that required owners to provide slaves with land for growing crops and rearing animals. However, these provision lands were also marginal and were often well away from slave villages. Over time, most slave villages evolved to exploit the landscape and to establish family space, gardens, and a hierarchical organization while maintaining individual and family privacy. On some islands and plantations, the planter class sought to create a strictly ordered village organization by enforcing housing arrangements and thereby decreasing freedoms within the slave community.

In this chapter, I present archaeological and historical data about the built environment of enslaved and freed Afro-Kittitians. The concept of built environment I use includes both tangible and intangible elements of houses and house yards. For this study of the built environment, I considered a variety of sources, including archaeological data from across the Caribbean, historic descriptions of the island, seventeenth- to nineteenth-century plats, maps, and paintings, and early twentieth-century postcards from St. Kitts. These sources show the range of housing types that enslaved people on this island likely used and provide context for my discussion of the spatial organization of slave houses and house yards at three sites on St. Kitts.

Finally, I discuss the historical and archaeological data within the larger context of the built environment before and after 1834, the year of emancipation on St. Kitts, including a discussion of overall spatial organization in slave villages and the potential explanations for house-yard organization at two structures on one site.

Archaeological and Historical Descriptions of Slave Housing in the Caribbean

Archaeological and historical studies of slave villages across the Caribbean have documented different housing traditions that can provide information on expected housing types on St. Kitts. The archaeological evidence for slave housing I use in this chapter mainly comes from the Bahamas, Barbados, St. Eustatius, St. John, and Montserrat. The historical data come from a variety of primary and secondary sources that describe general housing trends across the Caribbean and focus on St. Kitts.

Paul Farnsworth (1999, 2001) used historical documents and archaeological evidence to identify two housing traditions in the Bahamas. Farnsworth (2001) described walled structures made of stone for slave housing at Clifton Plantation. These buildings were constructed with mortared, unshaped limestone blocks and arranged along a road. The corners, windows, and door were made of cut limestone blocks and the walls were plastered. The buildings likely had a thatched roof and later a wooden-shingle roof. The buildings ranged in size from 15 by 20 feet to 17.2 by 28.5 feet. Farnsworth also notes the presence of post-in-ground buildings with walls coated in a mortar made of lime and sand (Farnsworth 2001, 259). Bahamian planters often allowed enslaved workers to organize their villages as they wished, but over time they promoted an ideal of placing houses in organized rows.

Descriptions of seventeenth- and eighteenth-century housing on Barbados indicate that the structures were either wattled or made of wattle and daub with thatched roofs (Bridenbaugh and Bridenbaugh 1972; Watts 1994; Carrington 2002). By the end of the eighteenth century, there was a movement toward neatly clad cabins with wooden siding and toward replacing thatched roofs with shingles (Carrington 2002). Handler and

Bergman (2009) used archaeological evidence to better characterize vernacular housing on Barbados. The archaeological evidence and the little historical evidence that are available show that the most common housing form during the period of slavery was a post-in-ground, wattle-and-daub structure with a packed-dirt floor and a thatched roof. In some houses, the wattle was constructed of small branches or trees; in others, it was made from cornstalks. The daub that was applied on the interior wall consisted of clay or mud; lime plaster was applied on later structures. Roof thatching was made from plantain leaves, cane trash, or palm fronds. Later houses were constructed of wooden planks nailed to posts or coral limestone blocks. Handler and Bergman (2009, 17–20) concluded that field slaves tended to live in smaller and less substantial homes than enslaved artisans, who had larger and better furnished homes.

On St. Eustatius, archaeological investigations at the Schotsenhoek slave village identified the remains of seven slave houses (Stelton 2015). The remains consisted of postholes organized in rectangular arrangements that ranged in size from 2.4 by 4.0 meters to 3.5 by 6.0 meters. One structure (Structure 5) had a subfloor pit that was 32 centimeters deep and contained fifty-three artifacts dating to the eighteenth century. Stelton (2015, 296–297) notes that in 1792, a traveler named Zimmerman l'aîné described slave houses on St. Eustatius as "little huts." His drawing of a slave village shows small houses with what appear to be thatched roofs. Stelton (2015, 303) believes the buildings were likely lightly built using wattle-and-daub or wood-board construction.

Kidd (2006) describes three structures on St. John with a stone foundation or sill that were most likely wattle-and-daub houses with thatched roofs. Kidd believes the stone foundation or sill helped protect the daub coating from eroding off the buildings. Structure 1 was 14.8 feet by 27.2 feet and had a stone and coral foundation or sill. Structure 2, which was L-shaped, was the largest of the structures. It also had a stone foundation or sill and measured 50 feet along the longest wall and 26.2 feet along the shorter edge of the L. A plastered floor measuring 10.1 by 14.1 feet was identified for Structure 3. Postholes on the edge of the plastered floor suggested a wattle-and-daub building.

Pulsipher and Goodwin (2001) investigated the Galways slave village on Montserrat and found evidence for several structures. They describe the remains of one building that included postholes cut in bedrock and an unmortared groundsill made of cut and uncut stone. Pulsipher and

Goodwin hypothesize that the building was a wooden structure elevated above the ground surface. The unmortared stone groundsill was laid under the structure's outer walls. The houses in the slave village at the Galways plantation ranged in size from 8 by 16 feet to 10 by 20 feet. The structures were informally arranged on hillside terraces.

Written descriptions of slave housing in the Caribbean are sparse. William Beckford (1790, quoted in Abrahams and Szwed 1983, 335–336) describes houses for slaves on Jamaica as having a central hall where cooking and socializing occurred and bedrooms on either side of the hall. Beckford noted that villages were either organized in straight rows or were "confusedly huddled together" (1790, quoted in Abrahams and Szwed 1983, 335). Joseph Barham described houses for slaves on Jamaica as a few wooden boards nailed to posts with roofing made of plantain leaves (Carrington 2002, 148). Dunn (1972, 248) suggests that some slaves in the Caribbean lived in "little oblong huts, built out of sticks and cane trash."

Limited records from St. Kitts and nearby Nevis provide some evidence about housing for slaves and Europeans of lower socioeconomic status. A description from Nevis indicates that slave houses on the island in the eighteenth century were post-in-ground structures with thatched roofs and walls made of cane trash (Hobson 2007). Although no specific description of slave housing on St. Kitts is available, we can use some passing references to infer what types of housing existed on the island. Rev. James Ramsay, who practiced medicine on several plantations on St. Kitts in the 1760s and 1770s, describes slave housing as being constructed of island timber that was cut and gathered from the mountains on Sundays, the typical day off for slaves (Ramsay 1784, 81–82). Ramsay noted that some planters would provide boards for doors and windows but added that these materials and nails were sometimes stolen from planters' supplies. Kittitian planter Clement Caines (1801, 207–208) claimed that in the late eighteenth century, slaves on the island took unused boards and staves from planters to make windows and doors and to cover their houses. He lamented this alleged theft and advised planters to keep their wood locked away and to count each board daily.

Daphne Hobson's (2007) analysis of information in contemporary documents listing the damage French raiders did to British plantations in 1706, found that some planters built "hurricane houses" that were post-in-ground structures with thatched roofs and caned walls (201–202). Hobson suspects that the caned walls were a variant of wattle-and-daub walls where sugar cane stalks or small-diameter trees and branches were placed horizontally between the posts and no daub was applied. The one- and two-room houses of small landowners on St. Kitts—which had timber posts, caned walls, and thatched roofs—may have been similar to housing for slaves. Some of the "finer" small houses for small landowners had a stone foundation with a brick or wooden floor (Hobson 2007, 206–212).

The best evidence for slave housing on St. Kitts comes from a variety of eighteenth- and nineteenth century maps, plats, and paintings. Most early maps of St. Kitts do not depict slave villages; they focus on great houses and the agricultural buildings on plantations. For instance, Samuel Baker's 1753 map, one of the most comprehensive mid-eighteenth-century maps of the island, shows the great houses, the boiling houses, and the mills on the island, but it does not depict any slave village locations.[1] This is typical of most islandwide eighteenth-century maps and plats that highlight British occupations without noting the location of enslaved African communities. A 1780s plat of Stephen Payne Galway's Pond Estate on St. Kitts shows a two-acre slave village located at the edge of the plantation along a public road.[2] The plat shows twelve houses in the slave village organized in two parallel rows of six structures. The doors to each building are on the gable end, which faces east. This plat suggests that the planter prescribed the arrangement of the slave village because the buildings are in two rows. The plat also shows eleven buildings with vertical lines that likely represent caned or thatched walls. One building does not have these vertical lines; it may have been a wattle-and-daub or possibly a wood-framed house.

Several 1782 maps of the French siege of Brimstone Hill Fortress show numerous slave villages in the area around the fortress. A map by Pechon shows the village houses formally organized in rows with some vegetation between the house rows.[3] All houses face the same way and are evenly spaced. The same villages depicted on a map in the Library of Congress by an unknown cartographer and on Nicholas's map housed in the National Library of France depict the village houses not in orderly rows but as unevenly spaced buildings facing different directions.[4]

A painting from around the 1790s of the Brimstone Hill Fortress attributed to Lt. James Lees in the holdings of the Brimstone Hill Fortress National Park Society depicts the commissariat's yard at the base of the hill with slave houses just outside the yard. These houses were likely occupied by slaves owned by the British government who worked at Brimstone Hill.

Each house appears to have a thatched roof, but the construction of the walls is difficult to discern. None of the houses appear specifically organized into rows and they all face in different directions. Another painting attributed to Lees of Brimstone Hill's southern flank in the holdings of Scotia Bank on St. Kitts shows a sugar plantation slave village with seventeen houses that are not organized in an orderly fashion and have ample vegetation between and around them. The houses all have a thatched roof and some may have caned, thatched, wood-plank, or wattle-and-daub walls.

The 1828 McMahon map of St. Kitts is the only islandwide map to depict the slave village locations across the island. However, because McMahon used a standardized template to denote slave villages, it is unclear if his map accurately portrays village organization or the number of slave houses. For instance, McMahon shows the Pond Estate village with twelve structures but does not depict them as being organized in an orderly fashion, as the 1780 plat of Galway's Pond Estate does.

Information on housing after emancipation is even more scarce than information on housing during the period of slavery. An 1846 painting of Brimstone Hill Fortress by Lt. William Mason Inglis, a royal engineer, shows a rare glimpse of Kittitian housing in the mid-nineteenth century (Figure 2.2). The painting shows five structures at the base of Brimstone Hill and some women working over a large pot in front of one building. It is hard to tell what type of siding is on these buildings, but it could be wood frame or wattle and daub. All of the buildings have a thatched roof.

Late nineteenth- and early twentieth-century postcards and photos provide some of the best evidence of housing on St. Kitts after emancipation. Photographer A. Moure Losada produced numerous postcards in the early twentieth century that depicted housing in St. Kitts (Figure 2.3). Chattel houses—wood-framed structures with horizontal-plank siding that was often covered with thatched wooden shingles—were typical of the late nineteenth and twentieth centuries and are most frequently depicted in these photos (Figure 2.3a). One house (Figure 2.3b) has horizontal-plank siding and a thatched roof. A postcard (Figure 2.3c) postmarked 1930 depicts a house made from bundled sugarcane that has a thatched roof. This structure may have been round. The other structure in this postcard (Figure 2.3c) is a horizontal-plank building with a thatched roof. An early twentieth-century postcard by M. D'Andrade shows a small house with what appears to be horizontal wood planks, some of which

Figure 2.2. An 1846 painting of Brimstone Hill Fortress by Lt. William Mason Inglis showing the postemancipation village. In author's possession.

are covered in stucco or daub (Figure 2.4a). This building is elevated on wooden piers. A glass magic-lantern slide by Williams, Brown, & Evans shows two wood-framed chattel houses (Figure 2.4b). These two structures have wood-post piers and are elevated above the ground surface. As this image and one of the Losada postcards indicate (Figure 2.3a), siding and roofing made with wood shingles were characteristic of many early twentieth-century chattel houses. A photo from 1932 by an unknown photographer shows a house with sugarcane stalks as the walls and a thatched or caned roof (Figure 2.4c). This building seems to be a post-in-ground structure.

These images focus on façades and suggest that the house yards around the fronts of buildings were swept clean. The M. D'Andrade postcard shows a table attached to the side of the house that holds buckets and other items. It seems that few activities occurred in the front yard and most activities occurred in the side and rear yards. Other photographs and postcards from this era depict similar house-yard arrangements and front yards that are virtually devoid of evident activity areas.

Historical evidence suggests that housing for enslaved St. Kittitians likely consisted of post-in-ground buildings with caned or wattled walls and thatched roofs. Caned buildings would have had stalks of cane or small-diameter trees and branches arranged vertically, while wattled

(A)

(B)

(C)

Figure 2.3. (*A*) Early twentieth-century postcard of Kittitian housing by A. Moure Losada; (*B*) Postcard of Kittitian housing by Losada, postmarked 1928; (*C*) postcard of Kittitian housing by Losada, postmarked 1930. Postcards in author's possession.

(A)

(B)

(C)

Figure 2.4. (*A*) Early twentieth-century postcard by M. D'Andrade illustrating Kittitian housing. (*B*) A glass magic-lantern slide of early twentieth-century Kittitian housing by Williams, Brown, & Earle, Inc. (*C*) A 1932 photo by an unknown photographer of a caned house on St. Kitts. All in author's possession.

buildings had horizontally arranged small-diameter trees or branches interwoven between vertical posts. From the documentary record, there seems to be little evidence to support the idea that many slaves built and occupied wattle-and-daub houses on St. Kitts. Slaves built and occupied wood-framed structures even less frequently during the period of slavery.

Maps and plats offer contradictory information about the spatial organization of slave villages. Some of these sources, such as the Pond Estate plat, show villages organized in parallel rows that reflect an arrangement imposed by the planter. However, the later McMahon map depicts an entirely different organization at the Pond Estate. The 1782 maps of the French siege of Brimstone Hill Fortress also show the contradictory nature of these sources: one map shows the slave villages around Brimstone Hill organized into rows and all facing the same direction but other maps show these same houses facing different directions and arranged nonlinearly. Lt. Lees' paintings of Brimstone Hill also suggest that slave villages did not always conform to imposed spatial arrangements.

Historical evidence for postemancipation housing suggests a change over time in housing methods. We have limited information about housing in the immediate postemancipation period. Continuity in housing forms from the period of slavery, when caned or wattled walls with thatched roofing were most common, is likely. In the 1846 painting by Lt. Inglis, the only evidence from that period, it is not clear whether the buildings were constructed with wood framing or with wattle and daub. Over time, as the postcard and photographic images suggest, a shift in housing occurred so that by the early to mid-twentieth century, the preferred Kittitian housing was a wood-framed chattel house with a shingled or thatched roof. Some buildings in this period had horizontal-plank siding, but most had wooden-shingle siding. Chattel houses typically were elevated above the ground surface on wood-post piers. Although buildings with caned walls appear to have been rare in the twentieth century, some Kittitians continued to use them.

Archaeological Investigations

Given the paucity of historical descriptions of Kittitian slave housing and the contradictory evidence in contemporary images and paintings, archaeological excavation may be the most effective way to understand slave housing on St. Kitts. Archaeological investigations on the southeast peninsula of the island have focused on several sites, including slave villages at one cotton (Site 6) and two sugar plantations (Sites 1 and 3) (Figure 2.1). These sites currently provide some of the best archaeological evidence for the lives of enslaved people who lived and labored on the many plantations of St. Kitts.

Site 6

Site 6, which is situated on a rocky hillside, was a small plantation that may have been occupied from as early as the 1750s but was most likely occupied from the 1780s to the 1810s. Because this site does not appear on any of the St. Kitts maps, little is known about it. Small plantations on the southeast peninsula likely raised cotton and required few enslaved people to tend the fields. Archaeological investigations in three areas (Figure 2.5) provide evidence about activities and structure types (Ahlman 2009). One structure, which may not be related to slave housing, was a 10.0-by-12.5-foot building with a mortared-stone foundation and thatched roof. The structure had a partial basement or cellar that was filled with a thick layer of ash overlain by a layer of burned thatching, suggesting that the building burned just before it was abandoned. The thatching was of bundled grass rather than plantain leaves or sugarcane stalks. Relatively few artifacts were found in the two excavation units around this building. The most frequently occurring artifacts were nails and fragments of marine shell. This building was most likely a wood-framed storage building with a thatched roof.

Based on the distribution of surface artifacts, there were at least two associated domestic structures. A surface scatter of artifacts indicative of domestic activities—primarily refined European ceramics, liquor-bottle glass, and locally produced Afro-Caribbean wares—were found about 25 feet northwest of the stone foundation. Two excavation units in this scatter produced primarily refined European ceramics and liquor-bottle glass. The few nails that were recovered from these units may have been from windows or doors. There was no surface indication of a foundation, suggesting that the building was a post-in-ground structure with caned or wattled walls and a thatched roof.

A second domestic building was situated about 75 feet northeast of the storage building. The recovered artifacts include relatively high frequencies of liquor-bottle glass and Afro-Caribbean ware and a low frequency

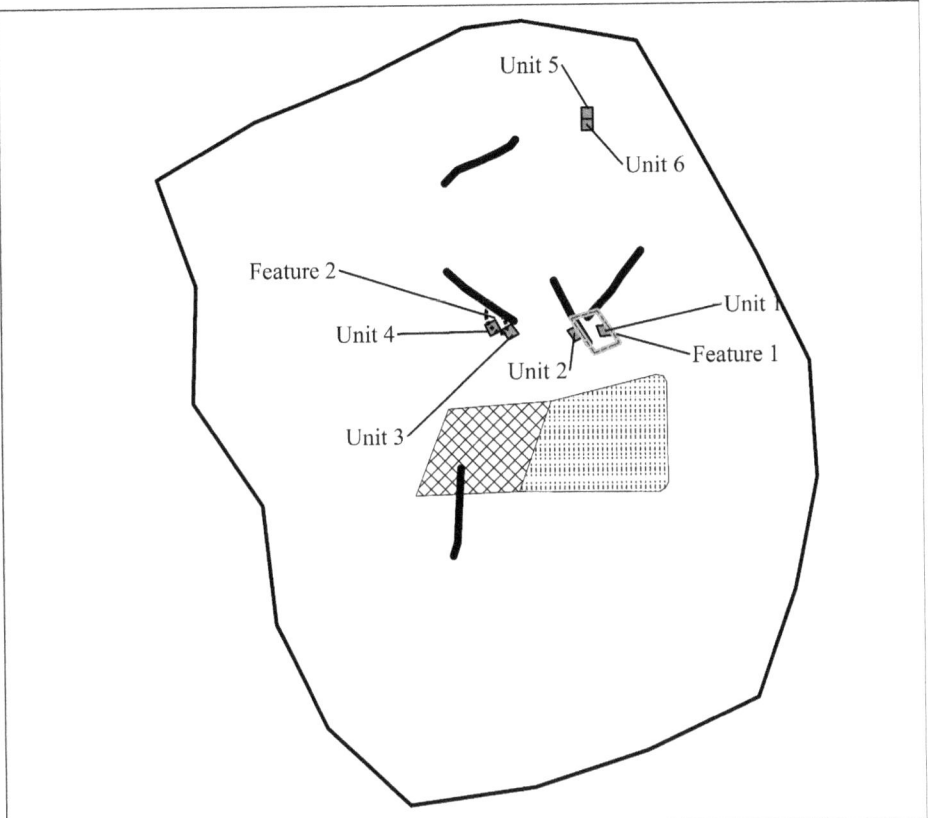

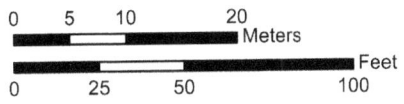

Figure 2.5. Plan view map of Site 6, a small cotton plantation, showing location of excavation units and features. Map created by Todd M. Ahlman.

of refined European ceramics. The highest concentration of stone and glass tools and lithic debitage from slave contexts on St. Kitts was recovered from this area, which suggests that the building was occupied by someone who made and traded fire flints (Ahlman et al. 2014). There were no surface indications of foundations, suggesting a post-in-ground structure. A higher frequency of wrought-iron nails was recovered from these two excavation units compared to the number of nails recovered from other excavation units at this site. The archaeological evidence suggests that this building may have been a post-in-ground structure with caned or wattled walls that had a shingled roof and framed doors and windows.

Site 2

Site 2 was a sugar plantation occupied by as many as 159 enslaved people from the late seventeenth century to emancipation in 1834 and an unknown number of Kittitians in the postemancipation period (probably through the 1850s). The only map evidence for the village location appears on the 1828 McMahon map, which shows sixteen houses in the village. This number of houses is likely low as the population of the village was around 159 in the 1820s; the number of houses probably should be closer to thirty.[5] This village occupied two sides of a plantation road; McMahon places equal numbers of structures on either side of the road. Archaeological investigations were undertaken on the eastern side of the road (Figure 2.6) because the village portion west of the road was destroyed by development in the 1980s and 1990s and could not be investigated.

Six surface scatters of artifacts were identified on the eastern side of the road that indicate disposal and activity areas around slave housing. Limited mechanical stripping and excavation units did not identify any subsurface features within these scatters. The scatters were located on the highest points of an undulating hillside, suggesting they were placed to take advantage of the prevailing winds. At this village, it is clear that the slaves who occupied the site arranged their village based on their own requirements, which in this case included taking advantage of a breeze, rather than in the orderly rows that may have characterized some sites.

A house platform was identified at the southern end of the village close to the plantation's windmill and industrial complex. An excavation unit in the center of the platform revealed a pit cellar where a wooden post was found. The wooden post suggests that the building had a raised wooden

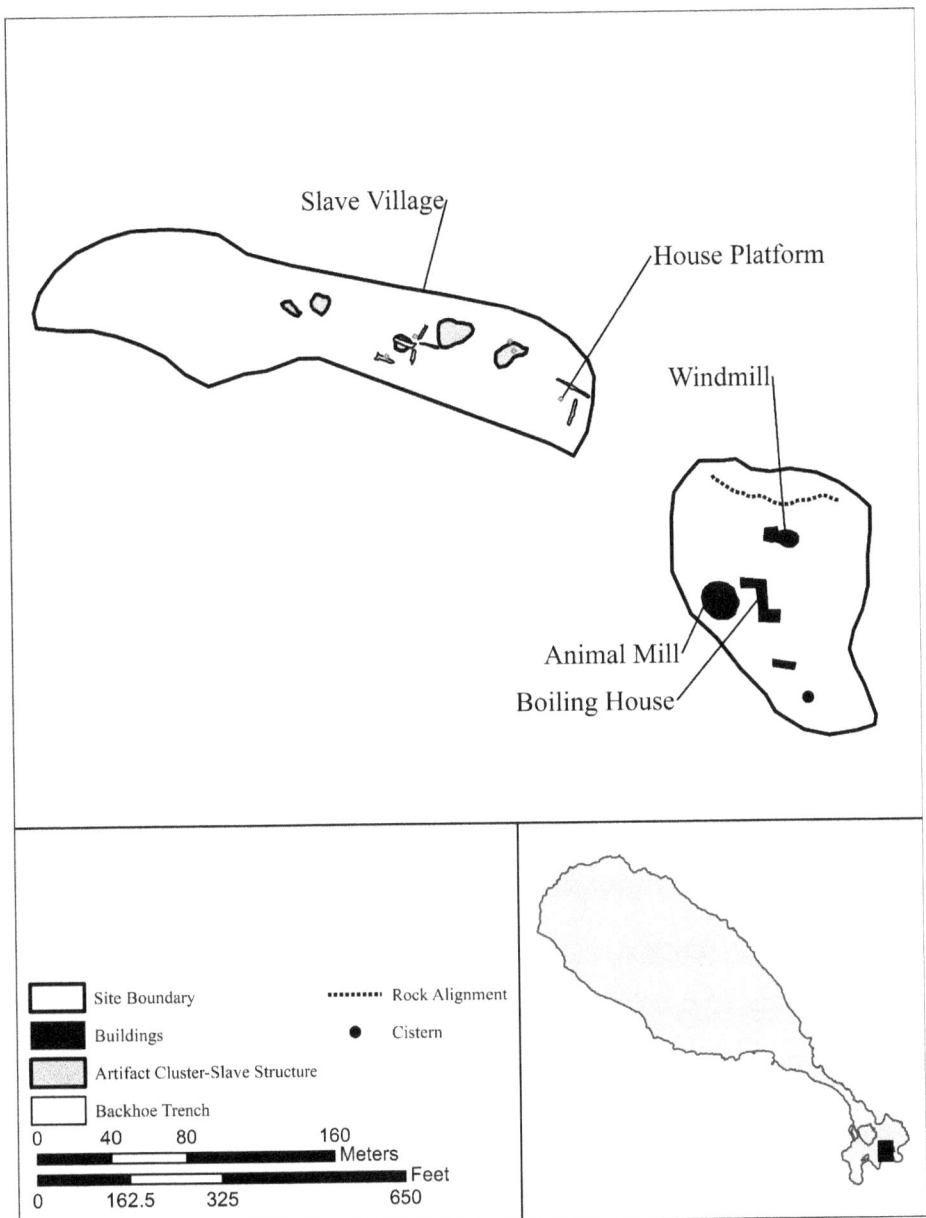

Figure 2.6. Plan view map of Site 2, a large sugar plantation, showing location of features and excavation units. Map created by Todd M. Ahlman.

floor at some point during its use. The recovered artifacts from the pit cellar are mostly liquor-bottle glass, refined European ceramics, and Afro-Caribbean wares. While the limited number of excavations do not allow for a full interpretation of the structure, it most likely was a post-in-ground building with a raised wooden floor. The relatively low number of recovered nails suggest that the structure's walls were either caned or wattled.

Site 1

Site 1 was a sugar plantation that was occupied from the late seventeenth century to the postemancipation period that consisted of a slave village and an industrial complex located on a hillside (Figure 2.7). Census records and plantation inventories indicate that there were anywhere from thirty-one to seventy-one enslaved individuals living at the site from the mid-1700s to the early nineteenth century and that by 1829 only forty-nine people were living in the village.[6] McMahon's depiction of fifteen structures in this location may be an overrepresentation of the actual number of houses, given that the population during the 1820s consisted of fewer than fifty-five people. It is more likely that there were ten or fewer houses in this village. The industrial complex is located on the lowest point and the houses of the village are scattered upslope to the west. The presence of surface scatters of artifacts suggests that the village had at least six terraced platforms on which slave houses were situated. Two structures have been investigated archaeologically.

Structure 1 is located on the lowest terrace, which is close to the industrial complex. This location indicates that Structure 1's occupants may have been involved in the oversight of sugarcane processing and may have had a privileged position in the slave village hierarchy. The structure was a 12-by-16-foot building with a groundsill or foundation made with unmortared, irregularly sized volcanic stones. A 70-centimeter-deep pit cellar was found in the middle of the foundation, which suggests that the building had a floor. The paucity of nails around the foundation implies the building was not framed and likely had caned or wattled walls. A row of shaped stones set on end on the building's west and upslope side was placed to prevent water from running underneath the structure and into the pit cellar. Few artifacts or evidence for activities were found in excavations west of the structure. A French coin dating to the late seventeenth

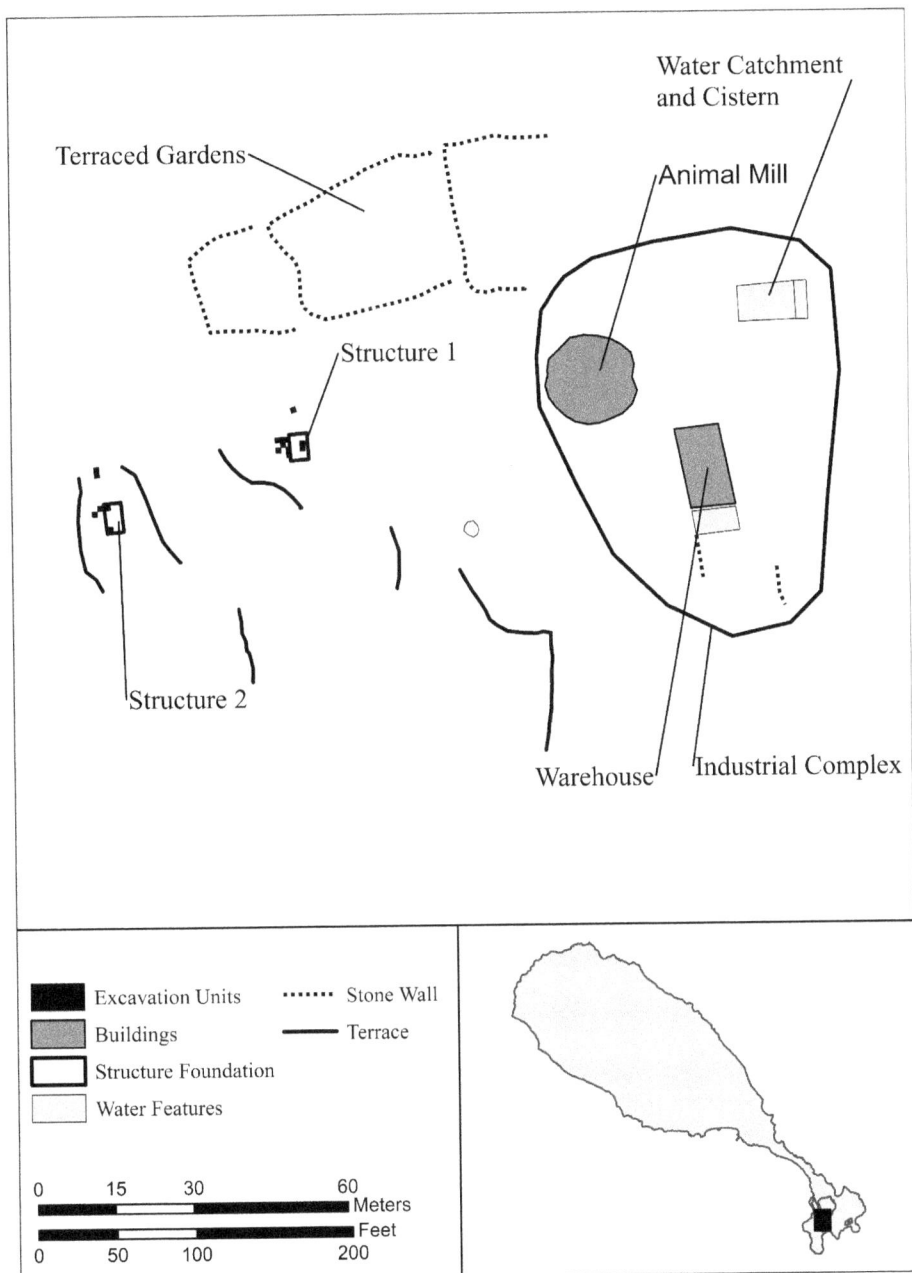

Figure 2.7. Plan view map of Site 1, a sugar plantation dating from the late seventeenth century to the mid-nineteenth century, showing location of structures, excavation units, and site features. Map created by Todd M. Ahlman.

century was found in the excavation units west of the structure. A dense surface scatter of artifacts indicative of activity and disposal areas was identified to the east of the structure, closest to the industrial area. A relatively high number of buttons and clothing items were found around this building, suggesting that an occupant or occupants were making or repairing clothes during the late eighteenth and early nineteenth centuries. The highest frequency of refined European ceramics and Afro-Caribbean ware on this site was recovered at this structure.

Structure 2 is approximately 120 feet uphill from Structure 1. Part of a mortared, shaped-stone foundation remains that measures approximately 10 by 18 feet. Excavation units on the structure's west side produced numerous artifacts, including refined European ceramics, Afro-Caribbean ware, glass, and faunal remains that are indicative of cooking and other household activities. A dense sheet midden of refined European ceramics, Afro-Caribbean ware, glass, and faunal remains was located about 12 feet northeast of the structure. These artifacts were generally larger than the ones to the west of the structure, indicating this location was a primary disposal area. Few artifacts were found to the east of the structure either on the ground surface or during mechanical trenching. The first building in this location was likely a post-in-ground structure with caned or wattled walls and a thatched roof that was replaced by a later structure that had a stone foundation. The recovery of numerous wrought-iron and cut nails in the upper 10 centimeters around the foundation suggests that the postemancipation building was a wood frame structure, perhaps a chattel house, that sat on the stone foundation. This building probably collapsed after the village was abandoned in the 1850s.

Discussion

Although historical evidence about the built environment of slavery on St. Kitts is scant, archaeological data can fill in gaps and provide a better understanding of the tangible and intangible elements of built environments. Historical documents (journals, travel accounts, paintings, plats, etc.) suggest that across the Caribbean, slave housing consisted mostly of post-in-ground, wattle-and-daub houses with some horizontal-plank structures and a few stone houses. Archaeological evidence suggests that in some locations, such as the Bahamas or Barbados, stone houses were more frequent in the later era of slavery than in earlier periods.

Several types of post-in-ground structures were likely in use during the period of slavery on St. Kitts, including wattle and daub, caned, and horizontal wood planking. The daub used in wattle-and-daub buildings was either lime plaster or clay. Lime mortar or plaster made from coral or limestone occurs widely in the construction of stone structures on St. Kitts. However, from the sample of housing for slaves examined thus far on the island, there is no evidence for the use of lime plaster to line walls. Although clay occurs throughout the southeast peninsula at the surface, buried in shallow deposits, or around the salt ponds, identifying soil-based daub is difficult because it is not likely to have survived to the present day and it would be practically indistinguishable from the natural soils unless the clays were heated or the structure had burned. It is also possible that daub was not used to line building walls so that air could flow through the structures. The southeast peninsula of St. Kitts is particularly hot and dry, so enslaved workers probably appreciated having a breeze flow through their houses. Several sources suggest that the walls on some buildings were caned.[7] Cane stalks were readily available for roofing and walls. Like daub, cane stalks would not have survived in the archaeological record and would be difficult to identify. The presence of cellars below two structures on St. Kitts indicates that some houses had an elevated wooden floor rather than a floor of hardened earth. Ground sills or foundations, which do not seem to have been common, served various roles, including preventing water from flowing under structures and keeping animals out of the houses.

Wood-frame chattel houses did not became a more common type of housing until late in the slavery period and after emancipation. Some enslaved and freed blacks who were able to earn money from the sale of commodities or from various specialized skills used that income for more permanent forms of housing. This display of wealth and rank reaffirmed their position in the community hierarchy. After emancipation, many Kittitians continued to live on the plantations where they had been enslaved and worked in the same fields where they had labored as slaves. The shift to a wage economy brought many hardships to the newly free Kittitians, but some were able to accumulate capital and invest their new income in tangible objects that benefited their household and perhaps displayed their relative wealth and position. Often this meant spending money on their home, a highly visible display to others in the village and to visitors from other parts of the island. When they did not own their land, however, they had to build a house they could move. That is why chattel houses became popular. The recovery of numerous nails in addition to the stone foundation at Structure 2 at Site 1 points to a wood-framed building in this location during the postemancipation era.

Although some maps suggest that Kittitian slave villages were organized in orderly rows, others depict a more irregular organization of houses that were not forced into rows. This latter pattern is likely most representative of Kittitian slave villages. Site 2 was organized so occupants of the village could take advantage of the prevailing breezes. At Site 1, the occupants terraced the hillside and created a village that assured privacy while maintaining the social hierarchy in the enslaved African community. These two villages demonstrate that enslaved Kittitians often organized their space according to their own ideals of community, privacy, and social hierarchy.

As the early twentieth-century postcards and photographs illustrate, front yards were typically kept clean and side and rear yards around the dwellings served as activity areas where people processed food, cooked, ate, and entertained. This is also a common pattern in archaeological findings from slave villages elsewhere in the Caribbean. The organization and use of space around the two structures investigated at Site 1 present some interesting insights into the use of house yards on St. Kitts.

Based on its location closest to the industrial complex, Structure 1 is interpreted as the residence of a enslaved person or family of relatively high rank and prestige in the plantation hierarchy. Structure 1 should have been oriented downslope facing the industrial complex, as this area was the most visible to people who worked in the industrial area and who traveled to the village. In that case, the yard on this side of the structure typically would have been kept clean and the uphill side of the structure would have been where household activities took place. However, there is a dense artifact scatter of ceramics, glass, and metal covering an area of over 2,300 square feet in the front of the dwelling and what was likely the rear of the house is practically devoid of artifacts. It appears that the front yard between the dwelling and the industrial complex, the side that was most exposed to the village occupants and to visitors to the site, was the locus of activities. This orientation meant that everyone who worked at and traveled to and from the industrial complex walked by or near this house and saw the activities occurring there. The recovered ceramics include a higher frequency of more expensive European ceramics, such as transfer-printed wares, than was recovered from Structure 2, which suggests that the occupants had money to acquire expensive goods more frequently than other village occupants. The activities that occurred in this yard probably included cooking and eating and displays of these more expensive ceramics and other objects. These displays and the larger size of the house yard signaled the privileged position of the occupants to the other villagers. This organization of the house yard of Structure 1 continued into the postemancipation period, when it appears that the occupants continued to live in a caned or wattled structure but purchased less expensive European ceramics such as sponge-decorated whitewares.

The organization of the house yard at Structure 2 suggests a clean yard around what was likely the front of the structure and a busy rear yard. In the rear yard, which was no more than 12 feet wide and about 1,600 square feet in size, the occupants cooked and ate sheep, goats, and local fish and shellfish. The frequency of Afro-Caribbean ware in this yard was more than twice as high as the frequency of refined European ceramics. At Site 1, the planter likely provided plain, edge-decorated wares and transfer-printed ceramics in the Willow pattern. At Structure 2, European ceramics have the highest relative frequency of these materials across the site. In the postemancipation period, Afro-Caribbean ware continued to be the most frequent ceramic type at Structure 2 and the most frequent European ceramic was sponge-decorated whiteware. In the postemancipation period, the organization of the house yard in which most activities occurred in the rear yard continued. The big change at Structure 2 after emancipation was that the occupants constructed a wood-framed chattel house on a mortared-stone foundation. The investment in housing rather than in ceramics shows that the occupants wanted to display the facts that they could buy the materials to build their own house and that they had mobility and could physically leave the former slave village.

Slave housing and how slaves organized house yards provided some sense of privacy and security. Enslaved people used the natural environment and vegetation to augment these arrangements. It should come as no surprise, therefore, that slave villages on St. Kitts were not as orderly and organized as period plats and maps suggest. Houses were placed to take advantage of local conditions, such as catching the prevailing breeze, or on terraced platforms to make topography conform to the occupants' needs. Village dynamics and the hierarchy in the slave community also played a role in spatial organization. For instance, the occupants of Sites 1 and 2, the houses closest to the industrial complexes, likely held a privileged position within the community hierarchy. At both sites, these occupants reinforced their position by purchasing and displaying expensive refined European ceramics and probably sharing liquor with other workers.

Conclusions

Most enslaved St. Kittitians built and lived in post-in-ground houses with either wattled or caned walls and a roof thatched with grasses or cane trash. Dirt floors were common, but some buildings had wooden floors that were elevated above the ground surface. While pit cellars across the wider Caribbean are rare, they appear to have been frequent on St. Kitts. This is evidence of elevated floors in dwellings. After emancipation in 1834, there was a gradual shift in Kittitian housing toward frame structures with horizontal-plank siding and thatched roofing. Some later houses in the twentieth century had wood shingle siding and roofing. Traditional caned and wattled housing continued into the twentieth century but appears to have been rare.

During the period of slavery (before 1834) there do not seem to have been many differences in housing styles based on prestige and social position in slave communities. For the most part, enslaved St. Kittitians did not have access to the materials or time they would have needed to construct wood-framed or stone houses. Data are too limited to make conclusions about the size of houses on St. Kitts or about any differences in housing that might be indicative of social standing or the ability to make money from tasks or selling commodities. Differences in the built environment that can be explored relate to material culture and the organization of house yards. While it may not seem that these two things are correlated, at least at Structure 1 at Site 1, it seems that the occupants organized their activity areas to display and highlight the fact that they were more able to purchase more expensive refined European ceramics than others in the community. This ability reflected their social standing in the plantation hierarchy and their ability to generate the income needed to purchase these items.

After emancipation in 1834, formerly enslaved people likely struggled to obtain clothing, food, and housing as they entered a wage-labor regime.

Immediately after emancipation, people likely used any income and time they had to obtain necessary items such as clothing and food instead of changing their housing to wood-framed buildings. By at least the 1850s, some Kittitians had reached a level of financial security through wage labor that they could invest in new, albeit inexpensive, ceramics and different, more expensive housing. More evidence is needed, but it seems that in the postemancipation period there may have been a shift in social dynamics in some villages as people grew into new roles in the postslavery plantation hierarchy.

Notes

1. Samuel Baker, *A new and exact map of the island of St. Christopher in America, according to an actual and accurate survey made in the year 1753. Describing the several parishes, with their respective limits, contents, & churches; also the high ways, the situation of every gentleman's plantation, mills, and houses; with the rivers, and gutts. Likewise the bays, roads, rocks, shoals and soundings that surround the whole* (London: Carington Bowles and Robt. Wilkinson, 1753), Geography and Map Division, Library of Congress.

2. Plat map of Stephen Payne Galway's Pond Estate, in Morne, Pond, and Salt Pond Estates, St. Kitts, MSS W. Ind. S. 73. Oxford University.

3. Pechon, *Plan du siége de St. Christophe, levé en 1782*, cartographic material, John Carter Brown Library, Brown University.

4. *Plan du siege de Brimston Hill*, 1782, Geography and Map Division, Library of Congress; Nicholas, *Plan du Siège de Brimston-Hill, investie le 12 Janvier et rendu le 13 Février 1782 à Monsieur le Marquis de Bouillé, Gouverneur général des Isles du Vent de l'Amérique et Commandant l'Armée*, 1782, Département Cartes et plans, GE D-15565, Bibliothèque nationale de France.

5. Slave Registers of Former British Colonial Dependencies, 1812–1834, accessed January 5, 2010, https://www.ancestry.com.

6. Slave Registers of Former British Colonial Dependencies.

7. E.g., the plat map of Stephen Payne Galway's Pond Estate and Lees' paintings.

3

The Present Past

The Design Legacy of Laborers' Housing in the Landscape of Vernacular Architecture on Nevis

MARCO MENIKETTI

Plantation environments consist of intersecting built landscapes that transform the natural environment to serve the needs of agricultural production. Elements of the plantation viewscape include the estate house and its associated structures, the processing factory and related facilities, and spaces set aside for the quarters for enslaved laborers. Although integral to the plantation landscape writ large, laborers' villages and housing constitute a distinct built space in the broader plantation environment that was recognized historically as an interaction zone of its own. This chapter will examine the relationship between pre-emancipation plantation housing and traditional forms that are still present on the landscape of the former British colony of Nevis, West Indies.

For two centuries, sugar production was the backbone of the economy on Nevis. Sugar plantations were in essence industrial landscapes: they had great swaths of land devoted to monoculture and areas designated for factories, specialized production, and storage. The transformation of local ecologies when plantations were established included obvious infrastructural changes, such as roads that linked shipping centers with estates and estates to other estates, and the introduction of nonnative animal stock. Less obvious changes were manifest in the partitioning and segregation of space that proscribed patterns of mobility and land use in the process (Leech 2008). Although the houses of the enslaved populations on Nevis were ephemeral, their sites constitute another built environment. The best that can be determined from archaeological evidence is that the houses for slaves were constructed from local perishable materials while plantation buildings were robustly constructed of local stone. However, the laborers' house form had an enduring legacy and influence over styles that are present on Nevis today. Analysis of this vernacular architecture in context may provide insights into the meanings this built environment had for the inhabitants and how they coped with the condition of bondage.

Houses are both elements of the landscape and important expressions of material culture. As such, they form a dynamic arena of social relations and negotiations of class, self, and community (Delle 1999, 136; Haviser 1999; Meniketti 2016). Houses are more than structures for sleeping or storing possessions; they may also function as loci for the formation and enactment of identity that was no less critical for people in bondage than it was for free citizens, and perhaps even more so (Battle-Baptiste 2011). For enslaved people, houses were spaces that offered refuge from the external world and allowed a brief respite from the surveillance of planters. Objects and landscapes can be imbued with meanings that legitimize certain social relations (Hood 1996, 124). As Ian Hodder (2012, 219) frames it, things simply need to be recognized as having enduring qualities to become entangled in cultural praxis.

Nevis, which the British colonized in 1628, was one of a trio of "mother" colonies of Britain in the Lesser Antilles; the other two were St. Christopher's (St. Kitts) and Barbados. A mountainous and rocky island that lacks streams or a year-round water supply and has only a lee shore as a harbor, Nevis would seem an unlikely location for a colony with an economy based on agriculture. Despite its small size of roughly 35 square miles, the island colony was a source of extreme wealth for white planters and was politically important for Britain well into the late eighteenth century owing to combined revenue streams from sugar production and the monstrously profitable slave trade. The history of Nevis, like that of other former and current colonial islands in the Caribbean, is one of resource exploitation, economic and military conflict among competing European interests, and the deeply embedded institution of slavery. During the first century of colonial development, Nevis escaped the majority of the disruptions military invasion from European rivals wrought that constantly beset the other colonies and the destruction of the estates that typically ensued. The fortunes of war, political economics, and rich volcanic soils (now depleted) allowed Nevis a prosperity that was out of proportion to its size.

Slavery and Housing on Nevis

The modern history of Nevis begins with the sighting of the volcanic island by Christopher Columbus in 1493 on St. Martin's Day. Over the next 130 years, the Spanish had a negligible physical impact on the island and a limited interest in the mineral-poor land. Slaving and disease, however, decimated the indigenous population severely in the sixteenth century, allowing the English to later easily colonize the virtually unoccupied island (Lowenthal 1972, 31). Nevertheless, remnant indigenous populations were present when a small band from Britain came ashore from the neighboring colony on St. Kitts. After a brief period of accommodation, the British enslaved them to work the first plantations (Hilton 1675). As late as 1675, indigenous Carib people were still enslaved laboring alongside Africans (Sainsbury 1893).

During the first years of the colony, there was little distinction in the dwellings of the adventurers who came to Nevis (Meniketti 2006), whose chief purpose was to earn quick wealth by producing luxury commodities such as ginger, tobacco, and indigo. None of the early settlers intended to remain on the island and they expended little effort on infrastructure. The first operations were small in scale and were manageable with a small workforce (Meniketti 2006). Tobacco houses were constructed alongside residences (Hilton 1675). As the realities of colonization took root, the distinctions between housing, spatial order, and social dynamics came to mirror, or at least to mimic, the hierarchical structure of England (Hicks 2007a). Although Hilton (1675) informs us of the broad-scale spatial divisions that dominated the colony, he is mute regarding plantation landscapes.

The first English settlers on Nevis cleared the rainforest with axes and fire and plantations were established as forest was cleared. Labor in the early colony was oppressive. Criminals, political prisoners, Indians, indentured servants, and Africans were all imported to clear the land. One important variant was that an indentured servant—if he was lucky enough to survive—might eventually come to own land and become a planter and possibly accrue enough wealth to return prosperous and with new status to England. Although such rags-to-riches stories did in fact occur, they were the exception (Leech 2008; see also Pares 1950). Most of the indentured servants and enslaved laborers were Irish during the first decades of development, before the large-scale introduction of Africans. The hardships they endured are evident in commentaries given in correspondence between colonial leaders and administrators (Fortescue [1901] 1964). Early house forms may have been based on types that were familiar to the English settlers and on those that were built during earlier plantation enterprises (Klingelhofer 1999, 2005).

By 1655, substantial storehouses had been built with stone and mortar foundations on Nevis in the shipping centers of Jamestown and Charlestown. Although these two towns emerged as important places of commerce, they remained a veneer along the coast; no towns were built in the interior. The progression of Nevis as a colony as John Hilton (1675) and other contemporary explorers relate it provides useful, if not altogether detailed information for analysis of the built landscape and the transformed rain forest environment as colonial settlement intensified and expanded (Sloane 1707; Churchill and Churchill 1732).

Capt. John Smith, who was on his way to Virginia, described the precolonial environment on Nevis as lush and wooded (Churchill and Churchill 1732). Hans Sloane, future founder of the British Museum, voyaged to Nevis in 1675 and later published his experiences and observations on natural history. Sloane described the character and scope of land clearing for sugar plantations and made caustic comments about Nevis's colonial society and about Nevisians (Sloane 1707). He reported that the island had been cleared nearly to the top of the mountain and that natural vegetation was to be found only in the higher elevations, where the climate and steep slopes made sugar cultivation unfeasible. He also wrote that the upper reaches of the mountain harbored "runaway negroes." Sloane observed that the inhabitants of Nevis had "small houses" that were "from Barbuda" (Sloane 1707, 42); presumably he meant that the materials used in construction had been imported. This was likely the case, as so many trees had been cut by the time of Sloane's trip that Nevisians were importing timber (Watts 1994, 395).

Because of the mountainous character of Nevis, seven distinct biomes exist that differentially influence rainfall, humidity, soil conditions, and wind. As a result, plantation productivity varied widely across the island. Sloane's observation of the encroachment of agricultural land to the upper slopes is supported by archaeological evidence of terracing and stacked-stone animal pens recorded above 2,000 feet (610 meters) above sea level on the mountain (Meniketti 2015). Also present in these upper elevation zones are remnants of house platforms and house clusters. Contemporary commentaries discuss the difficulties of clearing the forest, uncertainties about the weather, and worries about Spanish incursions or rebellion among papist Irish laborers (Headlam [1910] 1964). With time, the worries about Spanish attacks or Irish uprisings were replaced with worries about the ambitions of the French and the Dutch and the possibility that enslaved Africans would rebel (Merrill 1958, 67). Such concerns provided the motivation for building defensively. As a result, the built environment included forts, redoubts, and fortification walls that extended for miles along the western shore from Charlestown to Jamestown.

The Royal African Company, whose business was the slave trade, established its Caribbean headquarters on Nevis in 1675, thus ensuring that Nevis plantation owners had the first choice of the new captives. Complaints from colonial administrators on other islands ensued; they were particularly vitriolic from neighboring Antigua (Higham 1921, 151, citing Acts of the Leeward Islands). Meanwhile, the Royal African Company complained that Nevisian plantation owners were bypassing them and acquiring slaves from the Dutch on St. Eustatius (Fortescue [1899] 1964).

As Nevis prospered from 1655 to 1780, the African population steadily increased until more than 8,000 enslaved laborers toiled on more than 200 estates of varying sizes. Each of these persons required housing. The humble housing for plantation laborers was a vital element of the historic colonial landscape that until recently historians and tourists alike frequently overlooked. This feature is generally absent from the visual record or from modern reconstructions of estates, owing either to the perishable nature of the building material or the desire to gloss over or forget the legacy of slavery (Edwards-Ingram 1999). The plantation great house dominated the high ground in many cases. However, the habitations of workers were as much a fundamental unit of the built landscape of the plantation as great houses or windmills or factory buildings. The scale and spatial arrangements of buildings and the activities, conversations, family struggles, limited joys, and constant sorrows of a people that made their homes in these zones are as important for understanding the pre-emancipation agro-industrial world as are the more permanent structures and sugar factories.

Places, like houses, are both components of built environments and artifacts and therefore are expressions of material culture. It has become common in historical archaeology for landscapes themselves to be viewed as dynamic and transitory artifacts (Rubertone 1989, 50). The manner in which the island was partitioned and structured also contributed to unequal distribution of resources and is an "artifact" of the colonization process (Leech 2008). Dwelling places and the spaces they occupy are powerful focal points that are appropriate for the study of identity and cultural maintenance in colonial contexts. Although spaces are often examined through the framework of resistance, appropriating spaces to accommodate one's concept of self need not be viewed as an act of resistance; it can also be seen as human adaptation. As the slave-owners' objective was to hold people in subjugation, every "manifestation of will" on the part of slaves would be perceived or interpreted as resistance (Gaspar 1992, 135). In the eyes of the plantocracy, such behavior among enslaved populations as making the village space their own may have been resistance, but despite vigorous efforts to dehumanize Africans, humanity is not so easily dislodged.

Analysis of Vernacular Housing

Emancipation in the 1830s brought several changes to the social dynamics of Nevis society. An important outcome was the need for the formerly enslaved population to find land and housing away from the estate. Plantation owners were no longer obliged to provide either of these commodities and used this fact for leverage in negotiating with the newly free wage earners. However, labor was not without its own negotiating power and labor could be, and was, withheld at critical junctures, such as harvest time (Boland 1981; Gaspar 1992). Efforts by Nevisian plantation owners to collude to fix wages and to use other tactics to maintain control over the labor force ultimately failed. The most significant problem workers on Nevis faced was the lack of available land that resulted in an exodus of labor to other colonies in the Caribbean, such as Jamaica and British Guiana. This in turn led to a new labor shortage on Nevis in the decades following emancipation. This demographic shift reduced the population dramatically and had the unexpected effect of increasing the negotiating power of the labor that remained (Olwig 1995). Because building materials were expensive, housing continued to be a problem, but familiar house types were constructed on small plots and both the house and land became important family holdings.

During the first decades of colonization on Nevis, the housing of the original eighty settlers (and their unnamed servants) was essentially the same. People lived inside warehouses and huts built of locally cut timber. The earliest extractive practices required neither a large nor a skilled labor force. In contrast, sugar is costly to produce and requires both skilled labor and specialized equipment. As sugar production expanded and increasing numbers of entrepreneurs arrived in the colony to claim a share of the wealth that sugar was generating, shortages of labor became chronic. This was an intractable fact for all of the colonies. After 1655, sugar production eclipsed that of all other agricultural commodities and clear divisions in housing emerged that underscored distinctions based on status and wealth, even among planters. Enslaved Africans were imported in ever greater numbers, essentially replacing other labor sources to such an extent that administrators sought legislation to encourage the shipment of more white servants to the colony. By the mid-eighteenth century, the ratio of African to European had reached 8:1.

Here it is necessary to articulate certain assumptions that inform interpretations of laborers' housing on Nevis. Because we have found vernacular housing in the modern built landscape with links to the plantation past, we are asserting that for Nevisians, the house forms are not freighted with stigmatized social connotations. However, such spaces can be, and likely were, conceived as places for affirmation of self or served as domains where expressions of identity and autonomy could be achieved, particularly when these spaces housed families (Battle-Baptiste 2011). This concept of "homespace" as a "captive domestic realm" is not diminished by the character of the home (Battle-Baptiste 2011, 95) or the rudeness of construction. In the way that provision grounds came to be considered "property" and a "right" among enslaved workers, houses also constituted a vital element of personal space. In the context of slavery, such spaces may also have incorporated elements of African cultural heritage through familiar physical structures or uses of built space that stemmed from multiple origins (Ferguson 1992) and likely served important social functions that were beyond the influences of the planters (Haviser 1999, 359).

The dwellings of enslaved laborers on the Nevis sugar estates were temporary, impermanent structures that were functional yet fragile, built of perishable materials by planters who were loath to spend money even on clothes for the enslaved. These houses were as likely to deteriorate over time from natural rot as they were to suffer destruction during hurricanes. Unlike many house forms seen elsewhere in the Caribbean, where wattle-and-daub, earthfast, or masonry construction were common, such housing was rare on Nevis if it existed at all. An exception was the earthfast plantation house at the Hermitage, which suggests at least that the technique was not unknown (Leech 2005). A few household servants or kitchen staff who lived on the larger estates may have been quartered in a room in the great house, and there is evidence at two Nevis estates of servant quarters built of masonry that were similar to types noted on Barbados. However, there were few large estates on Nevis and fewer that had "great houses" deserving of the title. Detached masonry buildings that housed servants were uncommon. During the first half-century of the colony, the plantation owner's house on many estates was not significantly larger than accommodations for laborers. They were great in name only, although they were built with at least a ground floor made of local stone—which Nevis has in abundance—and a wooden second story (Meniketti 2015). These houses rarely had more than three rooms. Houses that qualify as "great" were constructed with multiple rooms, had expansive staircases and porches, and stood at least two or two and a half stories. The ground floor was generally of carefully finished masonry and the upper floors were built of timber and split-board siding. Porches may have had as many as three bays. After 1680, shingles and occasionally clay tile were used for roofing. The Pinney family mansion, Montravers, was a rarity. It was an edifice of imported brick that stood an impressive three stories tall (Pares 1950; Fradgley 2001; Townsend 2002). The kitchen house alone was larger than most great houses on Nevis. At such estates, servants might be housed in substantial masonry structures.

Analyzing Nevisian Housing

Analysis of housing is based on contemporary records, maps, and archaeological survey. Archaeological data from several plantation sites and five contemporary estate maps suggests that marginal spaces were commonly used for the dwellings of enslaved laborers on Nevis. The visual evidence of housing for enslaved plantation laborers comes in three forms: illustrations on estate maps, decorative borders on contemporary landscapes of Caribbean colonies, and as generic "African villages" depicted on island maps. Written accounts are generally too simplistic to be of much value for analysis. By comparing surviving images of dwellings shown on estate maps with archaeological deposits, we can describe the housing for enslaved workers with a reasonable degree of certainty. While only a few Nevisian estate maps have survived from the eighteenth or nineteenth centuries that depict laborers' housing, those that exist consistently portray the dwellings provided for enslaved workers as square or rectangular single-roomed wooden-sided structures. The huts or cabins are usually shown with thatched roofs. In many cases, furrows representing provision plots are shown alongside the huts. The majority of "cabins" have one door and a window on the side, but a few are shown with windows on either side of the entrance.

The eighteenth-century Clarke Estate map in the holdings of the Horatio Nelson Archives in Charlestown is particularly informative because it illustrates a cluster of houses, each with a plot for growing household produce (depicted as furrows) and each of uniform dimensions (Figure 3.1). These houses are situated on a parcel at a significant distance from the great house but with immediate access to the sugar works and the fields. The map legend labels these dwellings as "Negro Houses." Significantly, the cabins are not shown as orderly or in rows; they are widely spaced and share centralized provision grounds. The impression is one of community. The dwellings are located on the border of estate land adjacent to a drainage ravine. The general size of these structures conforms with findings in the archaeological record of dwellings I have recorded at three African village sites on Nevis. The Morgan's and Vaughn's villages are shown on a map drawn by Governor J. Alexander Burke Iles in somewhat generic form as square and in rows (Iles 1871). Assessment of the size of these houses was based on the signature footprint of these structures: rectangular, unnatural arrangements of stones or boulders that act as foundations that raised the floors above the ground (for a clear plan view see Meniketti 2015, 175). Measurements of the axis were made from the center of the stones both in sequence, diagonally, and longitudinally. Because it is likely that timber framing was balanced on the centers or crowns of the stones, these stones define the exterior dimensions of buildings. Propping up houses in this manner is a common practice today on Nevis, especially for "country cottages," as Nevisians refer to them. Figure 3.2 illustrates a hypothetical reconstruction of a typical dwelling with the archaeological footprint as found in the field shown next to it.

Figure 3.1. Hypothetical reconstruction of a laborer's house. Shown to the right of the house is the typical "footprint" of stones found on the landscape that is used to identify the house. Image created by Marco Meniketti.

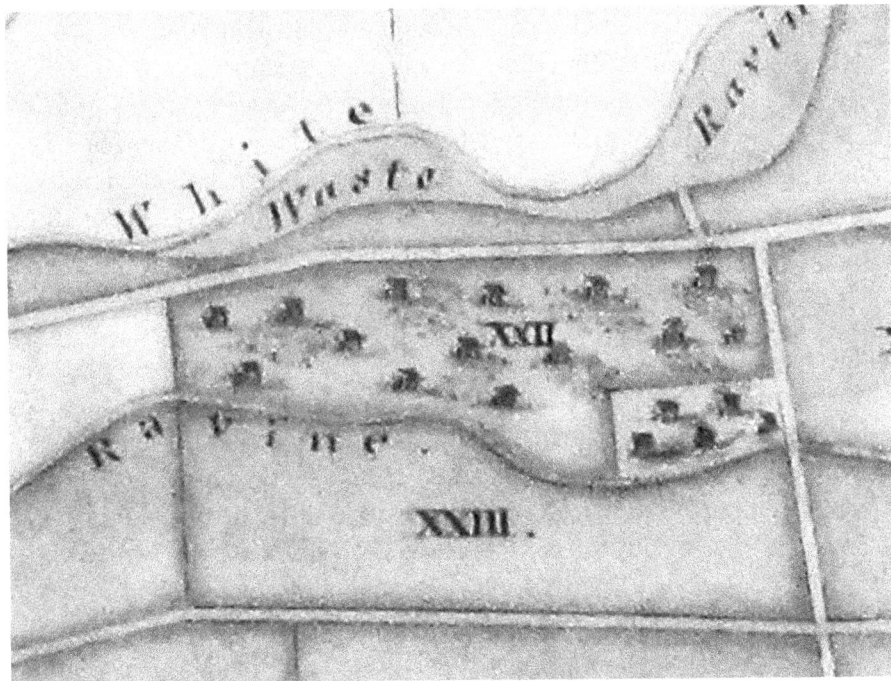

Figure 3.2. Closeup image from the Clarke Estate map. Used with permission of the Archives of the Nevis Historical and Conservation Society.

The dimensions of these houses are consistent with archaeologically recorded examples from Jamaica, although materials and construction methods differ significantly (Armstrong and Kelly 2000, 384). The lack of formality of house arrangement exhibited at Clarke's is also shown on a map of the Jessups estate on Nevis, where again the houses are scattered around provision grounds and trees.[1] As at other estates, the housing area borders a deep ravine (ghut). Of note on the Jessups map is the size of the houses. Many are shown as rectangular rather than square and with windows symmetrically placed on either side of the doors, but it would be a mistake to think of them as creolized Georgian architecture. A map depicting the Oliver estate, again from the eighteenth century, does not illustrate individual buildings, but a legend signifies the location of "Negroe Houses" adjacent to a ghut at the extreme end of the plantation, some distance behind the estate house (Oliver 1919; see also Meniketti 2015).

The use of thatch for roofing huts is not surprising, as this was a common practice for most structures on Nevis during the first century of settlement. The tradition of thatching roofs was not reserved for slave housing; the use of this material is as likely to have stemmed from European practices as from indigenous or African ones (Butzer and Butzer 2000, 21). Although it might seem compelling to do so, it cannot be argued that slave housing was constructed to mirror specific African patterns or to conform to familiar African types because more than one homogenous housing tradition can be traced to Africa. To make such an argument we would need to make assumptions about the common origins of all enslaved Africans brought to Nevis. In fact, many traditions would have been imported that represented the diversity of the enslaved population. Local tradition holds that most of the enslaved who lived on Nevis were of Yoruban heritage, a concept that is reinforced through poems and songs during the annual culture festival. Undoubtedly many were. However, the architectural evidence does not support this assertion as strongly as other elements of Afro-Nevisian culture. Although the typical structure for plantation housing on Nevis resembles one specific type of Yoruban housing—square and thatched—the particular form in Africa was commonly constructed asymmetrically of wattle and daub. This form is entirely absent from Nevis but is found elsewhere in the Caribbean. However one construes the use of thatch, this custom need not be associated with any particular group. It might as likely have its origin in the building traditions of the first wave of English and Irish settlers, who frequently used thatch to roof small houses at home. A more pragmatic view from this analysis suggests that expedience and economics were greater factors in the design of the first houses, which came to be the traditional form. A creolized aesthetic combined European elements that dated from before the import of Africans with elements that emerged later that were familiar to Yoruban and other ethnic groups as they appropriated the spaces and asserted their own sense of home-place. Of note is that screw pine (*Pandanus utilis*), an imported plant, is commonly found associated with village sites across the landscape. This flowering plant from the Old World tropics, which is not a pine at all, is excellent for thatch and basket weaving (Barlow 1993, 119).

Although thatch was a common material in construction, historic sources indicate that thatch was also perceived as a problem by colonial authorities when it was used in town. These sources tell us that thatch was used in architecture beyond the realm of housing. The Nevis Council issued proclamations that described the fire dangers the boiling of sugar syrup, the "dressing of victuals in the streets," and other open sources of fire posed to houses and places of business because most town buildings were built of wood and thatch.[2] An act of the council sought to remedy the source of the fire hazard by curtailing and confining such activities. Only in later years did the council press for an end to the use of thatch altogether, imposing fines for those who did not comply and requiring the use of shingles on all buildings within 200 yards of the main streets in towns. As late as 1699, the council felt the need to specify that the chimneys of cook houses and kitchens would henceforth be built "of brick or stones."[3]

Undoubtedly, the majority of mundane domestic activities of slaves were conducted outside the dwelling, a practice likely brought from Africa (Ferguson 1992; Haviser 1999). Cooking and other activities would take place in the yard. Nevis is, after all, in the tropics and it would have been uncomfortably warm indoors. The yards, not the houses, were important spheres of social interaction. Cooking outdoors was done with clay braziers and "monkey pots" best suited for stews. Activities might also be conducted behind the houses, shielded from view of the great house and incidental surveillance, a practice that has been described in Jamaica and elsewhere (Armstrong and Kelly 2000, 385). On Nevis it seems that housing was frequently beyond the view of the estate house; thus, activities might occur unmonitored anywhere on the grounds of slave dwellings. In fact, this arrangement may have facilitated the emergence of a community consciousness outside the realm of plantation surveillance—a subversive landscape that contributed to patterns of autonomy. What emerges is the idea of a "conceptualized landscape" that overlapped the built landscape and derived "localized meaning through social practices and experiences" (Knapp and Ashmore 1999, 11). In effect, the dwellings may have come to be perceived as property divorced from the plantation and dissociated from the condition of slavery for short periods of each day (Meniketti 2016). Travelers to the Caribbean occasionally reported in some locations that slave cabins were locked up tight like strongboxes, a clear sign of ownership (Berthelot and Gaumé 1985, 3).

The Clarke Estate map shows more than landholdings; it also illustrates the divisions of the estate into specific activity areas and offers insights into land management practices and to historical conceptualizations of space in the plantation context. Various treatises were written during the eighteenth century about how to lay out and manage plantation estates efficiently, such as that written by Bryan Edwards (1793) of Jamaica or Avalle (1799) of Saint Domingue. These often emphasized the efficient placement of workers' housing. These authors were participating in the early phases of the industrial revolution and the ascendency of capitalism, when such innovative concepts as standardization, efficiency, and land management were gaining traction in the world of commerce and business. Edwards wrote that houses on Jamaica were "seldom placed with much regard to order, but, being always intermingled with fruit-trees, particularly the banana, the avocado-pear, and the orange—the Negroes' own planting and property—they sometimes exhibit a pleasing and picturesque appearance." He went on to state that "allowing for differences in climate, they far excel the cabins of Scotch and Irish peasants" (Edwards 1793, 2:133–134). Although this statement in context was meant to simultaneously denigrate Irish and Scots and justify the existence of African slavery, it underscores important facets of the built environments of housing for the enslaved and the use of plots where such housing was sited for producing edible fruit.

Applying the principles of standardization and efficiency to plantations was viewed as a means of increasing productivity. The practice of standardization may have materialized on the plantations first in slave housing. In their cogent analysis of housing and social significance on Jamaica,

Armstrong and Kelly (2000, 378) cite Higman, who provided an account of an 1836 report to Parliament that remarked that "Negroe" houses on Jamaica were generally built near the center of plantations and not far from the works. The report clearly emphasized industrial efficiency. However, while such theories were no doubt put into practice in Jamaica or on French-controlled islands, there is little evidence on Nevis for the rapid adoption of such a model. Plantation owners on Nevis appear to have been more concerned with maintaining workers out of sight and housing there was more likely to be situated on marginal land that was unsuited for planting rather than on sites that provided efficient access to work zones. In fact, despite the tidy rows of African houses on Governor Iles' map, archaeological survey suggests otherwise. Iles may have been depicting what he thought an orderly postemancipation village ought to look like.

Archaeological Evidence

As no dwellings for laborers from the pre-emancipation era survive on Nevis, archaeological evidence of workers' housing is crucial to our understanding of the built environment. Archaeological investigations were conducted on three sites: Morgan's Village, Vaughn's Village, and Bush Hill. Table 3.1 provides the dimensions of stone features associated with slave dwellings. Measurements of platforms were made at five locations in three parishes from estates spanning two centuries. Additional data comes from samples from three village sites and three isolated finds that are not recognizably associated with a particular historic estate. The isolated structures are distinct from the typical village structures in that each is larger and exhibits a more defined rectangular platform. Artifact evidence suggests that each spanned the period of slavery to beyond emancipation. Artifacts used in this assessment were diagnostic ceramics, pipe stems, bottle forms, and iron objects, such as cooking utensils and pots. Just as important as the typical house size is the spacing of houses in the villages, which reflects the amount of living space any individual or family would have had and provides clues to population density. The average size of a house platform is 6 feet 4 inches × 9 feet 10 inches (1.9 meters × 3 meters) at the Morgan's Village site and 6 feet 11 inches × 10 feet 5 inches (2.1 meters × 3.2 meters) at the Vaughn's village site. The few house platforms

Table 3.1. Dimensions of house platforms at Morgan's village

Cluster	Width	Length	Number of stones defining shape	Location
Group 1	1.40 m (4.60 ft)	2.05 m (6.72 ft)	9	Morgan's Village
	1.25 m (4.10 ft)	2.60 m (8.53 ft)	5	Morgan's Village
	1.55 m (5.08 ft)	2.20 m (7.21 ft)	12	Morgan's Village
	1.30 m (4.26 ft)	2.95 m (9.67 ft)	17	Morgan's Village
	2.30 m (7.54 ft)	4.65 m (15.25 ft)	6	Morgan's Village
Group 2	2.50 m (8.20 ft)	2.65 m (8.69 ft)	6	Morgan's Village
	1.90 m (6.23 ft)	2.56 m (8.39 ft)	4	Morgan's Village
	1.90 m (6.23 ft)	2.95 m (9.67 ft)	12	Morgan's Village
Group 3	2.50 m (8.20 ft)	3.45 m (11.31 ft)	10	Morgan's Village
	2.75 m (9.02 ft)	3.80 m (12.46 ft)	8	Morgan's Village
Group 1	2.25 m (7.38 ft)	3.50 m (11.48 ft)	8	Vaughn's Village
	1.95 m (6.39 ft)	3.0 m (9.84 ft)	6	Vaughn's Village
	2.35 m (7.09 ft)	3.0 m (9.84 ft)	5	Vaughn's Village
	2.30 m (7.54 ft)	3.45 m (11.31 ft)	9	Vaughn's Village
	1.95 m (6.39 ft)	2.95 m (9.67 ft)	4	Vaughn's Village
Group 1	2.25 m (7.38 ft)	3.25 m (10.66 ft)	5	Bush Hill
	2.50 m (8.20 ft)	3.00 m (9.84 ft)	6	Bush Hill
Group 2	3.50 m (11.48 ft)	4.35 m (14.27 ft)	9	Bush Hill
	3.95 m (12.95 ft)	4.50 m (14.67ft)	11	Bush Hill
Brown Village	3.50 m (11.45 ft)	5.35 m (17.55 ft)	9	Hillside
Montpellier	4.25 m (13.94 ft	5.50 m (18.04ft)	10	Roadside
Cox Village	2.95 m (9.67 ft)	3.50 m (11.48 ft)	8	Roadside

at Bush Hill are slightly larger; they average 10.0 feet × 12 feet 5 inches (3.0 meters × 3.7 meters). The isolated finds averaged 11 feet 7 inches × 15 feet 9 inches (3.5 meters × 4.7 meters).

The arrangement of houses at the Morgan's Village site suggests a dense population. Houses were spaced unevenly on a terraced slope adjacent to a drainage ghut bordering the north side and a historic road defining its south side, which itself bordered a steep ravine (Figure 3.3). The road connected the Morgan's sugar works with an important thoroughfare of the plantation era. Terracing was constructed of stacked stone, small pebbles,

Figure 3.3. House platforms and terrace walls at the Morgan's Village site. Photo by Marco Meniketti.

and earth fill, creating flat areas large enough to support single structures with a few square feet to spare and giving the village the appearance of a staircase. Two pathways wound their way through the many terraces. Houses were close to one another; 15 feet (4.6 meters) was a typical spacing. No space was allocated for garden plots. However, several aged trees of domestic value were present adjacent to some of the terraces. According to an informant who lives on an adjacent property, furrowed land for garden plots at the bottom of the slope where the village apparently ended date to the 1920s. His grandmother worked the land near her cottage at the foot of the Morgan's estate and grew many traditional crops, having learned how from her mother.

The presence of domestically useful plants are an important indicator of former housing on the landscape. These include agave (*Agave caribae-icola*), commonly known as century plant; aloe (*Aloe barbadensis*), which, despite its name, is not native to Barbados; tamarind (*Tamarindus indica*); mango (*Mangifera indica*); and soursop (*Annona muricata*), three species of which are native to the Lesser Antilles. Guava (*Psidium guajava*), a native plant that earlier indigenous peoples cultivated, is also present. These plants all have household uses and most are not native to the Caribbean; they were introduced as ornamentals, as medicinals, or as supplementary food sources. Communities housed on marginal land had minimal space available for growing provisions and what they had was the least suitable for that purpose, yet they managed. Historic documents regularly refer to potatoes as the most common crop in the provision grounds (Gay 1929).

In overgrown regions of abandoned terrain that were once part of the plantation landscape, the presence of one or more of these plant species often hints at a former household. However, many of the plants described here are easily dispersed by the droppings of monkeys and the countless free wandering sheep and goats, so distribution alone is not an indicator of household production or planting. A careful search often reveals the signature stone arrangements in close proximity to these plants. Associated artifacts help confirm the assessment while providing suitable clues to dating. Dating the stone platforms with associated ceramics and bottle forms reveals that not all structures date from before emancipation, which strongly suggests continuity of housing and construction practices through the early twentieth century among poorer sectors of society. That house forms based on plantation dwellings continued in use is attributable to more than economics and at the least suggests that the type did not carry a distasteful stigma of plantation enslavement. Had a stigma been associated with the house form, carryover into a popular vernacular type would seem unlikely. Instead, the type was embraced and embellished.

The spacing of structures at the Vaughn's village site was similar to that at Morgan's and also made extensive use of terracing. The Vaughn's site has a gentler grade and is much larger spatially: as many as fifty dwellings were spaced across a landscape that also included stacked-stone animal pens and two masonry foundations that supported larger buildings about three times the size of houses. While the Morgan's Village houses were arranged vertically on a steep slope, the houses at Vaughn's assumed a horizontal arrangement that curved to conform to the contours of the landscape. Most of the houses at Vaughn's village were at the same level, whereas at Morgan's it would have been possible to peer over the roof of one's downslope neighbor. As was the case at Morgan's, Vaughn's village borders a ravine. The scale of the houses and the spacing between them are approximately the same at both villages. Artifacts suggest that some families resided at Vaughn's until at least 1930. Isolated house platforms are notable for being generally larger than the village examples, although the general rectangular shape is maintained (Meniketti 2015, 175). Artifacts are also more plentiful among these larger dwellings, and assorted iron nails, iron hooks, chain, and fragments of factory hardware point to adaptive reuse.

These huts can be contrasted in scale with an example of a probable masonry servant quarters dating to the eighteenth century at the Bush Hill estate. These lodgings contrast with detached housing mainly in materials. The Bush Hill estate may have begun operations in the 1680s under a different name, possibly in the possession of William Stapleton. What is certain is that George Clarke Forbes took ownership around 1780 with sixty-seven slaves. By 1830, close to 100 enslaved workers were present at Bush Hill, making it one of the largest factory concerns on the island (Meniketti 2006, 2015, citing Small and Eickelmann 2007).

The expertly dressed stone and mortared structure, which was close to the great house, was a combination single-story kitchen house, pantry, and living space with two rooms. The two rooms did not connect and had separate entrances. The two doors punctuated the north-facing wall. One opened to the kitchen while the second, spaced by a window between it and the first door, opened to a room separated from the kitchen by a masonry wall. The kitchen had two windows, one at the end on the east-facing wall and one next to the entry on the north side. Brickwork in the corner suggested the placement of an oven and chimney. This room measured 13 feet × 15 feet 4 inches (4 meters × 4.6 meters). The roof for the entire building is no longer extant, but notches in the masonry were clear indicators where ceiling beams were set to support truss work for a gabled roof, which likely matched the appearance of the great house.

The second room measured 20 feet 3 inches × 13 feet (6.1 meters × 4 meters). This room was also entered from a west-facing doorway after a rise of two steps. Excavation revealed a stone floor, but not the finely matched paving slabs found in the great house. Here the stonework was a mosaic of flat pieces of variable sizes recycled from other buildings. Plaster was present in patches on the walls and may have coated the floor as well. With walls averaging 2 feet (6 meters) in thickness and allowance for some rubble caused by growth of a strangling fig at the corner, the kitchen building/servant quarter measured 40 feet 10 inches (12.2 meters) in overall length. It should be noted that this larger room has evidence in the floor and walls of having been modified. A wall has been removed, suggesting that in a previous form the structure consisted of three rooms, each independent from the others. Where there is one room now, there were once two, each about 9 feet × 13 feet (2.75 meters × 4 meters) or just a little larger than the typical detached workers' house. The earlier configuration probably served as quarters for household servants. The structure was evidently modified during the postemancipation period, first into a storage facility and later into a medical dispensary (Meniketti 2015).

In the immediate vicinity of Bush Hill estate are two locations that have been identified archaeologically as areas set aside for laborers. Each of these spaces was in a marginal, topographically challenging location on rocky, slopped ground that was unsuitable for agriculture and might even be considered waste land as far as productivity is concerned. Yet small-scale housing was evidently possible. Stone platforms suggest buildings of the same scale as the rooms in the masonry servant quarters.

Place on the Built Landscape

Marginal land can be thought of as land that is too steep or too rocky for cultivating sugarcane or as land that is adjacent to areas that are subject to unpredictable events, such as along ghuts or drainage channels and ravines that are prone to flooding. In some cases, slaves were put to work building terraces to control flooding (Merrill 1958, 78).

During intermittent rainstorms, water can rush violently down ghuts and overflow with devastating effects. Housing was situated along such ravines at both the Morgan's Village and the Vaughn's village sites. The Morgan's Village site was also on very steep terrain with a slope approaching 30 degrees, necessitating terracing to create flat land for houses. The Morgan's Village site was situated downslope from the Morgan's estate sugar works, close enough to have pleased promoters of efficiency yet situated out of sight from the great house with its expansive view of Charlestown and the harbor. In each case, stones were arranged to serve as foundations, animal pens, and terracing. "This island grows stones," claimed one of my informants, reflecting on the volcanic nature of the island and the difficulty even today of clearing small garden plots. Stones cleared to make space for gardening were put to use for wall and animal pens, not simply piled up.

The term vernacular architecture has been in use since at least 1818, when architectural design theory began to gain prestige. In modern usage, architects often strive to find a "pure" vernacular type that can be stylized and accessorized. Hence, such forms as Tudor Revival, Victorian, Gothic, and Craftsman—to cite only a few—emerged as forms of their own but with a recognizable pedigree in simpler vernacular roots. Some of these styles have become iconic and have transcended the vernacular. By deconstructing contemporary forms, we find that on Nevis, the small cottages of today have their lineage in plantation housing. In their present form, imported materials are a necessity—especially timber—and corrugated tin roofing replaced shingles and thatch in the early twentieth century, yet the fundamental type remains consistent. The concept of vernacular forms as signifying a distinct archetype on which variations are based has immediate application on Nevis. Vernacular architecture is usually based on local needs and materials and is not constructed with formal plans but by traditional methods within traditional constraints or patterns. The architecture on Nevis, as on other islands, whether referring to the houses of European colonists or those of the enslaved population, is often in its original form an adaptation to a tropical climate or is a creolized architectural type based on familiar forms (Buisseret 1980). Although local materials were used, imported materials came to be incorporated in order to distinguish the status of the residents. The contemporary landscape of Nevis includes vernacular types that have their architectural heritage in the plantation dwellings at each end of the socioeconomic spectrum.

The housing types shown in the Clarke Estate map are standardized and conform closely to what is commonly referred to on Nevis today as a "country cottage." Most Nevisians think of country cottages as the quintessential "traditional" house style. The base form is a square or slightly rectangular house but with the addition of a porch and railing, often trimmed distinctively with decorative fretwork. A degree of symmetry is incorporated on the larger houses that have a window on either side of the entry door, each of which has wooden storm shutters. Strap hinges are used on doors and shutters. Traditional houses such as these are a popular motif for artists who seek a picturesque "quaintness" divorced from its architectural roots in slavery. The type is also a favorite subject of highly acclaimed traditional potters on Nevis, who replicate the vernacular houses with clay in miniature, fired with the distinctive red and black buff so typical of Afro-Caribbean ware (commonly known as colonoware). These models are occasionally enhanced with yards to show outdoor activities. Cooking and other necessary activities traditionally occurred outside the

Figure 3.4. A modern image of the manner in which stones are still used to support small houses without foundations. Also shown is the practice of joining separate structures. Photo by Marco Meniketti.

premises while the building itself served as sleeping quarters and living quarters with space to store personal belongings (see Ferguson 1992 for an example). Potters also occasionally model the typical brazier and gallipot.

Such vernacular "cottages" share several architectural elements with earlier forms, including the shape, the scale, the gabled roof, the window placement, and the practice of propping up the buildings above the ground level with readily available boulders or stones. No actual foundation supports the structure; instead, the corners of the house frames and floor beams are supported as level as is possible by piles of stone that are not supplemented by mortar. They are maintained in place by their own weight (Figure 3.4). No wooden beams are sunk into the ground. This use of stone also levels the buildings on sloped or uneven ground. The underside of the cottage is elevated above the ground to facilitate free circulation of air and reduce humidity-induced rot. This space also serves as a convenient place for storage. A large stone is also often found at the center of the arrangement to support the central floor beam that runs across the middle of the house on the long axis and prevents it from sagging. Such an arrangement of stones leaves its signature traces in the landscape long after the buildings have decayed or have been carted away to be used elsewhere. Some of these cottages are brightly painted and remain in use today, while others can be found decaying or in a dilapidated state in the bush.

A photograph in the Nevis Archives that was taken at the Bush Hill factory around 1900 clearly shows a similar house: a wooden-sided structure with a thatched roof. An Afro-Nevisian woman stands at the doorstep, an illustration that the form did not go out of style with emancipation and that Afro-Nevisians continued to use it for at least seventy years. A similar type of structure is also shown in stereo photographs from the 1910s on neighboring St. Kitts; one has a shingle roof while another is covered in corrugated tin.[4] The woman visible in the photograph is seen entering her front door in like fashion to the woman in the Bush Hill photograph, perhaps indicating a stock pose.

The structure has a single wooden shuttered window. The one corner of the building visible in the image is propped on stone, although the lower portions of the remainder of the building are cut off in the photo for the other corners. By manipulating the contrast of the image with a computer it was possible to determine that eight horizontally attached cut planks make up the sides of the house. By using a qualified estimate of 5 feet, 6 inches for the height of the woman pictured and the standard dimensions for doors, the approximate dimensions of the building could be worked out with reasonable certainty as consistent with the larger archaeological examples. The dimensions are estimated at 10 feet × 12 feet (3.0 meters × 3.7 meters). The door is at the center of the shorter side and a single window is centered on the long side.

By the time of the photograph, Bush Hill was mainly processing cotton. Although the image is obviously not that of a dwelling from the period of slavery, it is substantially the same in significant ways. The rocky uneven ground where the house in the photograph once stood is on a slope fronting the factory. This area was archaeologically investigated. The signature arrangement of stones suggests that at least five similar buildings occupied the area. Domestic artifacts collected at the site during archaeological survey span the entire nineteenth century.

The small size and impermanent nature of these houses had a practical benefit after emancipation: they were portable. Local informants describe how houses could be loaded on donkey carts and moved from one plantation to another during the period when laborers continued agricultural work but were no longer attached to any single plantation. This mobility of houses may have played an important role in labor negotiations after emancipation. After slavery ended in 1833, planters still conceived of the formerly enslaved as "their labor" and local officials enacted laws that severely restricted the opportunities of free laborers to agricultural work (Boland 1981, 594; Gaspar 1992). Plantation owners were no longer legally compelled to provide for workers and colluded to reduce worker unrest. However, laborers effectively undermined attempts to maintain them in agricultural servitude by moving their houses, playing one planter against another, or by settling on small plots of government land. In this interpretation, the cabins came to represent a symbol of independence in a changing colonial social landscape and sustained traditional patterns of domestic life (Trouillot 1996).

Conclusion

The housing of enslaved workers on Nevis was highly perishable and ephemeral, yet it was uniform in design and consistent in construction over time. Houses were tightly clustered, and while this served the spatial needs of plantation owners it may have also had the unintended consequence of fostering community. The archaeological remnants of housing for enslaved plantation workers is meager but discernible in former plantation landscapes and can be compared to historic and current vernacular architecture. The style of house had a lasting impact on vernacular forms of the Nevisian landscape. That housing types with foundations in the period of slavery continued to be used long after slavery ended and the gradual shift away from forced agricultural labor suggests that the stigma of bondage was disassociated from the architecture. Instead, we can posit that housing embodied different meanings that emancipated workers associated with independence, ownership, and community. Such a nexus has been demonstrated elsewhere in the Caribbean (Haviser 1999). The house form transitioned from its identification as laborers' housing to personal dwellings and from "plantation housing" to "traditional housing." The power of this transition is that it supported and reified concepts of self-worth and self-reliance in a changing and unstable social landscape at a critical historical juncture. The decades immediately following emancipation were a struggle on several levels as various sectors of society adjusted to new—and for some unsettling—social and labor relations. While control over one's destiny was not assured, control over the household in the form of a house became a reality. Over time, adherence to the style of the architectural archetype anchored the traditional form in a social context that remains a vital and even celebrated part of Nevisian culture today.

Although the main construction material used for homes on Nevis today is cinderblock, many houses continue to be built in the traditional fashion. Some have multiple rooms supported in the traditional manner. In a few cases, historic masonry foundations are appropriated and new houses sited on top of them. A second adaptation of the style in the vernacular is the practice of appending a second room of the same scale as the first that is not integrated with the first structure but is an attached building with its own gabled roof. This presents the double-gabled façade that is typical on Caribbean islands. While Nevisians do not necessarily aspire to live in small traditional homes, many people still do. These structures remain on the landscape not as reminders of a plantation past but as signs of cultural continuity and resilience.

Notes

1. Jessups Plantation, Digital Archaeological Archives of Comparative Slavery, accessed August 2016, https://www.daacs.org/plantations/jessups/#images.

2. "An Act for Suppressing Thatcht Houses and Erecting Brick or Stone Chimnies in All Towns," confirmed October 22, 1701, in Acts and Laws of Nevis, Horatio Nelson Museum, Charlestown.

3. "An Act for Suppressing Thatcht Houses and erecting Brick or Stone Chimnies in all Towns."

4. Copyright 1910 Keystone View Company, in author's possession.

4

Building a Better Village?

Transformations in French West Indian Slave Village Architecture from the Ancien Régime to Emancipation

KENNETH G. KELLY

Archaeological work on the context of plantation slavery in the French West Indies is particularly important. As the enslaved laborers were the overwhelming majority of the population of Guadeloupe and Martinique during the colonial period, their labor was the source of the wealth generated on the plantations. In addition, they are the ancestors of today's Antillais population. They are also virtually silenced in the historical record as they were unable to document their experiences and rarely passed oral histories from past generations to the present (Régent 2012, 12). Members of the elite who wrote about the conditions of life in the French West Indies rarely paid more than passing attention to the enslaved people who populated the landscape and to the built environment in which enslaved people lived. In some ways, this is all the more striking as slave owners exercised any control they wished on the placement and type of housing in which slaves lived, although enslaved people modified and repurposed that housing. With the advent of archaeological research focused on the daily experiences of enslaved Africans and their descendants on the plantation, we can now begin to (1) characterize the settings in which slaves lived on sugar plantations; (2) determine to what degree it varied through time and by place; and (3) commence a comparative study of slavery through the ancien régime, the revolutionary period, and the emancipation era.

The British occupied the French islands of Guadeloupe and Martinique during the Seven Years' War (1756–1763). In the years after the occupation, sugar production continued to expand on both islands (Blackburn 1997) and slave importations increased the numbers of enslaved people. Yet the trajectories of the two islands diverged widely in the revolutionary period of 1789–1804 (Blackburn 1988). Some of the dramatic events of this period were manifest in Guadeloupe and Martinique. The storming of the Bastille in July 1789 and the subsequent declaration of the Rights of Man caused shockwaves in both island societies as the planter class clashed with the free people of color who believed that the Revolution would afford them with new rights of citizenship, a process that was solidified for free citizens in the early 1790s. Likewise, rumors flew through the enslaved community that slavery had ended or that more free days had been assured (Dubois 2004, Régent 2004). These rumors and the fact the "promised" changes did not occur were likely behind a spate of planned, attempted, or realized slave insurrections, such as the 1789 insurrection in Martinique and in the 1790 uprising in Guadeloupe (Bénot 2003; Dubois 2004; Régent 2004). The August 1791 revolution in the Plaine du Nord of St. Domingue (present-day Haiti) and the subsequent upheavals there also probably influenced the 1793 insurrection of Trois Rivières and Sainte-Anne in Guadeloupe (Bénot 2003). British forces invaded and occupied Martinique and Guadeloupe in the spring of 1793, but Republican troops and newly freed slaves repulsed them from Guadeloupe. The de facto abolition of slavery in St. Domingue occurred in late 1793. By the end of 1794, Guadeloupe was in Republican hands and slavery had been abolished by decree from the metropole. However, as in St. Domingue, emancipation had come with the conditions of continued plantation labor for most (Dubois 2004, 167). This did not occur in Martinique, where British troops, in concert with the planters and free people of color, were able to retain control of the island and slavery continued unabated. Eight years later, as Martinique prepared to return to French control, the law of 30 Floreal year X (May 20, 1802) was passed, ensuring that slavery would continue as before. In contrast, on Guadeloupe, emancipation remained in effect until 1802–1803, when Gen. Richepance arrived with thousands of French troops. Seizing control of Guadeloupe, the French forces reimposed slavery on the population in 1803. Slavery endured in Martinique and Guadeloupe until its final abolition in 1848 (Dorigny 2003; Régent 2004).

Archaeological Insights about Architectural Changes on Guadeloupe

In 2001, I identified a series of slave villages associated with sugar plantations on Guadeloupe (Kelly 2002). Based on criteria of accessibility and
public ownership, I chose village areas on two estates for more detailed
archaeological work: Habitation Grande Pointe at the southern tip of
Basse Terre and Habitation la Mahaudière near the northern extremity of
Grande Terre (*habitation* is the French word for plantation). In both cases,
the village sites were reasonably well preserved because they were not
subjected to agricultural use after they were abandoned (Figure 4.1). Excavations at La Mahaudière demonstrated that the village site was occupied
before 1760 through the revolutionary period, when the plantation was
operated as a *sucrerie nationale*. It continued to operate in the nineteenth
century and was eventually abandoned late in that century as the plantation ceased to be profitable. The village at Grande Pointe had a shorter
period of occupation, from the very late eighteenth and early nineteenth
centuries through the mid-nineteenth century. Therefore, while the occupation of La Mahaudière clearly spanned the time before and after the
Revolution, it was less clear that this was the case at Grande Pointe. However, Grande Pointe proved interesting because of several unique features
of its slave village (Figure 4.1).

Habitation Grande Pointe is located in the commune of Trois Rivières
on an isolated coastal plain that is cut off from its nearest neighbors by
steep slopes. It is also about 3 kilometers from the center of the Trois
Rivières uprising of 1793, during which twenty-three members of the
planter class were killed (Dubois 2004, 129). The cause and purpose of
the uprising was complex: it was claimed that it was a response to a royal-
ist (counterrevolutionary) plot (see Dubois 2004 for a detailed account).
Regardless of the cause, it played directly into planter fears of murder at
the hands of their slaves. Our work at Grande Pointe revealed a unique
(at least in the French West Indies) masonry wall surrounding the slave
village and separating it from the nearby planter's house and sugar works.
Within this walled compound, the individual houses were largely built of
basalt rock, which is locally plentiful, and the houses were clearly placed in
regular rows in the village. This pattern of regular grid spacing of masonry
houses corresponds with a generalized pattern of village organization that
appears to have developed in Guadeloupe in the period immediately after
slavery was reestablished (Kelly 2008b, 66). The enclosing wall is unusual;

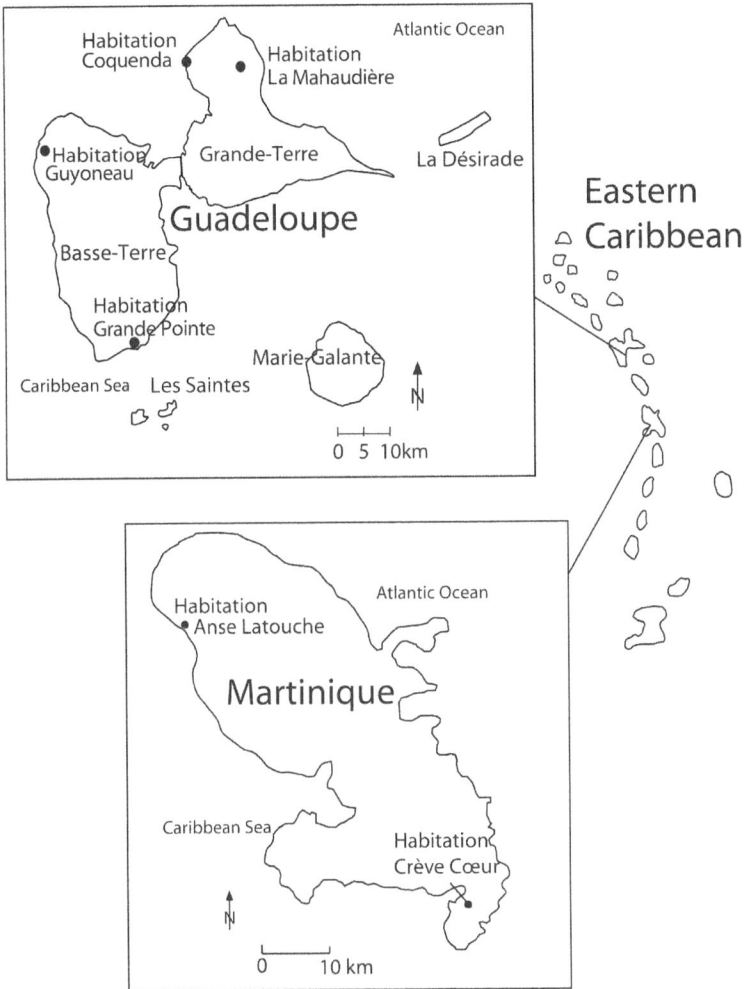

Figure 4.1. Map of Guadeloupe and Martinique. Created by Kenneth Kelly.

similar walls are reported for a very limited range of locales that includes Cuba (Singleton 2014, 2015) and St. Croix (Chapman 2010). This raises the question of why it is there. In Cuba, a walled village was found on a coffee plantation that was founded shortly after the Haitian Revolution. Theresa Singleton argues convincingly that the wall at Cafetal Santa Ana de Biajacas was built to permit slaveholders to lock up the residents of the village at night to guard against the possibility of insurrection (Singleton 2014, 193). The dimensions of the walls surrounding the slave villages at the plantations of Clifton's, Castle Coakley, and The Williams in St Croix are not well described, but they are associated with "improvements" to the villages that were instituted in the early years of the nineteenth century (Chapman 2010, 108–109). It is highly likely that planters made the "improvements" at the St. Croix estates and built the wall at Cafetal Santa Ana de Biajacas in part to improve their surveillance of and control over the captive population. Some scholars interpret centralized and organized settlements as a means of disciplining the landscape and its residents and providing better surveillance (Vlach 1995). I argue that the same process was under way at Grande Pointe, where the wall was built in response to a newly realized fear of slave revolt in a village that was established in the very late eighteenth century. The owners at this plantation, which was run by a Madame de Saint-Jours, may have felt particularly vulnerable due to its remote location (Flohic 1998, 359). The masonry wall, which still stands at over two meters tall in some places, would have permitted the planter to effectively control the movement of the enslaved villagers, particularly at night, adding a sense of greater safety for the planter (Figure 4.2). The village at Grande Pointe, which was established on a regular grid pattern, also conforms to the sorts of changes Chapman (2010) documents in the Danish Virgin Islands, which he associates with the slavery reform movement of the early nineteenth century, although an equally probable explanation is that the orderly layout of the village facilitated surveillance and order. While the walled village is the most explicit form of post-Revolution control seen on a Guadeloupean plantation, it is not the only one.

Habitation la Mahaudière was a large sugar plantation that was clearly active from at least the mid-eighteenth century. Archaeological work has revealed a continuous occupation for well over 100 years, until the late nineteenth century (Gibson 2007; Kelly 2011b). During the earlier period of occupation, housing was characterized by lightly built post-in-ground wattled houses, the *kaz en gaulettes* that are still seen in some areas of Guadeloupe. Archaeologically they are indicated by seemingly randomly placed arrays of postholes dug through the very shallow soils and into the limestone bedrock of the hillside where the village is located. These houses are clearly associated with the prerevolutionary period, as the artifacts in the postholes and associated features all date to the eighteenth century (Figure 4.3). In the nineteenth century, the village was located on the same site but the housing was built in a very different way. The

Grande Pointe works, *maison de maître*, and village

Water Mill

Maison de Maitre

Wall surrounding village

Wind Mill

Village

Caribbean Sea

Figure 4.2. Plan of Grande Pointe, Guadeloupe. Map created by Kenneth Kelly.

plantation established a series of uniform houses with masonry half-walls that were built in a gridlike pattern across the existing village site (see Gibson 2007 for details of chronology).

Architectural changes such as these, often referred to as "improvements" because they correspond to a growing discourse that sought to cast slavery in a more "humane" light, were double edged. I argue that the "improvements" at the village at La Mahaudière were part of a series of negotiations that were undertaken during the period when slavery was reestablished in Guadeloupe. A series of *arrêtés*, or decrees, promulgated between July of 1802 and April 1803 regulated the conditions of the reestablishment of compulsory work. Slavery was not formally reestablished until May 1803, when an *arrêté* decreed that the island would return to the statutes in force before the Revolution. The decrees required planters to increase allocations of clothing and food and to eliminate night work (Régent 2004, 427–432). The improvements of the new village at La Mahaudière predated the reform movement. Masonry buildings were said to be more healthful than wattled structures and the regular arrangement of the village meant that it was easier to keep it more orderly, which was supposed to promote cleanliness (Chapman 2010). However, the standardization of all of the housing eliminated opportunities for village residents to

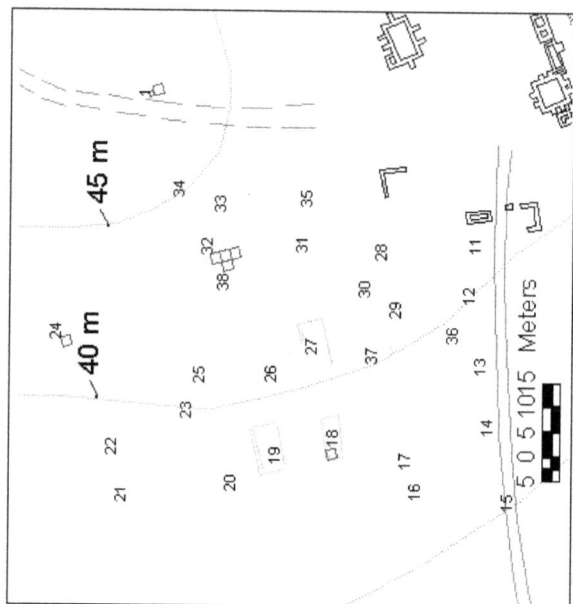

Village detail

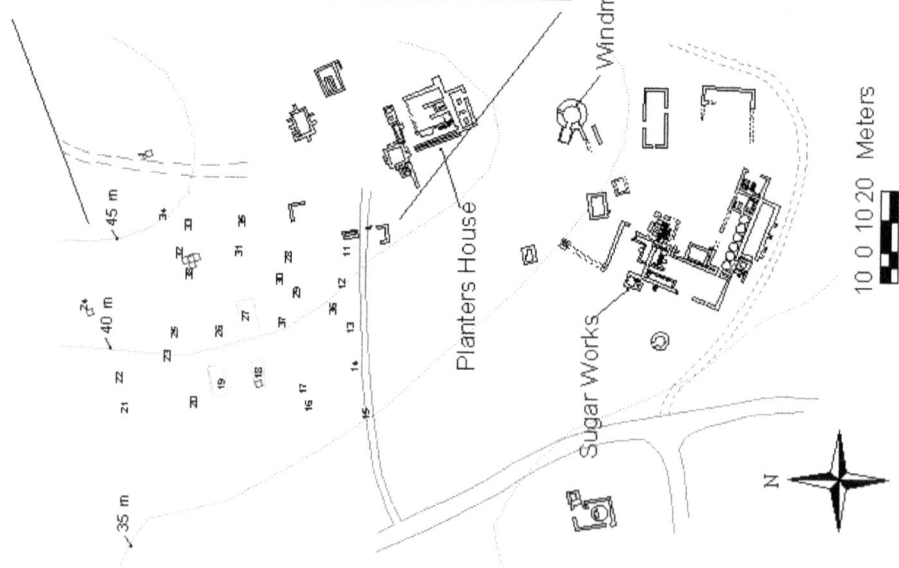

Numbers indicate house remains

Figure 4.3. Plan of La Mahaudière, Guadeloupe. Map created by Kenneth Kelly.

express themselves (see Armstrong and Kelly 2000). The close spacing of housing in the village also eliminated the yard areas surrounding the houses that enslaved people used to raise produce and medicinal plants (Handler and Wallman 2014). In addition, the regular spacing of slave houses made possible more efficient surveillance of the comings and go-ings of village residents and their self-discipline (Delle 1998). This last factor was probably very attractive to the plantation owners and managers as they worked to reenslave a disaffected population. Although there is no evidence that a wall surrounded the village such as existed at Grande Pointe, at both estates we see the same imposition of an orderly village arrangement coupled with "improved" housing.

The pattern discovered at the first two slave villages archaeologically investigated in Guadeloupe was not a chance occurrence. Additional evi-dence from Habitation Guyonneau in the northern Basse Terre commune of Deshaies supports these interpretations. In 2001, as part of my initial survey of slave village sites on Guadeloupe (Kelly 2002), I visited the lo-cation of the slave village for this estate as it was depicted on the "Carte des Ingénieurs du Roi," an unpublished map of the island that dates to the 1760s.[1] The village was located about 2 kilometers north of the Guyonneau main house and on the far side of the sugar works. A brief archaeologi-cal reconnaissance of the site revealed eighteenth-century ceramics and bottle glass and little else; other properties were more promising for my research goals. Several years later, archaeological research conducted in advance of property development on a location much closer to the main house at Habitation Guyonneau identified a nineteenth-century slave vil-lage site that consisted of masonry structures similar to those at La Ma-haudière that were arranged in a regular gridded fashion (Casagrande and Serrand 2008), again as seen at La Mahaudière and Grande Pointe. Thus, evidence at Habitation Guyonneau suggests that before the Revolution, the village was at some remove from the industrial and management cen-ter of the estate and that in the early nineteenth century, coincident with the reestablishment of slavery, the village was relocated to a more central location, "improved," and made more amenable to surveillance.

Another example of slave village relocation was identified at Habita-tion Coquenda in the commune of Anse Bertrand. Here, archaeologi-cal survey identified two village locations: one dating to the eighteenth century in the area indicated on the "Carte des Ingénieurs du Roi." This site of this village has been largely destroyed by cane cultivation but it remained identifiable because eighteenth-century artifacts were visible in the canefield. A second village site that dates to the nineteenth century is still preserved farther to the west. The evidence suggests that the village that dates to the eighteenth century was abandoned and a new village was established in a different location. While this nineteenth-century village does not appear to have been established on a grid pattern and we do not yet know how the houses were constructed, its presence confirms that Habitation Guyonneau was not the only plantation to have a slave village that was relocated at the end of the revolutionary period, around 1802 or 1803.

During the revolutionary period, plantations on Guadeloupe underwent a variety of transformations depending on their legal status. Some were abandoned when their owner fled or relinquished control, others were sequestered and their administration was handed over to members of the revolutionary government, and others continued to function, albeit at lower levels of productivity due to the challenges of securing sufficient labor. Although archaeological work on several other plantations has not identified the same types of transformations in housing, this may well be due to the variability of the revolutionary experience on Guadeloupe (Casagrande 2007; Henry et al. 2009). Several factors may explain this: it may be that these estates didn't face the same disruptions and need to reintegrate the working population and/or it may be that the archaeological work, which has been conducted from a French cultural resource management perspective, has not focused on the experiences of the enslaved workers and their villages (Kelly 2014b, 2014c). The experience of slavery is still not a key research focus for French archaeologists.

Laborers' Housing on Martinique

Fewer plantations on Martinique have been the subject of archaeological work than in Guadeloupe. However, one sugar plantation that dates to the eighteenth and nineteenth centuries, Habitation Crève Cœur, has been the subject of extensive excavation (Kelly 2014a; Wallman 2014). I have visited several other plantations with the consequences of the revolutionary period in mind, so I believe that some observations may be made with reasonable reliability.

Habitation Crève Cœur was a sugar plantation that was broadly comparable with La Mahaudière in size, scale, and duration of operation

(Barret 1990). Our archaeological work identified the slave village, which was located on a hill above and west of the main house and near the sugar works. Archaeological survey showed that the village was not established on a grid and that houses were placed on whatever level spaces could be found or created (Wallman 2014). There were no standing remains of slave housing and there are likewise no visible walls or foundations. All that is visible on the village site are the slight platforms that formerly supported houses. Excavations at a number of these platforms revealed the archaeological traces of lightly built wattled houses much like the *kaz en gaulettes* that were identified at La Mahaudière. These houses were indicated by a series of postholes dug into the subsoil and bedrock of the hillside, by the platforms, and in some instances by associated retaining walls and prepared floor surfaces.

Artifacts found in, on, and below the platforms demonstrated that we had a sample of houses that spanned the period from the late eighteenth century through the late nineteenth century (see Wallman 2014 for details of chronology). In 1822, Renouard observed that in Martinique, the majority of houses were of plank or wattle-and-daub construction and few were made with masonry (Renouard 1822, 108). In a departure from what has been identified in Guadeloupe at Grande Pointe, La Mahaudière, and Habitation Guyonneau, village housing remained the lightly built *kaz en gaulettes* (called *ti-baum* in Martinique) and never changed toward the more durable "improved" housing seen at the estates mentioned in Guadeloupe or in the Danish Virgin Islands (Figure 4.4). The work at Crève Cœur also opens the possibility that slave housing may leave very limited traces in steep settings, as the lightly built *kaz* may well have been elevated above ground, as is seen with houses in present-day Dominica. If that is the case, it has consequences for our interpretation of the living spaces surrounding such a house.

Archaeological work elsewhere in Martinique has been extremely limited and few projects have identified or focused on slave village areas. Work by the Institut national de recherches archéologiques preventives (INRAP, the French cultural resources management division) at Habitation Séguineau at Le Lorrain and Habitation De Luines at Le Vauclin has identified other slave village elements that reveal construction of lightly built wattled houses instead of the "improved" houses seen in Guadeloupe or in the former Danish Virgin Islands. Test excavations at Habitation Anse Céron at Le Prêcheur reveal that masonry housing (similar to that at

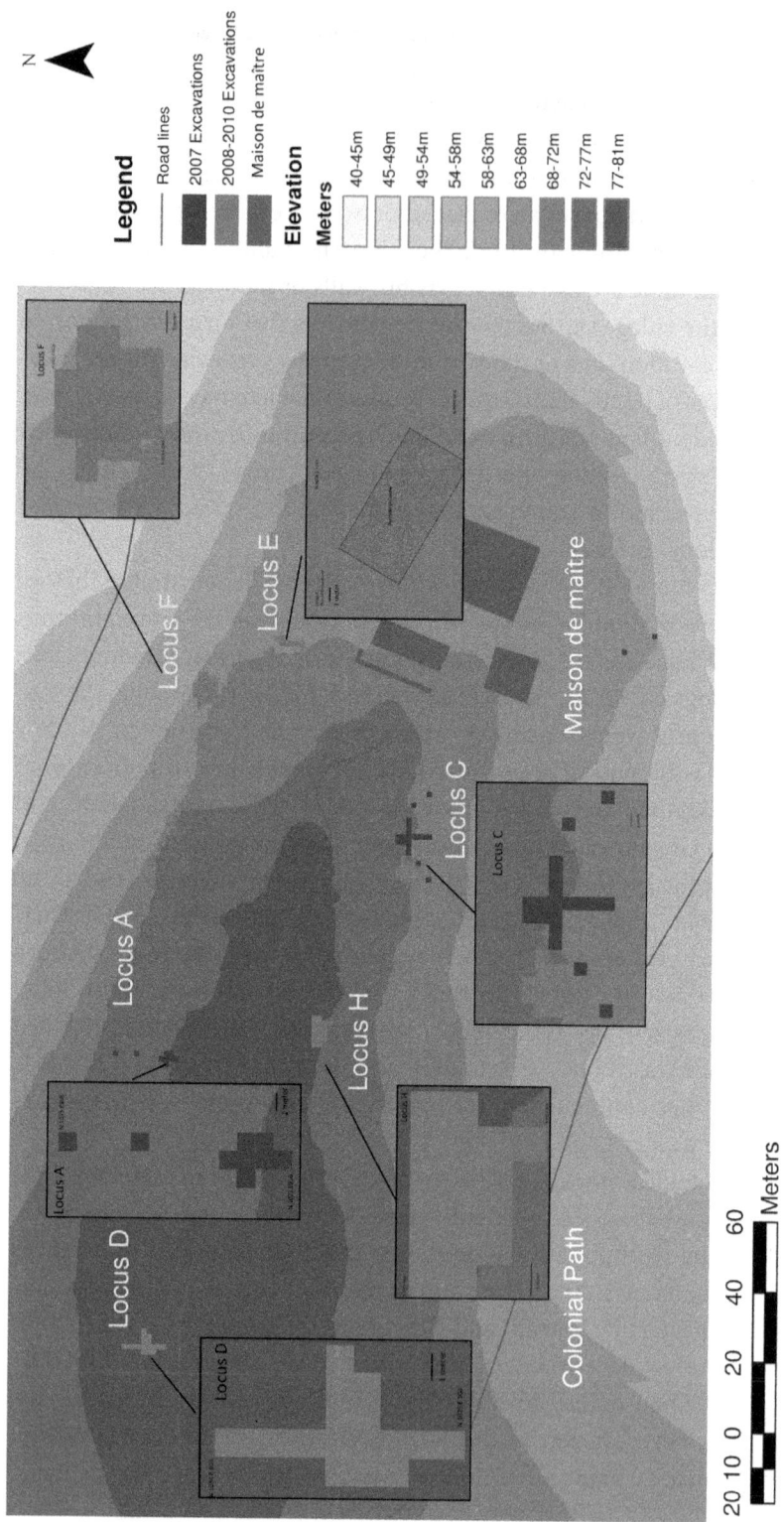

Figure 4.4. Plan of Crève Coeur, Martinique. Map created by Kenneth Kelly.

Guyonneau in Guadeloupe) was preceded by post-in-ground structures. This suggests that masonry structures, which were still in use in the early twentieth century, date to the postslavery period (Casagrande 2012).

Visits to a number of plantations and other locations that relied on a large labor force where archaeological work has not been conducted have revealed the presence of "improved" masonry housing, frequently constructed as multiple unit "tenements" (see Chapman 2010). However, in all cases these structures appear to date to the period after slavery, when plantation owners built structures to house the former slaves and keep them on the property (Christophe Charlery, personal communication, 2008). Examples of these tenements can be seen at the Trois Ilets pottery, where multiple rows of structures would have housed hundreds of workers. Less extensive multiunit worker housing structures that follow the same model are still extant at Habitation Pécoul at Basse-Pointe and at other plantations along the northeastern portion of Martinique.

Plantations throughout Guadeloupe and Martinique retain the remnants of workers' housing, whether they are small wattle-and-daub houses, "improved" masonry houses, or communal barracks-style structures. In all cases, the built environment of plantation villages included significant nonstructural elements that were as important for daily life as the structures themselves. The yard areas surrounding the houses where people lived were modified for use in a variety of ways, including gathering and socializing, preparing and consuming food, engaging in ritual activities, healing, and burying the dead.

"Missing" Yards at Crève Cœur

According to documentary sources, the enslaved population in the late eighteenth century on Habitation Crève Cœur numbered more than 150 individuals. The *Carte du Moreau du Temple* (Bousquet-Bressolier et al. 1998), which dates to the 1760s, depicts fourteen houses arranged in two parallel rows on the summit of the hill above the great house. A map from 1827 indicates thirty-two houses in the village, this time in four parallel rows.[2] The population of the village seems to have been larger than could have been accommodated in the number of houses depicted if they were limited to the two parallel rows.

Initial pedestrian survey revealed fourteen possible house platforms on the hilltop. Moving beyond a simple pedestrian survey, we initiated a shovel test survey of the entire hill. This shovel test array along and across the entire slope and summit of the ridge identified a number of platforms on the upper flanks of the ridge that were smaller than would accommodate a typical slave house.

Farther downslope, we encountered zones of deep deposits (with excellent preservation) on some of the steepest slopes of the hill. We estimated that these were refuse deposits that had been jettisoned over the side of the hill and accumulated at the base of the steep slopes. In total, the detailed mapping associated with the shovel test survey documented over forty potential house sites, including larger platforms and level areas such as on the summit and small ledges or retaining walls on the slopes. This number of potential house sites seemed to more accurately reflect the number of houses one would expect on a plantation of this size that was active for at least 150 years.

The diverse array of possible house sites we encountered scattered over the slope and summit of this hill led us to think differently about the yard areas and the built environments surrounding the houses. We were compelled to revisit the traditional interpretation of the house yard (Armstrong 1991) when we began to conduct some excavations on a variety of settings in the village area. Our excavations of platforms along the summit of the ridge generally revealed the type of house yard site we would expect: postholes that delimit the outline of the house set in a yard area relatively free of encumbrances where a host of activities associated with daily life would take place and were reflected in the artifacts.

However, when we began to excavate the smaller "platforms" that we identified along the upper slopes of the ridge, we were surprised by what we found. There was clear evidence of occupation, as shown by the kinds of artifacts present; the features, including postholes, some with nails in them; and indications of prepared surfaces. But these platforms were really more like ledges, not anywhere near wide enough to have supported a house. As we continued to excavate farther down the slope from the platforms, we continued to encounter postholes, including postholes with nails. Some of these postholes had been dug as much as one meter into the ground on slopes that were almost too steep to stand on. During the excavation, we had to create toeholds and handholds to keep from slipping down. Given the nature of these features and the household debris surrounding them there must have been some other type of structures on these slopes. It seemed unlikely that these were fence lines. Post-in-ground houses, such

Figure 4.5. Masonry houses at Anse Latouche, Martinique. Photo by Kenneth Kelly.

as the well-known wattled *kaz en gaulettes* or *ti-baum* (as had been exposed on the summit of the ridge) could not have left these sort of traces. I suspected that these postholes were associated with houses built up on pilings or stilts (Berthelot and Gaumé 2002), yet the ethnohistoric data on slave villages makes no mention of any such housing that I am aware of. There are some examples of slave villages built on very steep slopes—here I think of the village ruins still visible at Habitation Anse Latouche near St. Pierre, Martinique, where the masonry houses were literally perched on the steep slope, or of Morne Patate or Sugar Loaf in Dominica (Hauser 2015b), but in those cases the houses are set on platforms dug into the hillsides (Figure 4.5). Thus, it seemed possible that slave housing might have been established in such precarious places in other contexts, although I am unaware of any such archaeological evidence from other villages.

Of course, slave housing built on pilings over very steep slopes is not apt to have had the same sort of yard area surrounding it as is found in slave villages on flatter ground. At Crève Cœur, the small platforms may well have served as the entry to the houses and as a small area for cooking or other activities (some of the ledges at Crève Cœur had evidence of hearths). In these cases, the range of activities associated with

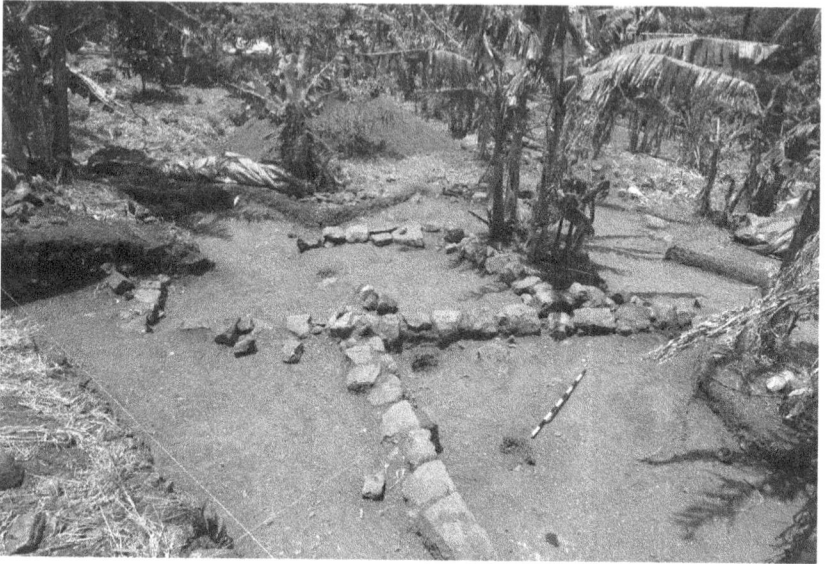

Figure 4.6. Morne Patate. Photo by Kenneth Kelly.

the yard areas would have had to have been conducted elsewhere (as at Morne Patate and Sugar Loaf, where the house was on one platform and the yard was on an adjacent platform [Hauser 2015b]), in a much more constrained space, or within the structure (Figure 4.6). The lack of yard space for these homes presents an interpretive challenge, as many of the activities we would expect to see in the yard would have taken place elsewhere and therefore the archaeologist would be confronted with an absence of evidence. In addition to the problem of associating activity areas with specific houses, there is also the challenge that anything that was left inside a piling supported house would not necessarily enter into the archaeological record (i.e., the ground) at that location. Furthermore, would not a house supported by pilings require a large quantity of nails (due to a framed construction) and thus be archaeologically visible? These were questions that occupied me as we worked to interpret the postholes and midden deposits we were identifying on the slopes at Crève Cœur.

Several years later I had the opportunity to spend a couple of weeks on Dominica assisting Mark Hauser with his geophysical project in the Soufrière enclave. During my stay, I became intrigued by the variety and number of houses I saw that were built on pilings and situated on very steep slopes. While clearly not as old as the archaeological house sites at

Crève Cœur, they were facing analogous circumstances and showing evidence of adaptation to these steep settings. I began studying them closely by ethnographically documenting houses and house yards in Dominica, in particular at the villages of DuBuc, Caulihaut, and Mahaut.

While many of these houses today sit on masonry bases or pilings, a number were on unmilled wooden pilings. Several elements became clear very early in my study of these structures. For one, although they were all built with board siding, it was clear from the interior and underneath that their framing, including how they were affixed to the pilings, was usually completed without nails. Thus, while nails were used to secure the planks to the walls and the shingles to the roofs, they were not necessary for the architectural integrity of the structure as a whole. The timbers of these frame structures were usually fastened with wooden pegs. Floors, necessarily made of boards, would not have required nails either, as gravity, pegs, or ties would have sufficed to keep them in place. Based on my observations of other structures built with wattled walls in Martinique and Marie Galante, I realized that wattled panels could have been inserted into the frame structures like those covered by boards in Dominica and that thatch roofing could certainly have been used, obviating the need for roofing nails.

Many of the structures I visited and studied in Dominica were on very steep locations, without any of the traditional yard area surrounding them (Figure 4.7). For some, the floor was on ground level only at the entrance (which was adjacent to a path or road that provided access to the doorway), a pattern much like the platforms at Crève Cœur. Some had adjacent cooking areas, but they were perhaps 2 to 4 meters below or above the level of the structure's living surface.

The pilings the framed houses sat on were also not integral to the structure but had notches at the top that the sills of the framed structure sat on (Figure 4.8). Frequently, wooden pegs connected the sill to the piling at the notches. This meant that pilings that decomposed could be replaced without endangering the integrity of the structure. According to local residents who built the houses and maintained them, the pilings might easily extend up to a meter into the soil if local conditions permitted.

The impermanent attachment to the pilings was also associated with another element, which I was unaware of when I began this project. In Dominica, much of the present-day occupation of the island is concentrated on a narrow ring of coastal land. This is because of several factors.

Figure 4.7. House on pilings, Dominica. Photo by Kenneth Kelly.

Clearly, being close to the coast provides easy access to the ocean and water-based transport. But following the abolition of slavery and the dissolution of many plantations, free laborers sought places to establish their own homes. Frequently, they did so by what amounts to squatting on land they did not own. The risks of investing money and labor in building a house on land that one did not own could be mitigated by building the houses in a way that permitted them to be moved if necessary. A number of photographs from the early and mid-twentieth century show small

Figure 4.8. Detail of pilings, Dominica. Photo by Kenneth Kelly.

houses being loaded onto trucks or trailers and moved to new locations. When a house is not tied to the land but is on posts that can easily be removed, it is much more portable (Watson and Potter 1993). The coastal location of many of these dwellings is explained because in French island colonies, which Dominica once was, 50 *pas du roi* ("steps of the king"; ~85 meters) from the shore were not owned by individuals but reserved as property of the Crown for defensive use. This land was thus more available to squatters. These areas are also frequently steep and difficult to use. Thus, houses on pilings would suit these locations for more than one reason.

On a steep hillside, the space underneath an elevated house can be useful, if not for people, then for storage. Ethnographic observations from many of the houses in Dominica show that lumber, boats, and other goods are frequently stored under houses. Furthermore, any sort of discarded item that might eventually have a use can be placed beneath a house, where it is protected from the weather and also clearly "owned." Modification made to the steeply sloping surface under or next to a house on pilings for the purpose of storage or to create a working area may also help explain another anomalous feature identified at Crève Cœur: a large expanse of steep slope that appeared to have been covered or "paved" with tightly packed fist-sized stones. This feature, which was initially rather confounding, may have been elaborated in order to protect materials stored under a house. The paving may have been under a house: several postholes penetrating the stone layer were identified. But it may also have been so placed to help protect the surface of the village from erosion, particularly during heavy rains.

Identifying this kind of hillside housing and recognizing it in the archaeological record pose a series of challenges to the researcher. Associating activity areas with specific households, always a difficult task, is made more challenging with the recognition that activities may have taken place at some remove from the house. However, because of the history of these types of houses, the researcher might consider that slave villages may have been in even more marginal locations than we expect and that activity areas may not be in a "yard" adjacent to the house. In short, archaeologists need to recognize the creativity and adaptation of freedpeople in the Caribbean (Mintz 1974).

Conclusion

Because the transition to "improved" housing did not occur before the end of slavery in Martinique in 1848, we see a very different pattern there than we see in the Danish Virgin Islands or in nearby Guadeloupe (Chapman 2010; Kelly 2011b). While all landscapes of slavery can be said to be "contested," as very different goals and desires structure the actions of different groups, how those contestations materialized in different locations depended on specific historical events and trajectories. In Guadeloupe, where the reimposition of slavery meant that plantation owners needed to take actions to bring people back onto the plantation village, planters ostensibly "improved" the housing in villages for the plantation labor force. These "improvements" came at a cost to newly reenslaved workers because they enabled the planters to better surveille them in a built environment that was more regimented and that curtailed the opportunities of enslaved workers to enact resistance to the plantation system. In Martinique, there is arguably less evidence of contestations on the part of the enslaved on the landscape, as the population there had not experienced emancipation during the Revolution, had not had opportunities to leave the plantation, and did not have to be pushed back into the slave village and plantation work. As a result, the ways the system was materialized in

Figure 4.9. "Improved" housing at Trois Ilets, Martinique. Photo by Kenneth Kelly.

terms of housing did not change until after slavery ended in 1848. Only then were estate managers compelled to consider providing "improved" housing to attract and/or retain a newly mobile labor force. Enterprises such as the massive pottery works at Trois Ilets constructed tenement housing that sheltered hundreds of workers and sugar estates that continued to thrive established tenement or otherwise "improved" housing for their workers, as seen at Habitation Pécoul or Habitation Gaigneron, where individual masonry houses still stand near the airport in Lamentin (Figure 4.9).

Slavery as practiced in Martinique and Guadeloupe was very similar to the slavery practiced elsewhere in the Caribbean. However, there were differences, some due to national cultures and others due to the manifestations of unique historical events, such as those associated with the period of the French Revolution. Now that several archaeological projects investigating French slavery have been completed, it is possible that a comparative approach to slave village architecture and the environments enslaved people constructed can identify the commonalities—and the divergences—in the materialization of the experience of slavery.

Notes

1. "Grande carte de la Guadeloupe" (par les ingénieurs géographes), 1763, Département Cartes et plans, Bibliothèque nationale de France, Paris.

2. Paul Monnier, "Atlas des côtes de la Martinique levées pendant les années 1824 et 1825," 1827, Département Cartes et plans, Bibliothèque nationale de France, Paris.

5

Asymmetric Architectures of Enslaved People in Jamaica

An Archaeological Study of Household Variation at Good Hope Estate

HAYDEN F. BASSETT

In the early 1790s, Jamaican planter Bryan Edwards (1794, 137) observed that among the island's plantations, "the cottages of the Negroes usually compose a small village." Each house, Edwards noted, was slightly different and "commensurate to the desires and necessitates of their inhabitants, who build them according to their fancy in size and shape" (138) The typical form was "an admirable shelter" supported by "hard posts driven into the ground" with a floor "of natural earth" and "a roof thatched with palm." As to the contents in each home, Edwards found that each household owned "a small table, two or three low stools, an earthen jar for holding water, a few smaller ones, a pail, and iron pot, [and] calabashes of different sizes" (138). The author continues by noting:

> This account of their accommodation, however, is confined to the lowest among the field negroes: tradesmen and domestics are in general vastly better lodged and provided. Many of these have larger houses, with boarded floors, and are accommodated—at their own expense, it is true—with very decent furniture: a few have even good beds, linen sheets, and mosquito nets, and display a shelf or two of plates and dishes of Queen's or Staffordshire ware. (Edwards 1794, 139)

Edwards's description of a typical house and village for enslaved laborers is not unique. Many of his observations echo those of other chroniclers in Jamaica (Dallas 1803; Stewart 1823). Nevertheless, in the last passage above, Edwards highlights a major distinguishing factor. He infers a spectrum of status among a plantation's enslaved population and suggests that architecture was one important medium through which people conveyed their position "at their own expense." While this account suggests that investment in dwellings was an important marker of asymmetric social relations, it is necessary to consider what other motivating factors influenced how an enslaved householder constructed his or her built environment.

Using archaeological evidence from Good Hope estate in northern Jamaica, this chapter assesses the variation in housing found within a single enslaved community and the significance of architectural expression to enslaved households. Three sites associated with Good Hope that were excavated in the period 2014 to 2016 are used to explore this significance. In doing so, this study builds on a canon of foundational work on the architecture of enslaved people in Jamaica (Armstrong 1990; Delle 1998, 2014; Higman 1998; Armstrong and Kelly 2000; Nelson 2011, 2016; Nelson et al. 2014). It continues and advances our understanding of the relationship between housing variation and social differences in a laboring community (Kelly 1989; Armstrong 1990, 2011; Reeves 1997, 2011, 2015; Higman 1998). The findings of this chapter assess variation in building practices as an important lens for understanding intracommunity social relations and how kinship, work roles, household composition, and whether a setting was urban or rural shaped architectural choices.

Historical Background of Good Hope

Established in 1744, Good Hope, an eight-square-kilometer (2,000-acre) plantation, was one of the largest and most productive sugar operations in Jamaica, exporting an average of 1,500 hogsheads of sugar each year. From the mid-eighteenth through the early nineteenth centuries, John Tharp, custos of Trelawny Parish and resident proprietor of eleven contiguous sugar estates and cattle pens, owned Good Hope. The plantation was centrally located among these landholdings, all of which lined the Martha Brae River from the interior of the island to Falmouth, the capital and principal port of Trelawny Parish (Figure 5.1).

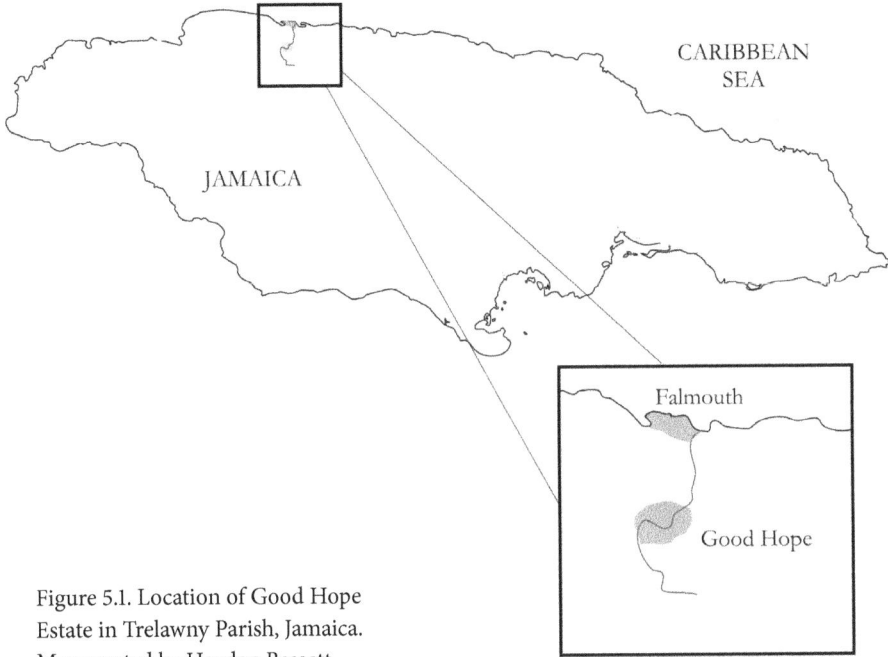

Figure 5.1. Location of Good Hope
Estate in Trelawny Parish, Jamaica.
Map created by Hayden Bassett.

Tharp operated the plantation from 1766 to 1804, when his nephew
William Tharp took over until 1838. William Tharp used Good Hope as
his place of residence while he presided over a collective 65 square kilometers (16,000 acres). Among these operations, John Tharp enslaved from
2,800 to 3,000 individuals at any one time; by the turn of the nineteenth
century he owned the most slaves of any planter on the island (Hart 1994;
Besson 2002). Few documentary records survive on enslaved life at Good
Hope in the late eighteenth century, though those that do reveal that a
labor force of more than 500 enslaved individuals lived and worked on
the plantation.

The vast majority of the enslaved people at Good Hope lived in a village
of 28,000 square meters (7 acres) near the center of the estate, close to its
industrial core. A 1794 plantation plat intricately recorded fifty small gable
dwellings surrounded by house gardens and fences beneath coconut trees
and other vegetation (Figure 5.2). Annual "Increases & Decreases" records for Good Hope indicate than an average of 414 enslaved individuals

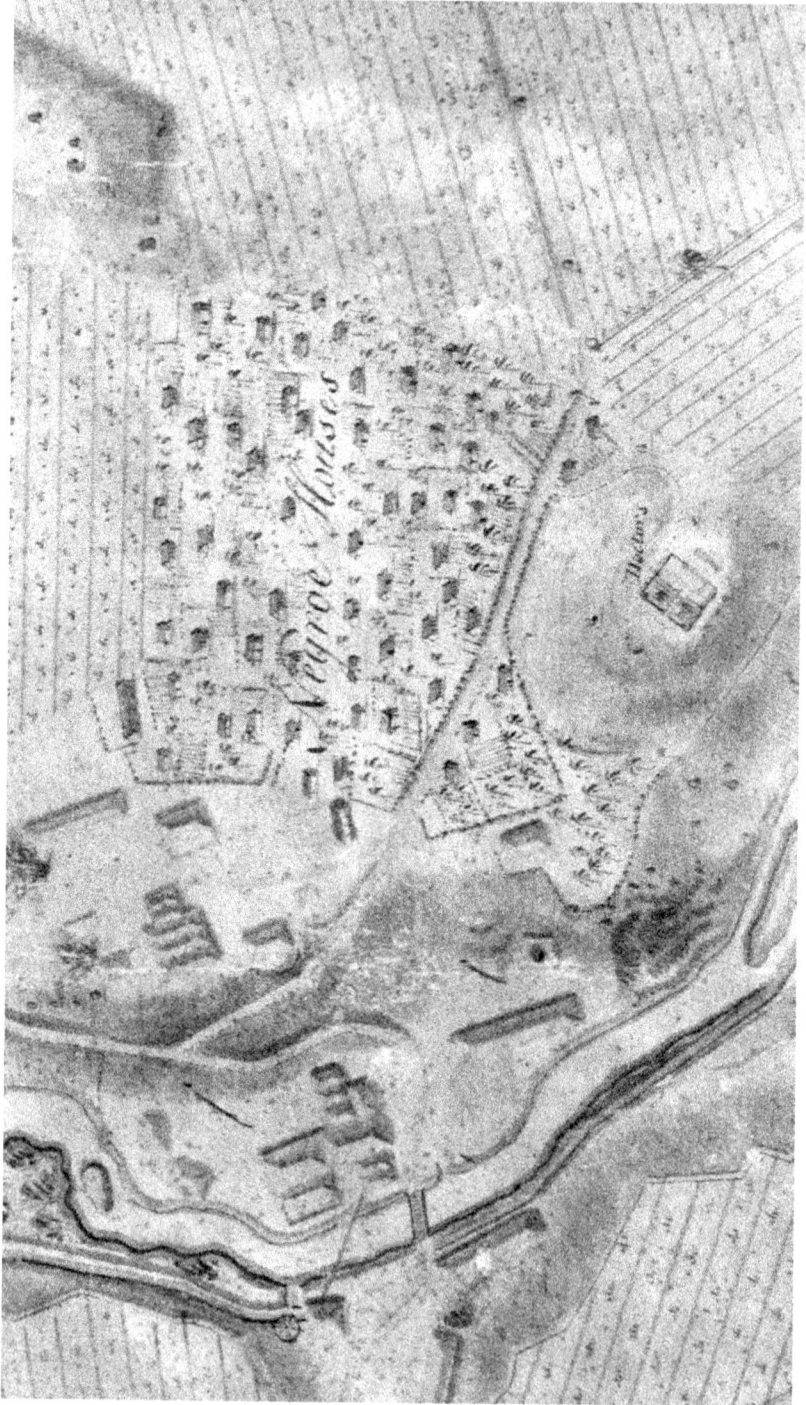

Figure 5.2. Section of 1794 Schroeter plat depicting the Good Hope slave village. Plat drawn by military engineer Capt. John Henry Schroeter. In private collection. Used with permission of Good Hope Estate, Jamaica.

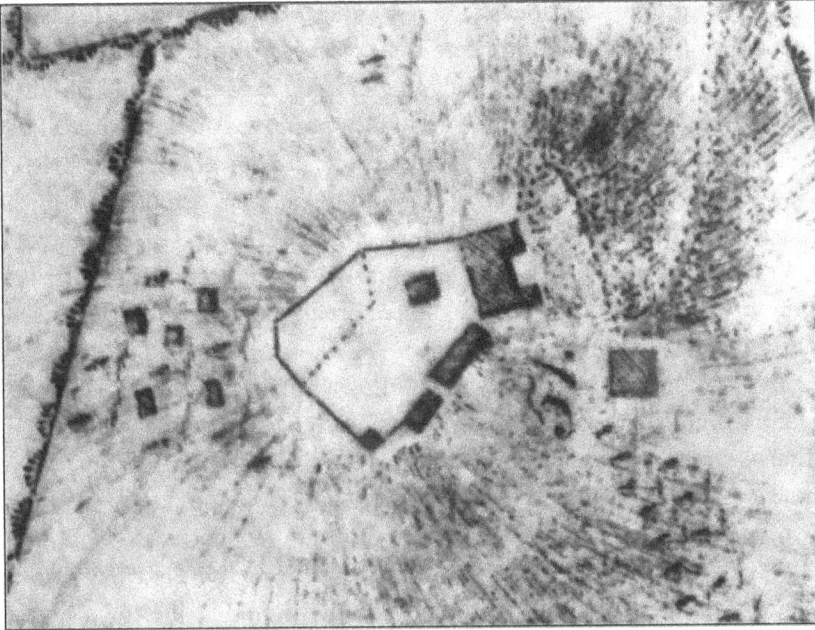

Figure 5.3. A map of the Good Hope Great House and domestic servants' village, anonymous, 1806. In private collection. Used with permission of Good Hope Estate, Jamaica.

likely lived in this village at any given time from the 1790s through the 1830s (Bassett 2017).

A small minority of Good Hope's enslaved population lived in a separate village at the north end of the plantation. There, eight to fifteen enslaved domestic servants occupied a group of houses immediately behind the great house (Bassett 2017). The small domestic servants' village is illustrated on two maps. One, dated 1794, depicted six dwellings; the other, dated 1806, depicted five (Figure 5.3). Probate records for 1804 indicate that approximately twenty-one enslaved individuals worked in and around the great house, although only eleven labored as cooks and house domestics (Bassett 2017). Given the number of houses and the near-continual demands of domestic labor, these eleven domestic laborers likely occupied the small village behind the great house.

At Good Hope, as was the case with most Jamaican sugar estates, the plantation did not end at its planted boundaries but relied on its connection to the sea. This connection was made possible through the port town of Falmouth, 7 miles north at the mouth of the Martha Brae River. There, Tharp constructed a large wharf for importing and exporting goods that included warehouses, docks, a store, and a network of roads to Good Hope. Produce accounts indicate that a large quantity of goods flowed in and out of Tharp's Wharf each year, serving nine of his sugar estates. Hogsheads of sugar and puncheons of rum produced on the Tharp estates were warehoused there before shipment to London, Liverpool, Bristol, New Castle, Glasgow, and New York. Lumber and provisions arrived primarily from Bristol and New York (Bassett 2016a, 2017). Household goods to resupply his properties were temporarily warehoused before distribution to the estates, and on at least three occasions, enslaved people were docked and sold there (Nelson 2016).

By 1790, the waterfront lot was outfitted with a large gentry town house from which Tharp occasionally oversaw shipment of sugar and rum. Tharp's highly skilled enslaved masons and carpenters constructed the house as a scaled-down version of the Good Hope great house; it had two chambers fronted by three large entertaining spaces (Nelson et al. 2014, 102; Nelson 2016). From the early 1790s through the late 1830s, John Tharp and his nephew William sporadically occupied the town house, from which they maintained a social, political, and economic presence in Falmouth during the last half-century of slavery on the island. On each occasion, eight to eleven enslaved domestic servants traveled from Good Hope to support the domestic needs of the town house.

At these three locations—Good Hope, the Good Hope great house, and the Falmouth town house—the enslaved people of Good Hope constructed and occupied their own built environments under varying conditions of enslavement. External constraints varied, including whether a person did fieldwork, trade labor, or domestic service and whether they lived in an urban or rural setting. Yet within these restrictions, enslaved people built and maintained internally defined social worlds. Archaeological evidence of their dwellings, their gardens, and their yards render this constructed world visible and paint a new picture of the various community dynamics people created under conditions of enslavement.

Fieldwork: 2014–2016

The Good Hope Archaeological Project began in 2014 as a plantation-wide survey of the domestic life of enslaved individuals on a large-scale sugar estate. In collaboration with Falmouth Heritage Renewal, I located and sampled villages and quarter sites associated with the plantation's enslaved labor force over the course of three seasons (Bassett 2017). Seasons one (2014) and two (2015) of the project focused on the two village sites at Good Hope and season three (2016) investigated the lives of enslaved people living in Tharp's town house in Falmouth.

During these three seasons, we successfully located domestic occupations for enslaved people at each site in addition to associated dwellings, yards, walls, and other landscape features. In addition to the built environment, the project uncovered over 22,600 artifacts from the eighteenth and nineteenth centuries (Bassett 2017), animating these spaces in ways that speak to the lives of the nearly 500 enslaved individuals who lived and labored at Good Hope at any one time from 1775 to 1838.

Village 1

In 2014, the project sampled the southwest corner of the primary village site at Good Hope. The village, labeled "Negro Houses" on a 1794 map, was located near the plantation's industrial core in a bowl-shaped depression known locally as a cockpit. Village 1 housed an average of 414 people in the period 1775 and 1838, the majority of the plantation's labor force. Documentation defined the demographic composition of the village by occupation; this population consisted of the plantation's field laborers, tradesmen, drivers, hospital workers, livestock keepers, grass cutters, cartmen, and boiling-house laborers, and those who were too old or too young to work.

The project team excavated a total of 184 shovel test pits at six-meter intervals and four 1 × 1 meter test units (Figure 5.4). Whereas the shovel test pit survey located individual houses and yards, the targeted units sampled three of the four house clusters uncovered in the survey. Geostatistical analysis of survey data revealed the presence of distinct size-sorting patterns in ceramics, rendering the taphonomic signature of regular yard sweeping around and between house sites (Bassett 2016b).

Swept spaces articulated the sample area's eight dwellings into four distinct domestic loci. Two loci suggest clusters of two to three houses, while the other two suggest isolated houses that were not connected to other dwellings by swept yards (Figure 5.5). Each house and housing cluster possessed a series of low, dry-laid stonewalls that likely outlined

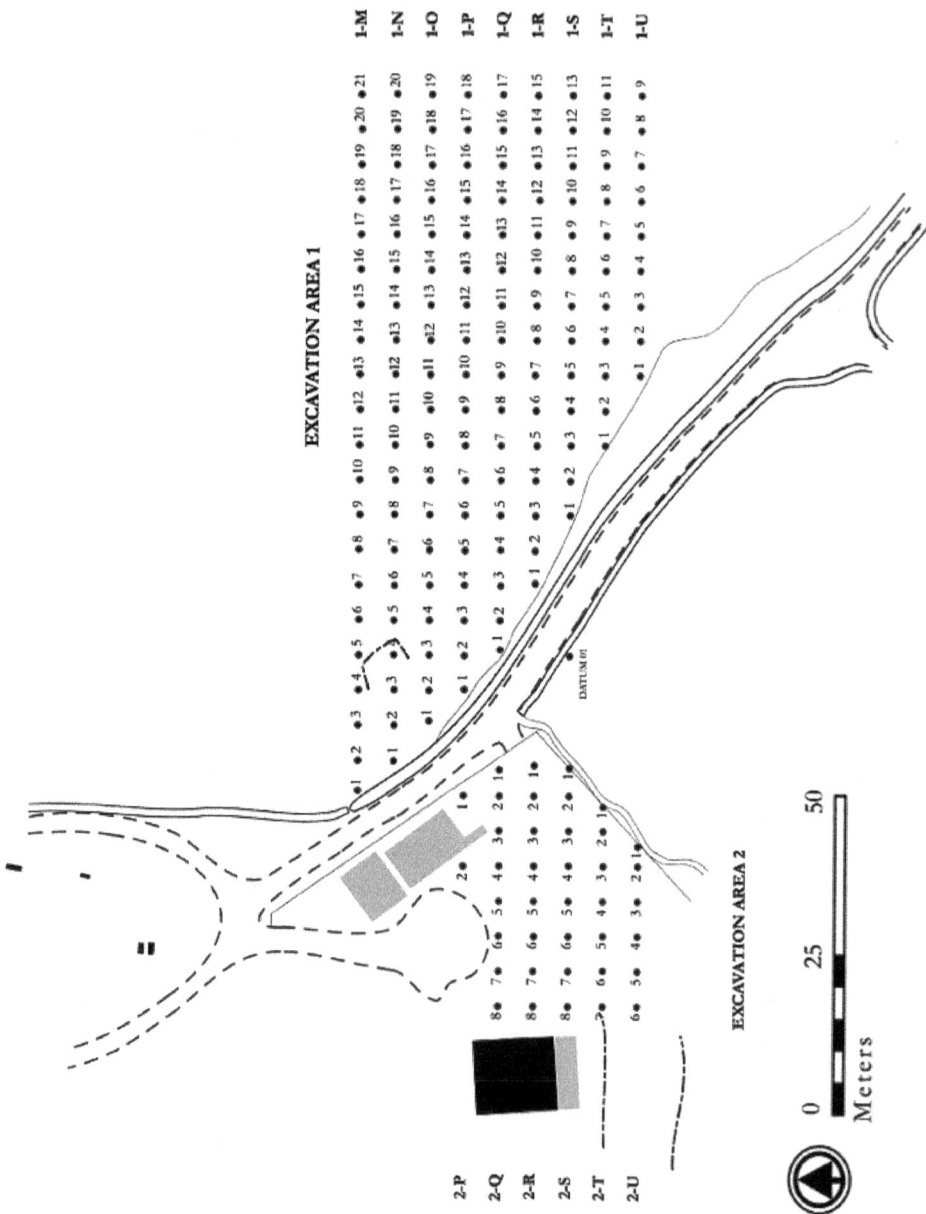

Figure 5.4. Archaeological site plan of Village 1 at Good Hope illustrating shovel test pit survey of the southeast corner of the village. Map created by Hayden Bassett.

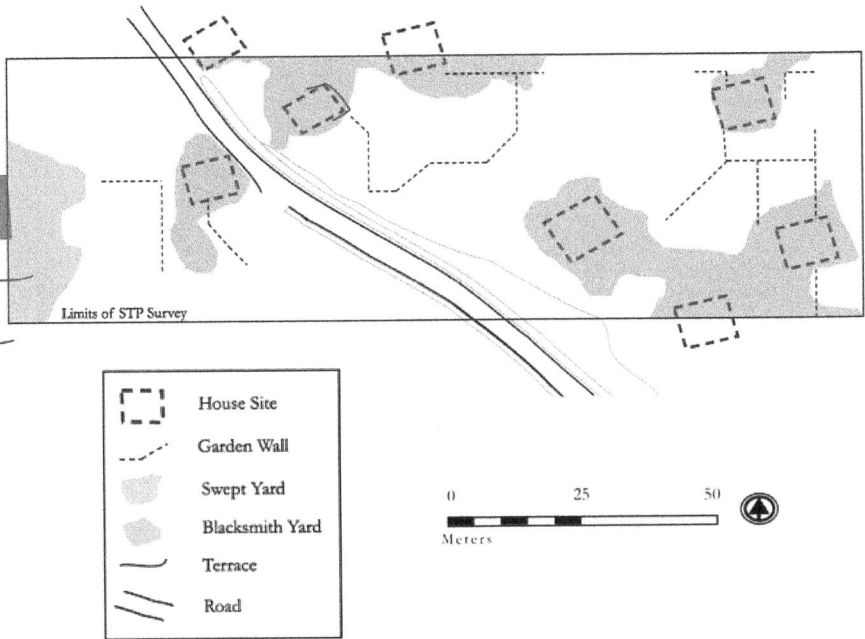

Figure 5.5. Reconstruction of Good Hope slave village site plan based on geostatistical analysis of shovel test pit survey data and stratigraphic sampling. Map created by Hayden Bassett.

individual and common house gardens. Unlike houses and yards, which existed throughout the period of occupation, stone walls demarcating space did not begin to appear until the turn of the nineteenth century.

Village 2

In 2015, the project focused on the small village for enslaved domestic servants northwest of the Good Hope great house. Surviving boundary walls and one remaining house foundation aligned with those illustrated on maps depicting the village from 1794 and 1806. This minimized the need for reconnaissance survey and helped determine the extent of the sample area (Figure 5.6). As with Village 1, the project used a survey of shovel test pits at six-meter intervals to locate subsurface deposits, establish a site

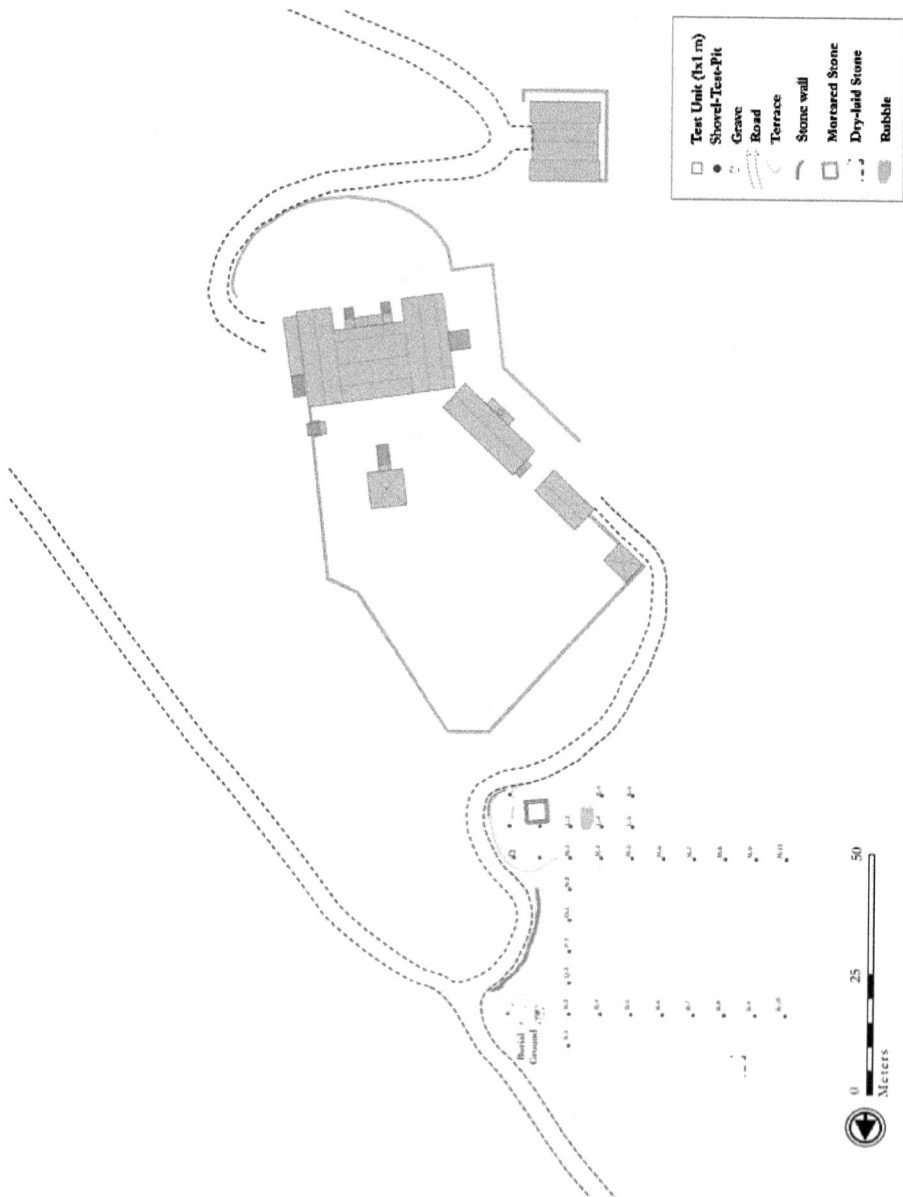

Figure 5.6. Archaeological site plan of Village 2 showing its relationship to the Good Hope Great House. Map created by Hayden Bassett.

Test Unit (1x1 m)
Shovel-Test-Pit
Grave
Road
Terrace
Stone wall
Mortared Stone
Dry-laid Stone
Rubble

Burial Ground

Meters
0   25   50

chronology, and record spatial variation across the extent of the village. A single 1 × 1 meter test unit was also placed in the yard boundary of the surviving house foundations. This provided a household and stratigraphic sample of the artifact-rich "toft-zone" (Hayden and Cannon 1983, 126), or peripheral area of swept accumulated debris that represents the range of household activities (Bassett 2016b, 2017).

As with Village 1, the project created detailed records of all above-ground architectural and landscape features. This included the village boundary wall, one intact stone foundation mortared in course, one dry-laid rubble foundation, one dry-laid cut-stone foundation, and a burial ground marked by low rectangular cut-stone monuments. Of these features, the stone foundations mortared in course represented the best surviving dwelling of an enslaved person on the plantation. The burial ground is situated in the corner of the village, which is an incredible survival, and is considerably smaller than the burial ground for the rest of the enslaved community at Good Hope. This suggests that enslaved domestic servants were segregated from the rest of the enslaved community in death as they were in life. While many similarities between the two villages are present, variation among their similar components, such as yards and dwellings, reveals much about social variation among enslaved people across the plantation.

Falmouth Town House

In 2016, the Good Hope Archaeological Project shifted its focus to an urban setting, the Tharp House in Falmouth. The archaeological investigation of the Tharp House targeted the building's rear yard (Bassett 2016a). As previous studies have shown (Wesler 2013; Nelson et. al 2014; Nelson 2016), enslaved people in Jamaica's ports typically occupied small dwellings or a range of quarters in the rear yards of urban houses. Today, the rear yard of Tharp's town house contains several remnant outbuildings and a central partition wall that divides the yard into two distinct spaces. An 1840s map depicting the space suggests that the masonry partition dates to the period of slavery, as do at least two additional outbuildings that are not visible on the surface.

The archaeological team used shovel test pits to determine the historical organization of people and activity across the yard through time. A total of forty-five shovel test pits at three-meter intervals (Figure 5.7)

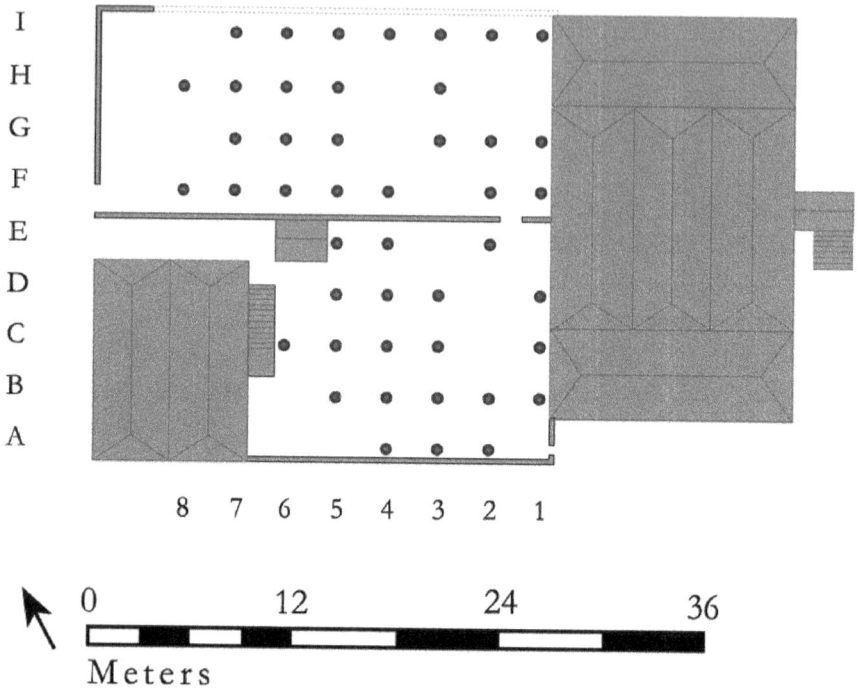

Figure 5.7. Site plan of rear yard of the Tharp town house illustrating locations of shovel test pits relative to standing architecture. Map created by Hayden Bassett.

produced approximately 4,476 artifacts dating from the mid-eighteenth to the late twentieth centuries (Bassett 2016a, 2). As expected, the project uncovered the subsurface remains of the two additional outbuildings dating to the Tharp period (1790–1838) located on opposite sides of the yard's partition wall. Analysis of the outbuilding deposits revealed that the building located in the south yard was historically used as a kitchen while the larger building in the north yard was residential and likely served as quarters for the enslaved house domestics.

Together, the three sample areas—Village 1, Village 2, and the Tharp House rear yard—represent three variable conditions of enslavement within the same plantation. In each location, enslaved people lived and labored in circumstances in which household size and composition, market access, labor demands, and control over domestic space varied. These characteristics each played a role in shaping the time, resources, and motivations enslaved workers had to construct a built environment to suit their different needs.

Architectural Variation at Good Hope

Archaeological findings from the two villages at Good Hope suggest that houses depicted in the 1796 survey plat of the plantation truly represent house locations in the late eighteenth century. However, the survey plat depicts village houses as separate and unarticulated from one another—each house an isolated unit with a small garden surrounded by a field-stone wall. Archaeological evidence reveals a different story in which most aspects beyond house location are simply stylized representations.

The most significant deviations from this representation were the con-structed spaces that extended beyond the walls of a dwelling, creating a domestic complex. Swept earthen yards surrounded each house and were likely constructed and maintained to support domestic tasks and establish relationships among dwellings. Adjacent to yards, low stone walls defined small garden plots that provided for the household, supplementing larger provision plots beyond the village boundaries. Together, the house, yard, and kitchen garden formed the basic domestic unit of an enslaved person's built environment. Elaboration, extension, and/or exclusion of one or more of these three elements created variation among the households of the enslaved community at Good Hope. This constructed variation became one of the many mediums through which social relations were established and negotiated among households of enslaved people.

Houses

Building materials uncovered during archaeological investigations sug-gest that construction varied from household to household. Boarded, nog (or Spanish walling), and wattle-and-daub dwellings stood side by side in the boundaries of Village 1. These findings are consistent with ar-chaeological evidence of nog and boarded houses at Marshall's Pen (Delle 2014, 166) and detailed records from Montpelier Estate. The latter record provides an important snapshot of the architectural variation in a typical village on a Jamaican sugar estate. For Montpelier in the 1820s, this break-down of house construction consisted of 64 percent wattled, 21 percent boarded, 2 percent shingled, 4 percent nog, and 9 percent stone (Higman 1998, 152). Evidence from the eight dwellings from the sample area of Village 1 at Good Hope suggests that board houses roofed in thatch domi-nated other housing types.

In Village 2, mortared stone foundations for a small dwelling now stand near the entrance to the site. This was the only foundation the project found with rough-cut stones mortared in course. In other examples from Villages 1 and 2, house foundations were typically dry laid and commonly took the form of a rubble terrace that leveled uneven ground. To create these forms, cobble- to boulder-sized stones were either stacked to the preconceived footprint of a house to support a sill or arranged around an earthfast frame of corner and ridge posts sunk into the ground. The mortared foundations from Village 2, a remarkable survival of the latter type, include hollow casts of principal posts, studs, and an intact door frame. These voids reveal that the corner and ridge posts were sunk 1.0 to 1.5 feet into the earth and that limestone foundations were laid around these posts in rough courses to just below the height of the floor. Studs were then inserted in regular intervals between the principle posts, connecting the roof frame to the foundations. An additional one to two courses of limestone were then laid to anchor the studs and provide support for a wooden floor. Two narrow slots were left open in the foundation to provide ventilation beneath the floorboards. Stratigraphic testing of this dwelling's yard suggests that the house was built in the late eighteenth century and remained occupied through the 1830s. Although this dwelling appears to represent a significant investment, other houses of this period follow this form within a small range of variation.

While house size can only be estimated for most dwellings, two extant foundations in the villages at Good Hope suggest that housing on the plantation for enslaved people fits islandwide trends. One common denominator emerges among such dwellings that have been excavated and reported on in Jamaica over the past sixty years. As with the two extant stone foundations at Good Hope, house footprints are typically defined by multiples of three feet. This measure is the standard English yard and suggests that most houses were likely constructed by or with the aid of skilled enslaved tradesmen fluent in English building measures. Housing dimensions ranged from 9 feet × 18 feet (162 square feet) to 30 feet × 30 feet (900 square feet). While the eighteenth-century sample is limited, four examples from Good Hope, Drax Hall, and Seville suggest that late eighteenth-century housing was generally smaller and of a more standard size than nineteenth-century housing (Table 5.1). From 1800 through emancipation, house dimensions varied more widely, generally becoming larger yet retaining the building block of three by three feet (Figure 5.8).

Table 5.1. Dimensions of published slave housing excavated in plantation contexts in Jamaica to date

Location	Century	Dimensions	Square Feet	Buildings	Source
Drax Hall	Late 18th	16.6 feet × 29.3 feet	486.38	1	Armstrong 1990, 101
Good Hope	Late 18th	14.5 feet × 15.8 feet	229.10	1	Bassett 2015
Seville	Late 18th	13.0 feet × 19.5 feet	253.50	1	Armstrong 1992, 55–56
Seville	Late 18th	16.3 feet × 22.8 feet	371.64	1	Armstrong 1992, 55–56
Drax Hall	Early 19th	11.4 feet × 19.5 feet	222.30	1	Armstrong 1990, 112
Good Hope	Early 19th	12.2 feet × 21.1 feet	257.42	1	Bassett 2014
Roehampton	Early 19th	16 feet × 24 feet	384.00	1	Higman 1998, 150
New Montpelier	Early 19th	9 feet × 18 feet	162.00	1	Higman 1998, 149
New Montpelier	Early 19th	12 feet × 24 feet	288.00	1	Higman 1998, 149
New Montpelier	Early 19th	15 feet × 18 feet	270.00	3	Higman 1998, 149
New Montpelier	Early 19th	15 feet × 21 feet	315.00	1	Higman 1998, 149
New Montpelier	Early 19th	15 feet × 25 feet	375.00	1	Higman 1998, 149
New Montpelier	Early 19th	15 feet × 28 feet	420.00	2	Higman 1998, 149
New Montpelier	Early 19th	15 feet × 30 feet	450.00	1	Higman 1998, 149
New Montpelier	Early 19th	18 feet × 18 feet	324.00	1	Higman 1998, 149
New Montpelier	Early 19th	18 feet × 21 feet	378.00	3	Higman 1998, 149
New Montpelier	Early 19th	18 feet × 25 feet	450.00	7	Higman 1998, 149
New Montpelier	Early 19th	18 feet × 27 feet	486.00	9	Higman 1998, 149
New Montpelier	Early 19th	18 feet × 30 feet	540.00	3	Higman 1998, 149
New Montpelier	Early 19th	18 feet × 36 feet	648.00	1	Higman 1998, 149
New Montpelier	Early 19th	21 feet × 28 feet	588.00	3	Higman 1998, 149
New Montpelier	Early 19th	21 feet × 34 feet	714.00	1	Higman 1998, 149
New Montpelier	Early 19th	25 feet × 25 feet	625.00	1	Higman 1998, 149
New Montpelier	Early 19th	25 feet × 30 feet	750.00	1	Higman 1998, 149
New Montpelier	Early 19th	27 feet × 30 feet	810.00	1	Higman 1998, 149
New Montpelier	Early 19th	30 feet × 30 feet	900.00	1	Higman 1998, 149
Islandwide estimate	Late 18th	15–20 feet × 15 feet	225–300	—	Edwards 1794, 164
Islandwide estimate	Early 19th	10–15 feet × 15–20 feet	150–300	—	Stewart 1823, 266

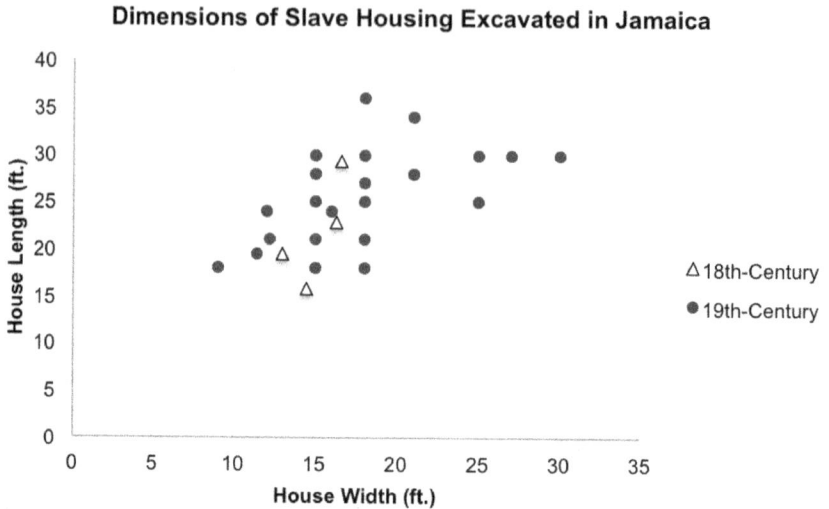

Figure 5.8. Scatterplot of length and width (in feet) for slave housing excavated in plantation contexts in Jamaica. Created by Hayden Bassett.

Two measurable examples from Good Hope, one from the late eighteenth century and one from the early nineteenth, are closer to the lower extreme of this range. These two examples align with period descriptions from Bryan Edwards (1794, 138) and John Stewart (1823, 266), who observed that the dimensions of most housing for enslaved people in Jamaica was ten to fifteen feet wide and fifteen to twenty feet long.

Functional analysis of artifact assemblages from Village 1 and Village 2 revealed several common characteristics among dwellings at Good Hope. Targeted unit excavation at sampled house sites yielded tightly dated stratified contexts associated with each house. Using Douglas Armstrong's (1998) functional categories adapted from South's (1977) categories and controlling for time from 1780 to 1830, each assemblage was placed in five categories, each of which contained three to five subcategories. Most relevant to this study is the "architectural" category, which includes all construction, hardware, finishing, and otherwise decorative material associated with the physical dwelling. At each of the four household loci investigated, architectural material constituted the majority of artifacts recovered.

Comparison of the range of artifact classes suggests that houses in both village sites were built from the same set of architectural materials. This implies that most variation in housing occurred as a product of crafts-manship rather than as a function of differential access to building materials. This is most evident in stone foundations. As previously mentioned, semi-cut limestone laid in course was used for at least one house in Village 2. However, these foundations suggest that this was more an investment in aesthetics than in structural integrity. At least two houses in Village 1 mimicked this aesthetic of cut stone by plastering over rubble foundations to create a smooth plane. This practice is still used in many parts of rural Jamaica and is amplified by scoring the smooth plane to the appearance of ashlar masonry.

Probate records for Good Hope's owners indicate that enslaved trades-men crafted some building materials specifically for the plantation's en-slaved community. An 1805 inventory for the blacksmith shop reveals a stockpile of door hardware referred to as "negro door hinges." This special genre of hardware likely indicates locally crafted strap hinges for use by enslaved people on their houses. Seven of these noticeably thinner strap hinges were recovered archaeologically from the two villages at Good Hope.

Yards

The distribution of ceramics in the village sample area reveals the practice of yard sweeping. For households of enslaved people at Good Hope, the maintenance of domestic space extended beyond the house interior to the exterior space surrounding the quarter. Yard sweeping, which is widely practiced among contemporary Jamaican households, is typically done multiple times a day. Historically, sweeping was done with hand brooms made from tightly bound palm fronds, or "broom thatch," which required its user to bend at the waist and sweep across the yard from center to pe-riphery. The practice removed debris, vegetation, and loose sediment to the edge of the yard, creating a clean exterior living surface for domestic tasks and social gathering. The aesthetic of the swept yard was amplified by the compaction of earth, which was created through a combination of sweeping loose sediment and the daily use of the yard's surface. By keep-ing floors and surrounding yards swept, Good Hope's enslaved house-holds left a distinctive archaeological pattern of small debris at the center of the yard surrounded by larger debris at the periphery. I have found that this signature is most visible spatially through the distribution of average ceramic sherd size.

Detecting yard maintenance through patterns of artifact sizes, or size-sorting (Wandsnider 1996, 341), has been successful in other archaeological contexts. Examples include Samson's (2010, 276) "systematic sweeping accumulations," Samford et al.'s (1986) sweeping-up effect, and Bon-Harper (2009, 2010) and Neiman et al.'s (2014) use of an artifact-size index. In both villages at Good Hope, larger ceramic sizes (greater than 25 millimeters) define the boundaries of these swept spaces, creating a substantial domestic footprint surrounding each dwelling (Figure 5.9). While yards were clearly visible in size-sorting pattern throughout Village 1, evidence for yard sweeping in Village 2 is most evident surrounding the two foundations nearest the road.

House yards and their organization have been viewed in many ways since Sidney Mintz (1974, 232) first observed that "together the house and yard form a nucleus within which the culture expresses itself, is perpetuated, changed, and reintegrated." Building on this observation, Armstrong (1991, 52) defined the house yard in archaeological terms at Drax Hall, noting that "within slave communities, house structures alone are not the primary residence unit. Rather, the house and surrounding yard combine to form an inside-outside house-yard activity unit and a distinctive house-yard pattern of activities and material use." Armstrong (2011, 87–88) later built on the study of house and yard at Seville, observing a shift to large communal yards shared by multiple households and the importance of common yards as spaces of "social interaction and discourse." At Good Hope, archaeological evidence suggests that activities in house yards included food preparation, cooking, house repair, and social gatherings organized around eating, drinking, and smoking. Notably, the sample area yielded no evidence for yard burials, as seen at Seville (Armstrong and Fleischman 2003).

Yards also provided the space needed to grow produce for both subsistence and surplus. As Delle (2014, 18) observes, "Yard spaces were loci of production for the local markets." Domestic tasks could be divided among the members of an extended household, freeing time for production activities and participation in market days. For Good Hope, this local market was the well-known Bend-Down Market in Falmouth, Jamaica, where goods for sale were referred to as "yard provisions" (as they still are today).

Average Ceramic Sherd Size (mm)

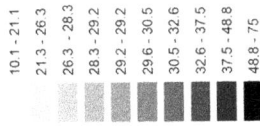

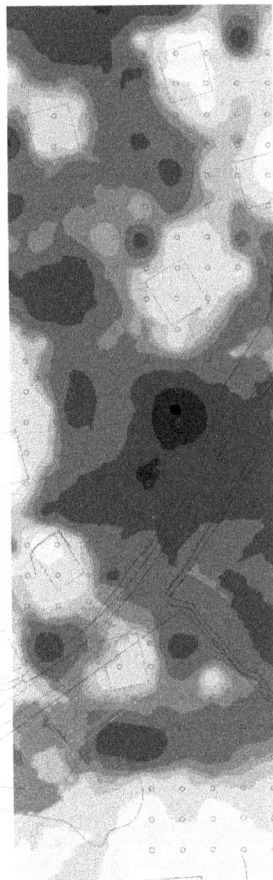

- 10.1 - 21.1
- 21.3 - 26.3
- 26.3 - 28.3
- 28.3 - 29.2
- 29.2 - 29.2
- 29.6 - 30.5
- 30.5 - 32.6
- 32.6 - 37.5
- 37.5 - 48.8
- 48.8 - 75

Household / House Yard Location based on Size Distribution (Sweeping Pattern):

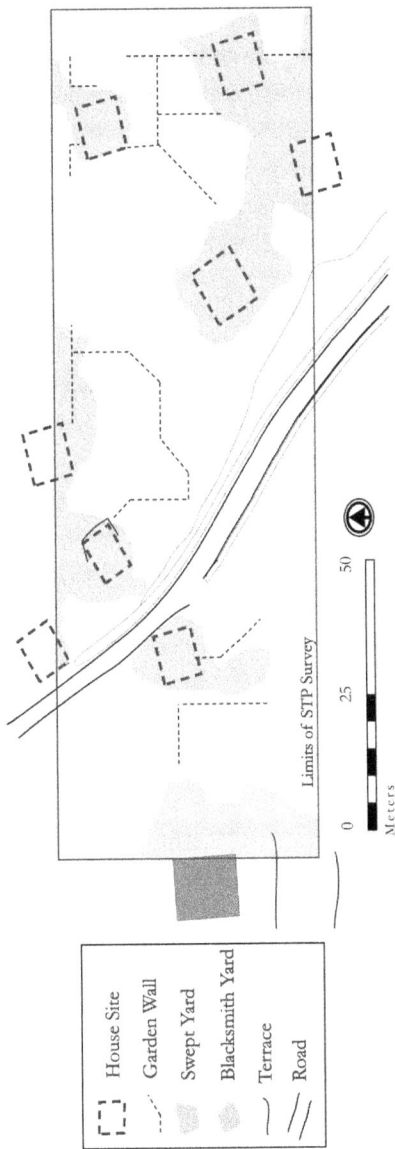

- House Site
- Garden Wall
- Swept Yard
- Blacksmith Yard
- Terrace
- Road

Limits of STP Survey

Meters
0   25   50

Figure 5.9. (*Top*) Spatial distribution of average ceramic sherd size in Village 1 at Good Hope with a gradient indicating ceramic sizes classified from small to large. (*Bottom*) Interpretation of geostatistical results illustrating locations of swept yards (based on kriging) and garden walls (based on subsurface features). Maps created by Hayden Bassett.

The house-yard evidence at Good Hope reveals two types of housing arrangement: (1) several houses arranged around a common yard; and (2) a solitary house with its own yard. The former—multiple houses sharing a common yard—closely aligns with the findings of other archaeologists in Jamaica, including Delle's findings (2014, 166) at the first village at Marshall's Pen, Armstrong's findings (2011) at the later village at Seville, and Higman's findings (1995, 168–171) at Montpelier and Sherwood. Variation between single houses and housing cluster arrangements was almost certainly linked to the household composition of those who occupied the structures. In a major demographic study of household composition, Higman (1995, 168) found that creole (or Jamaican-born) skilled tradesmen and their "dependents" were the most common occupants of housing clusters. Consistent with findings from Good Hope, housing clusters at Montpelier were limited to two to three dwellings per extended kin group.

Walls and Gardens

Alongside each house yard, evidence for household gardens manifests through remnant boundaries. As illustrated in the 1794 plantation plat, each dwelling in Village 1 had an adjacent house garden that was bound by stone walls. The pattern of dry-laid, stacked-stone features in shovel test pits and test units illustrates how houses, yards, and gardens created residential units formed through aggregation on available village land.

While the boundary walls that defined the extent of Village 1 appear to have been in place throughout the period of this study, stratigraphic testing in house-yard compounds suggests that stone walls that defined and subdivided individual house yards and gardens did not appear until after 1800. In the late eighteenth century, enslaved households at Good Hope began bounding and subdividing their allotted space with dry-laid low fieldstone walls. These walls were not substantial enough to keep animals in or out and appear to have been a visual demarcation more than a physical barrier. Such walls likely served to define garden land as a resource restricted to a single house or group of houses. It is likely no coincidence that the proliferation of these stone boundary walls coincides with major population increases in the village at Good Hope. Thus, the practice might suggest conflict surrounding land tenure among households of enslaved people.

In Village 2, the absence of garden plots is a significant deviation from the house, yard, and garden model. For enslaved people, house gardens were in large part utilitarian. The small plots of land were used to grow minor crops, spices, and medicinal herbs. These items were needed more frequently throughout the day than the produce grown in the more distant provision grounds. In both the gardens and the provision grounds, meeting the needs of the household and growing a surplus for market required a significant investment in time and labor. Archaeological evidence in Village 2 suggests that domestic servants spent very little time in and around their dwellings. In fact, comparison of the two village assemblages suggests that Village 2 was likely only used for sleeping and eating, in contrast to the evidence of a range of household activities seen in the assemblage from Village 1. This absence of agricultural and other household activities beyond sleeping and eating is evidence of the different demands of enslaved domestic service. Village 2 assemblages suggest that domestic service placed great demands on enslaved people's time.

Urban Slavery at the Tharp House

In northern Jamaica, the built environment of urban slavery departed significantly from that seen on rural plantations. Housing for enslaved people was in most cases designed into the house lot and was consistent in terms of the materials used and elevation with buildings surrounding it. In Falmouth (Wesler 2013; Nelson et al. 2014; Nelson 2016), as was the case in many port cities around the British Atlantic (Herman 2005), most enslaved people lived and labored in a collection of outbuildings in a wall-bound rear yard. At the Tharp House, workspace and domestic servant housing were collapsed into a square yard with a central partition located directly behind the great house.

On the south side of the masonry partition wall, a small work yard was organized around a central detached kitchen. The spatial distributions of artifacts suggest that the service route of house domestics moved from an east-facing door of the kitchen toward the back of the town house and up an external staircase to a central passage connected to entertaining rooms, bedrooms, and a large dining room (Bassett 2016a). The north side of the yard's partition wall was for the most part open and flanked by an L-shaped building to the west. Artifact distributions suggest that this long

L-shaped building was used for housing. The narrow footprint of the structure suggests a formal range of one-room quarters facing the open yard. Given the design of neighboring examples of early nineteenth-century domestic quarters (Nelson et al. 2014; Nelson 2016), this building almost certainly housed the eight to eleven domestic servants who would have been brought from Good Hope to support the town house when one of the Tharps was in residence.

As these spaces suggest, the built environment of urban slavery was both different and similar to that of the rural plantation. Each had the common elements of a work yard and residential "village," so to speak. Behind the town house, these spaces were collapsed into a single self-contained space that remained separate from the town house because it was contained by masonry walls.

These walls were common elements of the infrastructure of urban enslavement around the Atlantic by the early nineteenth century (Zierden and Herman 1996; Herman 2005; McInnis 2005). As McInnis (2005, 194) has observed in Charleston, South Carolina, "the architecture of the back-lot both ordered and regulated the relationships between master and slave and between slaves." These regulations extended to the quarters; enslaved domestics had little control over the residential spaces they inhabited.

Nevertheless, domestics carved out their own social space among these infrastructures of enslavement. Because the landscapes of enslaved domestics wove through, underlay, and creatively navigated the dominant white landscape (Upton 1984, Nelson 2011; Smith and Bassett 2016), these spaces were not so much constructed as they were shaped through practice. In many ways, they mirrored domestic spaces enslaved people created and maintained in Village 1 and 2 at Good Hope. In Falmouth, these constructed spaces began not in the quarter but in the yards just outside.

Analysis of the Tharp House rear lot using ceramic size sorting reveals that domestic servants maintained swept earthen yards as both a living and working space (Figure 5.10). One or more individuals frequently swept from the center to the periphery of the yard on both sides of the central partition wall, likely on a daily basis. In both the north and south yards, larger ceramics concentrated against the boundary walls and central partition and smaller ceramics remained in the yard interior. South of the partition wall, refuse from the kitchen and other parts of the formal work yard were swept clear. In this area, enslaved domestics labored to maintain their workspace. North of the partition wall, these

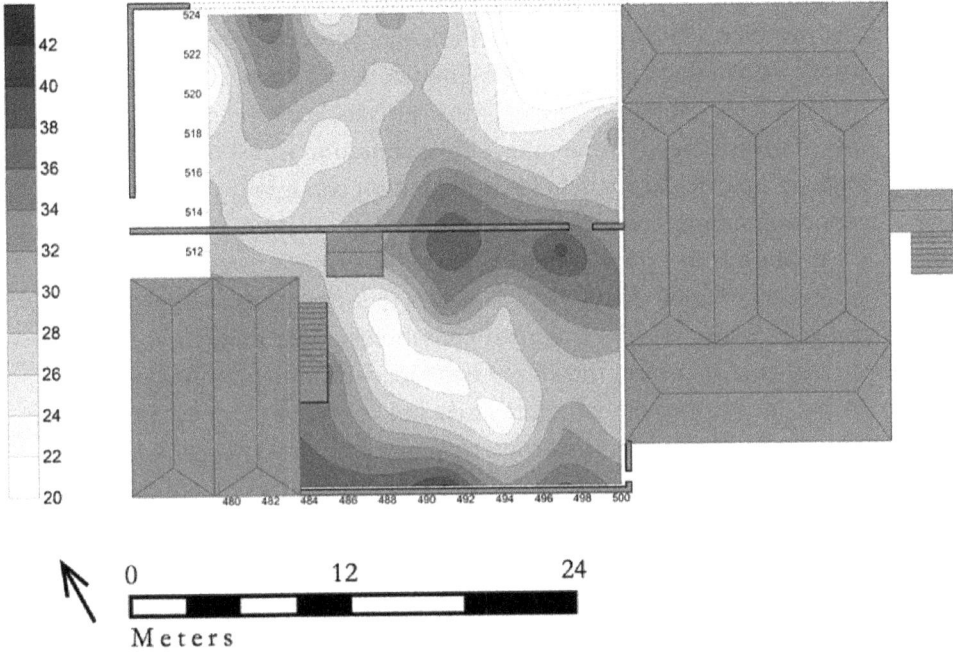

Figure 5.10. Spatial distribution of average ceramic sherd size (i.e., size sorting) in the Tharp House rear yard, indicating yard sweeping toward boundary walls and central partition wall. Lighter-shaded space indicates small ceramic sizes the broom left behind. Maps created by Hayden Bassett.

same individuals labored to maintain and construct space exclusively for their own needs outside their formal labor roles.

Asymmetric Architecture: Household Composition and Building Investment

In the quote that began this chapter, Jamaican planter Bryan Edwards (1794, 139) described a typical dwelling found in a plantation village. This common form, he said, was "confined to the lowest among the field negroes," noting that "tradesmen and domestics are in general vastly better lodged." This account appears to highlight social distinctions among enslaved people along the lines of plantation labor roles. From the viewpoint of this planter, such distinctions were manifest in material differences, notably in housing "at their own expense" (1794, 139).

In this final section, I use evidence from Good Hope to suggest that this variation was not a product of unequal access to market goods and resources and that architectural elaboration is not a reliable spectrum on which socioeconomic status can be measured across an enslaved community. Rather, I argue that architectural elaboration is just one investment strategy a particular household configuration commonly used regardless of socioeconomic standing.

At Good Hope, the fact that evidence for multiple dwellings exists together in common swept yards suggests that many enslaved people organized themselves into extended households under multiple roofs. The clustering of houses in the village was made meaningful through shared spaces such as central common yards and collective gardens. This finding supports the notion that contemporary households in rural Jamaica, which are commonly organized around "family land" compounds shared among extended cognatic kin, had its genesis in the period of slavery (Besson 2002).

Common house-yard compounds included up to three dwellings, each of which had a surrounding yard. These dwellings were interconnected by a central yard. The other form of dwelling arrangement found at Good Hope was the solitary house with its own swept yard and garden. Two of these solitary houses were uncovered in Village 1; the material assemblages of these houses were more similar to the solitary housing arrangement of Village 2. The presence of window glass in solitary houses provides compelling evidence for a greater emphasis on architectural elaboration among smaller households. Recent work by Matthew Reeves (2015) suggests that the ratio of nails to window glass is a consistent metric for measuring architectural refinement in slave housing. Solitary houses in Village 1 and 2 reveal a uniform presence of window glass that contrasts with the near-absence of window glass among larger multi-house compounds.

Differences in choices about material possession manifested in other household goods found in each village. Ceramic scaling based on decorative attributes (Miller 1980, 1991; Moore 1985) provides a useful measure of expense associated with refined earthenwares of the late eighteenth century through the 1830s (see also Kelly 1989, Armstrong 1990, Reeves 2015). Controlling for time from 1780 to 1830, the larger household compound in Village 1 exhibits greater investment in decorated ceramics than the housing of domestic servants in Village 2. This difference manifests in the top two pricing tiers of decoration: hand-painted and transfer-printed

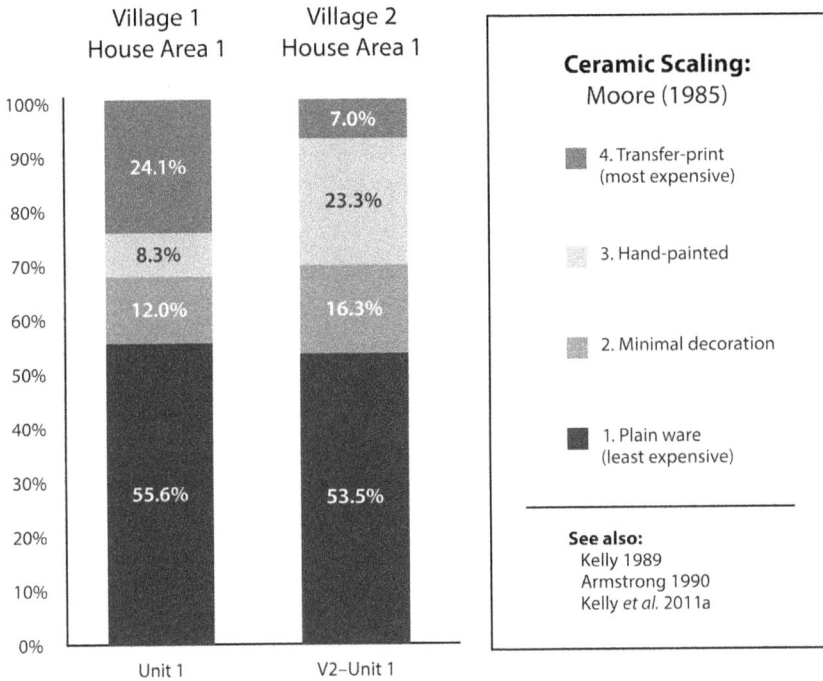

Figure 5.11. Ceramic scaling by decorative class in the yard of a multi-dwelling household in Village 1 at Good Hope and a solitary household of domestic servants in Village 2. Chart created by Hayden Bassett.

ceramics (Figure 5.11). This pattern of consumer goods remains the same even when one confines the sample to just pearlware in both contexts and when the sample is confined to single contemporaneous stratigraphic layers. This suggests that by the early nineteenth century, members of larger kinship compounds in the primary village at Good Hope were spending more on expensively decorated ceramics (a nonessential item) than individuals who lived in solitary houses in both Village 1 and Village 2.

In Village 1, one distinct area of investment stands out compared to larger extended household clusters. Using Douglas Armstrong's (1998) categories for functional analysis and again controlling for time from 1780 to 1830, domestic servants in Village 2 appear to have invested directly and indirectly in items related to personal adornment more than members of households in Village 1. In a functional analysis, this is seen in the

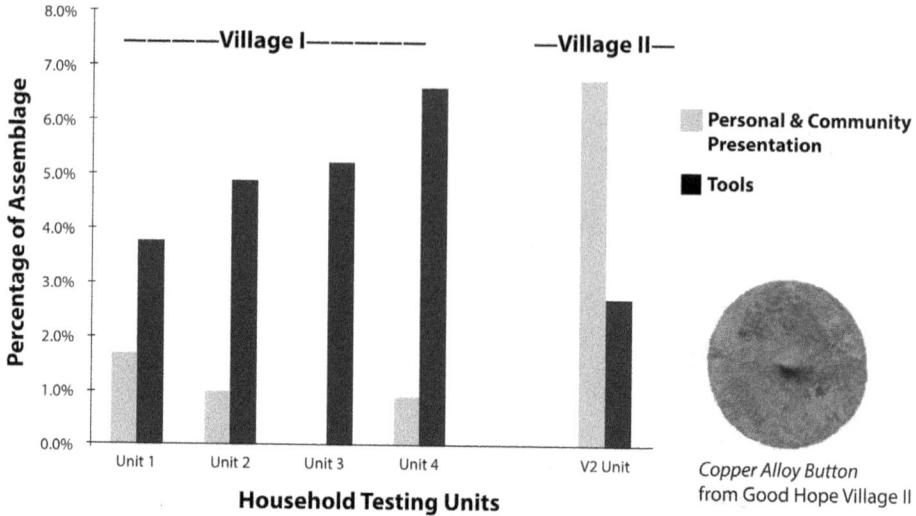

Figure. 5.12. Functional analysis of domestic artifact assemblages from Villages 1 and 2 at Good Hope, illustrating the percentage of artifacts in the category personal and community presentation and in the category tools within their one-by-one-meter unit assemblages. Bar graph and photo by Hayden Bassett.

overall percentage of artifacts in the "personal and community activities" category, largely because of the quantity of buttons present (Figure 5.12). The overall percentage of artifacts classed in the "tools" category includes household activities, sewing, animal tack, yard equipment, and so forth. As expected, these items are in the minority in the contexts of domestic servant housing.

Archaeologists and historians working in Virginia and the Caribbean have previously observed material variation between unrelated individuals and larger kin-based households. For example, at Thomas Jefferson's Monticello, Neiman (2008) found that enslaved people in kin-based housing constructed communal subfloor pits for common storage while those who lived in barracks-style housing apart from kin constructed individual storage pits for personal needs. Similarly, Jillian Galle (2011) suggests that investment in items of personal display like metal buttons reflects the signaling system of unmarried or unrelated individuals. In such cases, choices in material goods reflect multiple unrelated individuals who lived in close proximity to people with whom they had more ephemeral social bonds. Galle argues that such individuals may have felt a greater need to invest in themselves in order to negotiate the conditions of enslavement than members of larger social units, such as an extended household. At Montpelier in Jamaica, Higman (1998, 182) found a correlation between durable housing (i.e., stone) for individuals and flexible housing materials for larger extended kin groups. In the latter groups, flexible materials such as wattle, board, and dry-laid walls easily accommodated changing garden boundaries, pens, and house locations that followed ever-changing household relations between and among kin groups. Taken together with the findings from Good Hope, this suggests that domestic building practices were significantly shaped by choices related to household composition and concerns for the social unit more than they functioned as a recognizable proxy for social status.

Discussion

In contrast to the conventional narrative that enslaved domestic workers had the most material wealth, the archaeological evidence presented here suggests that the occupational hierarchy did not have a direct correlation with material wealth by any single measure (e.g., ceramics or architecture), particularly after the turn of the nineteenth century. Comparison of domestic servants in Village 2 and field laborers and tradesmen in Village 1 illustrates how kinship networks and time outside plantation labor might have played a more important role in shaping material conditions than the labor position itself. As a locally born creole population expanded in the late eighteenth and early nineteenth centuries, larger kinship groups emerged. At Good Hope, this developed unevenly. In the larger village at Good Hope, this change resulted in individual houses joined by common yards, forming clusters of extended households. Importantly, these kinship groupings afforded the possibility that kin could pool resources and allocate household labor more efficiently. This would have created more collective time to devote to provision grounds, raising animals, and participating in markets, among other activities that would have contributed toward a better quality of life. These means of gaining access to resources and the variations that are evident in the consumer decisions of enslaved people may point to a more significant division among enslaved people than occupation alone.

In their foundational work on household archaeology, Wilk and Rathje (1982, 620–621) noted two important concepts for understanding the relationship between houses and social collectives: the dwelling unit and the household. The concept of a dwelling unit relates to the number and social composition of those who live under one roof. In contrast, Wilk and Rathje define the concept of a household as "the social component of subsistence" that involved occupying one or more houses and forming "a domestic strategy to meet the productive, distributive, and reproductive needs of its members" (Wilk and Rathje 1982, 618). In functional terms, the distinction between these concepts highlights the fact that those who live under one roof do not necessarily constitute a household (Bender 1967; Goody 1972) nor is an entire household necessarily confined to one roof. This distinction is important for household archaeology, as Wilk and Rathje (1982, 620) note: "Archaeologists do not excavate households; they find the material remains of dwellings." Inferring the nature of the household from the material remains of a dwelling or dwellings is an analytical and interpretative act.

When considering architectural investment in domestic buildings, it follows that one must first consider the social unit that a building contains. The findings from Good Hope are useful for constructing a model of investment in architecture as it relates to the relationship between the dwelling unit and the household. Data from Good Hope suggest that when the dwelling unit, or those housed under a single roof, corresponds to the entirety of the household unit, the dwelling itself becomes a significant medium for investment choices and expendable resources. In such cases, elaboration of the physical house is one of the most significant and visible material expressions identifiable to the entire social unit. In contrast, when the household was bigger than the dwelling unit and its members occupied multiple adjacent buildings, investment choices appear to have been more flexible and distributed, focusing on obtaining items that benefited the larger group of related dwellings, such as sets of expensive ceramics like those found in Village I. Together, this framework allows one to reconsider single-spectrum proxies for measuring socioeconomic status and view architectural elaboration as one choice within a range of options that would have been beneficial to a particular form of household composition.

Conclusion

Matthew Reeves (2010, 5) suggests that "rather than seeing the [enslaved] community as unified," we should "seek the social relations inherent among a set of households who have both competing interests and commonalities both inside and outside of their core context." Understanding variation in housing for enslaved people and the connections and cooperations those spaces maintain is one way to render such social variation visible. At Good Hope, three village settings reveal three distinct patterns of living. Planters created varying conditions of enslavement that are manifest in different priorities for different segments of the enslaved community. For some enslaved people, such as domestic servants in Village 2 and the occupants of solitary houses in Village 1, investment choices appear to have focused on a smaller household unit. In these cases, the dwelling unit corresponded with the household unit and small numbers of people channeled their time and resources into the elaboration of their dwelling. At Good Hope, this was most visible archaeologically in houses with glass windows.

In extended family compounds, however, consumer practices appear to have focused on larger household units through more portable material goods shared between multiple dwellings, such as finer ceramics. Comparison to a related urban site demonstrates that these patterns, a product of relative control over constructed space and access to time outside labor, were in some settings restricted. Enslaved people moved in and out of varying circumstances, such as the domestic servants who traveled from Good Hope to Falmouth. Understanding architectural variation in the context of household composition and choice within a range of options reveals much about enslaved people's different motivations and priorities in varying conditions of enslavement.

6

Variation within the Village

Housing Enslaved Laborers on Coffee Plantations in Jamaica

JAMES A. DELLE AND KRISTEN R. FELLOWS

Quarters that housed enslaved laborers on colonial plantations have been an important focus of archaeological work for decades. Enslaved housing has long been interpreted as a physical manifestation of the control plantation owners and managers imposed on laborers (Delle 1998; Higman 1998; Orser 1990; Vlach 1993). However, under close inspection, features of housing construction and spatial arrangement can also be interpreted as evidence of varying degrees of autonomy and resistance.

This chapter considers housing at Marshall's Pen, a relatively late plantation in the uplands of what is now the parish of Manchester in central Jamaica, founded and owned by Alexander Lindsay, the sixth Earl of Balcarres, in 1813 and later owned by his son James Lindsay, the seventh earl. Alexander Lindsay served as lieutenant governor of Jamaica, the chief executive, from 1795 to 1801. When he returned to England, he became one of Jamaica's leading absentee coffee planters. As has been well understood for decades, the sugar economy, which was structured by large, privately held estates worked by enslaved laborers, dominated Jamaica from the late seventeenth into the middle of the nineteenth centuries. Some degree of temporal and regional variation existed in the physical manifestation of plantations in Jamaica, attributable not only to the individual predilections of plantation owners and managers, who exerted differing levels of control over the construction and layout of housing for enslaved workers, but also by changing economic realities that continually redefined the complex relationships between enslaver and enslaved.

Two events helped frame the layout, construction, and design of housing at Marshall's Pen. From the perspective of Caribbean planters, the first of these was the shocking success of the Haitian Revolution of 1791–1804, a complex struggle between various groups that sought to redefine social relationships in the French colonies in the wake of the French Revolution. The long struggle for control of what was then the wealthy and powerful colony of St. Domingue radically disrupted the colonial world of the Caribbean at the turn of the nineteenth century. In 1790, St. Domingue was the world's leading producer of sugar and coffee. The series of conflicts that unfolded on Hispaniola precipitated both crisis and opportunity for the planters of colonial Jamaica. European demand for coffee skyrocketed in the late eighteenth century. However, the majority of European colonies in the Caribbean had long been focused on sugar production and lacked the infrastructure or ecological conditions required to produce coffee. Jamaica was a notable exception. While the sugar economy dominated on the coast and in several large upland valleys, in 1790 there were still large tracts of undeveloped land suitable for coffee production in the highlands of the Blue Mountains and John Crow Mountains in the east and on the Dry Harbor and Manchester plateaus in north and south-central Jamaica. The collapse of the St. Domingue coffee industry resulted in a massive coffee boom in Jamaica in the 1790s and early 1800s as enterprising planters and new investors (many from Scotland) gambled that the infrastructure required for coffee production would develop rapidly. This included housing for enslaved workers (Delle 2014). Because most coffee plantations were established at elevations from 2,000 to 5,000 feet above sea level, new housing forms distinct from what was constructed on eighteenth-century sugar plantations were required to safely house the enslaved laborers who did the heavy work of clearing forests, caring for coffee trees, building mills, and transporting coffee down the often-treacherous slopes of highland Jamaica to the wharves scattered along the island's coast.

The second event that helped shape the form of housing at Marshall's Pen was the British government's abolition of the African slave trade in 1807. In the years following the abolition of the trade, it became increasingly difficult and costly to acquire labor gangs to work on new plantations. Those who sought their fortunes in the coffee industry after 1807 were generally required to purchase complete gangs from bankrupt or intestate plantation owners or lease gangs for the heavy labor required to establish a coffee plantation. In 1810, Lord Balcarres wrote a letter of advice to Robert Alexander Lindsay, a free young man of color under the earl's protection in Jamaica. Lindsay, a mason by trade, was seeking a way forward in his career and hoped to become involved in plantation management, a route that was not easily open to anyone in the 1810s, let alone a young man of color of limited property. The earl wrote, "Had the island remained as I knew it, negroes easily procured etc. your situation would have been . . . well understood by me. The abolition of the slave trade . . . [has] so changed the routine of a young man's career as to disable the fair judgment of those who have seen Jamaica under the Old Regime."[1] In this passage, Balcarres alluded to how it had been relatively simple to procure enslaved laborers in Jamaica while the African trade was still legally operating and to the difficulties those who wanted to become established as planters faced after the legal trade ended. After that, enslaved labor was expensive and difficult to acquire and the thrifty plantation owner well understood the necessity of keeping enslaved workers on plantations alive and ensuring that their population would increase through successful childbirth and childrearing, a process the planters called natural increase. Balcarres was keenly aware of the economic importance of keeping the enslaved population healthy. He wrote to his Jamaica plantation managers in 1810: "The increase of Negroes depends on the lightness of their labour. Whether that relief from overwork is to be procured by addition to the number of Negroes or decrease of labour, the result is one and the same to the question—natural increase of Negroes."[2]

In 1812, Balcarres and his agents agreed to establish a new coffee settlement on a property he owned in what is now the parish of Manchester. During the disruptive first decade of the nineteenth century, which was characterized by warfare among colonialist nations related to the Napoleonic Wars, Balcarres had sought to expand and intensify production in Jamaica in the hope of making a killing in the European coffee markets. This profit was highly illusory, however, and Marshall's Pen never quite lived up to the earl's expectations. One reason for this was the volatility of the European coffee market. The primary market for Jamaican coffee was mainland Europe, which happily paid a premium price to consume Jamaica's inferior crop. The resulting high price for coffee fell in 1807 when European ports were closed to British trade, including coffee shipped from Jamaica. During the latter years of Napoleon's reign, many coffee planters struggled mightily because of the resulting overproduction crisis. Hundreds of newly formed plantations were running at full tilt, but with the European ports closed to their product, there was no effective market for the generally low-quality coffee produced in Jamaica. The market price of coffee continually declined as supply continually outpaced demand and many indebted coffee plantations fell into ruin (Delle 1998). As his peers faltered and failed in a difficult market, Balcarres hoped to profit from his ability to wait out the crisis, during which he worked to acquire and develop more property. In the waning years of the Napoleonic era, Balcarres shrewdly anticipated an opening of the European markets by holding back his crops for future sale and developing new coffee settlements on his vast Jamaican estates. He established Marshall's Pen during this period. In 1812, Balcarres's agents began to develop a new coffee settlement on one of the earl's existing estates, known then as Martin's Hill; by 1814, this new settlement was known as Marshall's Pen.

The first evidence of housing at Marshall's Pen is found in a letter to the earl from his agents dated November 29, 1812. Reacting to the earl's instructions that a number of enslaved workers be relocated to Manchester from his failing Balcarres Plantation in the parish of St. George, his agents replied, "On the . . . important direction in your Lordship's letter, the removal of 80 Negroes from Balcarres to Martin's Hill, we have to express our perfect concurrence in opinion. . . . Negro houses are already prepared for part of them in the new settlement at Martins Hill," a reference to the settlement that would become known as Marshall's Pen.[3] The name "Marshall's Pen" first appears in a letter from the agents in Jamaica to Balcarres in April 1814: "We have removed the late purchase of Negroes to the new settlement of Marshall's Pen, where they are comfortably established, their grounds and houses having been previously put in perfect preparation for their reception."[4]

Over the course of the next several years, Balcarres and his agents worked to augment the labor force at Marshall's Pen by both relocating people from Balcarres Plantation and purchasing gangs of enslaved laborers, generally people whom the House of Atkinson, the Jamaican merchant house that managed the absentee earl's local affairs, had acquired through a variety of means. Although Balcarres made several such acquisitions to increase the population of the main settlement at Martin's Hill, within a few years he began to see the value of expanding the development of Marshall's Pen. In March 1817, his agents informed the earl that "we have made a purchase of a very fine gang of forty two Negroes, thirty workers and twelve fine, healthy children . . . The houses and grounds prepared since last year at Marshall's Pen for the Balcarres Negroes will be most conveniently occupied by the present gang" (Figure 6.1).[5] From this point forward, the population of Marshall's Pen, which was concentrated in this first village (which was constructed and settled in the period 1813 to 1817), consisted of from 110 to 120 people, although in 1821 and 1822 a considerable number of people were relocated from Martin's Hill to a settlement closer to Marshall's Pen known as New Green.

For about a decade following Napoleon's abdication in 1814, the European market for Jamaica coffee rebounded and Balcarres eagerly intensified his investment in Marshall's Pen. In October 1821, his agents informed him that the "field of coffee at Marshall's Pen looks very well." However, "the very great distance the chief strength of [laborers] was from the field (nearly 5 miles) has been a great impediment; we are now moving the people to a more centrical [sic] part of the property."[6] This new settlement became New Green, a village on the outskirts of the plantation where many of the laborers at Marshall's Pen relocated after emancipation and which their descendants occupy to this day.

After 1822, the correspondence between Balcarres and his Jamaica agents fell off, likely due to a debilitating accident the earl had suffered. He died in March 1825, bequeathing all of his Jamaican property to his heir, James Lindsay. Although he had briefly lived in Jamaica during his youth, the younger nobleman had had no dealings with the Jamaican properties until his father's death. His reaction to the state of affairs is evident in his correspondence with some of his acquaintances. The picture that emerges suggests that the estate managers had fallen into some questionable practices during the declining years of the elder earl. Even though the earl had made a vast investment of tens of thousands of pounds over decades, by the mid-1820s the three estates he had established—Balcarres Plantation, Martin's Hill, and Marshall's Pen—were barely clearing a combined annual profit of £1,000. James Lindsay, who succeeded his father as the seventh Earl of Balcarres and was later named twenty-third Earl of Crawford, was the absentee proprietor of Marshall's Pen through 1852, when for the first time after nearly three decades of his ownership, the costs of running his Jamaican estates exceeded the revenue they generated. The earl immediately moved to sell Marshall's Pen and the rest of his Jamaica

Figure 6.1. Plan view of the village of Marshall's Pen. Map created by James A. Delle.

property at auction, receiving a fraction of the investment his father had made when he established his Jamaican estates.

Although the seventh earl was interested in managing the property efficiently, there are only a few references in his correspondence to laborers' housing on his estates. In May 1832, George Brooks, who had recently been hired to manage Marshall's Pen, wrote to the earl: "The Negroes at Marshall's Pen have formerly been allowed to make [provision] Grounds where they pleased, the consequence is that they have taken the best lands near the works, leaving the Rocky Hills . . . for Coffee."[7] John Salmon, who took over the management of Marshall's Pen following Brooks's untimely death, corroborated this observation. Salmon informed the earl that "the property has been run over in a most unwarrantable manner by the Negroes—leaving scarcely an acre of virgin soil near at hand."[8] He later wrote that the "Marshalls Pen Negro houses are very badly situated and straggling. The Negroes some of them are 1½ miles from the works and 2½ perhaps from the field . . . losing from the situation of their house between two and three hours." As a result, plantation managers "oblige[d] them to get up by three o'clock to get their victuals and be in the field in time" to begin work.[9]

The issue of housing is largely ignored in the earl's correspondence until 1838, when the full abolition of coerced labor was enacted with the demise of the apprenticeship system. At this point, planters turned to the relationship laborers would have with their houses and provision grounds. Possession of houses and grounds was clearly a bargaining issue in the labor negotiations following the end of slavery. In June 1838, about two months before the final end of the apprenticeship system, Duncan Robertson, the new manager of Marshall's Pen, wrote to the earl about his intentions: "It is my intention in the first instance to offer them the use of their Houses, Gardens, and Provision Grounds, Medicines, & Medical Attendance for the labour of three days weekly," a sum that Robertson later estimated to be the equivalent of 10 pounds per year.[10] Thomas Fowlis, the earl's agent in London, articulated the importance of possessing land in the postemancipation era in a March 1839 letter: "One of the great evils in Jamaica is the independence of the Negroes, for [because of] their being able to support themselves by their provision grounds, and although they have no legal right to them, it will be difficult . . . to make a general ejectment of them by either a legal process or by force."[11] Later in 1839, while discussing one of the earl's other properties, Balcarres Plantation, Fowlis mentioned a report he had received that "the negroes are building new houses for themselves, which is probably to avoid the payment of rent and to be independent of their employer."[12] In disputes between labor and management, protecting access to land was crucial for both. In a letter that reported on the situation at Marshall's Pen following a visit in April 1839, William Morrice wrote that "the first complaint made to me was by a woman who said [Duncan Robertson, the manager] would not protect her grounds from neighbour's cattle, and she had lost her crop of yams worth £5. .6. .8." Morrice noted that "her house is 22 ft by 16, shingled and built by the estate. . . . The best houses and largest and best grounds are held by those that do not work [for the estate] at all. . . . Some of the houses are 40 feet long by 22 having four bedrooms and a large hall in the centre."[13] Residents who did not work on the estate were most likely formerly enslaved workers who maintained possession of their houses and grounds following emancipation. Likely concerned by these reports, the earl ordered his agents to establish a township at New Green. In the early 1840s New Green was subdivided into lots that the estate sold to the formerly enslaved people of Marshall's Pen and Martin's Hill. By the end of the 1840s, the original village at Marshall's Pen was abandoned. Residents who did not (or could not) move to the new township were likely evicted.

Freestanding Houses and House-Yard Compounds

The firsthand descriptions of housing at Marshall's Pen from the earls' correspondence reveals precious little about what housing on early nineteenth-century Jamaican plantations was actually like. While archaeological evidence clearly indicates that enslaved people at Marshall's Pen were living in freestanding structures, living spaces in Jamaica extended beyond these stand-alone buildings.

Research has shown that most activities likely took place out of doors in yard spaces (Armstrong 1990, 2011; Armstrong and Kelly 2000). Douglas Armstrong's (1990) work at Drax Hall, one of the earliest archaeological studies in Jamaica to pay attention to slave housing, provides information from ethnohistorical and archaeological records. He connected the importance of the house yard in the village to West African traditions. These yard spaces were not just open areas where people would congregate; they also were places where animals were penned, where cooking was done, where people were buried, and where people socialized (Armstrong 1990,

2011; Higman 1998; Armstrong and Kelly 2000; Armstrong and Fleischman 2003).

While Higman's (1998) research at Montpelier does not speak as directly to house-yard areas, he does refer to "multiple-house families" because kin groups that occupied more than one structure are described in the records of the plantation. It appears that it was not uncommon for these compounds to include houses of differing sizes and construction techniques. Delle's (2014) previous work at Marshall's Pen also noted the presence of house-yard compounds, some of which were delimited by stone fencing and/or contained animal pens. At Drax Hall, it appears that animal pens were constructed using wooden sticks, a more ephemeral and less labor-intensive material (Armstrong 1990). Excavations at Seville Plantation have also highlighted the importance of yard spaces, especially as they related to areas of control and autonomy for the enslaved population. In the original village at Seville, which was constructed under the supervision of plantation managers, houses were placed in linear rows. While this allowed for greater surveillance of the front of these structures, the backyard spaces, where laborers spent the majority of their free time, were hidden from view. The second village at Seville was constructed with less oversight. The spatial arrangement and variation in building techniques of the second village point to increased autonomy for enslaved laborers and the incipient Afro-Jamaican society that was developing in these spaces (Armstrong and Kelly 2000; Armstrong 2011). The larger size of house yards in this later village also speaks to their importance in Jamaican society (Armstrong 2011). It is important to consider the context of the immediate yard space and associated animal pens, and other structures that may be included in a house-yard compound, when studying the housing of enslaved Jamaican laborers.

Construction Techniques

Although freestanding structures were the typical housing arrangement for enslaved laborers in Jamaica, there was no standard footprint or building method. If for no other reason, Montpelier is a noteworthy site because of the architectural variety in the villages. Higman's (1998) monograph provides one of the most thorough overviews of building techniques seen on the island. Much of his data come from an 1825 report which indicated that walls were of five types—wattled, Spanish walled, boarded, shingled, and stone—and roofs were thatched or shingled. The only type of flooring identified was made of boards and this was found only in houses with boarded or wattled walls (Higman 1998, 151). Higman's work is an excellent resource for anyone interested in a more thorough discussion of each of these types of structures.

Both Armstrong (1990) and Higman (1998) thoroughly describe the techniques of wattle construction, which may or may not have used nails depending on availability, and used small round sticks woven between upright posts. Clay and earth daub would have been added to seal off the spaces between the sticks, then both interior and exterior walls would have been covered with plaster (see also Nelson 2016). This wattle construction technique is frequently referred to as wattle and plaster or wattle and daub. Wattle and plaster appears to be one of the most common forms of construction in Jamaican villages even when other building methods were present. This construction technique is not unique to Jamaica or even the Caribbean. Many of the Africans who were forcibly brought to the island would have had knowledge of this building technique (Armstrong 1990; Higman 1998; Nelson 2016). Both Armstrong and Higman also point out that wattle houses used materials that were locally found and easily accessible.

Spanish wall construction refers to a building technique that may have been first introduced to Jamaica during the sixteenth-century Spanish occupation of the island. These buildings began with a wooden frame. Spaces between the timbers were then filled in with stones and mortar and then plastered over. A timber frame is also the starting point for both board and shingle houses; wooden boards or shingles were then used to construct the walls by attaching them with nails to the frame (Higman 1998). It is important for archaeologists that the use of these two materials, boards and shingles, requires far more nails than any of the other building methods described. Shingle houses in particular make use of large numbers of small, rather uniformly sized nails to attach shingles to underlying weatherboards.

Perhaps unsurprisingly, the stone houses at Montpelier were likely "solid masonry structures making little use of other materials in their external walls" (Higman 1998, 164). It is significant for archaeologists to know that stone foundations have been used for houses whose walls were not made of stone; a stone foundation is not necessarily indicative of a stone house. As may be expected, variation in building methods creates differences that are sometimes subtle in archaeological signatures.

Regardless of construction methods and materials used, the vast majority of these structures had thatched roofs with a fairly significant pitch. Palm leaves were the primary materials used for the thatch and were twisted or plaited (Armstrong 1990; Higman 1998; Nelson 2016). Higman (1998, 156) provides a nice figure that details the manipulation of palm leaves for this purpose. He also describes how Guinea grass and cane trash were sometimes used as substitutes for palm thatching. However, these alternatives were less durable and would have needed to have been replaced more frequently. Shingles were another form of roofing (Higman 1998; Armstrong 2011). Some houses in the second village at Seville used this roofing technique. Interestingly, one house-yard area Armstrong excavated that dated to the period of slavery contained evidence of a kitchen shed that had a slate roof, although the nearby house had a thatched roof (Armstrong 2011). While thatched roofs dominated, there was some variety in roofing practices present on the island.

Flooring in these structures also differed among estates and even among and within structures. At Drax Hall, Armstrong (1990, 101) found evidence of several different types of flooring in the same relatively large house. He writes, "Large, flat limestone rocks (20–40 cm) and marl predominated in the room on the north side, while the floor in the middle (largest) room was covered with smaller limestone rocks, brick, and marl. The south room, on the other hand, had no surviving flooring. This area probably had a dirt floor." Other structures are thought to have had wooden flooring, which may be represented during excavation by an increased presence in nails (Armstrong 1990; Higman 1998). Portions of a plastered floor were uncovered at Montpelier, yet another type of flooring (Higman 1998). Possible flooring materials in the houses of estate villages seem to have included packed earth, limestone rock, and/or brick with marl, wood, and plaster.

The variability in the size of houses in village sites seems even greater than the variability in construction techniques. According to at least one ethnohistorical source, the most common arrangement was a two-room building that ranged from 15 to 20 feet long (Higman 1998; Nelson 2016), although other sources observe a 16 × 24 feet standard, 12 × 12 feet huts, and houses with a range of 10–15 feet × 15–20 feet (Higman 1998). The archaeological record has demonstrated that the size of houses for enslaved laborers truly did vary. At Montpelier, Higman (1998) recorded dimensions of structures that ranged from 9 × 9 feet all the way to 30 × 30 feet. Armstrong (2011) reports that at Seville the first village had a standard house size of 12 × 18 feet and the second village ranged from that size to a slightly larger structure of 15 × 21 feet. At Drax Hall, a three-room building with dimensions of 14.6 × 29.3 feet (4.5 meters × 9 meters) was excavated (Armstrong 1990). In our own experience excavating at Marshall's Pen, we have also encountered a range of structure sizes in the village. Based on the footprints of foundations, remains of steps, internal postholes, and floor remnants, the village at Marshall's Pen's had structures that ranged from one to three rooms. While some sites may have had a standard house size (e.g., the first village at Seville), many did not.

Variation in Housing Forms on Jamaica

Much of the variation in architectural techniques used in Jamaica can be seen through sketches, reconstructions, and photographs in some of the sources cited throughout this discussion. These images include archaeological maps of house foundations (Armstrong 1990; Higman 1998), elevation drawings or photographs of standing ruins (Farnsworth 2001; Nelson 2016), sketches from historical sources (Higman 1998; Nelson 2016), and projections or reconstructions of what housing would have looked like based on documentary or archaeological data (Higman 1998; Armstrong and Kelly 2000; Armstrong 2011; Nelson 2016). These figures are important for researchers, as they provide a way to visualize, and not just know or describe, the structures the people who were enslaved built and inhabited.

Armstrong's (2011) work at Seville has demonstrated that no two village sites are the same, even when they are located on the same plantation (see also Armstrong and Kelly 2000). The first village at this site showed great uniformity in the dimensions of structures, the two-room layout, the construction techniques used, and even the amount of space between the buildings. In contrast, excavations at the second village have revealed a variety of building methods, some variation in structure size, a notable increase in yard space, differences in the orientation of the buildings, and even differences in number of rooms. As Armstrong has explained, the variances between the two villages indicate that plantation managers supervised housing construction at the first village and that enslaved workers in the second village had greater latitude in terms of control and creativity (see also Armstrong and Kelly 2000). Many archaeologists argue that variation within a village is indicative of greater autonomy for the enslaved laborers. As Higman (1998) notes:

> The existence of diverse dimensions at New Montpelier is important because it suggests strongly that even the stone houses [which represent more traditional English building techniques] were not constructed according to designs taken from European pattern books or built to a single model under the direct supervision of the planter. . . . [Only] among the sets of houses laid out evenly spaced, parallel to the eastern boundary wall, did uniformity of spatial organization and uniformity of size and shape coincide, and only here is it possible to see the hand of an overarching authority at work. (150)

While plantations have long been the focus of historical archaeological research in Jamaica, the architectural features of the structures in the enslaved laborers' village have not always been central to the discussion. However, archaeological and documentary evidence shows that freestanding houses dominated, that yard spaces were important components of living situations, that structures ranged in size and layout, and that there were five primary modes of construction. Methods used for flooring and roofing also varied.

The built environment can reveal much about the social landscape of a plantation. Higman's work notably demonstrates the variation that can occur within and between sites. Armstrong's and Armstrong and Kelly's work at Seville has demonstrated both the importance of yard spaces in regard to living spaces and the differences that occur when enslaved laborers are able to exert more control over the construction of these spaces. Even the original village at Seville displays avenues of resistance to European notions of control and surveillance. Estate villages were indeed places of great importance in the colony.

The Village of Marshall's Pen

Based on their work at Seville Plantation, Armstrong and Kelly (2000) observed that Jamaican plantation villages in the early nineteenth century were organized either as linear rows of houses flanking a central road or

Figure 6.2. Negro House Hill as it appeared in 1999. Photo by James A. Delle.

path or clustered in compounds. Which design prevailed may well have been based on the intensity of surveillance the proprietor or managers of an individual estate demanded. Evidence suggests that at Marshall's Pen, the village was organized into compounds, while the later village at New Green was designed on the linear model (Delle 2002, 2011; Fellows and Delle 2015).

From 1999 to 2001 and then again from 2012 to 2016, Delle led field projects at Marshall's Pen, examining house areas within the bounds of the known village and outlying field houses on the estate (Delle and Fellows 2014; Fellows and Delle 2015). Archaeological data were collected from six houses representing three different house compounds in the village and three additional field house locations, one of which was likely occupied in the twentieth century. In 1999, the ground surface of the village was quite clearly visible, as the site was then used as a cow pasture and the bush was eaten low by cattle. This level of visibility allowed for detailed and controlled surface survey (Figure 6.2). One striking feature of the house compounds at this site is the extensive stone fencing used to create pens and to separate different house-yard complexes from one another.

The 1999 survey revealed that the village was in fact a complex of ten house compounds clustered on the crest of a hill, known locally to this day as Negro House Hill. The compounds each contain from one to six discernable structures, the majority of which are likely houses. The house compounds were bounded by stone walls and a gate in the stone wall provided access to them. A cart road that is still apparent provided access to the village from the south and southwest.

It has been argued elsewhere that two parallel, intertwined economies drove the plantation system of colonial Jamaica (Hauser 2008; Delle 2014). The overarching economy, of course, was based on the international exchange of commodities, including export crops from the Caribbean to feed European markets, the trade in human beings as commodities to work on the plantations, and the importation of textiles, iron tools, and machinery from Europe. The other economy was the internal trade in locally produced goods, both at local market towns and within and between plantation communities. This trade was largely controlled by enslaved and free people of African descent in Jamaica (Hauser 2008; Delle 2014). This latter economy depended on access to provision grounds and gardens where the enslaved could exercise a recognized right to grow food for themselves and their families and to sell anything they produced when they were not directly involved in labor for the plantation. Planters recognized that the enslaved could produce goods for sale in what were known as provision grounds—small farms where the enslaved grew staple foods such as plantains, tubers, and fruits. The enslaved also made use of the spaces around their houses to plant kitchen herbs and vegetables and perhaps fruit trees, coffee, or sugar. There was a spatial distinction between garden and ground, evinced by William Morrice's remarks about a visit to Marshall's Pen in which he focused on house gardens: "I . . . proceeded through the Negroe Houses which are of very superior description, and have large, rich gardens containing an abundance of oranges, plantains, mangoes, cocoa nuts, pines, etc. with coffee and very fine sugar sufficient for their own use."[14]

Given the presence of an internal economy and local markets, it is logical to conclude that people in the villages exchanged goods and services with each other, based on their individual skill and knowledge and the kinds of plants and animals they were able to raise in their yards, gardens, and grounds. House-yard compounds must not therefore simply be considered as areas of habitation; they must also be considered as sites of local production, exchange, and consumption. The concept of hospitality can tie habitation, relaxation, and social and material exchange together.

Bearing this in mind, the analysis of the following house-yard compounds considers not only the size and variation of the features investigated but also the types of social and economic exchanges that likely took place there, based on recovered archaeological material.

When the village of Marshall's Pen was established, much of the Manchester Plateau it is situated on was covered with old-growth tropical hardwood forests. The cultivation technique Jamaican coffee planters used in the early nineteenth century required their workforce to cut 40–60 acres of forest annually, as coffee needed to be planted in "virgin" soil that would support coffee trees for between five and ten productive years. Large coffee plantations like Marshall's Pen voraciously consumed the hardwood forest, leaving thousands of acres of scrub brush and grass pastures in their place. The destruction of the Jamaican rain forest on the Manchester Plateau left hundreds of thousands if not millions of board feet of tropical hardwoods lying on the ground. Much of this wood was burned into charcoal, some was exported as logwood, and much was also used to construct buildings, including housing for the enslaved. Available woods included mahogany and a local hardwood called bullet that was preferred for house construction because its heavy density made its timbers naturally resistant to termite infestation. Tropical cedars had also thrived in the Jamaican uplands and forest clearance provided an ample supply of water-resistant cedar shingles for cladding roofs and siding houses. Stone, mortar and plaster were also plentiful; the Manchester Plateau is a massive limestone conglomerate that was easily mined for cut stone and lime. Mortar and plaster made red by the bauxite-rich soils of the plateau were used to finish interior walls and create plaster floors; they were also applied as stucco on the exterior of Spanish-wall houses.

House Area 6

House Area 6 is the first yard compound one would encounter as one crested the hill where the village was situated. The compound is built on a shallow terrace that runs approximately 140 meters along the side of the hill. It is possible that what we have identified as a single house area was actually two compounds, although there is no visible indication of a boundary line bisecting the area. In field excavations, we considered the western half of the house area as a distinct cluster of features, which included a stone pigpen, two houses, and a large burned-earth feature.

Figure 6.3. House Area 6 under excavation. Photo by James A. Delle.

To the east is a second cluster of features consisting of four house plat-forms. The densest concentration of surface artifacts was located between the two clusters. It consisted primarily of domestic serving ware (bowls, plates, saucers), fragments of iron cooking pots, and the remnants of a bottle dump that consisted of fragments of dark-green wine bottles, case bottles, and stoneware jars. When we floated soil from the burned feature, we recovered the remains of several medicinal plants and common beans. Small artifacts, including several glass beads, were also recovered from this feature, as were fragments of iron spoons, forks, and cooking pots. The evidence suggests that this central area of House Area 6 was a locus of social interaction. The high density of bottles found indicate that sig-nificant alcohol consumption occurred on the site. This may be evidence that House 1 in House Area 6 was a rum or grog shop; the burned feature may represent a pit where pork was jerked for sale to the enslaved workers as they returned home from their labors in the fields.

One of the houses in House Area 6 was the focus of excavation (Figures 6.3, 6.4 and 6.5). The house was built into the side of the hill, and evidence indicates that the house featured a front wall made of cut limestone. Joists would have been placed on top of it to create a level floor surface. The distribution of nails indicates that the house was wooden, most likely clad

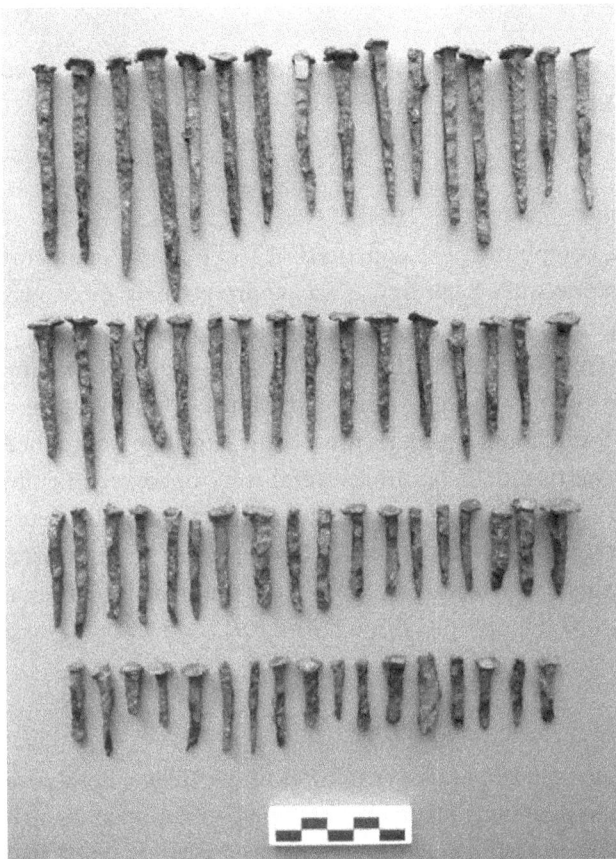

Left: Figure 6.4. A selection of nails recovered from House Area 6. The number of nails and variety of forms suggest this was a board house with a shingle roof. Photo by James A. Delle.

Below: Figure 6.5. A board house in Porus of similar dimension and likely construction technique to the houses that are archaeologically visible in House Area 6. Porus is a small town approximately 17 kilometers southeast of Marshall's Pen. Photo by James A. Delle.

with cedar boards or shingles. A sloped yard behind the house contained a small three-stone hearth.

House Area 1

House Area 1 is a compound that consisted of three house platforms surrounded by a stone wall. Each house was approximately three meters square. Remnants of Spanish wall were found with wooden framing pieces still adhered. Two of the three small houses featured flooring made of limestone cobbles packed with earth. House 2 was built on a dressed-limestone foundation. Although most of the cut stone was robbed out at the turn of the twentieth century, several were uncovered in situ during excavation. The third small house used part of a naturally occurring limestone outcrop for its foundation. A high density of wrought-iron nails suggests that this house featured a plank floor and may have been a board or shingle house (Figures 6.6, 6.7, 6.8, and 6.9).

House Area 2

House Area 2 contains the two largest structures in the village. Both were built atop foundation platforms made of limestone cobbles piled in such a way as to create a level platform. House 1 features a small veranda that looked out over cultivated fields to the overseer's house and may have been so situated to allow the enslaved to surveille the enslavers. Large postholes in the center of the house indicate that it consisted of three rooms (plus the veranda), and that these posts likely supported a significant roof feature. The prevalence of nails suggests that this was a board or shingle house. The floor was constructed of red plaster atop a small subfloor made of limestone pebbles.

House 2 was similarly constructed but contained a chimney base of 4 × 4 feet. It is the only structure in the village to feature such a chimney, although both the bookkeeper's house and what was likely once the overseer's kitchen feature chimneys with hearths. At just over 2,000 feet above sea level, it would not have been uncomfortable on most evenings to have an interior fire. However, the size of the feature may indicate an oven; if that is the case, this structure may have been used as a bake house. The population received rations of wheat flour, and while they could have

Figure 6.6. House Area 1 under excavation. The rubble piles are remnants of Spanish wall. Photo by James A. Delle.

Figure 6.7. A fragment of Spanish wall in situ in House Area 1. Fragments of wood can be seen adhered to the rubble fragment. Photo by James A. Delle.

Above: Figure 6.8. A Spanish wall house in Porus. Note the singled roof (*upper left*) and evidence for the Spanish wall (*lower left*) beneath the cracked stucco. This house is similar in size and likely construction technique to the houses in House Area 1. Photo by James A. Delle.

Left: Figure 6.9. Construction detail of a surviving Spanish wall house in Porus. Framing members, rubble infill, bauxite/clay mortar, and lime plaster stucco are visible. Photo by James A. Delle.

Figure 6.10. House Area 2 under excavation. The hearth foundation can be seen in the lower right. Photo by James A. Delle.

made dumplings in iron cooking pots, more refined bread products could have been baked for sale in House Area 2 (Figure 6.10).

The compound contained an elaborately terraced garden feature that cut into the side of the hill and was bounded at the edges by stone fencing. A small animal pen was also tied into this stone fencing. At the bottom of the garden was an abandoned above-ground tomb. Clearance and excavation of this latter feature clearly indicated that it was used as a grave, but it is likely that the occupant was removed with his or her family when the village was abandoned. The only artifact recovered from the tomb was a headless coffin nail.

Conclusion

Similar to other Jamaican plantations, housing forms at Marshall's Pen varied in terms of size, construction, and finishing details. Compounds varied as well, not only in size and structure but in terms of social use. House Area 1 seems to have been a residential compound. House Area 6 seems to have been an area for socializing that included a communal cooking feature and what may have been a grog shop. House Area 2, which had the largest and most complex houses and gardens, including a house with a chimney (that perhaps was a bake house), may have been a space reserved for drivers. Interestingly, although previous archaeological studies have shown variation in village housing, specialization within activity areas and architectural features has not been explored in depth. House compounds were not just the locus of residence and socialization; they were also an important element of the means of production and exchange for the villagers of Marshall's Pen.

Perhaps the word "village" is a more apt description of the conglomeration of house-yard compounds found in such spaces on colonial plantations than has ever fully been discussed. The various house areas excavated at Marshall's Pen show evidence of specialized activity areas and thus of specialized economic activities. Our archaeological investigations have provided evidence of a population that included skilled tradesmen who were filling economic and productive niches. Apparently, the structural constraints of slavery did not prevent such specialization from taking place in the villages of the enslaved.

Additionally, architectural features may be the material manifestation of social differentiation within the village. In his discussion of the village at Drax Hall, Armstrong (1990) suggests that differences between house sizes (i.e., the number of rooms) and appointments (i.e., furniture and other possessions) could speak to status differences within the enslaved population. The size and complexity of house-yard compounds also varied and perhaps reflected differences in social standing. Of course, internal status differences within the laborers' community would still have been tied to power dynamics between enslaved workers and plantation management. At Marshall's Pen, it is notable that the largest structure (House 1 in House Area 2), with multiple rooms and a veranda, also had the most labor-intensive floor (plastered) and was associated with the largest kitchen garden. This compound also had the best view, contained the only structure with a chimney, included an animal pen created with stone fencing, and featured a cut-limestone tomb. Although the archaeological data of Marshall's Pen is not sufficient to truly speak to social relations within the enslaved population, they do point to possible lines of inquiry for future researchers working in similar villages.

It has been argued that housing construction and the spatial arrangement of enslaved laborer villages can indicate both logics of control and surveillance on the part of European masters and overseers and degrees of autonomy and resistance on the part of the laborers. A more in-depth look at three house areas in the Marshall's Pen village has corroborated earlier discussions while also adding a new layer of nuance to the conversation. The layout of the Marshall's Pen village into house compounds that vary in size and architectural design and features speaks to the relative degree of autonomy this enslaved community had. Absentee planters, the transfer of the estate from the elder to the younger earl, turnover in estate managers, changing business plans based on the volatile coffee market, movement of laborers between estates (due in part to the end of the slave trade), and the more remote and often treacherous landscape of the upland location all led to a greater freedom in establishing the sociospatial dimensions of the village. The tremendous range of house sizes, construction techniques, and yard sizes and features present at the Marshall's Pen village may well be evidence of status differences within the enslaved community. Finally, these three house areas have also revealed differences between activity areas that speak to economic activities that tie this population to the larger system of internal trade in Jamaica. The potential bake house, the communal cooking feature, the terraced garden, animal pens, and a possible grog shop are the infrastructure enslaved people would have needed to produce and exchange goods. This village was a site where people lived, socialized, and produced what they needed to sustain themselves, but it was also a site where they engaged in economic production that extended beyond the plantation's primary function of growing coffee.

Notes

1. Lord Balcarres to Robert Alexander, November 5, 1810, Lindsay Family Papers 14th–20th Century, (hereafter Lindsay Family Papers), Earls of Crawford and Balcarres Records, Earldom of Crawford Muniments 14th–17th Century (hereafter Crawford Muniments), 23/9/515, Angus (Edzell, Glenesk, etc.), Fife (Balcarres, Leuchars, etc.) and Lancs (Haigh, etc.), Acc. 9769, Manuscript Collections, National Library of Scotland, Edinburgh.

2. Lord Balcarres to Atkinson, Bogle, and Company, June 30, 1810, Earls of Crawford and Balcarres Records, Lindsay Family Papers, Crawford Muniments, 23/14/16.

3. Atkinson, Bogle, and Company to Lord Balcarres, November 29, 1812, Earls of Crawford and Balcarres Records, Lindsay Family Papers, Crawford Muniments, 23/8/67.

4. Atkinson, Adams, and Robertson to Lord Balcarres, April 3, 1814, Earls of Crawford and Balcarres Records, Lindsay Family Papers, Crawford Muniments, 23/8/72.

5. Adams, Robertson, and Company to Lord Balcarres, March 26, 1817, Earls of Crawford and Balcarres Records, Lindsay Family Papers, Crawford Muniments, 23/8/89.

6. Agents to Lord Balcarres, October 10, 1821, Earls of Crawford and Balcarres Records, Lindsay Family Papers, Crawford Muniments, 23/8/107.

7. George Brooks to Thomas Fowlis, May 8, 1832, Earls of Crawford and Balcarres Records, Lindsay Family Papers, Crawford Muniments, 25/11/130.

8. John Salmon to Thomas Fowlis, July 2, 1832, Earls of Crawford and Balcarres Records, Lindsay Family Papers, Crawford Muniments, 25/11/134.

9. John Salmon to Thomas Fowlis, August 16, 1832, Earls of Crawford and Balcarres Records, Lindsay Family Papers, Crawford Muniments, 25/11/142.

10. Duncan Robertson to Lord Balcarres, July 25, 1838, Earls of Crawford and Balcarres Records, Lindsay Family Papers, Crawford Muniments, 25/11/274; Duncan Robertson to Lord Balcarres, Earls of Crawford and Balcarres Records, Lindsay Family Papers, Crawford Muniments, 25/11/497.

11. Thomas Fowlis to Lord Balcarres, March 11, 1839, Earls of Crawford and Balcarres Records, Lindsay Family Papers, Crawford Muniments, 25/11/290.

12. Thomas Fowlis to Lord Balcarres, April 2, 1839, Earls of Crawford and Balcarres Records, Lindsay Family Papers, Crawford Muniments, 25/11/294.

13. William Morrice to Thomas Fowlis, April 6, 1839, Earls of Crawford and Balcarres Records, Lindsay Family Papers, Crawford Muniments, 25/11/295.

14. Thomas Fowlis to Lord Balcarres, June 26, 1839, Earls of Crawford and Balcarres Records, Lindsay Family Papers, Crawford Muniments, 25/11/300.

7

Humanitarian Reform, Model Cottages, and the Habitational Landscape of Slavery on a Bahama Island

ALLAN D. MEYERS

During the last quarter of the eighteenth century, a reform movement arose in Britain that aimed to improve standards of material comfort for the working poor and destitute. Architectural literature featured new housing designs for laborers, particularly in rural settings (e.g., Kent 1776; Miller 1789; Plaw 1796). One of the more influential authors of this genre was John Wood the Younger (1728–1782), a respected architect from the city of Bath in southern England (Maudlin 2010). In 1781, Wood published *A Series of Plans for Cottages or Habitations of the Labourer*, which outlined what he felt were key principles of housing for cottiers. Wood's guidelines and the plans of model cottages that accompanied them were reproduced in a second edition in 1806 and a third edition in 1837.

This humanitarian concern with alleviating the deprivations of poverty stemmed, in part, from concerns about housing shortages in the face of rapid population growth in Britain (Crowley 2001, 218). It also arose from the needs of smallholders who had been displaced by the neoliberal policy of enclosure (Williamson 2002, 45–49). This policy subdivided communal lands across the English countryside and reconstituted them for ownership by individuals (Turner 1984). Such allotments had been carried out on a local scale since at least the early 1600s. Parliamentary acts of enclosure, designed to rationalize agricultural landscapes for food production needs accelerated privatization in the period 1750 to 1830 (Turner 1984, 17). Philanthropic partisans encouraged landlords who owned consolidated agricultural tracts to improve housing for the benefit of both laborers and proprietors.

The moral crusade for housing reform coincided with the rising tide of another humanitarian issue: abolitionism. In 1783, a committee of British Quakers distributed a petition against the slave trade to members of Parliament (D'Anjou 1996, 138). Rev. James Ramsay (1784) published a widely disseminated antislavery essay a year later, and the Society for Effecting the Abolition of the Slave Trade organized in London in 1787 (Hochschild 2005, 110). Within two decades, the transatlantic slave trade was outlawed. Understanding that complete emancipation would not happen immediately, activists lobbied for regulations that would force West Indian planters to decrease the severity of enslavement (Matthews 2006, 14). This led to parliamentary resolutions that called for the "amelioration" of the living conditions of slaves (Canning 1824). West Indian legislatures reluctantly passed a succession of reform acts in the 1820s that gave property ownership, marriage, and other new rights to slaves (W. Johnson 1996). These updated slave codes, which abolitionists viewed as precursors to emancipation, reiterated the slaveholder's duty to provide adequate food, clothing, and shelter to bondpeople.

In response to the abolitionist critique, some slaveholders began building model cottages that closely conformed to John Wood's recommendations. Both documentary sources and field studies of old plantations suggest that planters used the guidelines in reform literature to improve slave housing in parts of the West Indies (Chapman 1991). At some locations, masonry replaced wattle-and-plaster construction, dwellings with two rooms replaced the older style of one-room cabins, and multiunit row housing appeared for the first time. In the Bahamas, where British Loyalists in exile after the American Revolution established a plantation economy, the appearance of masonry slave dwellings has been linked to these reform impulses (Wilkie and Farnsworth 2005, 150). The presence of row housing, two-room cottages, and specific humanitarian design rules, on the other hand, has yet to be fully recognized. Farnsworth (2001b, 269) has even asserted that most Bahamian planters "had no impetus to build anything more complex than the simple [one-room] stone-built cabins. . . . As a result, the larger, improved housing units were not built." He speculated that planters in the Bahamas rejected many reform guidelines because local conditions there were different from those of the main sugar-producing islands.

Recent findings at Newfield Plantation, the early nineteenth-century estate of Henry Micajah Williams on Cat Island, force us to reconsider this limited view of Bahamian slave housing. Field surveys have documented masonry structures with floor plans and dimensions that are quite consistent with housing styles that humanitarian reformers recommended. Several forms reminiscent of John Wood's models—including the single-room cabin, the hall-and-parlor cottage, and the row house— were installed on the plantation premises for slave housing. These dwellings adhere closely to Wood's specifications. All the same, they are not direct copies of Wood's designs; they are adaptations of these models to the natural and social environments of a Bahama island.

Williams, a staunch apologist for slavery, could counter abolitionist criticism by showcasing paternalism at Newfield through progressive designs that were linked to improved health and the "cheerful" disposition of the inhabitants of such housing (Wood 1806, 5). Providing housing that conformed to high standards for the era was a visible expression of his benevolence and protection. Its intent was to obscure the tensions and degradations of enslavement (Vlach 1995, 119; Hicks 2007a, 221). In addition, the built environment reflected the highly stratified social order that Williams envisioned. While demonstrating that the Bahamas were not entirely beyond the reach of distant humanitarian movements, the habitational landscape at Newfield recalls the economic self-interest of a planter who sought to inspire compliant behavior in an enslaved workforce.

Principles of Humanitarian Housing Reform

As an authority on architectural standards, John Wood had exceptional credentials. His achievements included the much-celebrated Royal Crescent, a neoclassical focal point for the city of Bath that was completed in 1774. In attempting to raise standards for housing for the working class, he employed an approach that equated regularity with beauty and beauty with virtue (Maudlin 2010, 8). Wood fashioned cottages to fit rationalized landscapes. His conceptualizations contrasted with the aesthetics of an emerging picturesque movement that heralded variety, irregularity, and rustic decay. He also styled himself as something of a visionary. "No architect," Wood (1806, 3) stated at the outset of his pattern book, "had, as yet, thought it worth his while to offer the publick any well-constructed plans for cottages. . . . At the least, I should lead the way to some greater improvement." Yet, as Maudlin (2010, 14–15) observes, Wood's housing designs were less an innovation and more a codification of existing house types. After visiting the homes of poor cottiers in the hinterlands of Bath, Wood (1806, 3) outlined several problems that warranted remedy. Too many cottages were left damp from their situation on the landscape. The improper placement of doors, windows, and chimneys and inadequate wall insulation left too many dwellings poorly buffered from the elements. Additionally, few houses were spacious enough to afford a minimum level of privacy.

Wood (1806, 4–7) articulated seven principles for addressing housing deficiencies: (1) floors should be raised 16–18 inches above the natural grade to keep dwellings dry and rooms should be at least eight feet high for sufficient ventilation; (2) walls should be at least 16 inches thick to provide insulation and windows and doors should open to the south and east to avoid northerly drafts in winter and excessive afternoon heat in summer; (3) separate rooms should ideally exist for parents and children and for older male and female children; a porch or shed could offer additional storage; (4) dwellings should be no more than 12 feet wide for stability and roofs should be constructed with collar beams; (5) dwellings should be built in pairs, either a short distance from each other or adjoining one another as a row house; (6) dwellings should be built with solid walls using the best available materials; and (7) a yard or garden plot should accompany each house. To exemplify his architectural standards, Wood introduced four classes of model cottage that ranged in size from one to four rooms per dwelling. For each class, Wood illustrated plans for both individual cottages and row houses with adjoining cottages under one roof. He also envisioned one- and two-story versions of the three largest classes.

The two classes of cottage at the small end of Wood's spectrum apparently interested West Indian slaveowners. The smallest class included single-room cabins that varied in size from 144 square feet (12 feet × 12 feet) to 192 square feet (16 feet × 12 feet) on the inside. The second class included one-story cottages with hall-and-parlor layouts (Foster 2004, 90–92; Ellis 2010, 148–149). The hall was the larger room, accounting for approximately 60 percent of interior floor area. The parlor was a sleeping chamber, accounting for the other 40 percent of floor area. The interiors of these varied in size from 252 square feet (21 feet × 21 feet) to 348 square feet (29 feet × 12 feet). Wood (1806, 8) acknowledged that his designs were best suited to the countryside of southwestern England and that model cottages in other regions would need to be adapted to local conditions. He died just after the initial publication of his plans and did not have the opportunity to witness the full impact of his efforts at home and abroad. More than a dozen years after his death, a summary of his architectural principles was submitted to the Board of Agriculture as an enlightened and meritorious example of humane housing for the poor. In the report, a contributor identified "rough stone masonry" as the "strongest and most desirable" building material for such cottages (Crocker 1797, 114–117).

As Wood's ideas were finding resonance in Britain, anxiety over the imminent demise of the slave trade was growing in the West Indies. Bryan Edwards (1801, 178), a longtime planter in Jamaica, understood that such an outcome would "compel planters to cherish and husband their present stock [of slaves]; and sustain it in future by natural increase." In other words, the ways a planter could increase his slaveholdings would narrow significantly in the absence of an international slave trade. One way would be through increased birth rates among the slaves. Although the preoccupation of West Indian slaveowners with slave fertility was not a new phenomenon (Bardoe 2015, 69–70), more urgent considerations of the procreative health of the enslaved emerged during the era of antislavery activism. It was expressed in an 1803 treatise titled *Practical Rules for the Management and Medical Treatment of Negro Slaves, in the Sugar Colonies.* Ascribed to Dr. David Collins from St. Kitts, the manual advocated architectural standards like those John Wood recommended as a way of improving the health, safety, and productivity of slaves (Chapman 1991, 118).

Collins (1803, 134–135) argued that "next to hard labour, and scant feeding, nothing contributes more to the disordering of negroes than bad lodgings." He felt that the draftiness of many slave dwellings was unhealthy because a breeze blowing on perspiring or otherwise damp individuals was harmful. Collins (1803, 137) outlined three goals for slave housing: preserving health, protecting residents from storms, and providing resistance to fire. To achieve these objectives, he made recommendations about the placement and construction of slave houses and their proximity to each other. He recommended that when possible dwellings should be situated on the side of a hill that was protected from prevailing winds. However, he felt that they should not be too distant from plantation authorities so that the "proprietor, or his manager, may at all times have an eye to his gang" (Collins 1803, 138). Drawing on earlier ideas about regularity, linearity, and maintenance (Martin 1785, 3; Beckford 1790, 20), Collins advised that dwellings be spaced at least 30 feet apart and arranged in equidistant lines. He also recommended that the yard for each abode be shaded with plantain trees and that proper drainage channel wastewater away from quarters.

Collins suggested that each dwelling be built of stone to diminish the risk of fire. Where stone was not available or economically feasible, wattled walls with clay plastering for insulation and fire retardancy could be used. He recommended that stone walls be at least 20 inches thick and 5 feet high and have mortar at the joints for strength and stability. Floors were to be 6 to 8 inches off the ground and thatch roofs were to be hipped with a low pitch so they could better resist tropical storms. The interior was to be divided into two rooms by a wood or wattle-and-plaster partition. The rooms he recommended conformed to a hall-and-parlor plan; the hall measured 12 feet square and encompassed about 55 percent of the interior space. The smaller sleeping chamber measured 10 × 12 feet. Altogether, the floor area for an individual dwelling was just over 260 square feet.

Collins proposed that three dwellings could be placed under one roof in a masonry row house. In its dimensions and floor plan, Collins's row house strongly resembled the basic outline of the one-story "double cottage" John Wood recommended (1806, Plate 6, No. 1). Wood's plan for each hall-and-parlor unit measured 21 feet × 12 feet on the interior, whereas Collins described each unit as measuring 22 feet × 12 feet. Collins did not recommend several of the optional features Wood showed, such as pantries, sheds, privies, and door screens. Collins also did not mention the integrated fireplaces and chimneys that Wood deemed to be essential elements of dwellings in the British Isles, presumably because Collins found them to be less essential to slave life in the West Indies.

In addition to new housing forms, planters introduced broader changes to their settlement landscapes. Based on his study of plantation design at St. Croix in the U.S. Virgin Islands, Chapman (1991, 113–114) argues that a significant portion of slave dwellings on larger estates became divorced from the precinct of the planter's house in the early nineteenth century. These dwellings, which predominantly housed field hands, were concentrated some distance away in a new settlement or "village." The houses of domestic servants, or perhaps slaves who had some degree of authority or a specialized occupation, remained close to the owner's residence. The practical result was a bipartite habitational landscape. One complex of buildings, which was enclosed by fencing, served the proprietor and a minority of the slave community. Another settlement, which was also enclosed but was more distant, housed the majority of the enslaved population. The new village, which often sat downwind of the planter's house (Smith 1745, 225), was highly uniform in architectural design. Regimentation and European-inspired geometric order were imposed on the domestic lives of the enslaved, no doubt with the goal of influencing their behavior.

Bahamian Loyalists and the Slave Community at Newfield

The seeds of modern Bahamian society were sown in the period 1783 to 1790, when a wave of migration altered the demographic and physical landscapes of the archipelago. Roughly 1,600 British Loyalists fled the North American mainland after the American Revolution for territories still under the king's dominion, including the Bahamas. An estimated 5,700 slaves and free blacks accompanied them (H. Johnson 1996, 11).[1] With land grants from the Crown, these Loyalists established a plantation economy on several islands where only small or ephemeral settlements had previously existed. One of these locations was Cat Island, which assumed a prominent place among what one late eighteenth-century observer called the "Cotton Islands" (Wylly 1789, 4). However, the fortunes of many new settlers faltered within two decades due to pestilence and soil exhaustion (McKinnen 1804, 160, 170–171, 226–228). Emancipation in 1834 sounded the death knell for the economic regime most Loyalist families had imagined.

Among the immigrant Loyalists was Henry Williams, a native of North Carolina and captain in the king's Georgia militia during the Revolution (Troxler 1996). He was taken prisoner during the war, repatriated, and then evacuated with his family from the Georgia coast to British East Florida in the early 1780s. In 1784, Williams departed for the Bahamas, eventually settling his family on Watlings Island, now known as San Salvador. His youngest son, Henry Micajah Williams, came of age on Watlings and inherited seven slaves from his father's estate in 1791.[2] The younger Henry Williams became a prominent judicial figure and civil servant for the colonial administration. He was an attorney at the General Court in

Nassau as early as 1800 (Bahama Gazette 1800, 24), later holding judicial appointments on the General Court and the Court of Admiralty.[3]

Henry M. Williams likely established his property on Cat Island in the first or second decade of the nineteenth century, but the precise origins of what would become the Newfield estate remain unclear. The tract of an estimated 600 acres is located at the southeastern end of the island, 1½ miles (2.4 kilometers) west of the modern settlement of Port Howe (Figure 7.1). Williams owned forty slaves on Cat Island in 1822, presumably at the Newfield property.[4] By 1831, all sixty-two of his slaves lived on Cat Island. In July 1834, on the eve of emancipation Williams owned 74 enslaved persons, the third largest holding of bondpeople on Cat Island. His resident housekeeper, Susan Fountayne, owned an additional female slave.[5] If all of these individuals lived at Newfield, then the slave community there amounted to 75 people.

Slave registration returns shed light on the demographics of the Newfield community.[6] Six or seven nuclear families, averaging three to four children per couple, appear repeatedly in the returns. This core constituency accounted for 50–80 percent of the community, depending on the year of registration. Other members of the Newfield population are listed individually and the nature of their kin relations cannot readily be discerned. For most years, gender balance prevailed; only in 1834, when there was the equivalent of 8.5 males for every 10 females, was the ratio more decidedly unbalanced. Two-fifths of the Newfield population was younger than 15 years old throughout the era of slave registration. The high proportion of young people suggests a healthy fertility rate and is in line with higher relative fertility rates for the Bahamas overall (Higman 1995, 355–356).

The Newfield community was predominantly "creole," an official designation for African-descended people born in the Americas. In 1822, almost a quarter of the Williams slaves had been born in Africa, but that proportion fell steadily throughout the 1820s and 1830s. By the time of emancipation, just 10 percent had originated in Africa, and these were mostly persons of advanced age. A small segment of the Newfield community was considered "mulatto," a term used for those who were perceived to have been the issue of parents of both African and European ancestry. Mulattos consistently accounted for 6–7 percent of the Williams population through the 1820s and 1830s; across the colony, about 10

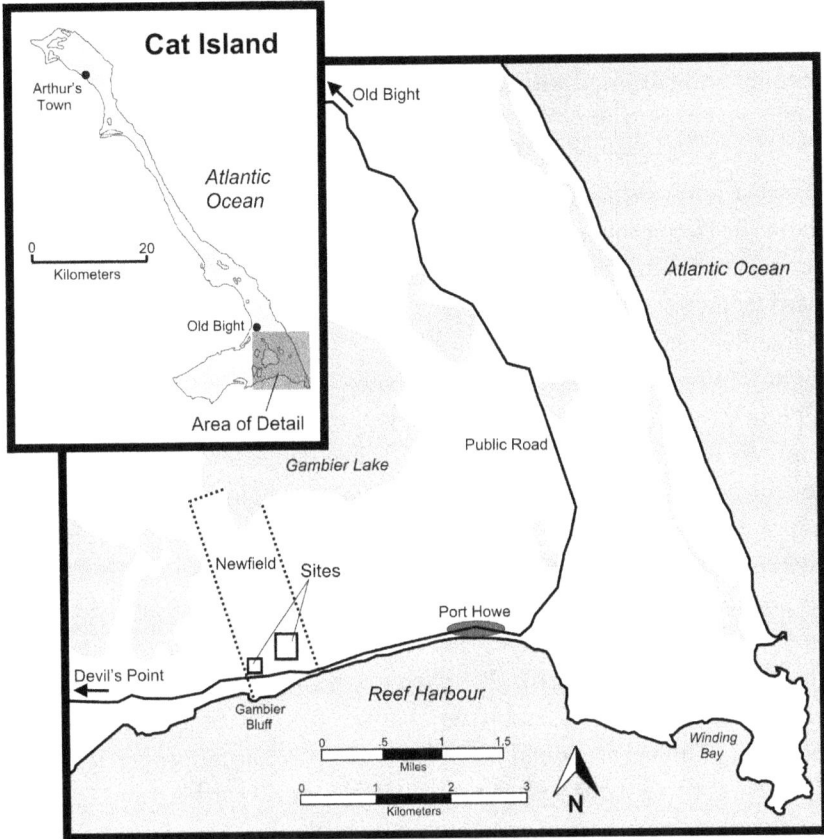

Figure 7.1. Location of Newfield Plantation archaeological sites at the southeastern end of Cat Island. Dotted lines represent the approximate boundaries of the estate tract. Map created by Allan D. Meyers.

percent of slaves were placed in that category (Craton and Saunders 1992, Table 10).

Although the initial agricultural strategy at Newfield is unknown, the 1830s operation centered on livestock and subsistence crops.[7] Among the fifty-nine able-bodied slaves of working age who lived on the Williams estate during the July 1834 registration, nearly 60 percent (n = 33) were described as field laborers.[8] Another 10 percent (n = 6) managed livestock. Roughly 12 percent of the working-age population (n = 7), all females, supervised young children. An additional eight percent (n = 5) were domestic servants, including a six-year-old male. Four men were listed as mariners or sailors and two others did gardening work and miscellaneous chores. Two men held the position of foreman or overseer. All of the fifteen individuals listed without occupation in the 1834 register were seven years old or younger.

During the years of accelerating abolitionism in Britain, Henry M. Williams ardently defended slavery. He was one of ten Bahamian signatories to an 1823 letter that protested against the Slave Registration Act and any proposals by the British government to enact emancipation. With standard language of apologists for slavery, the correspondence characterized Bahamian plantation slaves as well fed people who worked a judicious eight to nine hours per day and were subject to "humane and mild" discipline (Commissioners of Correspondence 1823, 25). When emancipation was finally enacted, the colonial government compensated Williams for the loss of his slaves. At the end of the transitional period known as apprenticeship (1834–1838), Williams retired from some professional activities and lived more regularly at Cat Island.[9] Before his death in 1843, he bequeathed the household furnishings and livestock at Newfield to his housekeeper, Susan Fountayne.[10] He also granted her occupancy rights to the estate for the near term. Fountayne, who was the daughter of South Carolina Loyalist John Armbrister and Caroline Thurston, a free woman of color, ultimately retained Newfield and two adjacent properties.[11] She consigned these lands to her brother, William Edward Armbrister. After she died, the Newfield settlement was likely abandoned.[12] Armbrister sold the lands to the Bahamas (Inagua) Sisal Plantation company, which operated from 1894 to 1911 (International Stock Exchange of the United Kingdom 1990).

The Habitational Landscape of Newfield

Two archaeological sites that once formed the habitational core of Newfield Plantation were surveyed from 2014 to 2016 as part of the Cat Island Heritage Project, which aims to document archaeological remains from the Loyalist period (1783–1838). One complex of ruins, known to local residents today as Newfield proper, lies on a wooded limestone ridge at approximately 75–95 feet above sea level. It consists of the remains of nine masonry buildings in a roughly ten-acre (four-hectare) space enclosed by stacked limestone rubble fencing (Figure 7.2). Five structures appear to have been residential and the others were likely used for storage, livestock,

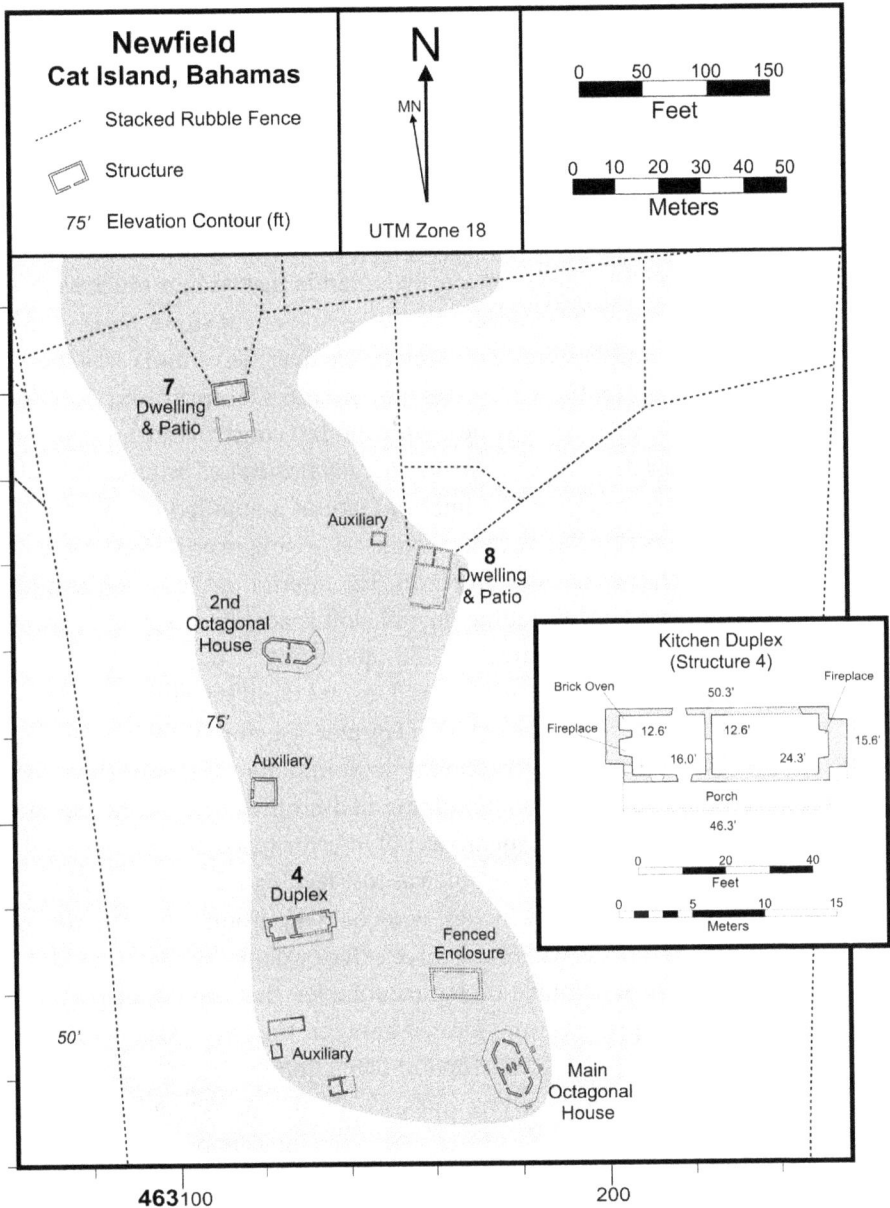

Figure 7.2. The main complex at Newfield Plantation, based on a 2014 field survey, with inset showing details of a duplex structure that functioned partly as a kitchen. Map created by Allan D. Meyers.

or auxiliary purposes. Cartographic sources suggest that this site was the planter's precinct, which Henry M. Williams occupied into the 1840s and Susan Fountayne occupied until her death.

Foremost among the structural remains is the presumed Williams house, the shell of which still stands. It was a distinctive octagonal edifice that could be seen from the public road. The symmetrical, eight-sided house was built predominantly of rubble masonry with smooth interior and exterior stucco; hewn stones appear at the joints. The walls, which are 11½ feet tall, sit atop an impressive veranda that rises as much as three feet and is accessed by several stairways made of cut stone. Square post-holes in the veranda masonry are evidence that the veranda was roofed. The veranda substantially increases the structure's footprint and elevation, giving what would otherwise be a more modest construction an imposing air. Six exterior doorways are symmetrically positioned around the walls. Each of the two rooms of the interior features a mantled fireplace made of cut limestone blocks. A central chimney, rising over 17 feet above the interior floor, serviced both fireplaces. The interior of the structure is just over 600 square feet, excluding possible loft space. However, the covered veranda swells the living area to 1,550 square feet.

Northwest of the main house was a second building with an octagonal plan, possibly the residence of Susan Fountayne before Williams died. Although its layout and construction style were similar to those of the main house, this second octagonal building had no fireplace and no elevated veranda and had just 460 square feet of interior space. Its exterior shell is largely intact; the walls rise as much as 10½ feet high. Remnants of a stone porch, elevated only a few inches, wrap halfway around the structure on the southeastern side, where the three exterior doorways are located.

The remains of a rubble-and-stucco duplex that served, in part, as a kitchen (see Figure 7.2) were located between the two octagonal houses. The building would have consisted of two adjoining units under a single gabled roof. The larger eastern unit was 306 square feet and the smaller western unit was 202 square feet. Each unit had its own fireplace and chimney; the western unit also featured a domed recess that resembles the brick ovens at other plantations (Gerace 1982, 219; Turner 1992, 35–36). The exterior walls that enclosed the western unit are largely intact; two doorways are located opposite one another on the north and south sides. The walls stand 7½ feet high and are 18 inches thick. The north and south walls of the eastern unit have mostly collapsed and precise locations of doorways and windows are uncertain. Although the floors of both units were raised more than 17 inches above grade, probing has revealed no detectable trace of plaster surfacing. The units were separated by a solid masonry partition with a small window. A cobble porch that is nearly flush with the ground runs the length of the building's south side.

At the north end of the planter's yard are the remains of two rectangular cottages that open to enclosed patio spaces off their south sides. Each had a yard in the rear defined by stacked rubble fencing. The northernmost of these ruins, Structure 7, has a standing structural shell that suggests a hipped-roof construction. The rubble-and-stucco walls are 7.2 feet high and 20 inches thick. At least five layers of interior wall resurfacing signal efforts to maintain and renovate the structure. Remnants of lime plaster flooring appear more than 18 inches above the ground surface. A single doorway opens to the south and windows are set in the south, east, and west walls. The interior was once divided into two rooms by a partition, as evidenced by a six-inch-wide remnant of lime plaster across the floor and by a vertical plaster line on the interior wall east of the doorway. The division results in a hall-and-parlor layout that compares favorably with a two-room model John Wood recommended (1806, plate 5, no. 2). The interior of the Newfield dwelling measures 12½ feet wide and is 285 square feet (Figure 7.3). The hall occupied 61 percent of the floor; the parlor occupied 39 percent. By comparison, Wood's cottage was 12 feet wide on the interior and occupied 300 square feet. Unlike the model cottage, the Newfield dwelling did not have a fireplace or shed. Collins (1803) did not recommend those elements to West Indian planters.

Gambier Bluff Settlement

Three-tenths of a mile (500 meters) southwest of the main Newfield complex is a site that likely served as a small settlement for field slaves (Figure 7.4). The forested location, which lies at an altitude of 80–100 feet above sea level, is known locally as Negroes Hill or variations on that name in local Bahamian dialect. Nine constructions, including five masonry dwellings with fireplaces and well-defined backyards, stand on a ridge leading to Gambier Bluff, a natural landmark that separates Flamingo Bay from Reef Harbour along the southern shoreline of the island. The maximum elevation of the ridge is downwind of but higher than the location of the main octagonal house at Newfield proper. None of the surface

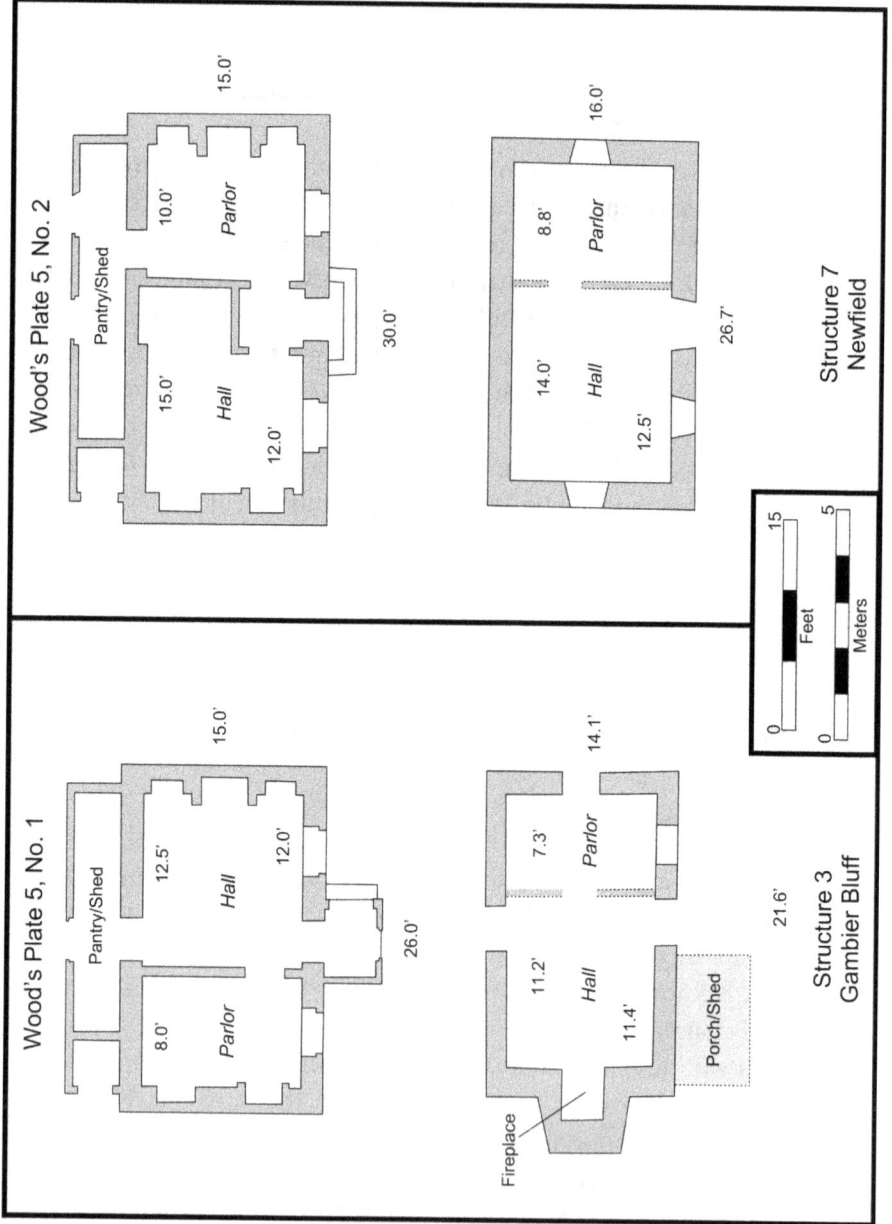

Figure 7.3. Plans of John Wood's second-class cottages compared to plans of hall-and-parlor dwellings at the Newfield and Gambier Bluff sites. Drawing by Allan D. Meyers.

Wood's Plate 5, No. 2

15.0'

Pantry/Shed

10.0'

Parlor

15.0'

Hall

12.0'

30.0'

16.0'

8.8'

Parlor

14.0'

Hall

12.5'

26.7'

Structure 7
Newfield

Wood's Plate 5, No. 1

15.0'

Pantry/Shed

12.5'

Hall

Parlor

8.0'

12.0'

26.0'

14.1'

7.3'

Parlor

11.2'

Hall

11.4'

Porch/Shed

Fireplace

21.6'

Structure 3
Gambier Bluff

Feet

0   15

Meters

0   5

artifacts observed around these ruins have production dates after 1840. In addition, the site is not depicted on maps dating to the late 1800s, which suggests that this portion of the Newfield estate was abandoned after apprenticeship ended in 1838.

Some combination of Wood's and Collins's recommendations seem to have informed the construction of the Gambier Bluff settlement. A row of three similarly planned dwellings was sited on a terrace on the protected northwest side of the ridge but still in view of the main house at Newfield. The dwellings, which were uniformly spaced 45 feet apart, had ground plans that approximated reform specifications. The walls regularly surpassed seven feet in height. Each house had a symmetrical interior that included a fireplace, a lime-plastered floor, and hall-and-parlor layout. The hall, which was always to the west, occupied roughly 60 percent of the floor area. The parlor included a window in the south or north wall. A partition was evidenced in each by vertical plaster lines on the interior walls just east of the north and south doorways. A third doorway opened to the east, and a small porch or shed abutted the south side of each dwelling. Each fireplace exterior rose only to the same height as the adjoining house walls and had no chimney stack. A yard delimited by rubble fencing was located off the north side of each dwelling.

The westernmost and largest of these three dwellings had 256 square feet of floor area and interior dimensions (22.7 feet × 11.3 feet) that were quite close to the recommendations of both Collins (1803, 142) and Wood (1806, Plate 5, No. 1). The other two dwellings had 210–215 square feet of floor area (see Figure 7.3). Wall thicknesses were 16–18 inches, conforming more to Wood's original specifications than to the later recommendations from Collins. None of the dwellings had windows or doors that opened to the west, a pattern that also conforms to Wood's standards. If cottages were to receive sunlight from the west, Wood (1806, 5) contended, "they will be so heated by the summer's afternoon sun, as to become comfortless to the poor labourer after a hard day's work." Overall, the built environment reflects a plan designed to order the landscape through rational geometry and mathematical balance.

The ruins of two other masonry cottages with a single-room layout lie near the highest point of the site. The westernmost of these dwellings—Structure 6—is the best preserved of the two. It measures 13.7 × 11 feet on the interior, just over 150 square feet (Figure 7.5). The rubble-and-stucco walls, which presumably supported a hipped roof, are 18 inches thick and

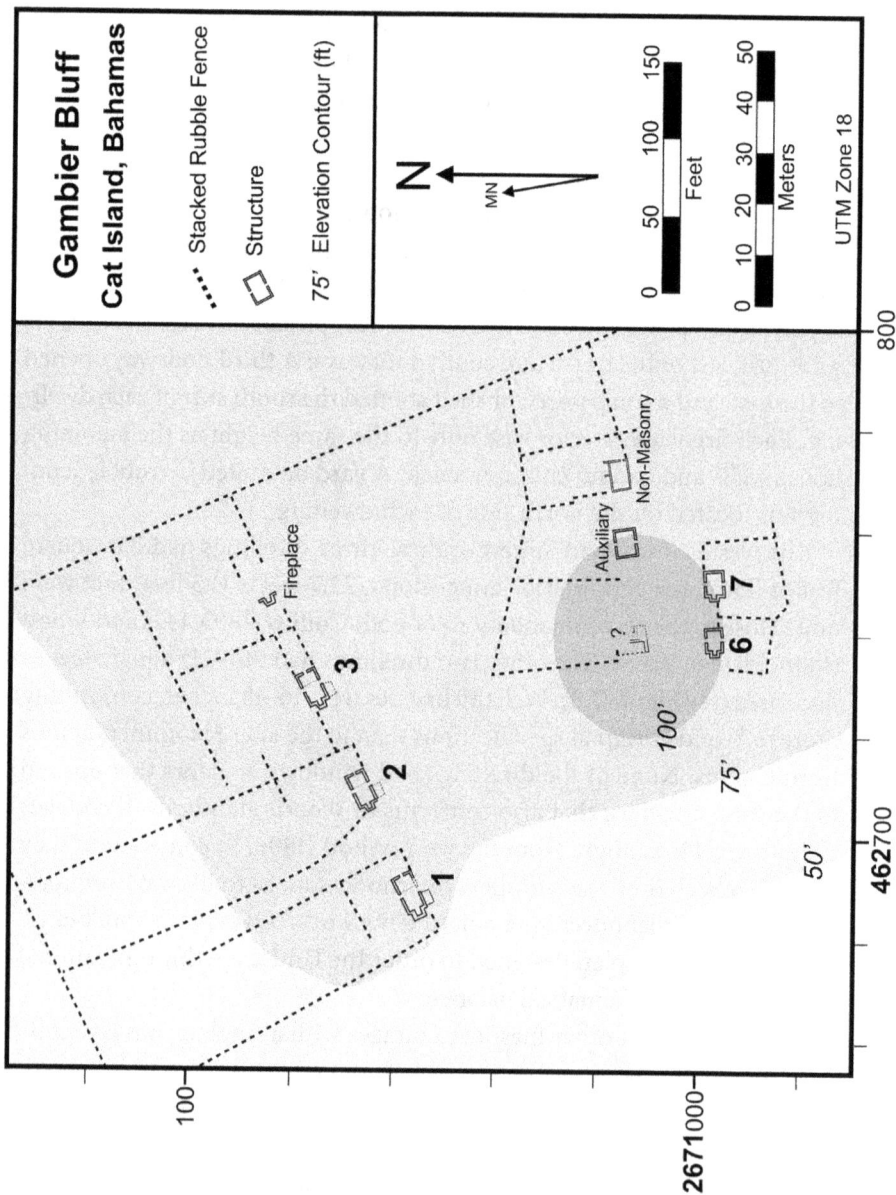

Figure 7.4. Plan of the Gambier Bluff site based on a 2016 field survey. Map created by Allan D. Meyers.

Figure 7.5. A single-room cabin at the Gambier Bluff site. Photo by Allan D. Meyers.

at least 6.2 feet high on the interior. A remnant of intact plaster flooring is raised nearly a foot above grade. The ground plan is symmetrical with doorways facing each other on the north and south sides; a single window is set in the east wall. Like other dwellings in the settlement, the fireplace with no chimney stack is located on the west wall. Beyond the rear doorway is a yard space defined by stacked rubble fencing that slopes downward to the south. However, unlike other dwellings at Gambier Bluff, there is no evidence of an exterior porch or shed.

A Built Environment of Inequality

The main Newfield complex and its Gambier Bluff subsidiary are both sited on hilltops and have maritime panoramas and comparable eminence. Gambier Bluff is actually a bit higher than the Newfield complex. This situation may seem counterintuitive in light of social dynamics on plantations, but it likely speaks to a concern for ecological adaptation irrespective of standing in the pecking order. Before the full development of germ theory, high elevation was thought to minimize the risks associated with miasma (Crowley 2001, 232–241). According to centuries-old ideas, miasma was putrid air resulting from excessive heat, dampness, and subterranean minerals. In the late eighteenth century, West Indian doctors attributed sickness and lack of vitality to the malignancy of air from stagnant ponds and swampy terrain. Yellow fever, in particular, supposedly emanated from "marsh exhalations." The *Bahama Gazette* spotlighted one military regiment's successful avoidance of the dreaded fever by stationing itself on a "high hill above the Town, removed from all exhalations."[13] Anecdotes such as this promoted the link between altitude and well-being, implying that a lofty perch offered greater benefit to mind and body. Moreover, breezy ridge tops meant improved ventilation, fewer insects, and practical safeguards against storm surges, seasonal flooding, and the accumulation of noxious wastewater.

Despite this topographic approach to maintaining health, dwellings in both settlement components remained embedded in a set of hierarchical relationships. In a very real sense, the cultural landscape was contoured for inequality. For example, while the main octagonal house was not at the highest natural point on the estate, it appears to have been the highest *visible* point. Its raised veranda, high walls, and even higher chimney achieved a commanding elevation among other components of the built

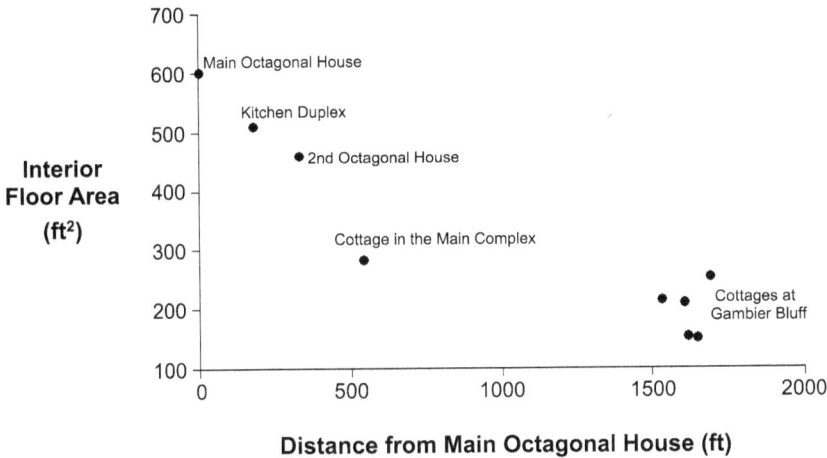

Figure 7.6. Relationship between house size and proximity to the main house at the Newfield estate. Chart created by Allan D. Meyers.

environment. Such visibility projected power and authority. The vantage point served as a panoptic position from which to observe the comings and goings of laborers. Strategic elevation also allowed the proprietor or his manager to be in visual contact with neighboring estates. This system of communication could have facilitated mobilization in the face of unrest among slaves (Delle 2011, 132–134).

Other dwellings played supporting roles in a hierarchical configuration that crossed two habitational nuclei separated by more than a quarter mile (500 meters). As distance from the main octagonal house increased, dwelling size generally decreased (Figure 7.6). The interior of the presumed Williams house was largest at 600 square feet. The nearby duplex, part kitchen and part residence, was second largest. The octagonal house that Susan Fountayne is thought to have occupied was third largest. The cottages at the rear of the main complex were 265 and 285 square feet. Although these were the smallest habitations in the planter's precinct, they were still larger than all the extant houses for low-ranking field laborers at the more distant Gambier Bluff. All in all, the relationship between architecture and proximity suggests that location symbolized a person's standing in the eyes of the master. Slaveowners such as Henry Williams manipulated the spatial and material circumstances of housing to underscore social inequality and express power (Orser 1988, 329).

Broadening Perspectives on Bahamian Slave Housing

The prevailing view in Bahamian historical archaeology is that early nineteenth-century slave dwellings failed to conform to most architectural standards humanitarian reformers outlined (Farnsworth 2001, 268). In this view, habitations did not have interior widths of 12 feet or less as Wood (1806, 6) and Collins (1803, 142) prescribed. Dwelling floors were not elevated, and hall-and-parlor layouts generally were absent. Farnsworth (2001, 267) noted that "we have yet to find in most of our cabins a partition into two rooms," adding that "thus far, we have not found any parallels to [multiunit row] houses on Bahamian plantations," although he raised the possibility of one on New Providence in a subsequent publication (Wilkie and Farnsworth 2005, 154). In light of the evidence for philanthropic slave housing on Cat Island, these summations warrant reconsideration. There was more habitational variety among the enslaved there than has been previously acknowledged.

Three types of masonry slave dwellings are present in the Newfield landscape: single-room cabins, hall-and-parlor cottages, and duplex row houses. The first two types are represented by five dwellings in the Gambier Bluff settlement, all of which are consistent with John Wood's housing standards. When capped with thatched roofs, they would have achieved the minimum room height of 8 feet that Wood proposed. All of the dwellings met or surpassed Wood's 16-inch standard for wall thickness and all were just under 12 feet wide on the interior. All were closed off on the west side, which Wood believed would shield against excessive afternoon heat in the summer. All were built in pairs or triples and all had well-defined adjoining yard spaces. All but one of the dwellings exhibited evidence of a roofed porch or shed abutting the exterior south wall, a supplemental feature Wood advocated. The hall-and-parlor dwellings had nearly identical spatial proportions to those Wood recommended.

Floor areas for the Gambier Bluff dwellings also fall in line with those Wood specified for his first two classes of cottage. Wood's smallest single-room cottage is 144 square feet and his smallest hall-and-parlor cottage is 252 square feet. The smallest one-room cabin at Gambier Bluff is 150 square feet and the two-roomed dwellings there vary between 210 and 256 square feet. The only one of Wood's basic tenets that was not fully implemented at Gambier Bluff was the elevation of house floors. In the two single-room cabins at the top of the hill, lime-plastered floors are

Figure 7.7. Recording the north exterior doorway of Structure 1 at the Gambier Bluff site. Photo by Allan D. Meyers.

raised as much as 11¾ inches off the ground. This accords with the recommendations for West Indian slave dwellings (Collins 1803, 139), but it falls short of the 16 inches Wood advocated (1806, 4–5). The other dwellings at Gambier Bluff had solid plaster floors about 4 inches thick that were installed directly on the ground surface. With or without raised floors, the settlement at Gambier Bluff would have outwardly exhibited many aspects of a model village that was designed in the humanitarian spirit of the age and showcased paternalistic concern for the enslaved population.

Although there was a strong British influence on housing design at Gambier Bluff, the dwellings there were not direct copies of model cottages. As John Wood (1806, 8) had anticipated they would be, his housing plans were adapted to local circumstances. This is perhaps best illustrated with the fireplaces. While each domicile had a fireplace on its western end, none of them had a chimney stack or flue, as would have been expected in the English tradition. Instead, some were capped with a low-profile masonry dome with an opening at the center; others were capped by several courses of dry rubble (Figure 7.7). The stacked-stone variation recalls local versions of rock ovens that generations of Cat Islanders have used for outdoor cooking. There also appears to have been little interest in closing off the north side of Gambier Bluff dwellings. All dwellings had doors or windows that opened to the north, contrary to Wood's prescription for the English countryside, where winter cold was a concern. In the Bahamas, the concern was with avoiding excessive heat rather than excessive cold.

The principles of housing reform were not limited to the domain of the field slave. They pervaded components of the Newfield landscape that were closer to the master's house. The hall-and-parlor cottage at the northern end of the planter's precinct addressed nearly every concern John Wood raised, although it was not completely closed off to the west, had no fireplace, and had an interior width that slightly exceeded 12 feet. Likewise, the kitchen duplex conformed to most of Wood's design principles, although it was not entirely closed off to the west and had an interior width of 12½ feet. The double chimney stacks of the duplex were perhaps more in line with British expectations, but its dwelling units were not equal in size; Wood always depicted his neoclassical row houses with equally sized units. The asymmetrical allotment of space in the Newfield duplex may have reflected the practicalities of a multifunctional building, an effort to economize, or some other adaptation to local conditions.

On the whole, the findings suggest an ordering of the habitational landscape that was intended to inspire domestic stability and compliance among the enslaved. Henry M. Williams was on record as an advocate of "sobriety and steadiness" among his slaves and he was willing to intervene in their lives by promoting early marriage to achieve it (Commissioners of Correspondence 1823, 27). For Williams, neoclassical design rules that linked regularity with virtue would have been another means to that end. At the same time, the landscape communicated Williams's image of the prevailing social hierarchy, no doubt with himself at the apex. Contemporaries understood well that plantation labor was stratified and that the lodgings and furnishings of enslaved tradesmen and domestics were often "vastly better" than those of field hands (Edwards 1801, 165; Roberts 2013, 202, 204). Joseph George Hunter, a Cat Island slaveholder and an acquaintance of Williams, told the Bahama House of Assembly that "Domestic Slaves are admired by all strangers that come to these islands. In no place are to be seen finer Negroes, or any so well clothed and found in necessaries" (Chalmers 1816, 48). Differences in house sizes on the Newfield estate and differences in closeness to Williams's house, emphasized that type of internal stratification by establishing symbolic distance between key groups in the plantation's operation. Conspicuous visual cues, such as the height of the Williams house, both reinforced and materialized those power relations.

More broadly, the residential architecture at Newfield illustrates the self-interest of a slaveholder who sought to extract labor from those he held in bondage. New housing standards may have rendered slave lodgings more aesthetically pleasing and resistant to fire and storm, but they also lent themselves to surveillance and the suppression of "turbulent contentions" (Collins 1803, 138). As an outspoken proponent of slavery, Williams sought to protect his investment in the regime by displaying socially progressive housing designs that were conceptually linked to the vitality and contentment of dwelling occupants. He signed a letter that encouraged critics in the metropole to experience for themselves the habitational landscapes of Bahamian slavery:

> Let our sainted persecutors only come among us for once at least; and we pledge ourselves that they will find in our field slave grounds, and in our houses, as healthy, sleek, and cheerful a peasantry, surrounded for the most with wholesome children, as are to be found in any part of the British dominions. (Commissioners of Correspondence 1823, 24–25)

In an era of intensifying antislavery activism, the model cottage was a political weapon that Williams and other slaveholders wielded in their battle to maintain the status quo. Installing such dwellings on their estates emphasized that they were fulfilling what they saw as a moral duty that exhibited concern for slave welfare while trivializing the antagonisms and dehumanizing nature of enslavement (Hicks 2007a, 221). The research challenge moving forward, as McKee (1992, 210) has articulated for the southern United States, is deciphering how the enslaved appropriated these architectural forms for their own sense of empowerment and cultural autonomy. Amelioration did not make the enslaved more contented. Instead, they became more restless, more emboldened, and more hopeful for freedom (Matthews 2006, 40–43).

Conclusion

Mounting evidence suggests that philanthropic slave housing at Newfield was not a Bahamian anomaly. Limestone masonry structures consistent with model cottage principles have been identified at several other Cat

Island sites and at sites on neighboring Long Island and San Salvador. The Cat Island Heritage Project, for instance, has recently recorded a seven-unit, rubble-and-mortar row house stretching 103 feet long on Joseph Hunter's Golden Grove plantation near Port Howe (Meyers 2015, 46). The nearby property of Lucky Mount features a four-unit masonry row house with a gabled roof structure. The basic floor plans of both buildings resemble the type of row house installed on a British-owned plantation at St. Croix during the era of humanitarian reform (Chapman 1991, Figure 6).

At Long Island, a surviving duplex made of cut stone blocks was apparently one of three such slave dwellings associated with the estate of Loyalist John Wood (Brooker 2011, 32–33); it features one-room units, each with a fireplace and chimney stack. On San Salvador, research at the nineteenth-century plantation of Charles Farquharson has revealed a line of four rubble masonry slave dwellings similar to the cottages at Gambier Bluff (Baxter and Burton 2011, 25). Each house ruin has a hall-and-parlor layout with a fireplace in the larger room. Given the limited field research that has been carried out on these old "cotton islands" (Wylly 1789, 4), future studies may well reveal philanthropic slave housing on an as-yet-unimagined scale. If that is the case, such findings will continue to propel scholarly discourse away from the notion that the colony was outside the full reach of humanitarian movements due to its social and demographic peculiarities (Farnsworth 2001, 269–270). Instead, researchers will have to reckon with a much wider variety of slave lodgings during the Loyalist era. This will require an approach rooted in the circumstances of individual islands instead of generalities about what a consortium of scattered Bahamian planters may or may not have endorsed.

Notes

1. Maya Jasanoff (2011, 356) estimates that 2,500 Loyalists and 4,000 slaves migrated to the Bahamas. However, her estimate doesn't include free blacks.

2. Last Will and Testament of Henry Williams Sr., March 17, 1791, Supreme Court Wills, Department of Archives, Nassau, Bahamas.

3. Blue Book of Statistics for 1834, 63; Blue Book of Statistics for 1838, 104–106, both in Records of the Colonial Secretary's Office, Department of Archives, Nassau, Bahamas.

4. Return of Henry M. Williams, 1822, Register of Slaves, Department of Archives, Nassau, Bahamas.

5. Return of Susan Fountayne, 1831, Register of Slaves, Department of Archives, Nassau, Bahamas.

6. Return of Henry M. Williams, 1822, 1825, 1828, 1831, 1834, Register of Slaves, Department of Archives, Nassau, Bahamas.

7. Inventory and Appraisement of the Estate of Henry M. Williams, 1843, 203–204, Estate Appraisals, Registrar General Office (1838–1853), Department of Archives, Nassau, Bahamas.

8. Returns of Henry M. Williams, 1834.

9. Blue Book of Statistics for 1838, 106.

10. Last Will and Testament of Henry M. Williams, March 19, 1842, Supreme Court Wills, Department of Archives, Nassau, Bahamas.

11. Return of Caroline Thurston, 1822, Register of Slaves, Entry 932, Department of Archives, Nassau, Bahamas; Riley (1980).

12. Last Will and Testament of Susan Fountayne, March 4, 1871, Supreme Court Wills, Department of Archives, Nassau, Bahamas.

13. "Memoir Respecting the Cause of Putrid Fevers," *Bahama Gazette* (Nassau), May 24, 1799.

8

Landscape and Labor on the Periphery

Built Environments of Slavery in Nineteenth-Century French Guiana

ELIZABETH C. CLAY

The spatiality of enslavement is a central theme of scholarship in the archaeology of Caribbean plantations, yet this topic remains poorly understood in the French Caribbean context. This chapter approaches the topic of built environments of slavery in the Caribbean through an analysis of plantation slavery in French Guiana using preliminary archaeological data collected in 2016. While intensive excavation has yet to take place, spatial and archival data from two nineteenth-century slave village sites will be presented in order to discuss how the built environments of domestic quarters were constructed to respond to planters' needs for social control and spatial order in a post-Revolution French colonial context.

Elsewhere in the region, space was primarily mobilized to facilitate the monocultural production of sugar and to control the growing population of the enslaved laborers who, by the end of the seventeenth century, constituted the primary labor force in the Caribbean (Mintz 1978; Curtin 1998; Higman 2000). Enslaved workers in French Guiana, however, labored on plantations that employed a more diversified agricultural scheme that included sugar but also relied on the production of cotton, cocoa, coffee, annatto, and spices. French Guiana was never seen as a "successful" plantation colony because of its failure to widely adopt sugar production and generate the wealth that came with it. However, the economy of French Guiana provided occasions for new colonial ventures. As a non-island member of the circum-Caribbean and a marginal space in the French Atlantic, French Guiana has a distinct history that contributes to the diversity of scholarship in the study of historic Caribbean plantation societies.

Historical Overview of French Guiana to 1848

In the colonial period, French Guiana was located at the frontier of France. Today, it still has that identity as an overseas department. A member of the Guiana Shield in northeastern South America, the department shares geographical characteristics with Guyana (formerly British Guiana[1]) and Suriname (formerly Dutch Guiana[2]), but its colonial history has more in common with French territories in the Caribbean Sea (Figure 8.1). However, compared to the French West Indies, French Guiana was a marginal colony that suffered from a lack of investment from France, a relatively small enslaved labor force, and the absence of initial development for cultivation (Redfield 2000; Mam Lam Fouck 2013). During the eighteenth century, investment in the region was limited because of several factors that included difficulty reaching the port of Cayenne by sea, the colony's distance from other French colonies, a generally poor return on investment, and limited interest in colonization (Figure 8.2). Following the disastrous 1763 expedition to Kourou, during which some 6,000 French settlers died, the area grew to have a reputation as an uninhabitable, disease-ridden colony that was unsuitable for European settlement (Lowenthal 1952; Redfield 2000). Limited colonization led to problems

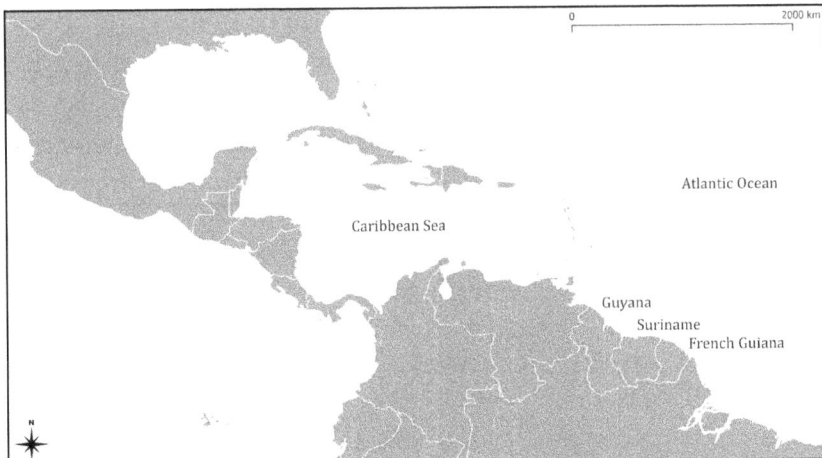

Figure 8.1. The circum-Caribbean location of French Guiana on the northeastern coast of South America. Map created by Elizabeth C. Clay.

Figure 8.2. An engraving of the port of Cayenne created in 1853. The protected harbor could only accommodate small boats due to its shallow nature; larger vessels were required to anchor offshore. Courtesy Coll. Archives territoriales de Guyane.

with securing enslaved labor. The slave ships that docked in Cayenne often did so because of a need to resupply or to avoid adverse weather. The captains of these ships were hesitant to sell to local planters for fear that they could not pay (Polderman 2004, 386). Nevertheless, slaves quickly came to outnumber all other groups and by 1750 French Guiana was home to 5,000 slaves and only 500 Europeans (Mam Lam Fouck 2013).

French Guiana's environment is characterized by the dense and humid forests of the Amazon, which cover over 90 percent of a region encompassing an area of 84,000 square kilometers (Barone-Visigalli et al. 2010; Rostain 2014, 67). An equatorial climate produces annual rainfall of 1,500–4,000 millimeters per year, distinct wet and dry seasons, consistent temperatures of 26 degrees Celsius, and humidity levels of 70–100 percent (Barone-Visigalli 2010; Rostain 2014). Three primary geographic zones define the region: the coast, a subcoastal zone that parallels the coast approximately 20 kilometers into the interior, and a vast interior region of rich neotropical rainforests (Tardy 1984). European colonization primarily took place along the coastal and subcoastal regions, while the densely forested interior remained home to a large number of indigenous groups and maroon communities. These two regions were historically referred to as the *terres basses* (lowlands) and the *terres hautes* (uplands), although elevations never exceed 600 meters and typically are less than 250 meters in height (Société d'Études pour la Colonisation de la Guyane Française 1843, 28; Barone-Visigalli 2010). Whereas the Dutch gained enormous wealth in the neighboring colony of Surinam by installing a system of dikes in the coastal lowlands where sugar was primarily grown, planters did not drain French Guiana's fertile swampy lowlands until the final decades of the eighteenth century. Throughout the history of the colony, polyculture was the norm. In the seventeenth century, planters grew tobacco, indigo, and sugar. In the eighteenth century, coffee and cacao dominated exports. In the nineteenth century, sugar, cotton, annatto, and clove grew in importance (Polderman 2004; Mam Lam Fouck 2013).

While the sugar economy of St. Domingue created enormous wealth for the French Crown in the eighteenth century, in French Guiana, sugar played a later role in the "relay race" of Caribbean sugar (Williams 1944 cited in Mintz 1961, 33). Following the Haitian Revolution, sugar production gained greater importance in French Guiana and took off after 1820 with the introduction of steam-powered mills for crushing cane (Mam Lam Fouck 1986). While sugar played a substantial part in terms of export value, it did not come to dominate the region because relatively few planters could afford to invest in its production (Mam Lam Fouck 1986). In the early 1840s, there were only forty to fifty large sugar estates in French Guiana. The rest of the plantations—approximately 569—cultivated some combination of annatto, cotton, clove, cacao, and coffee; most also devoted land to the production of foodstuffs and to pasturage (Société d'Études pour la Colonisation de la Guyane Française 1843).[3] Exploitation of some of these secondary crops, primarily annatto and cacao, could be undertaken with little financial and labor investment and thus provided a viable option for less wealthy planters (Mam Lam Fouck 1986; Polderman 2004). Because clove, annatto, and cacao were less labor intensive than sugar, planters could rotate the time and labor of their enslaved workers between these different crops and various growing seasons; production could likewise be taken up or abandoned as global prices rose and fell (Fabens 1853; Mam Lam Fouck 2013). Although by the mid-nineteenth century, the population of French Guiana was three times more numerous than it had been a century before, the economy still suffered from a lack of sufficient colonization and labor power. Planters lived dispersed from the principal city of Cayenne and some estates were isolated from others by many kilometers (Mam Lam Fouck 1996, 39; Polderman 2004).

Because of dense forests and numerous waterways, transportation of people and commodities was almost entirely water based in the colonial era (Société d'Études pour la Colonisation de la Guyane Française 1843, 31). There were few passable roads or paths in the colony except in the city of Cayenne. Subsequently planters established themselves on rivers and enslaved laborers dug canals for transporting products and people to and from Cayenne (Mam Lam Fouck 1996, 41). Mechanization increased in the nineteenth century. However, although mills were introduced for sugar, annatto, and cotton, planters often were not able to repay their creditors after installing them (Mam Lam Fouck 1996).

Clove and Annatto Production in French Guiana

French Guiana's environment and colonial history led to the cultivation of commodities that were unusual for South American and Caribbean colonies, notably clove and annatto. While the spatiality of Caribbean sugar production has been well studied, the organization of built plantation features on estates that specialized in diversified agriculture is less well understood. European competition for clove brought it briefly into play in the Atlantic world from the end of the eighteenth century until the abolition of slavery in Caribbean colonies. For over 150 years, the Dutch had a monopoly on clove until the French led an expedition to the Moluccan archipelago in present-day Indonesia in the 1770s. The expedition returned with the seeds of several prized commodities, including nutmeg, cinnamon, and clove (Lamendin 2014). The French began growing the spice in Indian Ocean colonies and also sent saplings to French Guiana with the explicit intention of dispersing production sites to various parts of the world to protect their control over the new commodity (Croucher 2015, 41). The equatorial climate of French Guiana was similar to the clove's native Moluccans and the trees thrived there. A colonial minister in 1816 reported to Paris that the soil and climate of the South American colony were entirely favorable to clove production and that the product from Cayenne was recognized as superior and even preferred to that from India.[4] In 1789, saplings from French Guiana were exported to Dominica, where William Buée, a planter on that island, experimented with clove agriculture for the benefit of the British Empire, which was looking for a way to profitably exploit the poor upland soils and mountain ridges that were unsuitable for sugar agriculture (Buée 1797). Buée concluded that

Figure 8.3. Postcard showing a twentieth-century clove plantation in Zanzibar, East Africa. In author's possession.

while clove trees could grow successfully on Dominica, they would need protection from wind, storms, and sea spray. These conditions did not threaten trees in French Guiana.

The marketable parts of the clove tree are the buds, which are harvested before flowering and then dried in preparation for market (Croucher 2015, 43). Production required caring for trees—which could exceed 40 feet in height—between harvests and picking buds by hand (Figure 8.3). While clove trees can be capped for ease of harvesting, in Cayenne they were allowed to grow and each tree was capable of producing 40–50 pounds of buds (Buée 1797). Clove trees in French Guiana were planted in rows laid out at intervals of approximately 20 feet and buds were picked at several harvest periods throughout the year using double ladders set up alongside the trees. The buds were then dried in the sun before being shipped abroad (Fabens 1853). Given the typical heavy rains in French Guiana, specialized structures for drying cloves called *sécheries* (drying houses) were constructed. These were roofed structures with rows of drawers that could be closed when the rains came to protect the drying buds from moisture and subsequent rot (Lamendin 2015). The environmental considerations that allowed cloves to thrive also favored other spices, including pepper, cinnamon, and nutmeg, although these were cultivated to a much lesser extent.

The annatto plant is native to French Guiana. Indigenous groups have used annatto for centuries as a dye, as an insecticide, and in craft production (Barone-Visigalli 2010). Planters in French Guiana began producing annatto as early as the seventeenth century; the crop was useful for mitigating economic crises involving other commodities (Le Roux 1994, 388). The product was used in Europe to dye fabrics in colors ranging from red to yellow and to add color to cheese and butter (Fabens 1853; Mam Lam Fouck 1996). As with clove trees, annatto grows best in the uplands of French Guiana and the plant (which grows as a shrub or a small tree) was historically planted in rows. To prepare annatto, seeds were separated from their pods, soaked in water for two days, crushed using wooden mortars and later by specialized crushing mills, soaked in water again, and then strained until all seed parts were removed. The pulp was pressed and left exposed until all water evaporated and then boiled for four or five hours to completely dry out the paste, which was then separated into rolls of four to five pounds, cooled and hardened, wrapped in banana leaves, and packed in layers in wooden crates for shipment (Fabens 1853; Royal Gardens, Kew 1887, 3–4). While annatto was also native to British Guiana, the industry never took off in that colony because of the success of sugar (Royal Gardens, Kew 1887, 8). Thus, French Guiana supplied the bulk of the annatto sold in Europe and the United States; Brazil was its only major competitor (Mam Lam Fouck 1996, 116).

Beyond weeding, not much care was required for annatto trees; fruit capsules were gathered when they were reddish in color and were dried in the sun for several days before processing began. Almost all colonists cultivated annatto to some extent alongside other commodities; the prepared paste could be stored until demand increased and harvests could go unprocessed during low periods in the market, which was quickly flooded solely by production in French Guiana (Mam Lam Fouck 1996, 116). As sécheries were essential to clove production, annatto preparation was accompanied by a specialized processing facility called a roucouerie, which was sited some distance from the main residential areas of a plantation and close to a water source. One roucouerie has been documented at a nineteenth-century French Guiana plantation site. It was a rectangular roofed structure with areas potentially reserved for drying buds and had ovens with in situ cast-iron kettles for boiling the annatto (Cazelles 2015). These iron kettles are the same type that were used for producing sugar cane and are found on sugar plantations in French Guiana and throughout the Caribbean region.

Despite the presumed ease of clove and annatto cultivation, which are harvested via a task-based rather than a gang-based labor regime, the fact that they were often grown in conjunction with other commodities may challenge the locally reiterated notion that slavery was in some sense easy. Furthermore, production in the nineteenth century may have been accompanied by increased surveillance and a harsher labor system overall, given the upheavals that followed the French Revolution and subsequent reenslavement of the workforce (Kelly 2008a). Task-based labor, the system associated with rice cultivation in lowland South Carolina and Georgia and with coffee production in the Caribbean, has long been characterized as a less brutal labor system because it allowed slaves greater control over their daily activities (Morgan 1982). However, some historians have cautioned against idealizing a complex labor regime that had its own inherent cruelties (Pruneau 1997; Schwalm 1997). Contemporary accounts of slavery in French Guiana are often contradictory: many state that the task system allowed enslaved workers to largely do as they pleased, while others describe excessive daily labor requirements and note that only the most physically fit could complete their work with time to spare (Ministre Secrétaire d'Etat de la Marine et des Colonies 1844, 145–146). Demographic differences in the archival record are clearer; on estates that did not produce sugar, there were fewer enslaved individuals and the division of labor was less specialized. While the enslaved population on sugar estates in French Guiana consisted of field laborers, blacksmiths, overseers, masons, coopers, carpenters, hospital workers, and wheelwrights, plantations that produced other commodities were primarily run by field hands, men and women identified in the written record as *cultivateurs* and *cultivatrices*. How these social differences may have manifested themselves materially in the form of the built environments of slavery is a primary research question of future excavations in the slave village context in French Guiana.

Nineteenth-Century Plantation Slavery in French Guiana: Habitations la Grande Marée and la Caroline

Archaeological investigations of plantations often focus on the spatial layout of villages, particularly whether the slave village was laid out in an orderly fashion or more organically organized. This latter characteristic is sometimes taken to correspond to lower levels of oversight during construction of slave housing and in plantation management generally (Armstrong and Kelly 2000; Delle 2014). Other scholars focus on how the layout of slave villages changed during moments of historical change or crisis. In the Caribbean, historical circumstances in the late eighteenth and nineteenth centuries led to a greater emphasis on providing adequate care for the slave population that may have influenced architecture and the use of space on plantations (Vlach 1995). Similarly, McKee (1992) demonstrates that slave quarters in the US South became more structured near the end of slavery, coinciding with the growing reform and abolitionist movements.

The unique circumstances surrounding the French Revolution and its aftermath had a profound impact on the plantation labor regime in French colonies and seems to have affected the spatial layout of nineteenth-century plantations. In Guadeloupe, this shift manifested in slave villages that were laid out in orderly rows and quarters that were constructed of durable masonry materials in contrast to eighteenth-century constructions, which were ephemeral. This may be indicative of a stricter labor regime and an attempt to impose order on both the landscape and the reenslaved workers and to increase surveillance in order to prevent uprisings (Kelly 2008a, this volume). While the end of the slave trade (which ended gradually in French colonies in the period 1814–1819) and greater attention to the care of enslaved workers may also have elicited architectural changes, Kelly (2008a, 399) notes that this shift was not found in Martinique, where the revolutionary abolition of slavery did not take place because the island was under British control. More durable architecture and organized village layouts thus may not be solely explained by concerns about health and well-being. In the nineteenth century, French Guiana was impacted by both the crisis in sugar cane production (following the Haitian Revolution) and the upheavals of the French Revolution.

In 2016, I directed archaeological survey at three nineteenth-century plantations in former slave villages to identify the material signature of enslavement in French Guiana. While one of these sites was a sugar plantation, the remaining two were more typical French Guianese plantations focused on a diversified agricultural and labor regime. These latter two sites, Habitation la Grande Marée and Habitation la Caroline, are located in the vicinity of Roura, a town located in the Oyak River Valley about 30 kilometers inland from Cayenne, at the center of the nineteenth-century

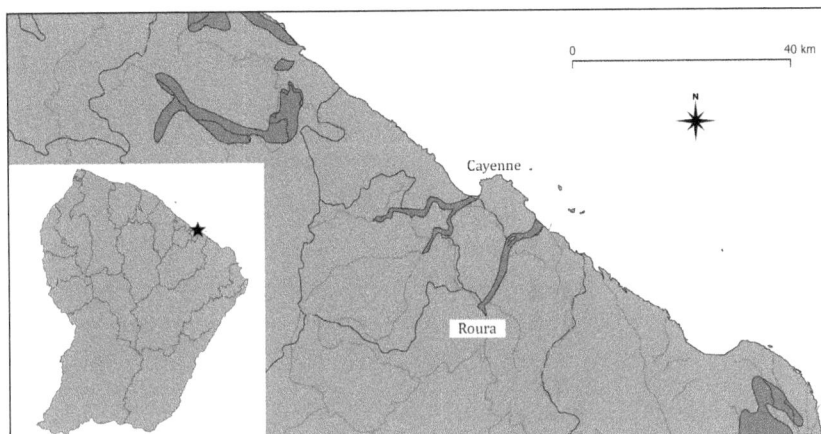

Figure 8.4. Roura, the center of the clove industry in nineteenth-century French Guiana and the site of Habitation la Grande Marée and Habitation la Caroline. Map created by Elizabeth C. Clay.

clove industry (Figure 8.4). The region of Roura is part of the subcoastal zone that is subject to unusually high rainfall of 3,500–4,000 millimeters per year (Sarge 2002). The Oyak River and additional manmade canals served to organize plantation space. Both La Grande Marée and La Caroline primarily produced clove and annatto, supplemented with other commodities. A *sécherie* for drying cloves and a *roucouerie* for processing annatto were present at both sites. Each plantation dates primarily to the post-Revolution period, after slavery was reestablished in French Guiana in 1803.

La Grande Marée first appears in the archival record in 1803. By 1829, the estate was described as having a master's house; nine slave houses, of which three were constructed on stone foundations and two covered in thatch; a *roucouerie*; and fifty-four slaves (Lamendin 2015). At the time of the abolition of slavery in 1848, La Grande Marée housed twenty-four enslaved individuals aged 14 to 70; the average age was 44. Sixteen were male and over 50 percent of the population had been born in Africa. Based on the family names and relationships recorded, four distinct family groupings are evident.[5] All individuals are recorded as *cultivateurs*, or farm laborers. In 1848, the fields at La Grande Marée were planted in clove, coffee, cinnamon, nutmeg, and manioc and other foodstuffs.[6] An inventory of the plantation also made that year noted seven wooden frame houses for the enslaved, each 10 by 5 meters, built on stone foundations

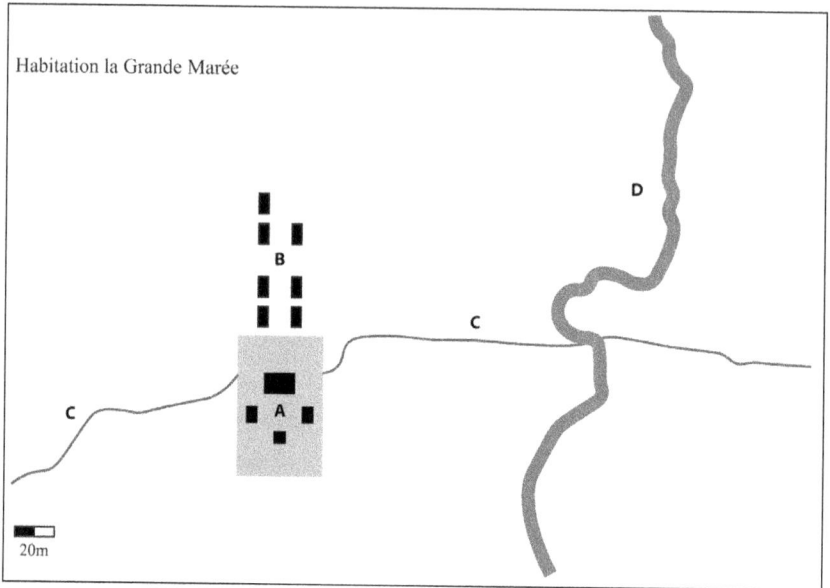

Figure 8.5. *A*, Elevated platform; *B*, slave quarter; *C*, paths; and *D*, waterway at Habitation la Grande Marée. Image created by Elizabeth Clay from LiDAR data (ALTOA/DAC Guyane 2015).

with shingled roofs (Lamendin 2015). All seven house foundations are visible on LiDAR imaging of the area undertaken by the French government in 2015 (Figure 8.5). The plantation was situated 100 meters from a small waterway, the Crique Saint-Martin, which was traversed by a major road that connected the site to nearby plantations (Lamendin 2010). In its present form, the planter's sphere includes the master's house, a kitchen, a hospital, a *sécherie*, and a handful of outbuildings, all located on a terrace. Because of the slope of the terrain, this part of the estate was leveled off and supported with a cut-stone retaining wall measuring approximately 1.5 meters tall. Cut into this wall is a small stone staircase that descended into the slave quarter area of the plantation. This area includes seven stone foundations of approximately 10 by 5.5 meters that were laid out in two parallel rows, perpendicularly aligned with the position of the staircase in the middle of the retaining wall. All structures at La Grande Marée were built with substantially sized cut stones made of laterite, the subsoil rock that is abundant in the hills around Roura. While these were likely quarried nearby and transported to the site by enslaved workers on the plantation, the quarry site has yet to be identified. Moreover, a skilled mason

Figure 8.6. Photo of House 2 in the slave village at Habitation la Grande Marée depicting the western foundation wall and stone staircase. Photo by Elizabeth C. Clay.

was probably employed at La Grande Marée. Removed from the site on the waterway is a rectangular building of approximately 34 by 11 meters that corresponds to the *roucouerie*. The building is located at the intersection of the creek and a drainage canal; water is required to produce *roucou* and the smells associated with its production necessitated a location far from the main plantation areas (Lamendin 2010).

During survey in 2016, six house foundations were identified. The first four were built on sloped terrain and were cut into the hill; their north-facing foundation walls were built as supporting walls for each foundation. Earth was piled in this built foundation and leveled off to create the floor surface of the house. The first four houses were constructed in a similar manner, while the remaining two were of shallower construction because they were built on more level terrain. Each house appears to have had a front or side porch area built into the foundation. Houses were separated from each other by about ten meters, which left ample yard spaces on all sides.

One of these houses, House 2, was chosen for limited excavation in 2016. This house was separated into two equally sized rooms by an interior wall; no visible interior entry connected the two rooms. The north, downslope wall supported a porch while the western wall included a

Figure 8.7. Coins dated 1818 and 1846 recovered at House 2 at Habitation la Grande Marée. Photo by Elizabeth C. Clay.

three-step stone staircase into the northernmost room and a doorway into the second room (Figure 8.6). We dug eleven 1 × 1 meter units in the house foundation in both rooms. No identifiable floor surface was uncovered, with the exception of limited evidence that ceramic tiles may have covered parts of the floor and then been removed when the house was abandoned. Otherwise, the construction appears to have been of packed earth. Very few artifacts besides nails and glass were recovered in the house, with the exception of two ten-cent French coins dated 1818 and 1846 (Figure 8.7).

Thomas Favard acquired Habitation la Caroline in 1792 and named it for his wife, Caroline Rouxel. Their son, Michel Favard, took possession of the estate after slavery was reestablished and developed it during the first half of the nineteenth century into a large clove plantation. Favard was a delegate to Paris and director of the interior for the colony for ten years. La Caroline was thus the country residence of a major player in regional and colonial politics in nineteenth-century French Guiana and someone with longstanding family ties in the colony. Following emancipation in 1848, Favard brought over laborers from East India to work the plantation until his death in 1863, at which point the estate was more or less abandoned (Sarge 2006). On the eve of abolition, La Caroline was home to 101 enslaved individuals. Some evidence suggests that at one time the estate was run by the labor of over 150 people. These figures make La Caroline one of the largest non-sugar-producing estates in the colony. While the population at La Caroline was much higher than at La Grande Marée, the proportion of males to females and of people born in Africa to those born in French Guiana are similar. The La Caroline population included sixty-seven males and fifty-seven individuals of African birth. Everyone at La Caroline is recorded as a farm laborer except for one married couple; both the husband and the wife were identified as carpenters. Documentary evidence also notes the presence of a woman named Magdeleine, the head cook and a surgeon whom Favard regarded highly until she was twice accused of poisoning a white overseer and expelled from the colony in 1831 (Tocney 2009). Within the population enumerated at emancipation, nineteen identifiable families are evident from surnames and recorded relationships.[7] Other than family groups, social organization in the village is less clear and will be a major research goal of future excavations. Because each house area was ostensibly constructed in a similar and strictly organized fashion at the discretion of the plantation owner, we do not know how each space was actually inhabited and appropriated by enslaved men and women.

La Caroline is located on comparatively flat terrain but follows a similar structural outline to that of La Grande Marée. A probate inventory taken following Favard's death in 1863, fifteen years after abolition, indicated that the plantation complex included a great house, a kitchen, a stable, a storehouse, a bookkeeper's residence, and a clove-drying house, all located on an elevated platform with a knee-high retaining wall. The plantation could be reached by water, which was the most accessible form of transportation in colonial French Guiana. A canal from the nearby Oyak River provided direct access to the estate; on disembarking, visitors would ascend a monumental staircase to the slaveowner's compound (Figure 8.8). On the opposite side of the platform, a small staircase descended to an elevated roadway approximately 10 meters wide that provided land-based access to the plantation and connected the slaveowner's compound to the rest of the estate. Two outbuildings, one a hospital and the other a building for processing manioc, were located at the base of the stairs on either side of the entryway. Shallow depressions of 3–4 meters on either side of the roadway separated the road from the house platforms

Figure 8.8. Monumental stone staircase leading to the planter's domestic sphere at Habitation la Caroline. Photo by Elizabeth C. Clay.

on either side and allowed for drainage. The road appears to have been made of packed earth. According to the probate inventory, there were twelve "workers' houses" present at Favard's death, eight of which were occupied after 1848 (Sarge 2006). LiDAR images of the plantation taken in 2015 indicate the presence of sixteen to eighteen foundations laid out in two orderly rows; surface survey revealed at least fourteen house foundations of similar size, 12 × 4.5 meters (Figure 8.9). Several of the extant foundations were completely intact on the ground surface while others are visible platforms. Foundation stones will likely appear with further excavation (Figure 8.10). Despite the limited archival descriptions of slave housing at La Caroline, I argue that construction was similar to that at La Grande Marée: wood frame houses built on stone foundations with

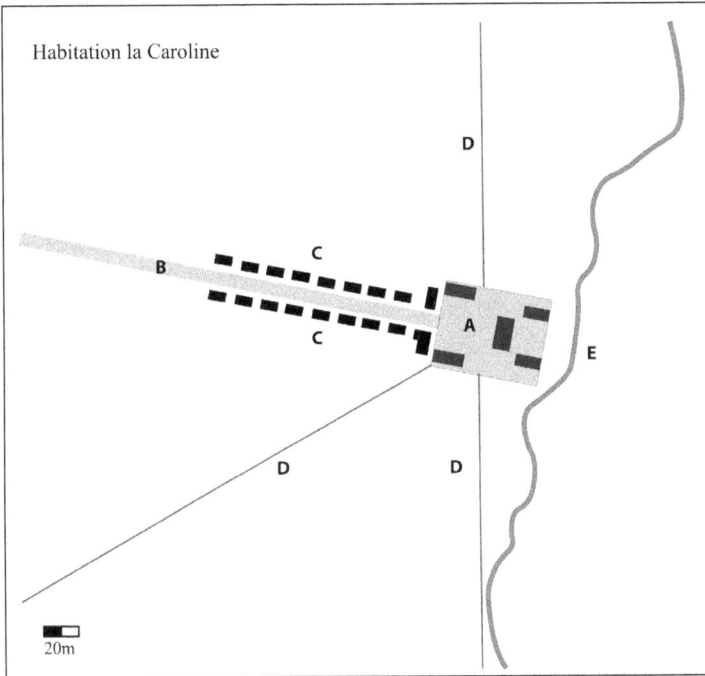

Figure 8.9. *A*, Elevated platform; *B*, roadway; *C*, slave quarter; *D*, paths; and *E*, canal at Habitation la Caroline. Image created by Elizabeth Clay from LiDAR data (ALTOA/ DAC Guyane 2015).

Figure 8.10. Corner of stone house foundation visible on the surface in the slave village sector at Habitation la Caroline. Photo by Jasper Colt.

shingle or thatched roofing. Two of the foundations were sampled with a total of eight 1 × 1 meter excavation units. House 1 was located next to one of the outbuildings adjacent to the planter's compound and included only part of a visible foundation wall. House 2 was farther away from the planter's domestic compound and in the middle of the row of slave housing. All four foundation walls were preserved and visible on the ground surface. Excavation revealed that the foundations were built in a single shallow construction of 20–30 meters deep. Foundation stones were less uniform at La Caroline and were a mix of cut laterite, large rocks, and cobbles interspersed with brick. It seems as though the foundation was built with a combination of specialized materials and whatever was on hand. At House 2, the more complete foundation, no evident entryways are apparent; these would likely have been formed by the wooden planks used to construct the walls of the house. The floors are of packed earth with the possibility that brick or tile covered some floor surfaces.

Houses in the village at La Caroline are separated from each other by only about 5.5 meters on either side and the road-facing wall of the house is likewise about 5.5 meters from the roadway. This would likely have restricted yard-space activities to the back of the house, since the entrance to each house would probably have faced the road. While French Guiana is not prone to seasonal hurricanes, as the Caribbean islands are, heat, humidity, rain, and vermin are a constant threat. Thus, despite the relatively large size of the houses at La Caroline, many activities would have taken place out of doors in yards kept clean to keep out snakes and other insects. Fruit trees were likely planted in yard spaces to provide additional shade and to supplement provisions.

Because each house appears to have been constructed in roughly the same manner and with identical dimensions, discerning any sense of social organization in house areas is difficult without excavation. Architectural artifacts recovered include nails, which point to wooden construction, large iron bolts and stakes, and iron window and door hinges. As at La Grande Marée, skilled carpenters at La Caroline would likely have directed construction of the houses. The fact that the organization and construction of houses were entirely of the master's making would certainly have impacted the sense of ownership that enslaved men and women had over their dwellings, yet it is likely that each house area was altered in some way to suit the needs of its inhabitants and/or the overall community. Even though social divisions are less apparent in the archival record on diversified agricultural plantations, it remains possible that certain people or groups of people would have been housed closer to or farther away from the slaveowner's house for reasons that remain unknown. These could include the individual's importance to the estate, such as might have been the case for Magdeleine, who was valued for her management of the plantation's domestic affairs and for her medical knowledge. This may have made her an asset both to the plantation master and within the enslaved community.

Plantations in French Guiana were much farther away from each other and from urban centers than was the case on island colonies such as Jamaica, so a marketing culture likely did not develop until the nineteenth century (Polderman 2004; Mam Lam Fouck 2013). Although the Code Noir made it illegal for French slaveowners to allow their slaves to grow their own provisions and to participate in local markets, documentary evidence indicates that the "free Saturday" system, which granted slaves a day to work their gardens, prevailed in the French West Indies because of the clear advantages it offered to planters (Mam Lam Fouck 1986; Tomich 2004; Gibson 2009). This was also the case in nineteenth-century French Guiana, where enslaved individuals were given every other Saturday off and spent their free time fishing, hunting, or caring for their gardens (Fabens 1853; Mam Lam Fouck 1986). Ethnographic accounts of creole life in the postemancipation period indicate a strong culture of self-provisioning that very likely began during slavery (Jolivet 1982). Whereas faunal remains in French Guiana are rare because the soil is highly acidic, archaeological evidence that fishing and hunting strategies were used to supplement the diet was confirmed by the presence of two types of lead weights, one for use with fishing lines and the other for use with nets. Despite the geographic expanse of the region, travel by boat to the markets in Roura or Cayenne was likely common and would have afforded enslaved people at La Grande Marée and La Caroline the chance to exchange goods and local news.

The assemblages recovered at both sites indicate strong commercial ties to France; most ceramics, pipes, and glass were made there. An ongoing analysis of nineteenth-century Cayenne shipping records confirms that coarse earthenwares were shipped from Marseille, fine faïence came from Nantes and Bordeaux, and a smaller proportion of refined earthenware and iron hardware came from Liverpool (Clay 2016). While scholars have long considered the internal markets of Jamaica (Mintz and Hall

1960; Hauser 2008; Bates 2016), much less is known about the marketing practices of enslaved people in French Guiana, including the extent of their participation in weekly markets, whether planters controlled the types of goods available to enslaved households as strictly as they did spatial organization, and whether locally produced ceramics were as important in French Guiana as they were elsewhere in the Caribbean.

Discussion

The social and spatial relationships of polycultural production are likely distinct from those of sugar. Future spatial documentation at La Caroline will clarify the size and layout of the entire village and spatial relationships within and between distinct house areas. Although ephemeral post-in-ground construction may have been the most common form of eighteenth-century slave housing in French Guiana (Hildebrand 2016), archaeological survey in 2016 found that even at smaller nineteenth-century plantation sites such as La Grande Marée, houses for enslaved laborers were constructed with stone. This could be because materials were abundant enough to produce cut-stone foundations on all plantation buildings. More robustly constructed houses could also have been the result of the abolition and reform movements of the nineteenth century that dictated that planters give greater care to the housing, subsistence, and health of slaves. The need to sustain the population following the end of the slave trade could also have led to transitions in housing construction. Durable architecture may also support hypotheses that slavery was more restrictive in the post-Revolution period of reenslavement in Guadeloupe and French Guiana to impose order and prevent uprising (Kelly 2008a, 399). While the slave village was out of sight on many colonial plantations, the villages at La Caroline and La Grande Marée follow an orderly layout and are integral components of the entire plantation design. Although contemporary visitors would likely have accessed the plantation by boat at both plantations, with the option of avoiding the sight of slave housing, the imposing nature of the elevated roadway at La Caroline seems to imply that this was also an official entrance, obliging those visiting by land to associate the enslaved with the material wealth of the entire establishment. The presence of this central roadway also supports hypotheses that yard-space activities took place in spaces behind the houses, out of view of passersby on the road. One archival image of slave housing in

Figure 8.11. Mid-nineteenth-century lithograph of housing for the enslaved at a plantation in Cayenne. Courtesy Coll. Archives territoriales de Guyane.

French Guiana supports the rectangular shape and alignment of housing observed at both La Grande Marée and La Caroline (Figure 8.11). It furthermore illustrates the wood-plank construction and thatch roofing that were likely used at both sites. The image additionally points to the organization of exterior spaces: areas for planting shade and fruit trees, raising pigs and chickens, and taking part in craft activities and socializing are all represented.

Most historical research about plantations in French Guiana argues that the task-based nature of production led to an easier, more relaxed system. However, the structured nature of plantation design at both La Grande Marée and La Caroline seems to question this assumption. The impact of this highly structured built environment on the daily lived experiences of enslaved men and women and how people may have modified these constructed environments to suit the needs of their individual households remain central research questions for future excavations in the region.

Conclusion

Because plantation slavery in French Guiana was different from that of the West Indies and the colony never attained the wealth of its island neighbors, its history has been continually shaped by founding myths, including that of a failed space where the plantation was never important. This assumption is largely sustained because the material remains of plantation agriculture persist on the contemporary landscape only in the form of ruins overgrown by the vegetation that overtook these structures when the plantation system was abandoned in the decades following abolition in 1848. Overlooking these spaces, however, risks overlooking the people who lived and labored at French Guianese plantations and their present-day descendants. The imposing structural features at La Caroline and La Grande Marée confirm that not all plantations were inconsequential establishments that left little in the way of material evidence. Instead, the French Guianese plantation offers a chance to approach labor in the Caribbean through a different lens. Caribbean anthropology has long held that labor—namely what enslaved people were working to produce—had an impact on daily life and the formation of creole Caribbean communities (Mintz 1978; Trouillot 1982; Mintz and Price 1992). To that end, future research and archaeological excavation will elucidate the unique experiences of labor in the French Guianese context while also providing further details about architecture and the use of space in individual house-yard areas.

This chapter briefly introduced spatial data about plantation organization in French Guiana. Initial conclusions support the idea that material conditions had parallels with plantations in Martinique and Guadeloupe, yet the many historical and environmental differences include a labor regime that was focused on diversified agriculture and the production of commodities that have not previously been studied archaeologically in the New World context. Despite French Guiana's geographic isolation and the relative lack of European investment in the region, the material signature of enslavement resembles that of the French and British Caribbean more broadly and suggests a shared logic of nineteenth-century slavery in which imported French material culture was significant and architectural durability and spatial control were important regardless of the commodity being produced. Further excavation in coming years will shed light on these unique experiences and contribute to the growing database of comparative Caribbean slavery.

Notes

1. Referred to as Surinam until the loss of the neighboring Dutch colonies to the British in 1814.

2. The Guiana Shield is a geological formation on the northeastern coast of South America. The British acquired Essequibo, Berbice, and Demerara, three formerly Dutch colonies, in 1814. They unified as British Guiana in 1831.

3. *Bixa orellana* is the plant commonly known in English as annatto, *achiote* in Spanish, and *roucou* or *rocou* in French. Nineteenth-century US merchants also typically referred to it as rocou.

4. Claude Carra Saint-Cyr and Benoit Cavay, "Proposition d'importer et de naturaliser à la Guyane Française un grand nombre de végétaux de l'Inde," February 25, 1816, D. F. C. Suppl. Guyane no. 34, Archives nationales d'outre-mer, Aix-en-Provence; Joseph Warren Fabens, "Speech Regarding Cayenne Economics and Politics," February 25, 1853, MH 94 Fabens Family Papers, Series VI: Joseph Warren Fabens (1821–1875) Papers, Business Records, Phillips Library, Peabody Essex Museum.

5. Registres de nouveaux libres, Roura, 1848, Archives territoriales de Guyane, Cayenne.

6. "Vente de l'habitation dite Grand-Marée," *Feuille de la Guyane française* (Cayenne), July 15, 1848.

7. Registres de nouveaux libres, Roura, 1848.

9

Royal Enslaved Afro-Caribbeans in Christiansted

Exploring the Archaeology of Enslavement in a Caribbean City

ALICIA ODEWALE AND MEREDITH D. HARDY

When African men, women, and children were first brought to the island of St. Croix on Danish ships in 1733, most entered through the port town of Christiansted and came directly from Africa (Highfield 2009, 90). Once ships were docked in Bassin Harbor, all of the commodities they carried, including human cargo, were processed, taxed, and weighed in the scale house. The enslaved Afro-Caribbeans setting foot on the island for the first time would have been bombarded with the sights and sounds of this burgeoning cosmopolitan port. They would have seen free and enslaved people of color going about their daily business alongside Danish officers and various individuals from around the world. Disembarking from the bowels of the ship, captives would have marched from the harbor to the customs house, then to the Danish West India and Guinea Company (DWIGC) warehouse, and then to auction yards scattered across the town. When they reached the company warehouse, they would have been cleaned, given tobacco and pipes, and then sorted according to nationality (Paiewonsky 1989, 91). Sources are not clear on exactly how long individuals were forcibly kept in the warehouse before sale, but most were taken to private auction yards throughout Christiansted and sold. Once these individuals were sold on the auction block as field laborers, domestic servants, artisans, or were retained for service to the Crown and DWIGC, they may have felt that the worst part of the journey was finally over. However, in many ways their travails were just beginning, especially for those who were forced to endure urban enslavement.

This chapter explores the world of the enslaved residents of the city of Christiansted who were the property of the Danish Crown. We start by examining the natural environment that threatened this seaside community and then explore the built environment of the site and the specific structures still standing today that can tell us something about urban slavery on this island. Finally, we examine new archaeological investigations at Christiansted National Historic Site in Christiansted, St. Croix, that illustrate the daily lives and activities of those who lived and worked in this compound.

The Built Environment of Urban Slavery in St. Croix

The United States Virgin Island group includes the islands of St. Croix, St. Thomas, and St. John, which from 1682 to 1917 were known as the Danish West Indies. The Virgin Islands are also said to have existed or been ruled under seven flags, given that at various moments, the islands were controlled by Spain, Holland, England, France, the Knights of Malta, Denmark, and most recently, the United States, which purchased the islands from Denmark in 1917 (Lewisohn 1970). St. Croix was under Denmark's control from 1733 to 1917, a period that encompasses the era of plantation slavery that concerns us here.

Christiansted, the first city established on St. Croix, was founded in 1735 after the DWIGC purchased the island and began construction on Fort Christiansvaern, a Dutch word meaning Christian's defense. The city was named for King Christian VI, who ruled Denmark from 1730 to 1746 (Westergaard 1917, 217). After this first structure was destroyed by a hurricane in 1738 and then rebuilt in 1749, the city began to take shape as the company warehouse; various churches of Lutheran, Dutch Reformed, Moravian, and Catholic affiliation; schoolhouses; roads; courtyards; docks; shops; taverns; theaters; seaside estates; and various houses of diversion began to dot the coast of the busy port town (Westergaard 1917, 248; Hall 1992; Haagensen 1994, 18; Highfield 2012; 2018). But the focal point of the urban landscape was Fort Christiansvaern, which was established as a preventive measure against attack from both land and sea. While it was specifically intended to counter the threat of pirates and slave rebellions, the fort was also used as an instrument of torture and punishment (Highfield 2012, 6; 2018, 124). This peculiar structure had two levels: the upper floors were reserved for the governor, his family, and various Danish officials, while the lower level served as a prison for both free and enslaved people. This is the place where Alexander Hamilton's mother was imprisoned on charges of adultery. The lowest dungeons of the fort were reserved for the enslaved (Haagensen 1994, 19). The fort, which was designed to protect Danish interests in the territory from Afro-Caribbean revolts, was no doubt built by Afro-Caribbean peoples; a large group of enslaved builders was captured and shipped to St. Croix explicitly for this building project after they were imprisoned for their role in the infamous rebellion in St. John in 1733, which successfully overthrew Danish rule on that island for almost a year (Highfield 2012, 6; Odewale 2016).

The first census taken in St. Croix, in 1742, reported an islandwide population of 2,080 people, which included a black population of 1,906 divided into the categories of "capable Negroes," "Manquerons or incapacitated," and children (Westergaard 1917, 319). A census for the city of Christiansted alone wasn't taken until 1745, when only forty people inhabited the city, twenty-seven of whom were labeled "Negroes" (Westergaard 1917, 319). By 1803, just over fifty years after the first census was taken, the population had swelled to 5,510, including 3,038 enslaved people, 1,407 free blacks, and 1,065 whites (Hall 1992, 88). According to a 1797 census, most of the enslaved community residing in the town were women (Hall 1992, 91). European colonists were a major part of this multicultural society, although the white community constituted only 6.5 percent of the population in 1803. The majority of these European settlers and planters were men who came to the island without their wives or children. Even though St. Croix was a Danish colony, most of the European residents were English, French, Dutch, or Irish (Dookhan 1994, 142). The bustling Caribbean city served multiple purposes for the island: it was a hub of commerce and military defense, the place where people were punished, and a center of residential life, worship, and entertainment.

On March 4, 1952, nearly forty years after the United States purchased the Danish West Indies, Christiansted National Historic Site was established as the Virgin Islands National Historic Site (National Park Service 2014, 3). The park was re-designated and received its current name on

December 24, 1960. It consists of approximately 7.5 acres on the waterfront of Christiansted Harbor (National Park Service 2014, 3). Christiansted National Historic Site is one of the most complete and best preserved Danish colonial administrative complexes in the New World (National Park Service 2014, 15). This site is unique for its six historic standing structures that are among the best surviving examples of Danish governmental architecture in the Caribbean: Fort Christiansvaern, the stable building, the steeple building, the DWIGC warehouse, the Danish Customs House, and the scale house (Figure 9.1).

The Christiansted wharf and the grounds of the fort and surrounding plaza have undergone many changes since the buildings were first erected at the beginning of the Danish era. In the first building phase, Fort Christiansvaern was completed in 1738 and then rebuilt following a hurricane in the 1740s. This was followed by the construction of the DWIGC warehouse complex (Cissel 2000; Lawson et al. 2004, 14; Highfield 2018). Since the fort was used primarily as a prison and Danish military depot, our focus is the DWIGC warehouse complex of buildings, where some of those Afro-Caribbeans enslaved by the Crown and by the royal bookkeeper lived and worked (George Tyson, personal communication, July 15, 2016). In a second building phase, in 1749, company slaves and artisans under the supervision of Chief Surveyor Johan Vilhelm Schopen built a warehouse complex that included offices and living spaces (Cissel 2000, 8). The warehouse was used to store both local and imported products such as sugar, molasses, rum, cotton, and tropical hardwoods and as housing for royal enslaved African men and women. Other buildings in the complex included kitchens, stables, baking ovens, residences for bookkeepers, several offices, and sleeping quarters for the enslaved.

Danish historical maps housed in the archival collections at the St. Croix Landmarks Society Whim Museum and at the Danish National Archives in Copenhagen include two depictions of the original warehouse complex, one dating to 1779 and the other dating to circa 1803 (Figures 9.2 and 9.3). Peter Lotharius Oxholm's 1778–1779 survey of the warehouse complex is the earliest account and provides a fairly detailed description of the use of specific rooms and particular buildings. This illustration identified a row of six single-story structures labeled as "Negro houses" (*Neger huuser*) located in the eastern half of the warehouse complex along the southern wall (Figure 9.2). This row of structures faced

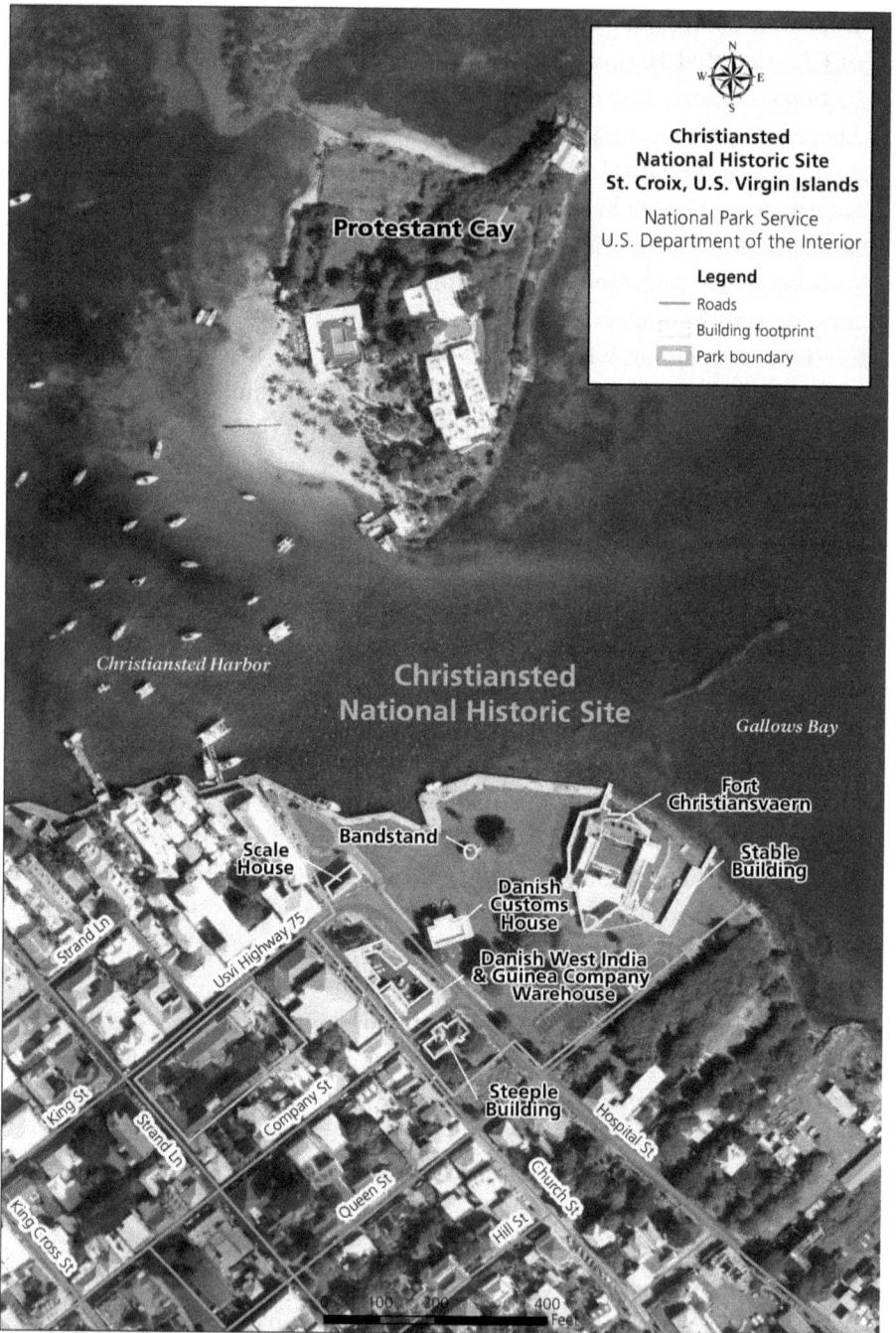

Figure 9.1. GIS map of six historic structures at Christiansted National Historic Site, St. Croix, US Virgin Islands. Map provided by the National Park Service.

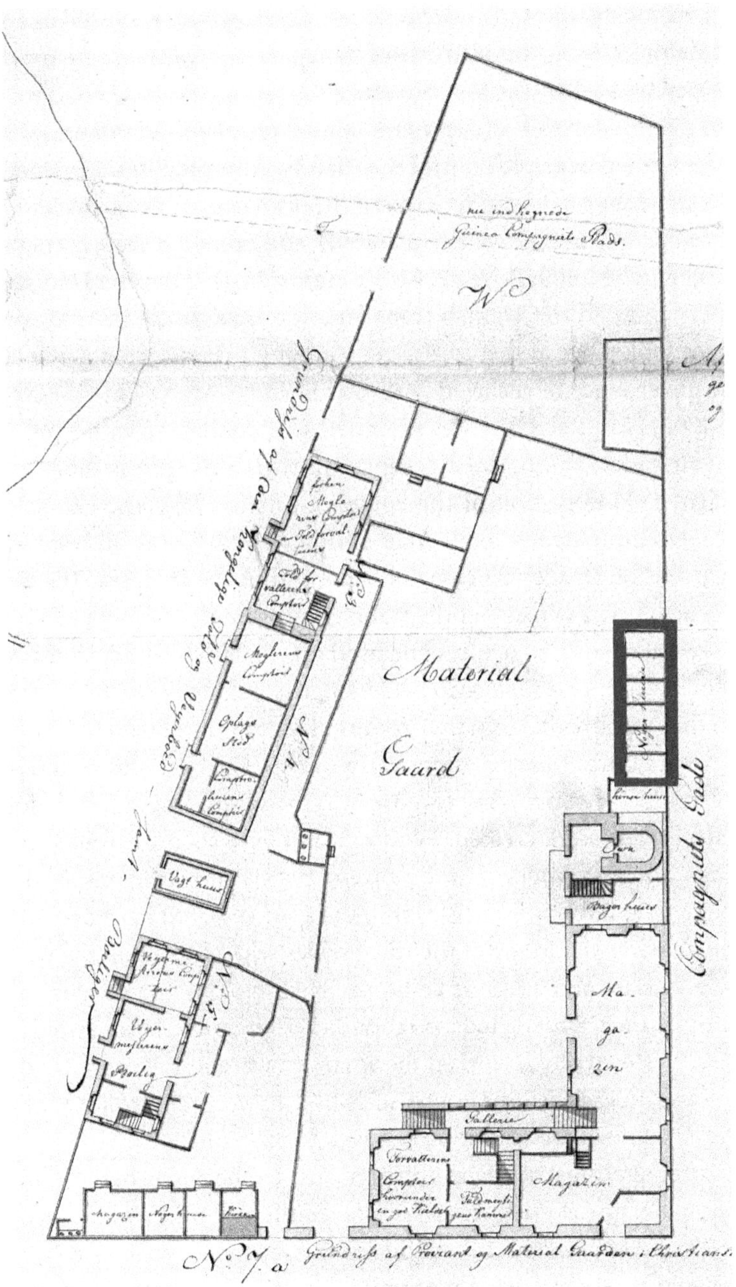

Figure 9.2. A 1779 map of the Danish West India and Guinea Company ware-house by Peter Lotharius Oxholm. The outlined section to the right is labeled "Neger Huuser" (Negro houses). Danish National Archives, no. 337,304.

the open courtyard of the warehouse complex, which was used as a work yard. Before 1754, it was also one of many auction yards where newly arrived enslaved Afro-Caribbeans were sold.

In 1754, Frederick V of Denmark bought out the shares of the DWIGC and the Crown began to control the islands. After that, trade opened and the local economy began to expand. Import-export firms began to sell enslaved people in their yards, in taverns, and even in private homes (Hall 1992; Highfield 2009; Boyer 2010, 37; Hardy 2011). After the Danish government banned the Danish trans-Atlantic slave trade in 1803, several changes took place at the warehouse building that reflected new policies in the governance of enslaved Afro-Caribbeans.

In 1796, Hospital Street was extended so it connected with King Street (Kongensgade), splitting the complex in two. This split is illustrated in the circa 1803 depiction of the complex (Figure 9.3). The extension of the street eliminated several small buildings and rooms, necessitating a reorganization and repurposing of space within the complex. The eastern half, which today consists of the standing customs house, was subdivided into several smaller structures enclosed by a shared wall that consisted of the stock warehouse (*oplage magazin*), a new baking house (*det nye bager huus*) that was divided into four rooms, the customs houses (*told-boden*), the broker's office (*magler comptoir*), an unspecified structure, and a new guard room (*nye vagt stue*) (Figure 9.3). New sleeping quarters for enslaved persons were created, as were a stable, a shed for water casks, a carriage house, a kitchen, and a privy. At this time, the enslaved men, women, and children who lived in these rooms would have been owned by the bookkeeper. Many of the royal slaves who worked on the wharf in the warehouses and at the scale house lived in a designated area located just east of town, as depicted in Oxholm's 1779 map of Christiansted (Martens 2016). Royal slaves worked the wharves, warehouses, military depot/storehouse, in the customs house, scale house (weigh house), the fort, and on the royal plantations that were leased to individuals.

This repurposing of space occurred just as the sugar-based economy started to decline at the turn of the nineteenth century (Westergaard 1917, xxiii, 253). As the market demand for Caribbean sugar began to wane, fewer captive laborers were required to work in the sugar fields and the constant purchase of enslaved men and women through the trans-Atlantic slave trade was no longer "profitable" (Westergaard 1917, xxiii, 253). In the decade before Denmark abolished the trans-Atlantic slave trade, nearly

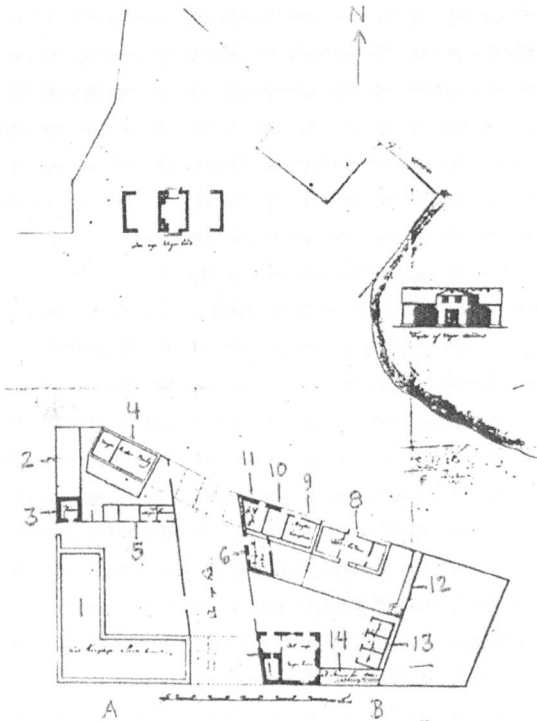

Figure 9.3. Plan of the Danish West India and Guinea Company warehouse, ca. 1803. *1*, Royal warehouse; *2*, unspecified structure; *3*, kitchen; *4*, weighing master's residence; *5*, first group of residential structures for Crown slaves; *6*, stock warehouse (*oplage magazin*); *7*, new baking house (*det nye bager huus*); *8*, customs houses (*told-boden*); *9*, broker's office (*magler comptoir*); *10*, an unspecified structure; *11*, new guard room (*nye vagt stue*); *12*, privy; *13*, second group of residential structures for Crown slaves. Danish National Archives, no. 337,304.

12,000 people were forcibly brought to the Danish West Indies as a means of bulking up the supply before access to this brutal system was cut off (Highfield 2009). On March 16, 1792, the Crown passed an abolition ordinance to ameliorate the conditions of enslaved peoples in Danish territories; this led to Denmark's abolishment of the slave trade in 1803. After that, the Danish government encouraged natural reproduction among the enslaved population to eliminate its dependence on international trading for enslaved laborers (Hall 1992, 84; Jensen 2012, 29; Highfield 2018). Danish officials began to encourage planters to take actions to preserve the health of and improve the living conditions of the enslaved population (Pope 1969, 155; Jensen 2012, 29).

In 1840, architect Albert Løvmand rehabilitated the customs house for use by government officials. In 1839, the carriage house, the stable, and the dwelling spaces for the enslaved were razed (Cissel 2000; Lawson et al. 2004). The customs house that stands today, which was completed in 1842, was built on the foundations of the residence of the DWIGC's bookkeeper.

Housing Conditions for the Royal Enslaved Afro-Caribbeans in the Danish West Indies

The constant threat of natural disasters posed a unique problem to enslaved communities on St. Croix and created the challenge of how to build housing that was both cost effective and able to sustain severe weather. Housing for the enslaved in Christiansted took many forms over time that depended on the occurrence of tropical storms, the materials available, and the affluence and disposition of the ruling classes. In 1829, Lt. Brady, a British naval officer, published an account that described housing for enslaved people owned by an "opulent master" in St. Croix that was mainly built of stone because of its "superior durability, dryness, and warmth" (Brady 1994, 9). He noted that these three qualities were the most important for protecting the body from atmospheric changes, which was a common problem on an island with frequent rains and the possibility of hurricanes every year. Lt. Brady observed that when a hurricane struck, over half of the houses not made of stone would be "unroofed" or completely destroyed but that stone houses were "seldom damaged" (Brady 1994, 9). Because of the expense of stone, coral, and masonry construction, poor and enslaved people were largely relegated to timber-frame or wattle-and-daub homes with thatched roofs. Estates that the Danish Crown leased to individuals established strict living conditions for their enslaved: masonry walls with wooden floors, separate kitchens, and tiled or shingled roofs (Hall 1992).

Christiansted was one of the first Caribbean towns to adopt a building code (1747) (Crain 1994, 48; Highfield 2012, 6). It included a town plan with a rectilinear design and mandated the use of building materials that were resistant to fires and hurricanes (Crain 1994, 50; Highfield 2012, 6). This prevented the fires that destroyed so much of the early architecture throughout the Caribbean and allowed for a remarkable preservation of the built environment of Christiansted and neighboring areas (Crain

1994, 50). The frequent use of wood as a building material is historically well documented in Christiansted, especially as window shutters, which were preferable to glass windows that were vulnerable to heat and high winds (Haagensen 1994, 18). Unfortunately, because wooden materials are susceptible to fire and decay, these remains are not visible in the archaeological record. However, the use of wood can be inferred through the presence of nails or pintles that once held the wooden shutters together. Additionally, the coral reefs that naturally form Bassin Harbor and provide protection to Christiansted produced an immense amount of broken coral, shell, and calcareous sand, all of which are potential building materials or can be used to level ground (Kidd 2006). As elsewhere around the Caribbean, stone, coral, clay, and the secondary products of plaster, mortar, and "quicklime" produced from shell, sand, and raw coral were popular building materials because they were locally available and resistant to the rigors of the tropical climate, storms, and other threats. Fire- and hurricane-resistant materials were developed out of necessity because of the high risk of damage from natural disasters and from the intentional and accidental fires that were all too common in the Danish West Indies and were especially threatening to those who lived on the coast. Christiansted's building plan based on masonry, coral, and clay construction was a direct response to the devastation that repeatedly visited Charlotte Amalie on St. Thomas, where the majority of homes were built of wood and were densely packed into the city center when it was first established. In 1804, the worst fire on record in Charlotte Amalie reportedly consumed 1,200 structures and claimed two lives (Highfield 2018, 217). Those who lived along the edge of Christiansted Harbor were the most exposed to tsunamis, hurricanes, invaders, and other natural and human threats (Odewale 2016).

We may never be able to produce an exhaustive list of the architectural materials used to create this built environment, but it is highly likely that even though the structures Danish soldiers and royal enslaved Afro-Caribbeans used were kept separate, the same building materials were used throughout the military compound. Sources indicate that skilled tradesmen and women within the enslaved community were the main builders of the compound and of the entire city of Christiansted (Highfield 2012). Excavations in and around the perimeters of the DWIGC warehouse complex have yielded evidence for architectural materials that include cut stone pavers, large blocks of coral, yellow and salmon-colored bricks, shell, mortar, clay, and slate roofing tiles. The low concentration of nails recovered from the excavations may also be evidence that both the earlier warehouse and the houses for enslaved workers were primarily built of stone, a stark contrast to the housing for enslaved workers in more rural locations on the island. For people living near the wharf, it would have been essential to use a variety of fire- and weather-resistant materials because they were exposed to the ocean's wrath if a hurricane struck.

It remains uncertain how much autonomy the enslaved community at Christiansted had about deciding how to build their homes, but most likely they were restricted to building within specific areas of the complex warehouse and would have been forced to adhere to the Christiansted building code and amelioration efforts. They were likely limited to specific materials, at least on the exterior surface of the home. However, archaeological evidence presented in this chapter may indicate that they had more autonomy about the materials they used inside these domestic spaces. The offer of better housing conditions and strict oversight over building plans as well as materials was yet another way that Danish officials exerted control over a captive population.

Beyond the challenges of building houses that could withstand hurricanes and following strict building codes, the enslaved community in Christiansted also faced problems associated with urban development, including access to clean water and increased exposure to diseases associated with densely concentrated housing. In 1758, Reimert Haagensen, a Danish planter on St. Croix, described how Europeans denied enslaved Afro-Caribbeans access to collected water that fed into large cisterns.

> Because there is such a lack of water, every inhabitant has his dwelling built in such a way that there are gutters below the roof for the collection of water for drinking, as well as for the preparation of food. . . . When a good rain comes, enough water can be collected in a short time from the gutters to serve the household for four to five months. This water is kept secure under lock and key. Neither slaves nor beasts get any of it to drink. (Haagensen 1994, 11)

Haagensen observed that drought conditions on the island in the 1750s led to a historic shortage of drinking water. Enslaved workers were forced to drink the same water as the livestock, a practice that increased the spread of disease (Haagensen 1994, 11). The cyclical pattern of tropical storms and drought also contributed to the spread of disease because the

Figure 9.4. Drawing by Frederik von Scholten entitled "Bitling near West-End, Santa Cruz Women," St. Croix, ca. 1844. The Danish National Archives, no. 000034248.

enslaved community, especially those in urban areas, was forced to depend on natural waterways for their water supply. These waterways were used for drinking, washing clothes, bathing, and watering the cattle (Figure 9.4) (Jensen 2012, 142).

To gain access to clean water, the enslaved community at Christiansted used their own material culture to survive in an European-dominated built environment. Recent excavations of Unit A of the DWIGC warehouse site revealed flat clay and slate roof tiles, a small amount of Afro-Crucian ware sherds from large pottery vessels, and a high proportion of glass fragments mainly from large wine bottles that were possibly used to collect, store, or purify water in this challenging environment (Odewale 2016; Table 9.1). Afro-Crucian wares are a type of colonoware, or handmade clay vessels using techniques enslaved people brought from Africa. African communities across the Caribbean region used the combination of flat roofing and large ceramic vessels to store water during the period of enslavement (Hauser 2017). Researchers have noted the same technique among historic communities in Dominica, where large handmade pottery jugs and glass bottles were often left on flat roofs as a natural system for collecting and storing water (Hauser 2017). Glass bottle fragments are one of the most abundant artifact classes recovered from Christiansted

National Historic Site (see Table 9.1). The high amount of glass found in the residential spaces of the enslaved community at Christiansted could support the hypothesis that these glass containers were used as a type of storage (Odewale 2016). The concept of glass wine bottles being used as storage originally came from Barry Higman (2000) and was then redefined by Mark Hauser, who claims that sites with the greatest access to water typically had a higher population of enslaved people and a higher frequency of glass bottles that were used for storage (Hauser 2015a). Hauser distinguished among different types of water including sweet, fresh, foul, clear, cool, and holy, and noted that each type required a separate kind of vessel for storage (Hauser 2015a). The biggest concern, especially for insular communities like those living on the edge of Christiansted Harbor, was transforming pond or foul water into clean water (Hauser 2015a). We do not know what purification process enslaved communities used. However, storing water would have posed a challenge for the Crown slaves in Christiansted since the Danish officers were the only ones who could store goods in the warehouse. In addition, the types of flooring used in all the residential structures for the slave labor force may have prevented an underground storage system. In such circumstances, glass containers may have been an excellent alternative to the subsurface storage systems that are commonly found at African diaspora sites in the southern United States (e.g., Singleton 1999; Samford 2007).

The high number of fragments of large wine bottles present in this assemblage may be linked to the scarcity of drinkable water on the island, since the enslaved community had access only to brackish water from open streams, rooftops, and shallow wells (Dookhan 1994,7; Jensen 2012). However, some of the glass fragments could also represent pharmaceutical bottles because at this point in the island's history, disease was a daily reality for both enslaved and free people (Hall 1992; Dookhan 1994; Tyson and Highfield 1994; Jensen 2012). We also cannot dismiss the idea that the wine bottles at one time held spirits, potable water, milk, seeds, or any other storable resource of importance to this community. Previous scholars have noted a tendency for researchers to link the discovery of wine bottle fragments at African diaspora sites to a belief that these communities had access to wine or alcohol (Smith 2008). This simplistic approach does not take into account that enslaved Afro-Caribbeans and African Americans commonly used bottles in ways that differed from how white Americans and Europeans used them. "To us milk bottles hold milk, beer bottles hold beer, and wine bottles hold wine; when the contents are gone they are usually thrown away. In contrast, slave-village containers like wine bottles were probably brought home whenever they were available to be used again and again to hold water, milk, juice, and even alcoholic beverages" (Ferguson 1992, 159). The multiplicity of uses for these glass vessels may never be known, but more detailed residue analysis may shed light on how this particular enslaved community used different types of bottles.

The Impact of the Natural Environment on the Lives of Enslaved Afro-Caribbeans in St. Croix

In 1738, a hurricane struck St. Croix, destroying the first commercial structures and the first Fort Christiansvaern (Tyson 2010). This disaster was compounded by a smallpox outbreak in 1739, which killed a large number of slaves, Danish government officials, and soldiers in the new town of Christiansted (Tyson 2010, 2).

In the period 1726 to 1848, St. Croix was hit with nine hurricanes, five droughts, and at least two major floods (Rogozinski 1992, 10; Armstrong 2001; Chenoweth 2006; Donoghue 2007; Jensen 2012). The Danish West Indies were also plagued by earthquakes, tsunamis, fires, drought, and insects that together created an unpredictable and calamitous environment for both enslaved and free people (Figure 9.5). Earthquakes and hurricanes were the most common natural disasters that affected this region during the era of Danish occupation. Primary sources from Moravian missionaries, planters' records, newspaper articles, and slave narratives record 174 hurricanes in the Caribbean region from 1492 to 1800 (Rogozinski 1992, 10). However, recent scholarship has uncovered evidence for 383 unique tropical storms and hurricanes across the Atlantic from 1492 to 1855 (Chenoweth 2006, 1).

There may have been a connection between the occurrence of slave uprisings and natural disasters. For example, the year of greatest destruction from natural disasters was also the year of the largest slave uprising in the Danish West Indies, the St. John rebellion of 1733. A series of catastrophic events occurred in the year leading up to the historic rebellion: a severe drought, two hurricanes, and a plague of insects that destroyed nearly the entire crop yield (Westergaard 1917, xi; Dookhan 1994, 167; Armstrong 2001, 147; Donoghue 2007, 26; Boyer 2010, 31). This was followed by the

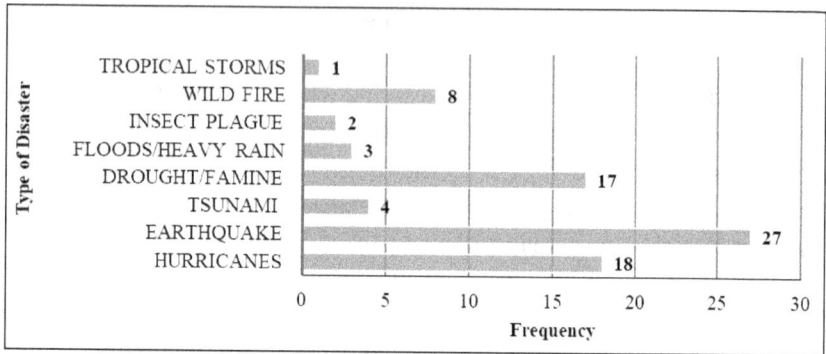

Figure 9.5. Bar graph of frequency of natural disasters in the Danish West Indies, 1720–1871. Source: Odewale 2016.

creation of the Gardelin Code, one of the most oppressive slave laws ever passed. It did not require planters to provide minimal food and clothing and it made it illegal for an enslaved person to offer any goods or produce for sale anywhere on the island without written permission from his or her owner (Boyer 2010; Odewale 2016). This code also institutionalized punishments against enslaved people who rebelled or committed crimes that included dismemberment, branding with hot irons, flogging, hanging, and castration. A slaveowner could exact any of these punishments without repercussions (Goveia 1993, 360). The combination of widespread starvation and devastation and the creation of a harsh new slave code created an environment that led to revolt. This observation brings into focus the role a hostile climate can play in triggering large-scale revolts. However, further research is needed to demonstrate any statistical correlation between the occurrence of natural disasters and mass rebellion in the Caribbean.

On St. Croix, as throughout the Caribbean, the months from July to October were known as hurricane months (Richardson 1983; Bossart 1987; Donoghue 2007; Jensen 2012, 36). Contemporary sources oscillated between blaming the "wrath of hurricanes" on divine and natural forces. However, it was common practice on St. Croix and St. Thomas to offer special worship services and prayers seeking mercy on June 25 before the start of the hurricane season and thanksgiving services on October 25 at its close (Schwartz 2015, 126). In the aftermath of catastrophe, the enslaved population paid the heaviest price. They had to recover from storm damage while also enduring the harsher restrictions Danish authorities instituted. For example, after the hurricane in 1772, new laws were passed that imposed a curfew and prohibited enslaved people from selling any-thing but produce in local markets. For months after a hurricane event enslaved people endured inadequate access to fresh water and fresh fruits and vegetables as they worked to rebuild destroyed homes, mourn those they had lost, and clear debris around their dwellings (Nissen 1838, 12–14). Sources claim that during a 1785 storm, damages amounted to more than 2.5 million Danish rigsdalers, which would have totaled close to US$60 billion today (Schwartz 2015, 104).

Droughts, hurricanes, and sporadic heavy rains often led to starva-tion because they destroyed provisions and alternative sources of food (Westergaard 1996, 57). Additionally, during hurricane season, imports to the islands were delayed or completely disrupted and food prices were severely inflated. These conditions could be fatal for slaves in the Danish West Indies and other Caribbean territories (Richardson 1983, 70). Many planters were unwilling or unable to pay higher prices for imported corn for slave rations and essentially used starvation as a way to reduce their slave holdings during these lean times (Westergaard 1996; Donoghue 2007, 161). They simply allowed their slaves to die, claiming that they had become too expensive to support (Richardson 1983, 70).

Earthquakes would have been just as devastating as hurricanes and droughts to the food and water supply of the enslaved community. An article published in the St. Croix *Avis* on December 10, 1867, noted that "ever since the earthquakes, the water from all the wells here in town and elsewhere is salt" (quoted in Watlington and Lincoln 1997, 88). An ar-ticle on December 13, 1867, stated that "following a severe shock of earth-quake . . . business [is] partly suspended, trade impeded and many—we speak without shame—are without the proper means of support for their daily sustenance" (quoted in Watlington and Lincoln 1997, 90).

Members of the enslaved community faced many social challenges as they tried to piece their world back together after natural disasters. Af-ter any hurricane event, the government's first priority was to reestablish European control and social order on the island. After a series of devas-tating hurricanes struck in the 1770s, the government refused to see the enslaved population in these territories as anything but a threat to society and never offered any aid to help them (Schwartz 2015, 81). Reports of looting, revolt, and discontent after hurricanes often led to harsher slave laws in the Danish West Indies (Schwartz 2015, 81). Such laws were passed to prevent looting and the sale of stolen goods and stemmed from European settlers' underlying fears about potential slave revolts (Schwartz 2015, 81). Those who lived and worked in close proximity to Danish officials in Christiansted would have been watched even more intently.

Occupational Hazards

Many occupational hazards burdened both rural and urban slaves, all of whom toiled in strenuous conditions in the Danish West Indies. Work-related injuries such as abscesses, sprains, fractures, amputations, lesions, hernias, and wounds were common among the slaves who worked in the warehouse at Christiansted and those who were forced to labor in the fields (Jensen 2012, 85–86). James Williams, a formerly enslaved man from Jamaica, said that after being sentenced to the treadmill at "St. Ann's Bay workhouse," he experienced back and knee injuries, reporting that "the mill-steps keep on batter their legs and knees and the driver with the cat keep on flog them all the time till them catch the step" (Williams 1834, 7).

Crown slaves in Christiansted worked in every part of the built landscape the Crown owned: the hospital, the warehouse (*pakhuset*), the harbors, the weigh house (*vejerboden*), the provisions depot (*proviant-gården*), and sugar estates (Haagensen 1994, 25; Martens 2010, 31). These workers were commonly referred to as "Company Negroes," "His Majesty's Negroes," or "packinghouse workers." From the 1790s to 1848, over 400 lived and worked in warehouses and weighing houses on St. Croix (Martens 2016). They worked in the company warehouse, they built works of "fortification and defense," and they worked on the wharf as packers, porters, and loaders (Dookhan 1994, 150). For Crown slaves who worked in Christiansted, the risk of injury was not much different than it was for field laborers (Pope 1969). Those who worked in the royal warehouses, on the docks, and in the scale houses primarily carried cargo to and from the ships that docked at the harbors (Pope 1969, 145). Poul Erik Olsen described the amount of strength needed and the degree of danger in this working environment in his book *Customs in the Danish West Indies, 1672–1917* (Olsen 1988 cited in Martens 2010, 36). Those who worked in the warehouse and the weigh house loaded and unloaded various goods and ballast stones from ships, transported heavy sugar casks to store-rooms or ships, and marked sugar casks with brands in preparation for export (Martens 2010, 36). Royally enslaved Afro-Caribbeans were re-garded as the most valuable for their strength, which was regarded as a skill (Martens 2016).

The trade in cotton also placed an enormous burden on warehouse workers. Crown slaves who worked on the docks were required to trans-port cotton sacks weighing nearly 400 pounds onto ships (Haagensen 1994, 40). Unloading roofing tiles shipped into St. Croix from New Eng-land or New York would have been just as demanding as handling sugar casks and bales of cotton (Haagensen 1994, 18). Work-related injuries would have been common among the enslaved warehouse workers (Jen-sen 2012, 85–86).

Slave narratives from the Caribbean often mention fever, rheuma-tism, and consumption. Rheumatism and the swelling of limbs and joints would have been common given the menial labor this community was forced to endure, and such conditions likely often became incapacitating. Those who were exposed to salt water every day, such as workers in salt mines, female launderers, or those who loaded goods on and off ships in the harbor, would have developed lesions or ulcers on their legs that had the potential to eat through to the bone with daily exposure to more salt water and would thus remain open, often resulting in eventual amputa-tion. In *The History of Mary Prince*, a formerly enslaved woman from Bermuda provided a detailed description of this ailment as a result of working in the salt works on Turks Island, where she was forced to stand in knee-deep pools of salt water for more than ten hours a day:

> I was immediately sent to work in the salt water with the rest of the enslaved Africans. This work was perfectly new to me. I was given a half barrel and a shovel and had to stand up to my knees in the wa-ter, from four o'clock in the morning till nine, when we were given some Indian corn boiled in water, which we were obliged to swallow as fast as we could for fear the rain should come on and melt the salt. We were then called again to our tasks and worked through the heat of the day; the sun flaming upon our heads like fire and raising salt blisters in those parts which were not completely covered. Our feet and legs, from standing in the salt water for so many hours,

soon became full of dreadful boils, which eat down in some cases to the very bone, afflicting the sufferers with great torment. (quoted in Salih 2000, 10)

One can imagine a similar condition developing for the Crown slaves who worked in the scale house and the warehouse along the docks of the Christiansted Harbor, where shallow amounts of salt water likely nipped at their heels and ankles as they carried loads to and from cargo holds.

Another hazardous aspect of working conditions for the Crown slaves who worked near Fort Christiansvaern was the close proximity of Danish soldiers and government officials, who were anxious to keep the majority black population of St. Croix under control. Some sources indicate that "His Majesty's slaves" were the ones who suffered the greatest from measures of social control because authorities were quick to make an example of them. Reimert Haagensen, a plantation overseer who lived in St. Croix from 1739 to 1750, described an execution he witnessed in front of Fort Christiansvaern: "On this occasion one of His Majesty's slaves was executed. He was taken from the fort and placed in the hangman's cart to be pinched with red-hot tongs, he acted in an extremely impudent manner, not only laughing and making merry but also calling the Governor and the Town Sheriff names of the worst kind. . . . He was pinched more than 100 times until he died" (Haagensen 1994, 54). Haagensen also recounted that every time an execution like this was carried out, the prisoner was marched from the fort to the gallows in public view and the fort was subsequently locked so that no one could enter or exit the facility until after the execution. Armed white citizens then surrounded the fort and Gallows Bay in anticipation of a revolt (Haagensen 1994, 54). Crown slaves lived closest to this world of heightened scrutiny and punishment under the watchful eye of the Danish military. Executions were a constant reminder of what happened to individuals who pushed back against the Crown's authority. The royal enslaved Afro-Caribbeans who lived close to Fort Christiansvaern would have witnessed individuals being beaten, chained to a "justice post," marched to the dungeons, or executed in the now-infamous Gallows Bay on the eastern side of the Christiansted harbor (Haagensen 1994; Highfield 2012; 2018).

Excavations of Slavery in Christiansted

Most of the artifacts recovered during the 2015–2016 field excavations at Christiansted National Historic Site were discovered in the areas where Crown slaves lived and worked. The assemblage reflects the activities of daily life in this complex. Many artifacts relate to domestic activities such as cooking, mending clothes, making buttons, and smoking tobacco. The presence of both Afro-Crucian ware and refined European wares in the assemblage signifies an exchange relationship between urban and rural enslaved communities; urban dwellers possibly traded pipes, buttons, and jewelry for locally made earthenwares with their rural counterparts, who had better access to clay.

The 2015–2016 excavations targeted the 1779 and 1803 floor plans of the warehouse complex and areas where anomalies had been identified in the ground-penetrating radar surveys the National Park Service's Southeast Archeological Center conducted in 2000 and 2015 (Lawson et al. 2004; Hardy 2011). Excavation units were placed in the approximate location of the two living areas on the 1803 map that largely corresponded with magnetic anomalies (see Figures 9.3 and 9.6). During two field seasons, archaeologists from the Southeast Archeological Center and the University of Tulsa and students and interns from the University of the Virgin Islands and Aarhus University conducted the fieldwork and analyses.

Four one-by-one meter excavation units and twenty-one shovel tests uncovered over 5,000 artifacts (Table 9.1 and Figure 9.6). The most abundant artifact class was metal, which constituted 23 percent of the assemblage by count and nearly 23 percent by weight. The second most abundant artifact type was glass, which constituted 23 percent of the assemblage by count but only 10 percent by weight. Fragments of shell constituted 15 percent by count and 7 percent by weight (Table 9.1). High concentrations of metal, glass, and shell were present throughout our excavations, with the exception of Unit F, in the approximate location of the baking house on the 1803 map (see Figures 9.3, 9.7, and 9.9). In Unit F, we recovered a high percentage of metal utensils such as latches, knife blades, and handles; clothing hardware such as buttons and buckles; horseshoes and snaffle bits; and architectural materials such as nails and metal spikes. These items constituted 62 percent of the assemblage by count and 88 percent by weight (Figure 9.8 and Table 9.2). The inclusion of this large proportion of

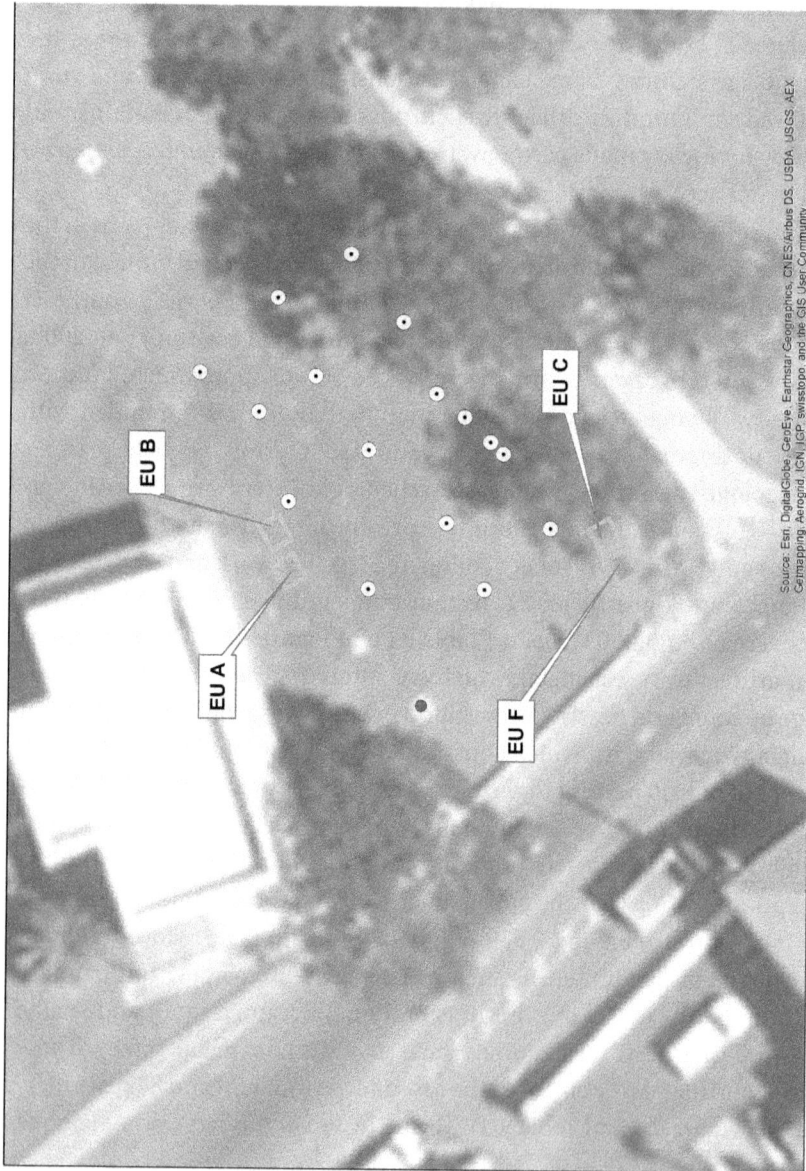

Figure 9.6. Map of 2015–2016 excavation units and shovel tests conducted for this project at the Christiansted National Historic Site showing the location of excavation units (EU) A, B, C, and F. Created by Alicia Odewale.

EU B

EU A

EU C

EU F

N

Source: Esri, DigitalGlobe, GeoEye, Earthstar Geographics, CNES/Airbus DS, USDA, USGS, AEX, Getmapping, Aerogrid, IGN, IGP, swisstopo, and the GIS User Community

● 2015 Datum

⊙ 2015_Odewale STP

0   12.5   25   50
Feet

0   4   8   16
Meters

Table 9.1. Total artifact inventory for 2015–2016 excavations

Artifact Class	Count	Percent	Weight	Percent
Afro-Crucian Ware	38	0.7	281.2	0.4
Brick	292	5.6	8,514.2	13.4
Ceramics	453	8.7	2,232.1	3.5
Charcoal	497	9.6	465.2	0.7
Coral	169	3.2	5,577.2	8.7
Fauna	164	3.2	235.9	0.4
Glass	1,195	23.0	6,459.4	10.1
Lithics	265	5.1	17,361.8	27.2
Metal	1,172	22.6	14,625.7	22.9
Mortar	143	2.7	3,192.6	5.0
Pipe Fragments	36	0.7	41.6	0.1
Roof Tiles	11	0.2	217.7	0.3
Shell	759	14.6	4,539.2	7.1
Wood	1	0.0	18.0	0.0
Total	5,195	99.9	63,761.8	99.8

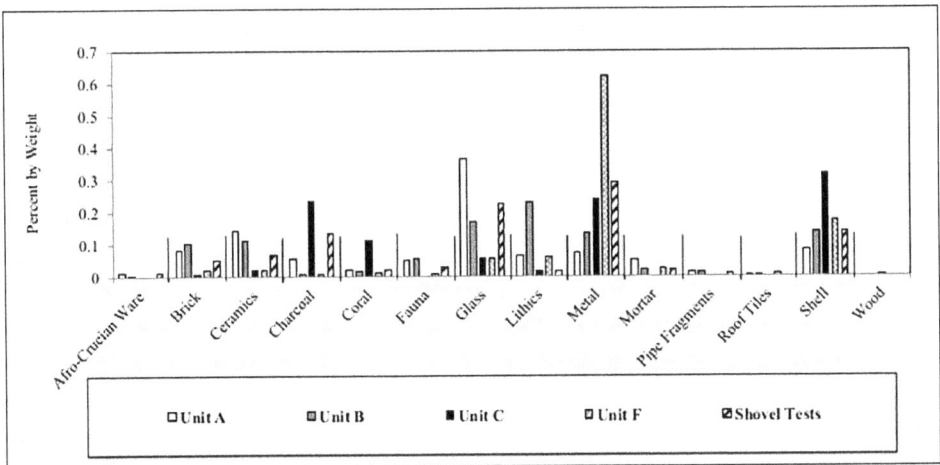

Figure 9.7. Bar graph showing artifact frequency by excavation unit conducted for this project within Christiansted National Historic Site, St. Croix, U.S. Virgin Islands. Created by Alicia Odewale.

Table 9.2. Count and weight of artifact categories by excavation unit (percent)

	Unit A		Unit B		Unit C		Unit F		Shovel Test Pits	
	Count	Weight	Count	Weight	Count	Weight	Count	Weight	Count	Weight
Afro-Cruzan Ware	1	1	0	0	0	0	0	0	1	1
Brick	8	5	10	10	1	11	2	0	5	28
Ceramics	14	10	11	4	2	0	2	0	7	1
Charcoal	5	1	1	0	24	1	1	1	13	1
Coral	2	6	2	1	11	17	1	3	2	5
Fauna	5	1	5	1	0	0	1	0	3	0
Glass	36	27	17	16	5	1	5	1	22	6
Lithics	6	7	23	42	1	54	6	3	1	25
Metal	7	13	13	14	24	11	62	88	29	28
Mortar	5	8	2	8	0	5	2	1	2	3
Pipe Fragments	1	0	1	0	0	0	0	0	1	0
Roof Tiles	0	1	0	0	0	0	1	2	0	0
Shell	8	21	14	3	32	1	17	2	14	2
Wood	0	0	0	0	0	0	0	0	0	0

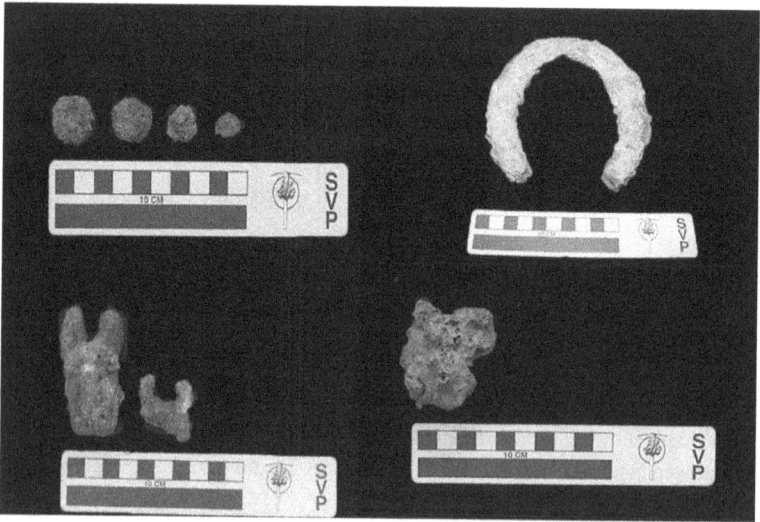

Figure 9.8. Metal artifacts recovered from Units C and F. *Clockwise from top left*: Metal buttons; horseshoe; slag; two-pronged forks. Photos by Alicia Odewale.

Figure 9.9. Remains of the possible base of a baking oven filled with and surrounded by gray ash from Unit F. Photo by Alicia Odewale.

finished metal artifacts inside the location of the baking house indicates that this built structure served multiple functions, possibly as a kitchen, a storage house, and a residential space for enslaved Afro-Caribbeans.

We organized the artifacts in this assemblage by material type and artifact class rather than by function because such items were commonly reused, modified, and repurposed in African diaspora sites. This practice means that single-use artifact classification systems are unsuitable for African diaspora sites, where enslaved people often created symbols of resistance or defense using both everyday objects and European-American materials such as high-fired ceramics, mass-produced tobacco pipes, and glass bottles. Many scholars have noted that in the African diaspora, relatively commonplace objects served dual purposes or carried muted messages of resistance or indicated the retention of African customs (Ferguson 1992, 118; Orser and Funari 2001; Weik 2012). For example, on the Garrison plantation in Maryland, archaeologists found two pewter spoons that retained traces of inscribed geometric designs that were similar to those contemporary Maroon communities in Suriname used to decorate spoon bowls and handles (Klingelhofer 1987, 114). These spoons were both functional eating utensils and carriers of possible symbolic messages.

Another important aspect of the archaeological research at Christiansted National Historic Site is the process of documenting the remains of historic structures and specific activity areas inside the complex that are no longer visible on the ground surface level. To that end, a shovel test survey was conducted at Christiansted National Historic Site followed by an excavation of specific areas that shovel testing identified as containing the remains of possible structural features. At a depth of 50 centimeters below surface, the floor space of Unit A was heavily disturbed by in-ground electrical conduits, but the partially preserved corners of the unit revealed a concentration of charcoal and faunal remains followed by a hard-packed layer of conch shell (Odewale 2016). In Unit B, the flooring space was too heavily disturbed by electrical lines and underground water pipes to provide any evidence of intact structural features (Odewale 2016).

In Unit C, at the approximate location of the residential spaces noted on the 1803 map (see Figures 9.3 and 9.6), we encountered what appeared to be a floor made of ballast stone set in mortar. This feature was remarkably similar to the intact ballast stone floor in the carriage building in the stable yard at Fort Christianvaern. Under normal circumstances, the combination of this discovery and an abundance of metal recovered from this area that included both finished products and unformed slag would suggest that this structure was not used as a residential space. In this case, though, it may be an indication that individuals were forced to live close to where they worked or that the building burned down at some point during its use. More research is needed to determine why a space designated as residential on historic maps would have so many finished and unformed metal fragments.

Excavations at Unit F, located next to Unit C, revealed the foundation or base of the baking oven that is indicated on the 1803 plan of the warehouse compound (see Figures 9.3 and 9.9). The location of this baking oven in close proximity to possible dwelling spaces of enslaved Afro-Caribbeans and the bookkeeper's residence suggests that this structure functioned as a workspace where members of the enslaved community prepared meals for the Danish officers, the bookkeeper and his family, and others who lived in the bookkeeper's residence. On the 1803 map, two other large areas were partitioned off outside the baking room that could have served as residential areas (see Figure 9.3).

Archaeologists in another urban context, the Royall estate near Boston,

Massachusetts, identified a similar structure that housed an "out kitchen" and living areas. This estate was originally owned by Antigua native Isaac Royall Sr. Next to the estate's mansion, a two-story brick kitchen was erected in 1739 that served as a space where the enslaved community prepared food for themselves, the Royall family, and any seasonally hired labor working at the estate (Chan 2007, 42). This structure had several partitions around the baking oven and a second floor where enslaved men, women, and children lived (Chan 2007, 43). A similar shared kitchen and housing structure may have been erected in Christiansted in 1803 after the construction of Hospital Street, which bisected the original site in the same location as the 1779 "Negro houses." When the street bisected the site, the two different residential areas were connected to a single baking house, which possibly created a shared space for food preparation and housing for the lead baker and the other enslaved laborers who prepared food for the compound. The discovery that the foundation for the baking oven was possibly still intact after 215 years was remarkable given the significant structural changes and acts of nature that Christiansted National Historic Site has endured in that span of time.

Summary and Conclusion

The Danish West Indies were characterized by a high mortality rate—estimated to be 35.7 per thousand during the years 1780–1790 (Hall 1992, 85)—that prevented the natural growth of the enslaved population. After the Danish slave trade ended in 1803 and even after all of the Crown's amelioration efforts, the years leading up to emancipation in St. Croix in 1848 were characterized by hazardous working conditions that were compounded by recurring natural disasters, widespread disease, harsh slave codes, and the decline of the market for sugar (Perry 2011, 28). The combination of environmental and social challenges was amplified in enslaved communities when planters began to cut back on "housing, sanitation, and health care" in the 1830s in an effort to cut costs as the international demand for Caribbean cane sugar continued to wane in favor of sugar from beets (Perry 2011, 28). These communities were plagued most often by the interrelated challenges associated with urban enslavement: harsh Danish rule, the natural Caribbean environment, the spread of disease, a tropical climate that exacerbated already hazardous working conditions, malnutrition and starvation, natural disasters, overcrowding, unsanitary housing, poor medical treatment, and lack of access to clean, potable water.

Units C and F in the warehouse complex revealed a wealth of information about the daily lives of the people enslaved by the Crown who lived and worked in this compound. The artifacts we recovered offer a glimpse into spaces where enslaved men and women of remarkable skill were busy building what would become the city of Christiansted while they were building their own community, even in a space surrounded by Danish soldiers.

The Crown slaves who lived and worked in the warehouse complex used European trade goods such as pipes, refined ceramics, belt buckles, and various glass wares. The presence of Afro-Crucian wares at the site indicate that slaves in the Danish West Indies, likely those living in plantation contexts, produced pottery. The Crown slaves at Christiansted could have acquired these wares through trade at the Sunday market or through daily interactions with soldiers and officers or with the bookkeeper's family, which lived near the warehouse compound. While they used a variety of tools, the assemblage indicates a heavy dependence on metal tools for completing daily tasks. Evidence from the ceramic assemblage recovered around the warehouse suggests that the people enslaved by the Crown had access to a wide variety of refined European ceramics, including annular-style creamwares and pearlwares dating to the period of occupation. This could be evidence that this population selected materials according to their aesthetic preferences or that they used household goods to express cultural identity, as is seen in ceramic assemblages at other Caribbean sites (Wilkie and Farnsworth 1999). Or perhaps these ceramics are simply what was available at the time of acquisition.

Another important part of daily life in the enslaved community in Christiansted involved acquiring essential resources like water. At first glance, the large amount of glass fragments recovered from Christiansted National Historic Site seems to indicate that enslaved people had access to alcohol. However, these bottle fragments may have been recycled to store water, even when cisterns and wells were accessible.

The partially intact ballast stone floor that was uncovered in Unit C is clear evidence that this potential dwelling space for people enslaved to the Crown was not designed for comfort. The remains of this residential area show no evidence of raised flooring, but a ballast stone floor was possibly laid down out of necessity. Ballast stones could have been chosen simply because they were available when these structures were built. However, it could also have been a deliberate choice within the enslaved community to repurpose the ballast stones they were forced to load on and off ships. It is also important to note that the ballast stone floor in the areas used by the enslaved contrasts starkly in quality to the paved stone floors of the Danish officer's stock warehouse (Odewale et al. 2017). It is also possible that the ballast stone floor was part of a stable yard built in the area next to DWIGC warehouse complex in the period 1810 to 1820 (Olsen 1960, 105). However, one reason we believe the flooring in Unit C could represent choices the enslaved community made is that this repurposing is similar to the repurposing of conch shell that Ken Wild discovered during the course of previous excavations in the same courtyard area at Christiansted National Historic Site in the 1980s. After hurricane Hugo struck the island in 1989 and uprooted a large mahogany tree near the location of the 1803 enslaved housing structures in Christiansted, salvage excavations around the fallen tree revealed an intact conch shell floor (Hardy 2011; Odewale 2016; Odewale et al. 2017).

Ken Wild's 1989 excavations (Hardy 2011) identified the use of ballast stone and conch shell in flooring as a standard construction method for historic buildings in Christiansted. This may indicate that the structures identified as part of the 1779 plan for the DWIGC warehouse complex were used as storage space or as stables, but they could also have served a dual purpose as residential housing. It is also possible that the purpose of these structures changed over time; many buildings in the warehouse complex have undergone several rebuilding phases and changes in use from residences to offices and storage. The exact function of these spaces is still being explored in ongoing excavations. As National Park Service archaeologists uncover the remains of more structures, the various functions of each room will become clearer. Future investigations may consider the diversity of materials this enslaved community used in interior spaces as a way to explore whether those spaces they used were less heavily regulated than the exterior surfacing that had to match Christiansted town building standards.

The archaeological evidence uncovered during these excavations offers a new perspective on the experiences of enslaved Afro-Caribbeans in St.

Croix (Hall 1992). We can now better imagine this waterfront landscape. Even though life for this enslaved community was challenging, it appears that this group of enslaved people had abilities that were necessary for the smooth operation of the company warehouse, the customs house, the fort, and the wharf (Tyson 1996, v; Odewale et al. 2017). Developing skills in carpentry and masonry provided a basis for trade and access to food, pottery vessels, and handmade wares from rural estates on island (Lawaetz 1991, 106; Tyson 2010). Without the skills and daily labor of enslaved individuals, the Danish operations in St. Croix and the bustling port of Christiansted would not have been possible.

10

Households and Dwelling Practices at the Cabrits Garrison Laborer Village

ZACHARY J. M. BEIER

The imposing defensive works of the Cabrits Garrison are a reminder of the measures the colonial British Army took to establish a formal presence on the island of Dominica in the middle of the eighteenth century. Within the walls of the fort, just beneath the present-day ground surface, is evidence of the pluralism, resistance, and freedom that emerged in military settings across the Caribbean during this tumultuous period. Caribbean forts integrated the social policies of the army administration and the surrounding plantocracy, resulting in socially engineered settings that served as meaningful points of contact, interaction, and transformation for diverse military communities (Figure 10.1).

The policy of using enslaved laborers in auxiliary roles and later as soldiers in the West India Regiments (WIR) is documented in the extensive archival record of the Cabrits Garrison, which the British Army occupied from 1763 to 1854. The dynamics of this changing military labor regime are also evident in the built environment at the household level. Like other contributors to this volume, I see this environment as composed of both structures built on the land and less durable spaces created through daily practices. Household archaeology at military sites is particularly significant because of trends in the interpretation of these sites. Previous scholarship on the built environment of Caribbean military sites has mainly focused on the defensive and technological qualities of bastions, ramparts and on officers' quarters and soldiers' barracks (see Buisseret 1971, 1980, 2008; Crain 1994; Buckley 1998; Douet 1998; Gravette 2000). The investigation of housing for enslaved and lower-status members of

Figure 10.1. View looking north along the coastline of Portsmouth and Prince Rupert's Bay in Dominica. The Cabrits peninsula is featured in the background. Photo by Zachary J. M. Beier.

a military community illuminates patterns of human behavior and the complex network of social relations that existed during the eighteenth and nineteenth centuries and how these arrangements and their associated meanings differed across space and changed over time (see Wilk and Rathje 1982; Allison 1998, 1999; Hendon 2008; Pluckhahn 2010; Carballo 2011; De Souza 2016 for discussion of household archaeology). The Cabrits Garrison presents a rare opportunity in historical archaeology to study a changing labor force that lived in a separate settlement within the walls of a British colonial fort in the Caribbean.

My investigation of the Cabrits village, where enslaved members of the British Army were housed, relies on archival and archaeological evidence to document the architectural character and the sociocultural and chronological content of these residential quarters. My understanding of this space is also aided by Henri Lefebvre's (1991, 38–46) "spatial triad." This model relies on three interrelated kinds of space. Spatial practice or perceived space is created through the contradictions between the ideal and actual use of a certain place. It provides structure and ensures the continuity and cohesion of everyday activities in wider socioeconomic contexts. Conceived space is the dominant space in any society based on its connection to the relations of production and the hierarchical order these relations impose. Planners, architects, and administrators create this space in order to produce particular exchange values. It is most often associated with socially segregated places and restrictions on the ability of certain groups to appropriate space or turn it into lived space. The third type of space in Lefebvre's triad, lived space, connects living spaces to social spaces by situating the active elements of material culture, including cultural practices and social relations, in the spaces that are central to domestic life and human experience (see Berdoulay 1989; Hanks 1990; Rothschild 1991; Rodman 1992; Robin and Rothschild 2002; Ng et al. 2013).

In a deliberate move away from viewing this fort as a monument to European expansion and colonialism, this chapter is concerned with what household architecture reveals about the varying modes of social construction and experience in the laborers' village at the Cabrits Garrison. It compares ways administrators in the British Army conceived of domestic areas in the Cabrits Garrison laborer village with how these spaces were actually lived in by enslaved and other lower-status inhabitants. This household-level analysis provides a vantage point that links spatial practices at a fort in Dominica to wider trends in the study of enslaved environments throughout the Atlantic world.

War and Slavery in Caribbean Archaeology

In 1975, in *The Problem of Slavery in the Age of Revolution, 1770–1823*, David Brion Davis lamented the fact that the question of the effects of war on slavery had not received the attention it deserved. Various historians have contributed to this emerging area of scholarship by investigating the systematic use of African and African-descended slaves in the imperial war apparatus in the Americas (see Buckley 1979, 1998; Handler 1984; Voelz 1993; O'Shaughnessy 1996; Vinson and King 2004; Brown and Morgan 2006; Dubois 2006). Moors and Spaniards originated this practice on the Iberian Peninsula during the first half of the sixteenth century. The Spanish military used slaves during its expansion into regions like the Greater Antilles of the Caribbean and Spanish La Florida before the advent of intensive agro-industrial production (see Deagan 1988, 2010).

The consensus among military historians is that blacks were primarily involved with the construction and maintenance of defense works during this period. However, blacks also served in military roles as militiamen, as sailors, as regular soldiers, and in special military units (Voelz 1993). Once a military labor system was in place in the Caribbean, it created new hierarchical social relations among indigenous people, Europeans, Africans and African-descended people.

By the eighteenth century, the military use of slaves was commonplace in all American colonies, especially in the Caribbean, where the combination of a dwindling white population and colonial wars meant that a portion of the slave population became more mobile (Handler 1984; Buckley 1998, 5). Officers in military outposts recruited local slaves for military duties. Some of these military personnel owned local estates that provided slaves as needed to local armies. In many cases, military officials and planters cooperated to create policies that were designed to subordinate and control laborers. At the start of the nineteenth century, the British colonial administration formally acknowledged the military potential of African slaves with the formation of the highly controversial WIR, which served in overseas conflicts and in various Caribbean forts until the British Army abandoned these installations in 1854. In the Caribbean, military forts were dynamic sites characterized by social changes that effectively transformed these settings into black garrisons—one of the first formalized spaces in the Caribbean for the beginnings of interracial societies.

Although historians, architects, and archaeologists have studied the military sites across the Caribbean, interpretations have changed over time (see Armstrong and Hauser 2009, 587–589). Prior to the local rule of the mid-twentieth century, historical research and preservation efforts focused on the imperial power of European nations for tourism and nationalistic purposes. Following independence in the Caribbean, archaeologists added investigations of the social and cultural dimensions of domestic life at Caribbean military sites, especially among enslaved or otherwise coerced indigenous and African laborers and lower-status military personnel who lived in and around forts (see Deagan 1988, 1995, 2010; Goucher 1999; Morris et al. 1999; Deagan and Cruxent 2002; Schroedl and Ahlman 2002; Ahlman et al. 2008, 2009; Haviser 2010; Leech 2010; Beier 2011, 2014, 2017; Odewale et al. 2017). As research reveals, significant themes in the study of the African diaspora are readily accessible through the archaeological investigation of colonial fortifications.

Situating Enslaved Labor at the Cabrits Garrison

From 2007 to 2011, I directed excavations at archaeological sites in the Cabrits Garrison, a 200-acre British military complex in a hilly peninsula along the northwestern coast of the Commonwealth of Dominica, which is positioned between the French islands of Martinique and Guadeloupe in the Lesser Antilles. The fort is spread out across two hills. The Inner Cabrits is sited from 450 to 515 feet above sea level and the larger Outer Cabrits rises to about 630 feet above sea level. It overlooks Prince Rupert's Bay, which is located near the town of Portsmouth and is the best harbor on the island. Portsmouth is the former capital of Dominica and is currently the second largest town on the island. Like other Atlantic world forts, the Cabrits Garrison was not particularly active in terms of its intended purpose of defense despite its strategic location. For example, during the Battle of the Saintes in April 1782, the French fleet traveled past Dominica on its way to engage the British fleet but the actual battle took place closer to Île des Saintes and Guadeloupe, well outside the range of the cannons at the Cabrits. This was an important naval victory for the British against a French fleet intent on expanding France's territorial holdings in the region (Honychurch 2013, 93–97). Additionally, in April 1802, the Eighth West India Regiment revolted against their white officers at the Cabrits in a brief but significant event that was reportedly the regiment's response to the army's use of its members for nonmilitary purposes (i.e., manual labor) and their fear that they would lose their status as British soldiers (Buckley 1979, 76; 1980). Other than these violent episodes, the Cabrits Garrison was most active as a hub for labor and community life (Figure 10.2).

People associated with colonial fortifications generated extensive documentation. Planners, architects, and other administrators created much of this record in their efforts to effectively manage or make sense of various labor projects and social hierarchies. Maps, administrative correspondence, and personal narratives of a variety of colonial elites and agents document how they conceived of enslaved laborers (Beier 2017, 83–124).

For instance, military personnel believed that it would not be possible

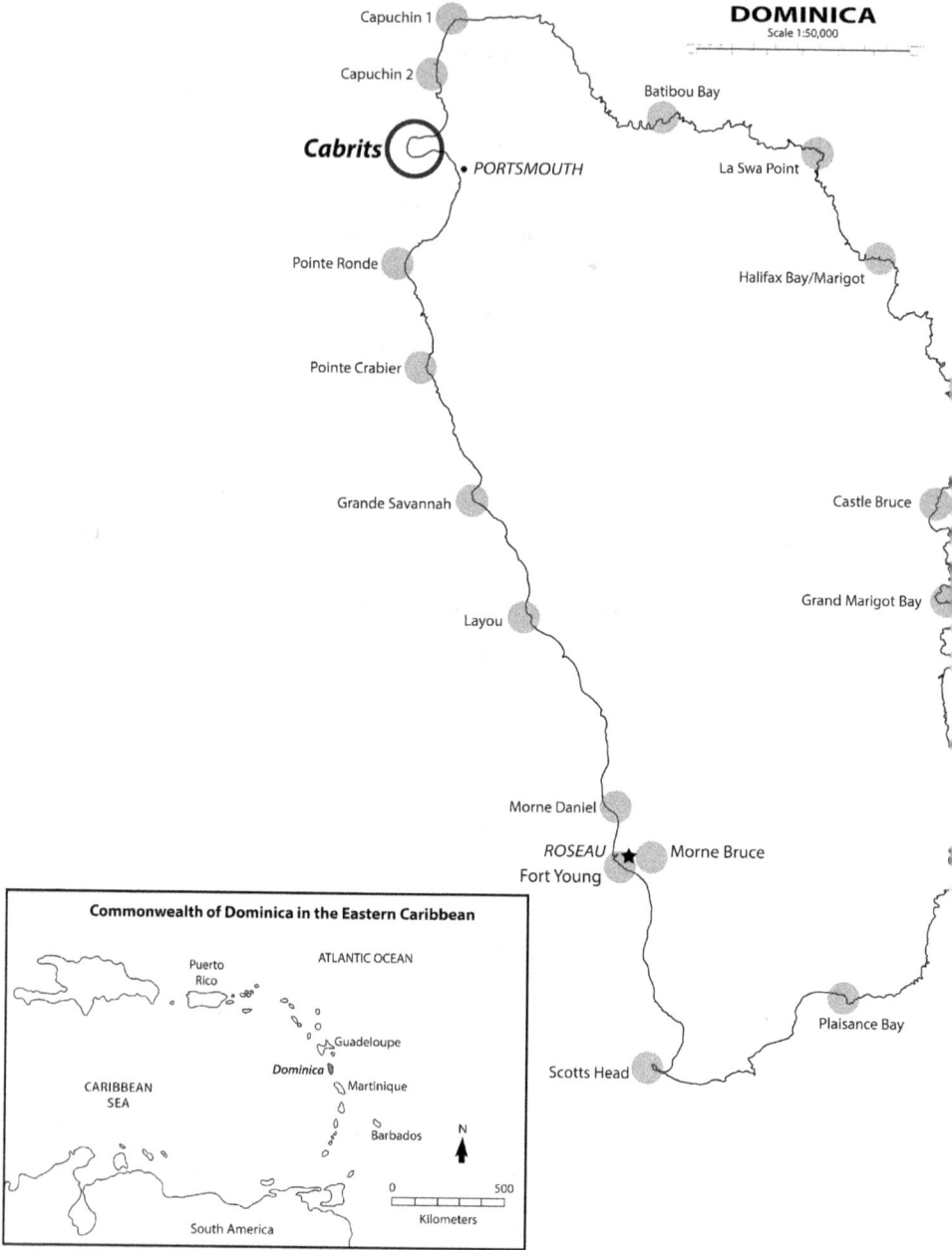

Figure 10.2. Map of Dominica and its location in the eastern Caribbean. The map features the Cabrits Garrison, other signal stations, and coastal batteries in operation from the mid-eighteenth to mid-nineteenth centuries. Map created by Zachary J. M. Beier.

to build and maintain the Cabrits Garrison and the other principle military posts on Dominica without the assistance of enslaved laborers. In a 1772 report to London, Capt. Robert George Bruce, an engineer, outlined the architectural plans for the defense of the island, which included an extensive garrison overlooking Prince Rupert's Bay. Bruce regarded the garrison as "the first and most important object to be secured by Fortifications in the island of Dominica."[1] He specifically mentioned that "Negro Artificers" usually built such fortifications because they were more readily available than white workers and cheaper to employ, costing five shillings per day as opposed to ten for white laborers. This reliance on enslaved labor for construction and other auxiliary tasks is documented throughout the military occupation of the Cabrits Garrison and was reinforced by popular beliefs of the period about racial inferiority and biological fitness in tropical conditions. By the end of the eighteenth century, the British Army had begun to recruit black regiments from the local slave population and from men recently arrived from the west coast of Africa. At the Cabrits Garrison, the army integrated black slaves into most of its lower-ranking military positions.

Jonathan Troup, a physician from Scotland who lived at the Cabrits Garrison in 1790 and 1791, took a keen interest in describing and sometimes drawing the black bodies he encountered. His diary provides a worm's-eye view of Dominican society and an unfiltered snapshot of the community at Prince Rupert's and the role of slavery in Caribbean military life during a period of intense construction at the fort.[2] He noted that dances at the Cabrits Garrison involved "gentlemen from Cabbrits," including British officers and planters, and he described enslaved women and a girl born into slavery at the fort and a "negroe dance" that took place in the valley between the Inner and Outer Cabrits, where the laborers' village was located (Troup quoted in Beier 2017, 119). Troup also paid attention to the daily work of enslaved individuals. On February 23, 1790, he wrote that "15 Negroe women carry the coral lime from the [Hill] to the works. The Driver walks behind." He comments further that "Black Negroes shine in the Sun[; the] replication [of] Dark is very great from a Negroe's body, very little from a white person. These bodies are not half as dry as ones from the absorption of [heat]."[3] He also noted a variety of injuries linked to the lifestyle of enslaved military laborers, including "pains in loins and head from carrying heavy burdens . . . up hills." In his opinion, these loads were "enough to kill the strongest animals." In his entry for

March 5, 1790, Troup stated that "two Negroe Boys got sore throats from the Damp office houses having their feet to the wall in night time." The unfinished clay floors and poorly insulated walls that were characteristic of the houses military administrators provided for enslaved laborers created a health hazard for these boys.[4]

Dr. Troup's diary is significant because his comments reveal that the labor of enslaved people was integral to the development and maintenance of the fort. Troup, who interacted with several prominent planters during his stay in the Prince Rupert's community, observed that most of these workers were hired from surrounding plantations. The ethnographic details Troup recorded highlight important demographics of this labor force (ethnicity, age, gender), the central role the valley played in the life of the Cabrits Garrison community, and his implicit racism, which naturalized this unequal social setting in the conceived landscape of British imperialism.

Perhaps cartographic evidence is most important for understanding labor at the Cabrits Garrison. Maps present a rare opportunity in the study of enslaved labor at Caribbean military sites because these settlements were typically ephemeral and were not often identified. The garrison occupied a wide and diversified space that could have housed 500 troops (Honychurch 2013, 74). The laborers' village is present on at least four maps of the Cabrits Garrison that were produced from 1791 to 1812 (Figure 10.3).[5] When these structures are labeled, they are identified as "negro huts," "pioneer huts," or "workshops." The exact number of these structures is unclear, but no more than twenty structures are indicated during occupation at the fort (Figure 10.3).

Other studies of slave housing at Caribbean plantations have documented features that are important to consider at colonial forts that used slave labor. Slave laborers lived in settlements located between where they worked and the offices of those who managed them. These settlements varied in arrangement and configuration (Handler and Lange 1978; Armstrong 1990; Delle 1998, 2011, 2014; Higman 1998, 2001; Armstrong and Kelly 2000; Gibson 2007). The proximity of the laborers' village at the Cabrits to the engineers' yard, civil administrators, and the Fort Shirley battery align with the Caribbean plantation model of economic efficiency. Located in the lowest portion of the fort, the village was situated downwind from the Fort Shirley battery, where soldiers, officers, and other administrators would have had a clear view of this settlement from the

1791

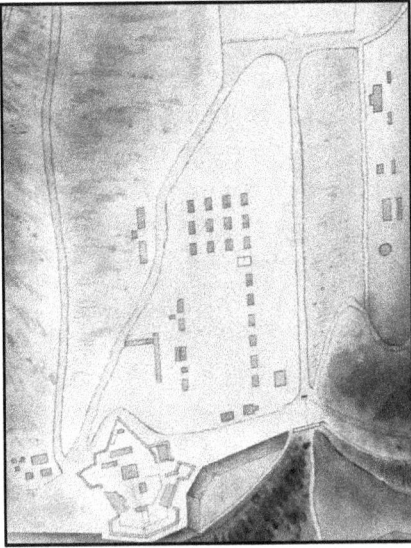

1792

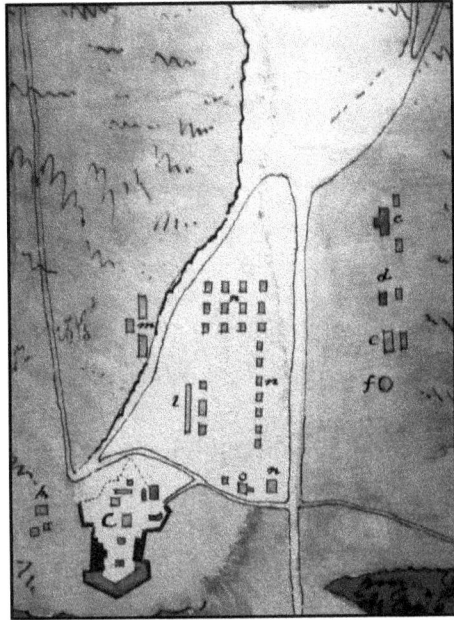

1799

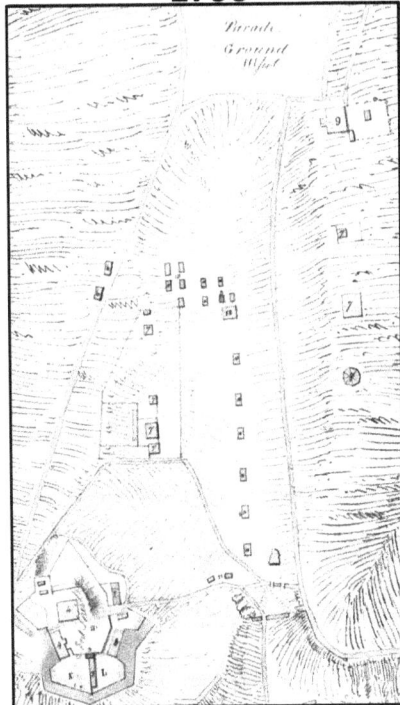

1812

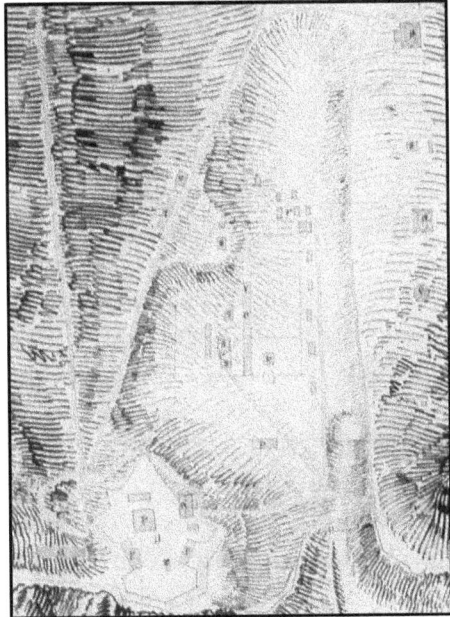

Figure 10.3. Maps featuring the Cabrits Garrison laborer village in the late eighteenth and early nineteenth centuries. Sources: *Clockwise from top left*: Project for the defense of Prince Rupert's Head, Dominica, 1791; Sketch showing the state of the post at Prince Rupert's Head, 1792; General plan of Prince Rupert's Head, December 1, 1799; and Plan of Prince Rupert's Head, 1812. Image created by Zachary J. M. Beier from maps in The National Archives (UK).

commanding heights of this headquarters. The engineers' yard, which included ordnance quarters, storehouses, and workshops, was directly above the laborers' settlement. A wall separated the laborers' settlement from what would have been the primary workplace for this community. Significantly, a forge located in a central point of the laborers' village was equipped with defensive features that included gun loops (see Figure 10.3; the forge is number 12 on the 1799 map). These tactical walls were presumably designed to prevent an invasion over the Inner Cabrits or an insurrection from within the laborers' village.

Maps and administrative documents demonstrate the initial presence of enslaved laborers in the final decade of the eighteenth century and the integration of other military personnel into this area, including regular infantry of probable African descent, in the first half of the nineteenth century. For instance, by 1812 most of the structures in the valley are identified as being associated with the Ordnance Department (see Figure 10.3). In that year, the vertically aligned buildings that had been marked as huts for laborers on previous maps were unidentified and were coded in the same pink color as buildings newly labeled in this settlement as "Barracks for troops of the line" ("p"). By this time, the Cabrits Garrison was widely referred to as a black garrison in primary sources, which suggests that the laborers' village was an important venue for interactions between different and emergent segments of the British Army.

Military Labor and Settlement Archaeology

Site survey and mapping of the settlement area associated with lower-status laborers at the Cabrits Garrison occurred from 2008 to 2011. In my estimation, this study area contains at least six of the structures identified as laborers' households or workshops on historic maps (see Figure 10.3). Two domestic areas in this site were extensively excavated (Structure 1 and Structure 2; see Figure 10.4).

Significant clusters of stones and other architectural features were documented across the surface of this settlement area; the heaviest concentration was in the southern portion of the site. A total of fifty-six seemingly anomalous surface features were identified that can be classified into several functional types. For instance, sequences of stone piles constitute what appear to be terraces that formed housing platforms and drainage channels. At least four terraces in a north-to-south alignment across the

CG-1 SURVEY MAP
Laborer Village

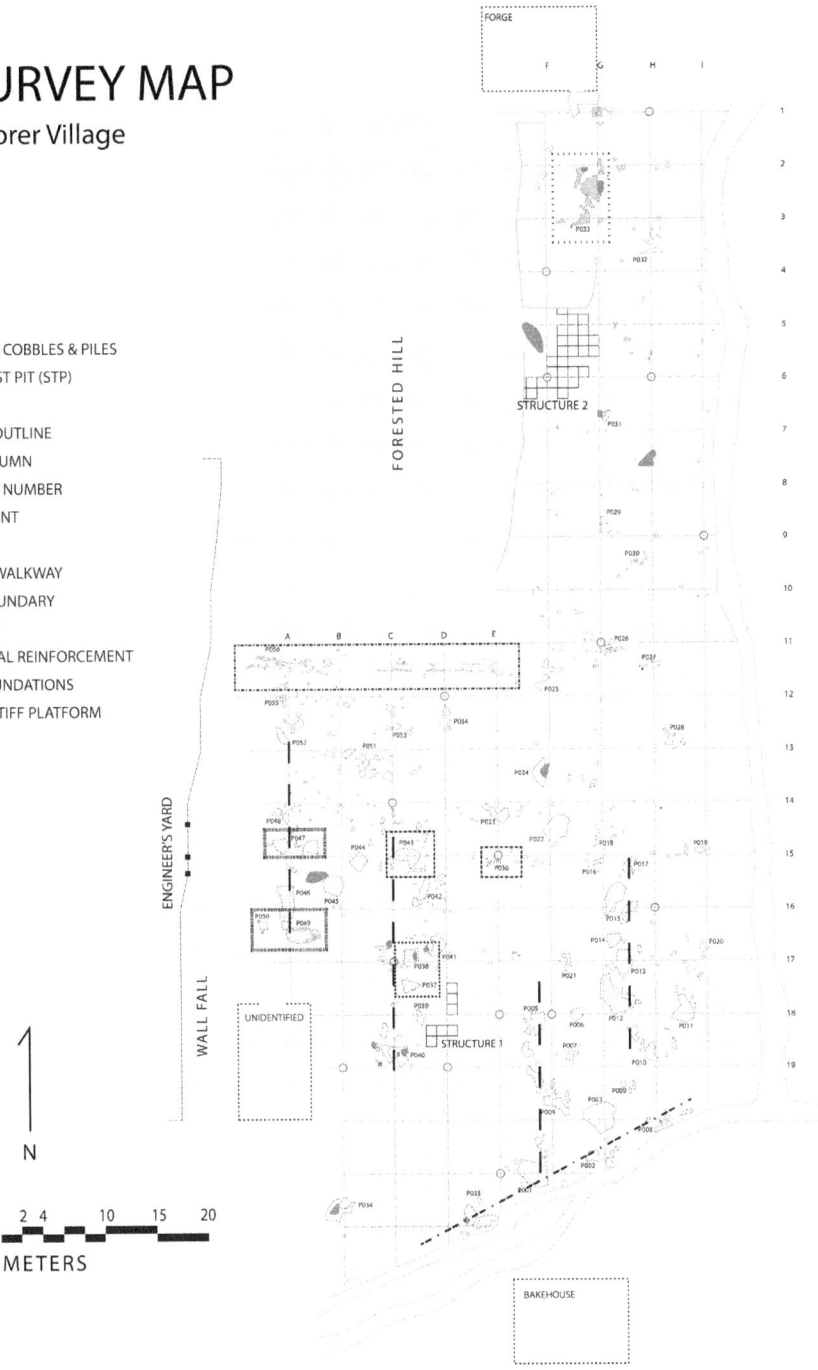

FORGE

F G H I

STRUCTURE 2

FORESTED HILL

P033

P032

P031

P029

P030

◯ ◡ = LIMESTONE COBBLES & PILES

◦ = SHOVEL TEST PIT (STP)

······ = RAVINE

······· = BUILDING OUTLINE

• = STONE COLUMN

P010 = STONE PILE NUMBER

▦ = DATUM POINT

— = TERRACE

▢ = DRAIN OR WALKWAY

·—··—·· = RAVINE BOUNDARY

▢ = ENTRYWAY

▢ = STRUCTURAL REINFORCEMENT

▢ = STONE FOUNDATIONS

▢ = VOLCANIC TIFF PLATFORM

A B C D E

P056

P055

P052

P051

P053

P054

P024

P048

P047

P044

P041

P023

P022

P018

P019

P050

P017

P046

P045

P042

P016

P015

P020

P050

P049

P041

P014

P021

P013

P011

P038

P037

P039

P008

P006

P012

P010

UNIDENTIFIED

P040

STRUCTURE 1

P007

P009

P063

P004

P008

ENGINEER'S YARD

WALL FALL

P002

N

P034

P033

P001

2 4 10 15 20

METERS

BAKEHOUSE

P026

P027

P025

P028

Figure 10.4. Survey map of the Cabrits Garrison laborer village (CG-1) highlighting the location of the two excavated domestic contexts (Structure 1 and Structure 2) and the different types of settlement features. Map created by Zachary J. M. Beier.

site were identified from sequences of cataloged piles, including 037–043, 046–048, 010–015, 001, and 004–005. Piles also constituted drains (056), served as boundary reinforcement for ravines (008, 002, 035), and once acted as stairways or walkways that crossed terraces and connected surrounding work areas, such as the engineers' yard, to the laborers' settlement (047 and 049–050).

Other piles appear to have been specifically suited for integration into a building plan. In some cases, piles with straight edges may have been used as structural reinforcement (037, 038). Other archaeologists working on British military sites in the tropics (Allen 1973) and on Caribbean plantations (Pulsipher and Goodwin 2001) have described this tactic of buttressing a side of a house using unmortared stones. This technique is also observable among certain communities in Dominica that have maintained this style of vernacular architecture. Additionally, certain piles exhibited a more evenly spaced alignment that resembled a line of stones for building foundations (036, 043), like the architectural outline documented in excavations of Structure 1. Other piles displayed the same volcanic tiff surface composition that was observed during excavations of Structure 2 (033), which required the presence of a bedrock layer of this material for its posthole style of construction.

In addition to their use in architecture, these piles are testament to water management strategies (see Pulsipher and Goodwin 2001; Espersen 2013). Extensive areas of land were routinely cleared around the Cabrits headlands, and the abundance and orientation of these features at the laborers' village no doubt reflect the need to counteract the effects of erosion in a tropical mountain setting. Cisterns, drains, and terraces made of stone piles identified at the Cabrits Garrison would have channeled water away from areas such as the engineers' yard, through the lower-lying laborers' village, and into the surrounding ravines, where it was directed outside the gates of the fort through a system of stone conduits.

Perhaps most important, this evidence demonstrates that the residents of the laborers' village had a lower economic status than other groups at this site and that they exercised some control over the design of their living spaces. In many ways, this area lacks the institutional aesthetic apparent at other settlements throughout the fort. Like other Caribbean slave villages (see Armstrong 1990, 97), the Cabrits Garrison laborers' village is characterized by a series of house-yard areas connected by narrow lanes. These living spaces often included separate enclosures for cooking, preparing and storing food, and working. Because administrators at the Cabrits Garrison never explicitly considered the military labor of enslaved workers at the Cabrits Garrison, gaps exist in knowledge about the number of laborers employed at the fort and the nature of their daily lives. An estimated 50 to 150 men and women, primarily slaves, likely inhabited and modified this living space by the end of the eighteenth century. Archaeological survey and excavation in this area reveals settlement features that are germane to assessments of the lived space of this community. This is a far more complex settlement arrangement than what is illustrated on maps of the fort from the period. Each structure excavated in the laborers' village exhibits features that connect varying forms of household architecture to the broader house-yard area.

Built Environments and Dwelling Practices at the Cabrits Garrison Laborer Village

Architectural material culture provides a primary link between artifacts and the living spaces they were associated with. Evidence for domestic architecture at the Cabrits Garrison includes a variety of local and imported resources, including coral and mortar, earthenware bricks and tiles, nails and other fasteners, hardware, window glass, and other material types. This artifact group constitutes the largest portion of the total artifacts recovered from excavations at the Cabrits Garrison (n = 5,776; 49,288.1 grams). Evidence from the laborers' village contributes the greatest percentage of this material (n = 4,912; 45,127.7 grams), while the shovel test pit survey in the Outer Cabrits soldiers' barracks, which is not included in the scope of the present chapter, recovered substantially less architectural evidence (n = 864; 4,160.4 grams) (see Beier 2017, 182–197, 199–200, 223–226). This discrepancy is no doubt related to the fact that area excavations were not situated in this portion of the Cabrits Garrison. The density and diversity of architectural evidence and other artifact classes in the laborers' village is also suggestive of a greater degree of variation in the construction materials and practices and household behaviors in this settlement than the apparent unity in construction techniques and daily practices documented at the soldiers' barracks. Insights gleaned from the two households excavated in the Cabrits laborers' settlement are significant for understanding the experience of slaves who lived at forts, on plantations, and at other sites throughout the Caribbean. This evidence demonstrates how lower-status and enslaved workers at the Cabrits Garrison rejected the standardized landscape and rigid social identities British colonialists imagined in favor of living spaces they actively shaped.

Structure 1

This structure is characterized by a foundation of rectangular cut stone and mortar that measures seven and a half meters long and just over five meters wide for the north wall, as revealed by extant surface architecture and area excavations. The seven 1 meter × 1 meter units placed in the northwest half of the structure resulted in the collection of 2,259 architecture-related artifacts (13,957.3 grams). Excavations also sought to collect information from an exposed section of wall and more accurately define the western portion of the foundation. The units bisecting the northern foundation (Units 33 and 34) provided the clearest information about the foundation, which measures approximately 32 centimeters in thickness and extended approximately 40 centimeters below the ground surface. Earthenware bricks make up a substantial part of the collected data (404; 4,226.6 grams) and were used in combination with cut limestone for the foundation. Excavations inside the structure did not reveal any floor surfaces or room partitions. The high frequency of wrought-iron nails (n = 1,119; 4,260 grams) compared to what we recovered from Structure 2 makes it seem likely that there was a wood floor and frame. Ceramic roofing tiles (n = 340; 2,685.4 grams) documented on the ground surface and during excavations suggest that this material was used for roof covering. Along with the ceramic brick, this distinctive orange roofing tile would have created a unified institutional aesthetic that the buildings situated in the lower and more visually accessible portions of the fort shared, including those in the Fort Shirley battery and the surrounding civil and engineering departments in the valley (Figure 10.5).

Mapping of the exterior foundation of the structure further aided in the description of the design, composition, and orientation of Structure 1. The low height of the stone-and-mortar foundation suggests that the building was one story and was built with timber framing. This assumption aligns with archaeological findings at other Caribbean military sites where slave life has been studied (Schroedl and Ahlman 2002, 40). The density of building materials varied from the eastern side of the structure to the west. This composition alludes to the orientation of Structure

CG-1 STRUCTURE 1

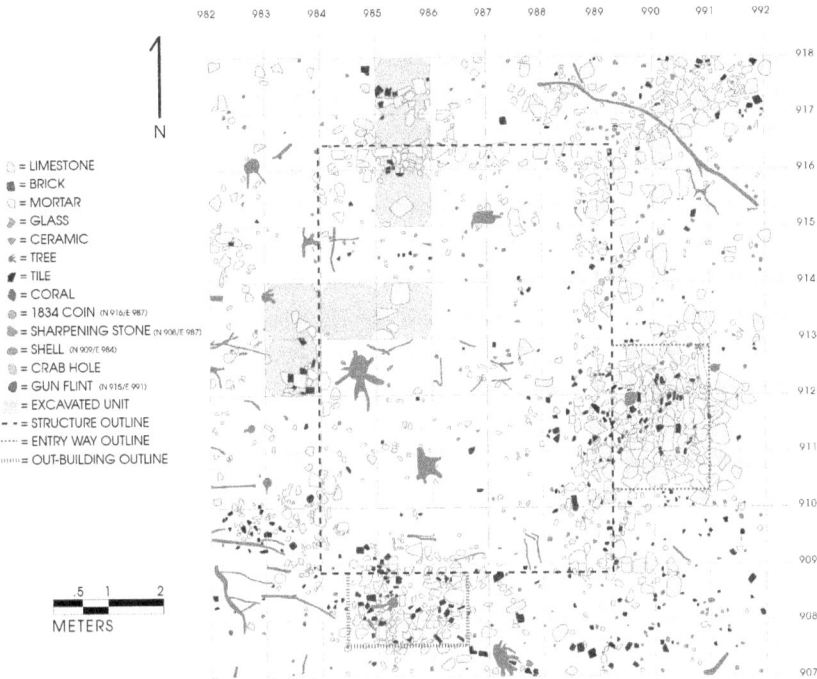

Legend:
- ⬠ = LIMESTONE
- ▪ = BRICK
- ◗ = MORTAR
- ◗ = GLASS
- ▾ = CERAMIC
- ⋆ = TREE
- ▮ = TILE
- ◗ = CORAL
- ◉ = 1834 COIN (N 916/E 987)
- ◗ = SHARPENING STONE (N 906/E 987)
- ◗ = SHELL (N 909/E 984)
- ◗ = CRAB HOLE
- ◗ = GUN FLINT (N 915/E 991)
- ◗ = EXCAVATED UNIT
- – – = STRUCTURE OUTLINE
- ⋯⋯ = ENTRY WAY OUTLINE
- ⊪⊪⊪ = OUT-BUILDING OUTLINE

METERS

Figure 10.5. (*Top*) Plan map of Structure 1 in the Cabrits Garrison laborer village (CG-1). (*Bottom*) Structure 1 in the Cabrits Garrison laborer village looking south over the north wall of this stone foundation building. Map and photo by Zachary J. M. Beier.

1; the built-up eastern side would have served as the front of the house and would have faced the prevailing winds from the east (see Armstrong 1990, 104). Along the eastern-facing wall of Structure 1 is a dense pile of stones, bricks, and ceramic roofing tiles. This feature no doubt served as the entryway and part of the terrace that formed the platform the structure was built on. Another external feature of Structure 1 is located near the southwest corner of the building. While no excavations were carried out in this area, this feature matches some of the descriptions of a "kitchen area" or "cooking shed" that Armstrong (1990, 103–104) provided, including its orientation behind the house and the presence of a sharpening or grinding stone identified less than a meter away during surface survey.

Descriptions of Structure 1 in the cartographic record are inconsistent, but an 1812 map of the fort may include this building as a "barracks occupied by the Troops of the Line" (see Figure 10.3).[6] Mean ceramic dating places the structure at 1796.04. While there is a certain degree of crossover in the occupation of Structure 1 and Structure 2, it is clear from collected diagnostic artifacts, including a coin dated to 1834 and a comparatively high concentration of pearlware (n = 331; 775.1 grams) and whiteware (n = 23; 27.7 grams), that Structure 1 was occupied following the construction of Structure 2 and was inhabited until the second half of the nineteenth century. The combination of this later occupation date and a formal style of architecture that featured a higher-quality cut-stone foundation suggests that this household was occupied by regular infantry, a European artisan, or wage laborers following emancipation. The structure likely served a domestic function; a high number of artifacts were associated with domestic purposes, such as ceramic tableware (n = 659; 1714.1 grams). The absence of tools and ordnance from the collected assemblage suggests that this structure was not likely used for storage or work.

Structure 2

This structure is characterized by a raised platform documented near a volcanic tuff ridge with noticeable wear patterns from human modification. Twenty-seven 1 × 1 meter units were placed in an area that measured approximately eight and a half meters from north to south and seven meters from east to west. Excavations in open areas recovered 2,387 (27,003.8 grams) of architecture-related artifacts and clarified the nature of this housing platform and architectural style. Mean ceramic dating places the occupation of this structure at 1794.24, slightly before Structure 1. Like the assemblage recovered at Structure 1, wrought-iron nails (957; 3,146.2 grams) and earthenware bricks (n = 133; 8,052.6 grams) and roofing tiles (545; 10,470 g) were among the most common artifacts collected and are indicative of the principal elements used to build this structure. Additionally, a total of twenty-one features were identified, including a series of postholes (F001–F008, F010–F014, F020), a trench cut into the volcanic bedrock platform along the E996 transect line (F021), and an oven carved into the volcanic ridge along the western boundary of the site (F009; see Figure 10.6).

The identified features demonstrate an architectural pattern in which builders made use of an area with a preexisting flat surface and workable volcanic bedrock. The posthole construction of this structure resembles descriptions of wattle-and-daub walls with posts placed every few feet to support the structure. Other archaeological investigations in the Caribbean have identified this architectural style in a variety of household contexts (see Armstrong 1990; Farnsworth 2001; Pulsipher and Goodwin 2001; Gibson 2007; Handler and Bergman 2009 for noted examples). Postholes were dug or carved into the volcanic bedrock, a technique other historical archaeologists working in the Lesser Antilles have described (Pulsipher and Goodwin 2001; Gibson 2007). These postholes share some commonalities, including their circular plan shape and flat-based V profile, but for the most part they vary in depth, in arrangement, and particularly in size; sizes range from 14 centimeters by 11 centimeters (F008) to 51 centimeters by 52 centimeters (F001).

The trench feature (F021) is either a drain or architectural footing for a wall. As discussed earlier, water management issues would have been a pressing concern for inhabitants of the laborers' settlement in the valley of the Cabrits because of its low situation. Dr. Jonathan Troup noted in his entry for January 23, 1790, that "some drains are made round the huts" at surrounding plantations to reduce the dampness of the clayish soils in and around these structures.[7] The trench may very well be this type of drain, which was commonly referred to as a "soak away." It may also have served a more architectural function to support thinner, vertically aligned posts through which wattle was woven (see Gibson 2007, 141–142). While the excavated trench feature (F021) at Structure 2 is wider than those documented in other contexts, the posthole (F012) located inside this feature is compelling evidence for the use of this construction technique.

CG-1 **STRUCTURE 2**

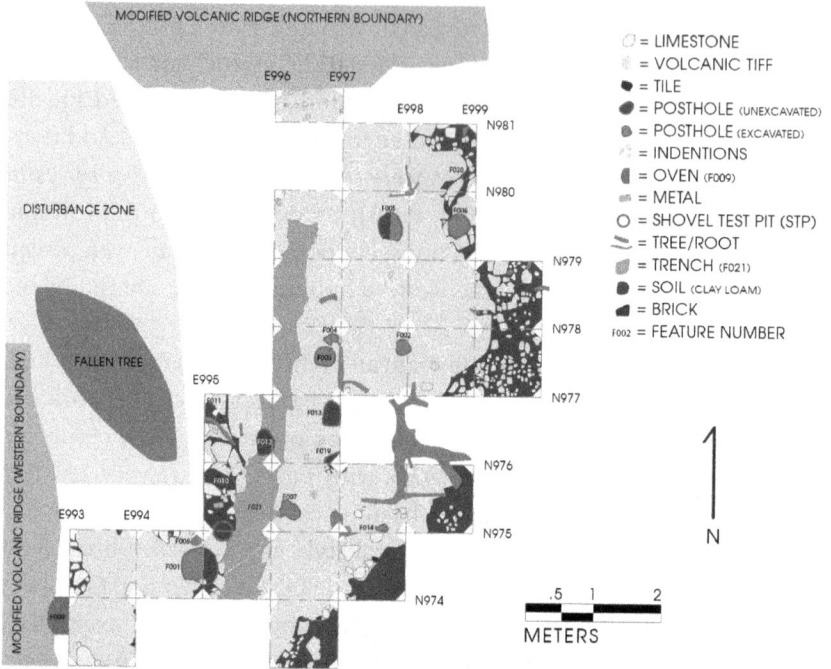

MODIFIED VOLCANIC RIDGE (NORTHERN BOUNDARY)

E996   E997

E998   E999

N981

F020

DISTURBANCE ZONE

N980

F005   F016

N979

N978

FALLEN TREE

E995

N977

F011   F013

F019

N976

F010

E993   E994   F021   F007

F004   F014

N975

F008

F001

N974

F003

MODIFIED VOLCANIC RIDGE (WESTERN BOUNDARY)

F014   F002

F006

F018

○ = LIMESTONE
 = VOLCANIC TIFF
● = TILE
● = POSTHOLE (UNEXCAVATED)
● = POSTHOLE (EXCAVATED)
 = INDENTIONS
◖ = OVEN (F009)
 = METAL
○ = SHOVEL TEST PIT (STP)
 = TREE/ROOT
 = TRENCH (F021)
● = SOIL (CLAY LOAM)
▰ = BRICK
F002 = FEATURE NUMBER

N

.5   1   2
METERS

Figure 10.6. (*Top*) Plan map of Structure 2 in the Cabrits Garrison laborer village (CG-1). Created by Zachary J. M. Beier. (*Bottom*) View looking south over the volcanic bedrock that served as the platform for Structure 2. Two large postholes are visible in the foreground, the trench feature is visible in the center, and the oven feature is visible in the back-right corner. Map and photo by Zachary J. M. Beier.

Lastly, the oven feature (F009) is like those European militaries used and is referred to as an "earthen camp kitchen" or "excavated kitchen" (Rees 2002). Excavations identified noticeable grooves running around the extent of the interior and a deeper groove in the center of the oven. The grooves and the shape of the oven suggest that it was used for boiling pots, even though faunal and botanical remains were not recovered from this context. Access to controlled and covered fire sources would have aided in the comfortable preparation of military rations and other acquired food. This is the only oven feature identified in proximity to households in the Cabrits village, suggesting that lower-status laborers centralized food preparation around Structure 2. Additionally, this feature likely added cooking smells and smoke linked to creole foodways that reinforced the distinctive character of this domestic context in the institutionalized space of the British Army (see De Souza 2016, 159).

It is clear that the standardized rectangular structure label used to identify laborers' housing on maps of the Cabrits Garrison does not provide a sufficient basis for assessing the complex layout, composition, and function of Structure 2. The concentration of architectural features, especially the postholes, confirms the presence of at least one structure in this area but the outline for this building is difficult to infer from the available evidence. Excavation units did not confidently narrow in on any type of floor surface distinct from the documented stratigraphy of the site. More than likely, a thin layer of hard-packed clay covering the volcanic bedrock served as a floor. It is also possible that the malleable volcanic layer of bedrock acted as the primary floor surface for Structure 2. The recovery of wrought-iron nails inside this structure does not rule out the presence of a raised wooden floor, although these were more likely associated with postholes in the construction of walls with wattle. The high frequency of roofing tile recovered during excavations reveals the possible covering used for this structure. While this artifact type could have been blown into the site with hurricanes over the years, the large postholes associated with Structure 2 could certainly have supported a ceramic tile roof. The large postholes and use of a heavy ceramic roof is unique and may allude to a more barracks-style of living in a space that integrated vernacular construction with the aesthetics of military administrators, cultural knowledge, and institutional control.

Finally, the comparatively high yield of agricultural and construction tools (n = 5; 2,373.5 grams) and ordnance (n = 6; 3,322.3 grams) recovered at Structure 2 suggests that it may have been used as a workshop or storage shed. But like Armstrong's (1990) assessment of a workshop at Drax Hall, Structure 2 is associated with a range of domestic materials that blur interpretations of its function, including a mixture of imported and locally produced ceramic vessels (n = 858; 2,273 grams), a high concentration of bottle glass (n = 1,836; 7,235.6 grams), and military accouterments and an oven feature. I submit that the mixed-material assemblage of Structure 2 and its location close to the forge and the engineers' yard suggests a space that was used for domestic and work purposes. In other words, former inhabitants of the structure lived where they worked and worked where they lived. Structure 2 also displays the dual roles of enslaved military labor at the site; it combines the material cultures of laboring and soldiering. A Sixth West India Regiment buckle dating to 1808–1809 was found during excavations. This is the only direct evidence of the presence of enslaved soldiers found during archaeological investigations.

Conclusion: Households and Military Sites in the Colonial Caribbean

Colonial military sites in the Caribbean have traditionally been considered as monuments to European expansion, technology, control, and competition. This emphasis on institutional qualities, central figures, and battlefields has contributed to narratives that overlook the diverse communities that came together at military sites. This chapter demonstrates the important contributions the investigation of both the conceived and lived spaces that lower-status military personnel inhabited within the walls of Caribbean fortifications can make to African diaspora archaeology. The settlement, architectural, and other forms of archaeological data related to the dwellings described in this chapter indicate a diversity of construction techniques and local and imported resources at the domestic contexts excavated at the Cabrits Garrison laborers' village. Household-level analysis recognizes the institutional impacts and local negotiations that the archaeological record of dwelling practices suggests. At the Cabrits, household variability reflects changes in military labor strategies over time, intrasite social differences, and interactions between lower-status and enslaved inhabitants of an increasingly diversified British colonial army. Examinations that rely on the available historical and archaeological record are necessary to provide a window into the process of design, construction, and use of these imperial-sponsored buildings in the broader context of Caribbean society.

Notes

1. Captain Robert George Bruce, "Report of the Island of Dominica with the nature and circumstances of its Coasts Towns & Harbours together with the Fortifications & Batteries necessary for their Security & defense as well as to make a secure Place of Arms either at Prince Ruperts Bay or Roseau so as the same may be defensible against any Attack from the Neighbouring Foreign Islands," March 27, 1770, Series WO 55/1553/4, The National Archives, Kew, London.

2. "Journal of Jonathan Troup, Physician, of Aberdeen, Scotland and Dominica, West Indies, 1788–1790, 1790, MS 2070, Library, Special Collections and Museums, University of Aberdeen, Aberdeen, Scotland (hereafter Troup Diary).

3. Entry for February 23, 1790, Troup Diary.

4. Entry for March 5, 1790, Troup Diary.

5. See "Three Sheets of Drawings Illustrating a Project for the Defence of Prince Rupert's Head, Dominica, to Accompany Reports by the Board of Officers Appointed to Examine the Works in the West," 1791, Series MPH 1/184; Lieutenant Richard Fletcher, "Sketch Shewing the Present State of the Post at Prince Rupert's Head in the Island of Dominica," 1792, Series CO 700/DOMINICA8; Lieutenant Colonel Charles Shipley, "General Plan of Prince Rupert Head Dominica dec 1st 1799," 1799, Series MPHH 1/18/2; and Capt. Henry Hobbs, "Plan of Prince Ruperts Head Dominica," 1812, Series WO 78/2508. All at The National Archives, Kew, London.

6. Hobbs, "Plan of Prince Ruperts Head Dominica."

7. Entry for January 23, 1790, Troup Diary.

11

Built Environments

Slavery, Materiality, and Usable Pasts

MARK W. HAUSER

One of the aims of this volume is to document the remarkable variation in how enslaved people engaged with their environment across the
Caribbean from the seventeenth to the nineteenth centuries, primarily
through houses, yards, gardens, and plots. Some of these engagements
appeared as isolated instances, some were part of large housing schemes
associated with single phases of construction, some occurred simultaneously, and others were separated by long periods of time. Thus, some
early-eighteenth-century housing was built with techniques and ideas
carried in the minds of enslaved people and organized around principles found in West Africa (Armstrong 1992; Pulsipher 1994), while other
highly ordered villages were laid out to optimize efficiency of movement
and the use of materials (Higman 1998). A century later, one regime that
was entwined in the politics of slavery and abolition, concerned about
the appearance of slave conditions and the reproductive success of the
laboring population, introduced measures to improve hygiene including
the regulation of villages (Handler and Bergman 2009), while another regime, smarting from the humiliating loss of a colony due to a rebellion by
slaves and their masters, began commissioning housing that was equally
regulated (Kelly 2008a).

No single story can describe the environments of the Caribbean that
were built and occupied during slavery. There was no single culture to
be housed and no pattern of spatial proxemics such as that early scholars of vernacular architecture, including Vlach (1976), Deetz (1977), and
Glassie (1976), proposed. Each structure built by a slave was shaped by

a combination of environmental factors, personal choice, and historical forces. Thus, each, in order to be properly understood, must be placed in its own context, which is what these essays endeavor to do.

There are reasons for documenting the varieties of housing found in the material record of slavery. For one thing, such an exercise can reshape social relations that are commonly rendered as monolithic and that draw on legal definitions of chattel property that form the foundation for the alienating process of "social death" (Patterson 1982). Information developed from Caribbean cases can also correct the propensity to write about slavery using facile categorizations such as slave dormitories and family households. Postulating the household as the antithesis of the dormitory encourages the idea that those who lived in dormitories did not have families. As Barry Higman points out, studies of households can exclude extended family networks and relationships that were not co-residential (Higman 1978). Studies of the liminal legal state of formerly enslaved laborers in the period 1834 to 1838—known as the apprenticeship period in the British Caribbean—show that the house, the yard, and the plot were fraught sites where struggles over self-definition and the relationship to the state took place. Missionaries educated legally emancipated people about "moral" lives as their status shifted from property to subject. While this was happening, prerogatives that slave codes had ensured, such as access to provision grounds and secure housing, became part of a negotiated labor arrangement between newly emancipated individuals and the people who owned the land on which they lived and made a living (Turner 1982). This predicament (sensu Brown 2009) sometimes translated into collective action, as was the case in the Morant Bay rebellion in Jamaica in 1865 (Heuman 1994).

The study of housing, as understood through the material record of slavery, has ideological implications. What is more, scholars must contend with the overwhelming, almost hegemonic, presence on the landscape of industrial buildings and estate houses, which are more visible, easier to render, and of greater interest to the governmental and commercial organizations that manage national patrimony. While authors in this volume do not question the value of the industrial archaeologies of factories and estate houses insofar as they help us better understand the built landscape, many reject attempts to describe slavery or its effects through such a narrow lens. Instead, they attend to expanding the conceptual range of the built landscape as a unit of archaeological analysis.

Terms

The contributors to this volume use terms such as "house," "yard," and "gardens" to consider the term "built environment" as it pertained to the enslaved. But what did such terms mean, and to whom? What did these spaces share that merits calling all of them "built" when we do not use such language to describe other areas such as tended woodlands or pelagic fisheries? Importantly, how do contributors use the term "built?" Conspicuously few authors venture any definitions of their own or rely on those found in the literary record of enslavement. This might suggest that what the term means is taken for granted. It might also derive from a hesitancy among historical archaeologists to venture into terrain long trod by scholars in other areas of study.

Nonetheless, it is appropriate to discuss how the contributors to this volume understand and deploy the term. Speaking very broadly, the cases presented in this volume interpret the built environment as human-made landscapes that are separate and distinguished from the natural environment. This definition is not intended to be sufficient to describe all of its applications in the existing literature and it is not meant to render the distinction between human-made and natural as settled issues. Rather, it is an attempt to characterize the landscapes contributors describe when they speak of housing and the labor they write about when they discuss plantation society. Offering this definition may or may not describe all of the features of the built landscape and its actors or encompass all of the historical particularities that gave rise to these places and people. Instead, it is a prompt that invites particular questions about what might be distinctive about the built environment of slavery and what knowledge these cases might lend to other instances where landscape and inequality are bound in such ways.

To paraphrase something I have written previously, the built landscape as an archaeological problem introduces several key questions that require resolution (Hauser 2017). What "cultural" and "natural" features do we consider important when we document the landscape and how do we interpret and analyze them in relation to other landscape features (Clement 1997)? Add to that, in what ways can houses as a fundamental unit of analysis—with their attached yards, gardens, or grounds—provide insight into the array of contextual factors that shape the indeterminacies of everyday life such as background, national affiliation, or long-term practices

(Singleton 2001, 2015; Tomich 2005)? Finally, how do these documented features and units create a competing geography (Camp 2002) to the geography that colonial administrators wrote about or that plantation plats represented (Hauser 2008)? Some studies gesture toward new considerations of social space through analyzing settlement patterns in light of geographic features such as wind, water, and ease of access (Higman 1987; Handler 2002). Dan Hicks (2007b) has considered these regionwide analyses in terms of deliberate economic coordination among planters. James Delle (1998) has highlighted security and the role of intervisibility in his analysis of planters' concerns.

Contributors to this volume have produced highly nuanced accounts of enslavement, enslaved life, and colonial society that reveal that what Trouillot (2002) identified as North Atlantic universals did not describe the world as much as offer particular visions of the world. We have to ask ourselves what it is that archaeologists can contribute beyond highly detailed descriptions. Is it enough to document the location of factories and assume patterns of land use and land tenure without exploring the relationship between those buildings and other landscape phenomena, such as water access, sacred groves, or refugia? What made the work of Lydia Pulsipher, Jerome Handler, Barry Higman, Theresa Singleton, and Douglas Armstrong useful and legible beyond archaeology was its attention to what the material record can speak to. In what follows, I discuss three realms of investigation through which the built environment can be more fully explored: world archaeologies, materiality, and usable pasts. Some of these explorations can rely on the toolkits and literatures already described in the text above while others require that we take these questions more seriously and learn, perhaps, from colleagues who study pasts in the absence of a documentary record.

World Archaeologies

There is a missed opportunity to think more globally about how the built landscapes of Atlantic slavery might translate to other times and other places. How might our understanding speak to, for example, Roman slavery? Conversely, in what ways does the housing afforded to people legally defined as slaves mirror other built landscapes where slavery might not be legal but some of its predicaments are nonetheless present? Considering slavery in the vein of world archaeology might be productive, but first it requires an unpacking of terms. One of the unfortunate things about referring to slavery in a title is the enormous ideological baggage it carries. Historian Joseph Miller (2012) has described the term slavery as a historical problem. It is big and vague and it introduces anachronisms and obscuring processes for which the term has become shorthand (Miller 2003). Although it has the appearance of a transhistorical institution and invites comparison across times and spaces, its workings are best understood by studying it in a particular time and place (Finley and Shaw 1998).

All attempts by archaeologists and historians to compare arrangements of labor, belonging, and commerce in the Atlantic world of the eighteenth century with the Mediterranean world of the first century have run into difficulties of basic questions: who owns what, who does what, who gets what, and what does it mean (Taylor 2005; Mattingly 2008; Webster 2008; Marshall 2014)?

There is also the issue of scale. That is, slavery was a constellation of activities that included human trafficking, violence, commodified labor, and captivity, but many of those actions can be understood only at macroscales while their effects were felt at the most intimate levels. Although Caribbean archaeology has only a few examples of interred human remains of people who were enslaved (Corruccini et al. 1982; Watters 1994; Armstrong and Fleischman 2003; Courtaud et al. 2004; Schroeder et al. 2014), those individuals have shown how the slow violence of malnutrition and intense, repetitive labor affected the human body. Other forms of evidence are less sensitive to how such activities embodied themselves in everyday life. Lange and Handler (1985) famously cautioned archaeologists studying slavery that while "relative social/economic status or rank can be defined archaeologically," "legal or imposed status cannot" (16). We need to continually remind ourselves of this in the context of Atlantic world slavery.

In a 2009 article that challenged a long-used definition of slavery as "social death" (Patterson 1982), Vincent Brown argues that scholars need to move "from seeing slavery as a condition, to viewing enslavement as a predicament, in which enslaved Africans and their descendants never ceased to pursue the politics of belonging . . . and regeneration" (2009, 1249). This shift in focus is particularly helpful for two reasons. First, it asks us to interrogate the differences between the discourses that surrounded slavery from different vantage points. Second, and more subtly, it demands that we ask very relevant questions about agency. The built environment has been a particularly useful way to examine such questions.

It is perhaps fitting that so much of the conversation in this volume centers on the house and its social meaning because so much of the practice of historical archaeology has been concerned with the house. Whether as a unit of observation or a point of theoretical departure, the houses where enslaved peoples lived have been a central part of archaeology's interrogation of the colonial past for nearly half a century. Archaeologists have relied on the built environment as a main point of entry into understanding slave life and the African diaspora, whether as a unit of analysis for studying the settlements where slaves lived (Handler and Lange 1978), a framework for mapping the ways of doing things that enslaved people brought with them from Africa (Armstrong 1992), or a means of identifying features in a larger landscape through which enslaved people carved out their own cultural worlds (Pulsipher and Goodwin 1999).

The contributors to this volume remind us that enslaved people were found in housing that was sited across the colonial landscape, including rural (Meneketti) and urban (Odewale and Hardy) settings, colonial strongholds (Delle and Fellows), and peripheral holdings (Clay). These individuals also occupied different positions on the social spectrum, including as enslaved laborers (Kelly), as free people of color (Ahlman), as field hands (Bassett), and as artisans (Beier). This variation reminds us that the predicaments of slavery touched many people, including those who were not defined as property or never wielded a cutlass to harvest sugar cane. The predicaments of slavery ranged so considerably that it is difficult to rely even on the term "slave life" as a concept that fits all situations. Elizabeth Clay makes this important point in her exploration of the spatial data from preliminary research in French Guiana. Despite a shared spatial logic that paralleled those found in other peripheral colonies and colonies more central to France's colonial project, she posits that we have to consider the unique experiences of labor in a colony where plantations were considered failed.

What happened to the predicaments that shaped the lives of the enslaved when a shift in the legal status that established these predicaments occurred? Ahlman explores this as he discusses yards and their meanings before and after slavery. With the shift in status came a shift in lives and livelihoods of people who labored on the land. Where once they had invested income from gardening and other wage-earning activities

244 · Mark W. Hauser

into household ceramics and other forms of portable material goods, after emancipation, they invested resources in housing materials. Ahlman describes how households converted what rural sociologists have called natural capital (labor and market activities) into financial capital and in turn transformed that into social capital. I bring this up not to question such transformations—indeed, they are the stuff of household economies. Instead, I would like to ask why some decided to transform currency into shingling and others decided to hoard their coins. What do these transformed spaces enable and constrain that previous iterations do not?

Allan Meyers considers this question in his discussion of housing reform that was wrapped up in the politics of slavery and abolition in the last Bahamas. As Jerome Handler and Stephanie Bergman (2009) observed in the British West Indies, planters who wanted to placate those in the metropole who were concerned about the quality of life of the enslaved and who articulated a growing awareness of hygiene implemented a series of amelioration acts that included improvements to slave dwellings. Meyers shows how such acts appeared to have improved the condition of slave life while simultaneously conspiring to increase surveillance over the everyday activities of enslaved people. For Meyers, this means that we have to move away from broad generalizations and consider more carefully the specific relations of slavery.

These are not just methodological considerations; they have consequences about what these spaces mean. Interpretation of the built landscape is not self-evident, and yet contributors to this volume are engaged implicitly or explicitly in a project in which the built prompts questions, creates inferences in new combinations of events, and enables archaeologists to determine which questions deserve attention.

Materiality

For me, considering the built environment of slavery is conducive to thinking through materiality and slavery. Here I am using the term materiality as shorthand for the relations people have with and through things, building on a meaning Daniel Miller developed. In Miller's theory, materiality recuperates a dialectic of "objectification" in which we create "things that in turn create us." When I employ materiality in this way I index the form and substance of the context of material use over time and at specific moments when people interact face to face. This usage builds on a long tradition in historical archaeology and material culture studies. Another way that my use of the term departs from Miller's is that I favor the more loaded term "fetish" for the set of interested positions that people take with objects that Miller calls materiality.

Take Meniketti's (2006, 2015) detailed descriptions of sugar factories on Nevis. The strength of this work is the degree to which he understands the mechanism through which labor operated a factory on a plantation. One cannot help but recall the classic work by Manuel Moreno Fraginals, *El Ingenio*, which described crushing mills as "huge grinders which chewed up blacks like cane" (Fraginals 1978, 143). Here not only does the human work the machine but the machine also works the human. I wondered about the fields and landscape features outside the plantation core. Archaeologists whose methodology engages with historical and political ecologies have provided important methods for mapping the difference between theory and practice (Kosiba and Hunter 2017). As has been accomplished in other places and times, scrutinizing elements of the environment that are often hidden in plain sight, such as water, shows that land did not always yield to colonial desire (Higman 2000; Hauser 2017).

In this regard, two chapters struck me as important methodological contributions. Kenneth Kelly describes variation in a unit of analysis that many archaeologists might have too easily taken for granted: the house yard. In an essay from his seminal work *Caribbean Transformations*, Sidney Mintz (1974) explored the social functions and symbolic meanings of gardens and yards among Caribbean peasants, highlighting house yards as a spatial entity that was integral to the organization of peasant life. Mintz's most enduring insight is that daily life—cooking, cleaning, playing, independent production—took place in a yard; the house that stood in the yard was a place where people stored things and slept. In their use of this social form to analyze slave contexts archaeologists have assumed that not all yards were made the same. Geographic conditions such as slope and soil and social contexts such as population density and law contributed to differences that affect the observations archaeologists make in meaningful ways. How do we know the shape of a yard, the amount of area that needs to be covered, and what those spatial arrangements mean? In mountainous Martinique and Dominica, the cases Kelly relies on, such details were determined by the angle of a slope.

In flatter contexts, as in the location Hayden Bassett considers, such delineations are more difficult. Borrowing techniques first advanced in household archaeology of the Maya Region (Robin 2013), Bassett looks at distribution densities to map architectural and spatial variations of the yard. His work provides a caution for those of us (and I include myself) who have in the past relied on samples of features and artifacts to describe the housing of entire communities that were far too limited. Scalar fallacies are not unique to Caribbean archaeology, but what is unique is the degree to which a planter elite invested in ideologies of labor (slavery) and identity (race) deployed scalar fallacies. Bassett's chapter shows us how we might be able to generate ways to think through such relationships.

There is a tension among many of the contributions to this volume between two poles: (1) archaeology that documents built landscapes that are evident but easily overlooked because of taphonomic processes and the incompleteness of the archaeological record; and (2) archaeology that is conditioned by and works within the grand narratives that shape both archaeological and popular understandings of the built environment. The difficulty is that the first type of archaeology takes the boundary between the built and natural environments as given, while the second takes the boundary as constructed—or at least our observations of it. Considering the built environment is a crucial element of mapping the boundary between nature and culture. This is not just an intellectual project; it gets to the very heart of what made colonies that relied on the labor of slaves work.

Delle and Fellows make this point by considering the built environment as a medium through which relations of power are exercised. This chapter builds on a long-term engagement with landscape and slavery in Jamaica that views the environment as an unwitting accomplice in the workings of slavery (Delle 2014). Where previous work looked at how people attempted to manipulate "nature" to produce networks of visibility and render insecure labor relations stable, this chapter looks at how people appropriated the spaces they inhabited. By relying on a system of auto-provisioning (Hartnett and Dawdy 2013), Jamaican common law attempted to create slaves as a kind of colonial subject through the soil they tilled, the water they channeled, and the produce they raised to support themselves. Yet if we describe the environment as part of a set of discursive strategies that engendered slavery, we should also ask what else is in the field of power relations. That is, what else is hidden in plain sight?

Usable Pasts

This book is concerned with how power was exercised through buildings, features, and other kinds of landscapes. It builds on long-standing traditions in social archaeology, a subfield that compels the archaeologist to scrutinize the schematic frameworks that must be used to make sense of people's material worlds (Meskell and Preucel 2008). It requires archaeologists to interrupt assumptions and preconceived categories and exposes unexplored spaces where familiar taxa don't hold. As it interrupts, it opens up new possibilities that can be extended into different spaces and times, move into different levels of generality, and be considered from different vantage points. Work of this sort is intrinsically presentist in that it situates the past as addressing present-day concerns about "human rights, the environment, and socio-economic development" (Lane 2011, 260). While this type of scholarship has taken on a much greater role in other world areas, it can also situate archaeological research in the Caribbean.

One path forward is to acknowledge that the practice of archaeology today is inextricably caught up with similar discursive acts and explore the role of archaeology in considerations of contemporary built environments. Land is increasingly a contested resource in many parts of the Caribbean today. Growing populations, increasing urbanization, and the demands of new crops and the tourism industry have put tremendous pressure on the land and its resources. In addition, high-convection weather patterns have led to increased intensity in droughts and precipitation that have led to landslides. All of these changes have been especially difficult for the many people who still make a living on land they do not own and those who are vulnerable to changes in housing stock.

Since the 1960s, housing schemes in Caribbean nations have led to new communities in the former hinterlands of island cities in the Bahamas, Barbados, Cuba, Dominican Republic, Jamaica, Guyana, and Trinidad. While some of these schemes have happened because of a need for social housing in light of increased urbanization (Donovan and McHardy 2016) and others because of market demands from expatriates taking advantage of tax laws and banking schemes, they have resulted in an increase in housing stock where policymakers are sometimes more sensitive to political and economic expediency than they are to environmental sustainability. While there is always the risk of introducing anachronisms when one draws analogies from events in past centuries (Logan 2016), there are lessons to be gleaned from the archaeological record.

Archaeology is a database of solution. Take the example of pre-Columbian settlement patterns and material use over the long term. There is some consensus that changing climate conditions shaped those patterns. Over the past 5,000 years, sea levels have diminished, water sources have moved, and weather patterns have changed in intensity and frequency. Where people placed settlements and how they built them show responses to environments and considerations of future planning that take the vagaries of weather patterns, increased intensity of high-energy storm events, and loss of soils into account (Cooper 2012). One can also consider how people captured fresh water from precipitation in locations where there was no ground water or surface water for drinking. For example, on beachfronts, where harvesting water can be a problem because of salt, one method people used was to bury bottomless pots stacked one on top of the other. The effect of this was twofold: it created a kind of cistern and it formed a column of water where the light fresh water would rise on top of the heavier salt water (Hofman and Hoogland 2015, 109). Archaeology has shown that people create inventive ways to solve problems.

The Anthropocene has introduced new concerns that the built environment of slavery might be able to address. Thinking through recent political tragedies where hurricanes led to a loss of land, livelihoods, and lives in Dominica, the Virgin Islands, and Puerto Rico, we can ask ourselves what solutions existed in past built environments that might lend themselves to the present. Many of the chapters in this volume describe housing schemes developed in response to pressures from market and social reformers. These arrangements materialized in relatively short order and required people to make do—in the case of those categorized as slaves, in seemingly impossible conditions by today's standards. Yet through improvisational strategies (Dawdy 2008) and finding solutions to problems (Hauser 2017), enslaved people made living in those conditions possible. I would challenge future scholars to think through such solutions as we face some of our own predicaments.

References

Abrahams, Roger D., and John F. Szwed. 1983. *After Africa: Extracts from British Travel Accounts and Journals of the Seventeenth, Eighteenth, and Nineteenth Centuries Concerning the Slaves, Their Manners, and the Customs in the British West Indies*. New Haven, CT: Yale University Press.

Ahlman, Todd M. 2009. "Archaeological Investigations at Site 6 for the Proposed Christophe Harbour, St. Kitts, West Indies." Report to KHT Joint Venture, LLC., and Environmental Management Consultants (Caribbean) LTD. Missoula, MT: Historical Research Associates, Inc.

Ahlman, Todd M., Bobby R. Braly, and Gerald F. Schroedl. 2014. "Stone Artifacts and Glass Tools from Enslaved African Contexts on St. Kitts' Southeast Peninsula." *Journal of African Diaspora Archaeology and Heritage* 3(1): 1–25.

Ahlman, Todd M., Gerald F. Schroedl, and Ashley H. McKeown. 2009. "The Afro-Caribbean Ware from the Brimstone Hill Fortress, St. Kitts, West Indies: A Study in Ceramic Production." *Historical Archaeology* 43(4): 22–41.

Ahlman, Todd M., Gerald F. Schroedl, Ashley H. McKeown, Robert J. Speakman, and Michael D. Glascock. 2008. "Ceramic Production and Exchange among Enslaved Africans on St. Kitts, West Indies." *Journal of Caribbean Archaeology* 2: 109–122.

Allen, Jim. 1973. "The Archaeology of Nineteenth-Century British Imperialism: An Australian Case Study." *World Archaeology* 5(1): 44–60.

Allison, Penelope M. 1998. "The Household in Historical Archaeology." *Australasian Historical Archaeology* 16: 16–29.

———. 1999. "Introduction." In *The Archaeology of Household Activities*, edited by Penelope M. Allison, 1–18. New York: Routledge.

Anderson, Nesta. 2004. "Finding the Space between Spatial Boundaries and Social Dynamics: The Archaeology of Nested Households." In *Household Chores and Household Choices: Theorizing the Domestic Sphere in Historical Archaeology*, edited by Kerri S. Barile and Jamie C. Brandon, 109–120. Tuscaloosa: University of Alabama Press.

Armstrong, Douglas V. 1985. "An Afro-Jamaican Slave Settlement: Archaeological Investigations at Drax Hall." In *The Archaeology of Slavery and Plantation Life*, edited by Theresa A. Singleton, 261–287. Orlando: Academic Press.

———. 1990. *The Old Village and the Great House: An Archaeological and Historical Examination of Drax Hall Plantation, St. Ann's Bay, Jamaica*. Urbana: University of Illinois Press.

———. 1991. "The Afro-Jamaican House-Yard: An Archaeological and Ethnohistorical Perspective." *Florida Journal of Anthropology*, special publication 7: 51–63.

———. 1992. "African-Jamaican Housing at Seville: A Study of Spatial Transformation." *Archaeology Jamaica* 6: 51–63

———. 1998. "Cultural Transformation within Enslaved Laborer Communities in the Caribbean." In *Studies in Culture Contact: Interaction, Culture Change, and Archaeology*, edited by James G. Cusik, 378–401. Carbondale: Center for Archaeological Investigations, Southern Illinois University Press.

———. 2001. "A Venue for Autonomy: Archaeology of a Changing Cultural Landscape, the East End Community, St. John, Virgin Islands." In *Island Lives: Historical Archaeologies of the Caribbean*, edited by Paul Farnsworth, 142–164. Tuscaloosa: University of Alabama Press.

———. 2011. "Reflections on Seville: Rediscovering the African Jamaican settlements at Seville Plantation, St. Ann's Bay." In *Out of Many, One People: The Historical Archaeology of Colonial Jamaica*, edited by James A. Delle, Mark W. Hauser, and Douglas V. Armstrong, 77–101. Tuscaloosa: University of Alabama Press.

Armstrong, Douglas V., and Mark L. Fleischman. 2003. "House-Yard Burials of Enslaved Laborers in Eighteenth-Century Jamaica." *International Journal of Historical Archaeology* 7(1): 33–65.

Armstrong, Douglas V., and Mark W. Hauser. 2009. "A Sea of Diversity: Historical Archaeology in the Caribbean." In *International Handbook of Historical Archaeology*, edited by Teresita Majewski and David Gaimster, 583–612. New York: Springer.

Armstrong, Douglas V., and Kenneth G. Kelly. 2000. "Settlement Patterns and the Origins of African Jamaican Society: Seville Plantation, St. Ann's Bay Jamaica." *Ethnohistory* 47(2): 369–397.

Ashmore, Wendy, and Richard R. Wilk. 1988. "Household and Community in the Mesoamerican Past." In *Household and Community in the Mesoamerican Past*, edited by Richard R. Wilk and Wendy Ashmore, 1–28. Albuquerque: University of New Mexico Press.

Avalle [habitant cultivateur de Saint-Domingue]. 1799. *Tableau Comparatif de productions de colonies fraçaises aux Antilles avec celles des colonies anglaises, espangnoles et hollandaises, de l'année 1787 à 1788*. Paris: Goujon fils, Debray, Fuschs.

Bahama Gazette. 1800. *The Bahama Almanac and Register, for the Year 1800*. New Providence, Nassau: Office of the Royal Gazette.

Bardoe, Samantha R. 2015. "Resistance and Reform: Landscapes at Green Castle Estate, Antigua. In *The Limits of Tyranny: Archaeological Perspectives on the Struggle against New World Slavery*, edited by James A. Delle, 65–91. Knoxville: University of Tennessee Press.

Barlow, Virginia. 1993. *The Nature of the Islands: Plants and Animals of the Eastern Caribbean*. Dunedin, FL: Cruising Guide Publications.

Barone-Visigalli, Eglé, Kristen Sarge, and Régis Verwimp. 2010. *Histoire et archéologie de la Guyane française. Les jésuites de la Comté*. Matoury: Ibis Rouge.

Barret, Jean-Baptiste. 1990. "Crève-Coeur, Sainte-Anne, Martinique—site d'archéologie industrielle." In *Rapport de fouille no. 3. janvier, février, mars*, edited by Centre d'études et de recherches archéologiques. Fort-de-France, Martinique: CERA.

Bassett, Hayden F. 2016a. *Phase I Archaeological Investigation of the Tharp House Rear Yard, Falmouth, Jamaica: Archaeological Site Report Prepared for the Jamaica National Heritage Trust*. Williamsburg, VA: College of William and Mary.

———. 2016b. "The House-Yard Revisited: Domestic Landscapes of Enslaved People in Plantation Jamaica." Paper presented at the annual meeting of the Society for Historical Archaeology, Washington, DC

———. 2017. "The Archaeology of Enslavement in Plantation Jamaica: A Study of Community Dynamics among the Enslaved People of Good Hope Estate, 1775–1838." PhD diss., College of William and Mary.

Bates, Lynsey A. 2016. "Provisioning and Marketing: Surplus and Access on Jamaican Sugar Estates." In *Archaeologies of Slavery and Freedom in the Caribbean: Exploring the Spaces in Between*, edited by Lynsey A. Bates John M. Chenoweth, and James A. Delle, 79–100. Gainesville: University Press of Florida.

Bates, Lynsey A., John M. Chenoweth, and James A. Delle, eds. 2016. *Archaeologies of Slavery and Freedom in the Caribbean: Exploring the Spaces in Between*. Gainesville: University Press of Florida.

Battle-Baptiste, Whitney. 2007. "'In this here place': Interpreting Enslaved Homeplaces." In *Archaeology of Atlantic Africa and the African Diaspora*, edited by Akin Ogundiran and Toyin Falola, 233–248. Bloomington: Indiana University Press.

———. 2011. *Black Feminist Archaeology*. Walnut Creek, CA: Left Coast Press.

Baxter, Jane, and John Burton. 2011. "Farquharson's Plantation Revisited: New Historical and Archaeological Insights from Two Seasons at Prospect Hill." *Journal of the Bahamas Historical Society* 33: 17–26.

Beaudry, Mary C. 2015. "Houses beyond the House: On the Archaeology and Materiality of Historical Households." In *Beyond the Walls: New Perspectives on the Archaeology of Historical Households*, edited by Kevin R. Fogle, James A. Nyman, and Mary C. Beaudry, 1–22. Gainesville: University Press of Florida.

Beckford, William. 1790. *A Descriptive Account of the Island of Jamaica: With Remarks upon the Cultivation of Sugar-Cane, throughout the Different Seasons of the Year, and Chiefly Considered in a Picturesque Point of View*. Vol. 2. London: T. and J. Egerton.

Beier, Zachary J. M. 2011. "Initial Feasibility and Reconnaissance at the Cabrits Garrison, Dominica." In *Proceedings of the XXIII Congress of the International Association for Caribbean Archaeology, June 29–July 3, 2009, Antigua*, edited by Samantha A. Rebovich, 233–243. Antigua: Dockyard Museum, English Harbor.

———. 2014. "The Cabrits Garrison." In *The Encyclopedia of Caribbean Archaeology*, edited by Basil Reid and R. Grant Gilmore III, 83–84. Gainesville: University Press of Florida.

———. 2017. "'All the King's Men': Slavery and Soldiering at the Cabrits Garrison, Dominica (1763–1854)." PhD diss., Syracuse University.

Bender, Donald. 1967. "A Refinement of the Concept of the Household: Families, Co-Residence, and Domestic Functions." *American Anthropologist* 69(5): 493–504.

Bénot, Yves. 2003. "The Chain of Slave Insurrections in the Caribbean, 1789–1791." In *The Abolitions of Slavery: From L. F. Sonthonax to Victor Schoelcher, 1793, 1794, 1848*, edited by Marcel Dorigny, 147–154. New York: Berghahn Books.

Berdoulay, Vincent. 1989. "Place, Meaning, and Discourse in French Language Geography." In *The Power of Place: Bringing Together Geographical and Sociological Imaginations*, edited by John A. Agnew and James S. Duncan, 124–139. London: Unwin Hyman.

Berthelot, Jack, and Martine Gaumé. 1985. "Introduction." In *Caribbean Style*, edited by Suzanne Slesin, Stafford Cliff, Jack Berthelot, Martine Gaume and Daniel Rozensztroch, 1–3. New York: Clarkson Potter.

———. 2002. *Kaz Antiyé jan moun ka rété*. Guadeloupe: Editions Perspectives Créoles.

Besson, Jean. 2002. *Martha Brae's Two Histories: European Expansion and Caribbean Culture-Building in Jamaica*. Chapel Hill: University of North Carolina Press.

Besson, Jean, and Janet Momsen, eds. 2007. *Caribbean Land and Development Revisited*. New York: Palgrave MacMillan.

Blackburn, Robin. 1988. *The Overthrow of Colonial Slavery, 1776–1848*. London: Verso.

———. 1997. *The Making of New World Slavery: From the Baroque to the Modern, 1492–1800*. London: Verso.

Boland, Nigel. 1981. "Systems of Domination after Slavery: The Control of Land and Labor in the British West Indies after 1838." *Comparative Studies in Society and History* 23(4): 591–619.

Bon-Harper, Sara. 2009. "Spatial Variation and Activity Areas at Monticello's Site 8." Poster presented at the annual meeting of the Society of American Archaeology, Atlanta.

———. 2010. "Yard Space: Comparisons of General Activity Areas Between Historic Period Social Groups." Poster presented at the annual meeting of the Society of American Archaeology, St. Louis.

Bossart, Johann Jakob, ed. 1987. *C. G. A. Oldendorp's History of the Mission of the Evangelical Brethren on the Caribbean Islands of St. Thomas, St. Croix, and St. John*. Translated by Arnold R. Highfield and Vladimir Barac. Ann Arbor, MI: Karoma Publishers.

Bousquet-Bressolier, Catherine, Monique Pelletier, and Danièle Bégot. 1998. *La Martinique de Moreau du Temple, 1770*. Paris: Comité des travaux historiques et scientifiques.

Boyer, William W. 2010. *America's Virgin Islands: A History of Human Rights and Wrongs*. Durham: Carolina Academic Press.

Brady. 1994. "Observations upon the State of Negro Slavery in the Island of Santa Cruz, the Principal of the Danish West India Colonies: With Miscellaneous Remarks upon Subjects Relating to the West India Question, and a Notice of Santa Cruz." [1829]. In *The Kamina Folk: Slavery and Slave Life in the Danish West Indies*, edited by George F. Tyson and Arnold R. Highfield, 159–180. Charlotte Amalie, USVI: Virgin Islands Humanities Council.

Bridenbaugh Carl, and Roberta Bridenbaugh. 1972. *No Peace beyond the Line: The English in the Caribbean, 1624–1690*. New York: Oxford University Press.

Britt, Sean F. 2010. "Fueling the Fire: Examining Caribbean Colonial Relations between Humans and the Environment." *Historical Archaeology* 44(3): 54–68.

Brooker, Colin. 2011. "John Wood on Long Island, the Bahamas, 1790–1802: Preliminary Notes on the Architecture of a Loyalist Plantation." *Journal of the Bahamas Historical Society* 33: 28–37.

Brown, Christopher Leslie, and Philip D. Morgan, eds. 2006. *Arming Slaves: From Classical Times to the Modern Age.* New Haven, CT: Yale University Press.

Brown, Vincent. 2009. "Social Death and Political Life in the Study of Slavery." *American Historical Review* 114(5): 1231–1249.

Buckley, Roger Norman. 1979. *Slaves in Red Coats: The British West India Regiments, 1795–1815.* New Haven, CT: Yale University Press.

———. 1980. "'Black Man': The Mutiny of the 8th (British) West India Regiment: A Microcosm of War and Slavery in the Caribbean." *Jamaican Historical Review* 12: 52–76.

———. 1998. *The British army in the West Indies: Society and the Military in the Revolutionary Age.* Gainesville: University Press of Florida.

Buée, William Urban. 1797. "A Narrative of the Clove Tree in the Island of Dominica." *Journals of the Assembly of Jamaica* 10: 70–74.

Buisseret, David. 1971. *The Fortifications of Kingston, 1655–1914.* Jamaica: Bolivar Press.

———. 1980. *Historic Architecture of the Caribbean.* London: Heinemann.

———. 2008. *The Fortifications of Jamaica.* Elsa Goveia Memorial Lecture series. Kingston: Department of History and Archaeology, University of the West Indies Mona, Kingston.

Butzer, Karl, and Elizabeth Butzer. 2000. "Domestic Architecture in Early Colonial Mexico: Material Culture as (Sub)Text." In *Cultural Encounters with the Environment: Enduring and Evolving Geographic Themes,* edited by Alexander B. Murphy and Douglas L. Johnson, 17–37. Lanham, MD: Rowan and Littlefield.

Caines, Clement. 1801. *Letters on the Cultivation of the Otaheite Cane; The Manufacture of Sugar and Rum; the Saving of Melasses; the Care and Preservation of Stock; and the Attention and Anxiety Which Is Due to Negroes.* London: Robinson.

Camp, Stephanie M. H. 2002. "'I could not stay there': Enslaved Women, Truancy, and the Geography of Everyday Forms of Resistance in the Antebellum Plantation South." *Slavery and Abolition* 23(3): 1–20.

Canning, George. 1824. *Speech of the Right Hon. George Canning, Secretary of State for Foreign Affairs, &c. &c. &c. on Laying before the House of Commons the Papers in Explanation of the Measures Adopted by His Majesty's Government with a View of Ameliorating the Condition of the Negro Slaves in the West Indies, on Wednesday, the Seventeenth of March, 1824.* London: Hatchard and Son.

Carballo, David M. 2011. "Advances in the Household Archaeology of Highland Mesoamerica." *Journal of Archaeological Research* 19(2): 133–189.

Carrington, Selwyn H. H. 2002. *The Sugar Industry and the Abolition of the Slave Trade, 1775–1810.* Gainesville: University Press of Florida.

Casagrande, Fabrice. 2007. *Saint-Claude "Bélost-La Diotte."* Paris: Institut national de recherches archéologiques préventives.

———. 2012. *Habitation Céron, Martinique, Le Prêcheur*. Paris: Institut national de recherches archéologiques préventives.

Casagrande, Fabrice, and Nathalie Serrand. 2008. *Deshaies Guyonneau, Rivière Forban*. Paris: Institut national de recherches archéologiques préventives.

Cazelles, Nathalie. 2015. *Les habitations coloniales de la commune de Montsinéry-Tonnégrande: La roucouerie de l'habitation Risquetout, la sucrerie de l'habitation la Charlotte*. Cayenne: Service régional de l'archéologie Guyane.

Chalmers, George. 1816. *Proofs and Demonstrations How Much the Proposed Registry of Colonial Negroes Is Unfounded and Uncalled For: Comprehending, the Reports and Resolves of the Bahama Assembly, on the Principle and Detail of the Proposed Registry*. London: Luke Hansard & Sons for Thomas Egerton.

Chan, Alexandra. 2007. *Slavery in the Age of Reason: Archaeology at a New England Farm*. Knoxville: University of Tennessee Press.

Chapman, William. 1991. "Slave Villages in the Danish West Indies: Changes of the Late Eighteenth and Early Nineteenth Centuries." In *Perspectives in Vernacular Architecture*, vol. 4, edited by Thomas Carter and Bernard L. Herman, 108–120. Columbia: University of Missouri Press.

———. 2010. "Slave Villages in the Danish West Indies: Changes of the Late Eighteenth and Early Nineteenth Centuries." In *Cabin, Quarter, Plantation: Architecture and Landscapes of North American Slavery*, edited by Clifton Ellis and Rebecca Ginsburg, 99–120. New Haven, CT: Yale University Press.

Chenoweth, Michael. 2006. "A Reassessment of Historical Atlantic Basin Tropical Cyclone Activity, 1700–1855." *Climate Change* 76(1–2): 169–240.

Chivallon, Christine. 2007. "The Contested Existence of a Peasantry in Martinique: Scientific Discourses, Controversies, and Evidence." In *Caribbean Land and Development Revisited*, edited by Jean Besson and Janet Momsen, 159–173. New York: Palgrave MacMillan.

Churchill, Awnsham, and John Churchill. 1732. *A Collection of Voyages and Travels, Some Now First Printed from Original Manuscripts, Others Now First Published in English*. Vol. 3. London: Walthoe, Wotton, Birt, Browne, Osborn, Shuckburgh, and Lintot.

Cissel, William Fleming. 2000. "The Danish West India & Guinea Company Warehouse, Christiansted National Historic Site, Proposed Restoration and Slave Trade Museum." Unpublished manuscript.

Clay, Elizabeth C. 2016. "From the Margin of Empire: Clove and Cacao Production in French Guiana, 1802–1848." Paper presented at the biennial meeting of the European Early American Studies Association, Paris.

Clement, Christopher Ohm. 1997. "Settlement Patterning on the British Caribbean Island of Tobago." *Historical Archaeology* 31(2): 93–106.

Collins, David. 1803. *Practical Rules for the Management and Medical Treatment of Negroe Slaves, in the Sugar Colonies, by a Professional Planter*. London: J. Barfield for Vernor and Hood.

Commissioners of Correspondence. 1823. *An Official Letter from the Commissioners of Correspondence, of the Bahama Islands, to George Chalmers, Esq., Colonial Agent Concerning the Proposed Abolition of Slavery in The West Indies*. Liverpool: S. H. Hankey.

Cooper, Jago. 2012. "Fail to Prepare, Then Prepare to Fail: Rethinking Threat, Vulnerability, and Mitigation in the Precolumbian Caribbean." In *Surviving Sudden Environmental Change: Answers from Archaeology*, edited by Jago Cooper and Payson Sheets, 91–114. Boulder: University Press of Colorado.

Corruccini, Robert S., Jerome S. Handler, Robert J. Mutaw, and Frederick W. Lange. 1982. "Osteology of a Slave Burial Population from Barbados, West Indies." *American Journal of Physical Anthropology* 59(4): 443–459.

Courtaud, Patrice, Thomas Romon, Lot Belmont, and Maison Jersier. 2004. "Le Site d'Anse Sainte-Marguerite (Guadeloupe, Grande Terre). Presentation d'un cimetiere d'époque coloniale." *Journal of Caribbean Archaeology* 1: 58–67.

Crain, Edward E. 1994. *Historic Architecture in the Caribbean Islands*. Gainesville: University Press of Florida.

Craton, Michael. 1978. *Searching for the Invisible Man: Slaves and Plantation Life in Jamaica*. Cambridge, MA: Harvard University Press.

Craton, Michael, and D. Gail Saunders. 1992. *Islanders in the Stream: A History of the Bahamian People*. Vol. 1. Athens: University of Georgia Press.

Crocker, A. 1797. "On Cottages." In *Communications to the Board of Agriculture; On Subjects Relative to the Husbandry, and Internal Improvement of the Country*, vol. 1, 114–117. London: George Nicol.

Croucher, Sarah K. 2015. *Capitalism and Cloves: An Archaeology of Plantation Life on Nineteenth-Century Zanzibar*. New York: Springer.

Crowley, John E. 2001. *The Invention of Comfort: Sensibilities and Design in Early Modern Britain and Early America*. Baltimore, MD: Johns Hopkins University Press.

Crumley, Carole. 1987. "A Dialectical Critique of Heterarchy." In *Power Relations and State Formation*, edited by Thomas C. Patterson and Christine Ward Gailey, 155–169. Washington, DC: American Anthropological Association.

Crumley, Carole, and William H. Marquardt. 1990. "Landscape: A Unifying Concept in Regional Analysis." In *Interpreting Space: GIS and Archaeology*, edited by Kathleen Allen, Stanton Green, and Ezra Zubrow, 73–79. London: Taylor and Francis.

Curtin, Philip D. 1998. *The Rise and Fall of the Plantation Complex: Essays in Atlantic History*. Cambridge: Cambridge University Press.

Dallas, Robert Charles. 1803. *The History of the Maroons: From Their Origin to the Establishment of Their Chief Tribe at Sierra Leone*. London: A. Strahan Publishing.

D'Anjou, Leo. 1996. *Social Movements and Cultural Change: The First Abolition Campaign Revisited*. New York: Aldine de Gruyter.

Davis, David Brion. 1975. *The Problem of Slavery in the Age of Revolution, 1770–1823*. Ithaca, NY: Cornell University Press.

Dawdy, Shannon Lee. 2008. *Building the Devil's Empire: French Colonial New Orleans*. Chicago: University of Chicago Press.

Deagan, Kathleen A. 1988. "The Archaeology of the Spanish Contact Period in the Caribbean." *Journal of World Prehistory* 2(2): 187–233.

———. 1995. *Puerto Real: The Archaeology of a Sixteenth-Century Spanish Town in Hispaniola*. Gainesville: University of Florida Press.

———. 2010. "Strategies of Adjustment: Spanish Defense of the Circum-Caribbean Colonies, 1493–1600." In *First Forts: Essays on the Archaeology of Proto-Colonial Fortifications*, edited by Eric Klingelhofer, 17–39. Boston: Brill.

Deagan, Kathleen A., and José María Cruxent. 2002. *Archaeology at La Isabella: America's First European Town*. New Haven, CT: Yale University.

Deetz, James. 1977. *In Small Things Forgotten: The Archaeology of Everyday Life in Early America*. New York: Anchor Books.

———. 1990. "Landscapes as Cultural Statements." In *Earth Patterns: Essays in Landscape Archaeology*, edited by William M. Kelso and Rachel Most, 1–4. Charlottesville: University Press of Virginia.

Delle, James A. 1994. "The Settlement Pattern of Sugar Plantations on St. Eustatius." In *Spatial Patterning in Historical Archaeology: Selected Studies of Settlement*, edited by D. W. Linebaugh and G. G. Robinson, 33–61. Williamsburg, VA: William and Mary Center for Archaeological Research.

———. 1998. *An Archaeology of Social Space: Analyzing Coffee Plantations in Jamaica's Blue Mountains*. New York: Plenum Press.

———. 1999. "The Landscapes of Class Negotiation on Coffee Plantations in the Blue Mountains of Jamaica, 1790–1850." *Historical Archaeology* 33(1): 136–158.

———. 2002. "Power and Landscape: Spatial Dynamics in Early Nineteenth-Century Jamaica." In *The Dynamics of Power*, edited by Maria O'Donovan, 341–361. Carbondale: Center for Archaeological Investigations, Southern Illinois University Press.

———. 2011. "The Habitus of Jamaican Plantation Landscapes." In *Out of Many, One People: The Historical Archaeology of Colonial Jamaica*, edited by James A. Delle, Mark W. Hauser, and Douglas V. Armstrong, 122–143. Tuscaloosa: University of Alabama Press.

———. 2014. *The Colonial Caribbean: Landscapes of Power in Jamaica's Plantation System*. Cambridge: Cambridge University Press.

Delle, James A., and Kristen R. Fellows. 2014. "Death and Burial at Marshall's Pen, a Jamaican Coffee Plantation, 1814–1839: Examining the End of Life at the End of Slavery." *Slavery and Abolition* 35(3): 474–492.

Delle, James A., Mark W. Hauser, and Douglas V. Armstrong, eds. 2011. *Out of Many, One People: The Historical Archaeology of Colonial Jamaica*. Tuscaloosa: University of Alabama Press.

De Souza, Marcos André Torres. 2016. "Behind Closed Doors: Space, Experience, and Materiality in the Inner Areas of Brazilian Slave Houses." *Journal of African Diaspora Archaeology and Heritage* 5(2): 147–173.

Donoghue, Eddie. 2007. *Negro Slavery: Slave Society and Slave Life in the Danish West Indies*. Bloomington, IN: AuthorHouse.

Donovan, Michael G., and Pauline McHardy. 2016. *The State of Social Housing in Six Caribbean Countries*. IDB Monograph 426. Washington, DC: Inter-American Development Bank.

Dookhan, Isaac. 1994. *A History of the Virgin Islands of the United States*. Kingston: Canoe Press.

Dorigny, Marcel, ed. 2003. *The Abolitions of Slavery: From L. F. Sonthonax to Victor Schoelcher, 1793, 1794, 1848*. New York: Berghahn Books.

Douet, James. 1998. *British Barracks, 1600–1914: Their Architecture and Role in Society.* London: Stationery Office.

Douglass, John G., and Nancy Gonlin. 2012. "The Household as Analytical Unit: Case Studies from the Americas." In *Ancient Households of the Americas*, edited by John G. Douglass and Nancy Gonlin, 1–46. Boulder: University of Colorado Press.

Dubois, Laurent. 2004. *A Colony of Citizens: Revolution and Slave Emancipation in the French Caribbean, 1787–1804.* Chapel Hill: University of North Carolina Press.

———. 2006. "Citizen Soldiers: Emancipation and Military Service in the Revolutionary French Caribbean." In *Arming Slaves: From Classical Times to the Modern Age*, edited by Christopher Leslie Brown and Philip D. Morgan, 233–254. New Haven, CT: Yale University Press.

Dunn, Richard S. 1972. *Sugar and Slaves: The Rise of the Planter Class in the English West Indies, 1624–1713.* Chapel Hill: University of North Carolina Press.

Dunnell, Robert C. 1992. "The Notion Site." In *Space, Time, and Archaeological Landscapes*, edited by Jacqueline Rossignol and Luann Wandsnider, 21–41. New York: Plenum Press.

Edwards, Bryan. 1793. *The History, Civil and Commercial, of the British Colonies in the West Indies, in Two Volumes.* Vol. 1, 2nd ed. London: John Stockdale.

———. 1801. *The History, Civil and Commercial, of the British Colonies in the West Indies, in Two Volumes.* Vol. 2. 3rd ed. London: John Stockdale.

Edwards-Ingram, Ywone. 1999. "The Recent Archaeology of Enslaved Africans and African Americans." In *Old and New Worlds*, edited by Geoff Egan and R. L. Michael, 156–164. Oxford: Oxbow Books.

Ellis, Clifton. 2010. "Building for 'Our Family, Black and White': The Changing Form of the Slave House in Antebellum Virginia." In *Cabin, Quarter, Plantation: Architecture and Landscapes of North American Slavery*, edited by Clifton Ellis and Rebecca Ginsburg, 141–155. New Haven, CT: Yale University Press.

Espersen, Ryan. 2013. "Water Use at Palmetto Point and Middle Island, Saba, Dutch Caribbean: A Modeled Approach for Settlement Viability." *International Journal of Historical Archaeology* 17: 806–827.

Fairbanks, Charles H. 1974. "The Kingsley Slave Cabins in Duval County, Florida, 1968." *Conference for Historic Sites Archaeology Papers* 7: 62–93.

Farnsworth, Paul. 1999. "From the Past to the Present: An Exploration of the Formation of African-Bahamian Identity during Enslavement." In *African Sites Archaeology in the Caribbean*, edited by Jay B. Haviser, 94–130. Princeton, NJ: Markus Wiener.

———. 2001. "'Negro houses built of stone besides others watl'd + plastered': The Creations of a Bahamian Tradition." In *Island Lives: Historical Archaeologies of the Caribbean*, edited by Paul Farnsworth, 235–271. Tuscaloosa: University of Alabama Press.

Fellows, Kristen R., and James A. Delle. 2015. "Marronage and the Dialectics of Spatial Sovereignty in Colonial Jamaica." In *Current Perspectives on the Archaeology of African Slavery in Latin America*, edited by Pedro P. A. Funari and Charles E. Orser, 117–132. New York: Springer.

Ferguson, Leland. 1992. *Uncommon Ground: Archaeology and Early African America, 1650–1800.* Washington, DC: Smithsonian Institution Press.

Fesler, Garrett R. 2004. "From Houses to Homes: An Archaeological Case Study of Household Formation at the Utopia Slave Quarter, ca. 1675–1775." PhD diss., University of Virginia.

Finley, Moses I., and Brent D. Shaw. 1998. *Ancient Slavery and Modern Ideology*. Princeton, NJ: Markus Wiener.

Flohic, Jean-Luc, ed. 1998. *Le patrimoine des communes de la Guadeloupe—Antilles*. Charenton-le-Pont, France: Editions Flohic.

Fortescue, John W., ed. (1899) 1964. *Calendar of State Papers, Colonial Series, America and West Indies: 1685–1688*. Vaduz: Krauss Reprint LTD.

———, ed. (1901) 1964. *Calendar of State Papers, Colonial Series, America and West Indies, 1689–1692*. Vaduz: Krauss Reprint LTD.

Foster, Gerald. 2004. *American Houses: A Field Guide to the Architecture of the Home*. Boston: Houghton Mifflin.

Fradgley, Nigel. 2001. "Montravers House 2001." In *Nevis Heritage Project Interim Report 2001*, edited by Elaine Morris, Roger Leech, Andrew Crosby, Tessa Machling, and Bruce Williams, 76–80. Southampton: The Nevis Heritage Project, University of Southampton.

Fraginals, Manuel Moreno. 1978. *El ingenio: complejo económico social cubano del azúcar*. Havana: Editorial de Ciencias Sociales.

Franklin, Maria. 2004. *An Archaeological Study of the Rich Neck Slave Quarter and Enslaved Domestic Life*. Williamsburg, VA: Colonial Williamsburg Foundation.

Galle, Jillian E. 2011. "Assessing the Impacts of Time, Agricultural Cycles, and Demography on the Consumer Activities of Enslaved Men and Women in Eighteenth-Century Jamaica and Virginia." In *Out of Many, One People: The Historical Archaeology of Colonial Jamaica*, edited by James A. Delle, Mark W. Hauser, and Douglas V. Armstrong, 211–242. Tuscaloosa: University of Alabama Press.

Gaspar, David Barry. 1992. "Working the System: Antigua Slaves and Their Struggle to Live." *Slavery and Abolition* 13(3): 131–155.

Gay, Edwin F. 1929. "Notes and Documents: Letters from a Sugar Plantation in Nevis, 1723–1732." *Journal of Economic and Business History* 1: 149–173.

Gerace, Kathy D. 1982. "Three Loyalist Plantations on San Salvador, Bahamas." *Florida Anthropologist* 35(4): 216–222.

Gibson, Heather R. 2007. "Daily Practice and Domestic Economies in Guadeloupe: An Archaeological and Historical Study." PhD diss., Syracuse University.

———. 2009. "Domestic Economy and Daily Practice in Guadeloupe: Historical Archaeology at La Mahaudière Plantation." *International Journal of Historical Archaeology* 13(1): 27–44.

Glassie, Henry. 1976. *Folk Housing in Middle Virginia. A Structural Analysis of Historic Artifacts*. Knoxville: University of Tennessee Press.

Goody, Jack. 1972. "The Evolution of the Family." In *Household and Family in Past Time*, edited by Peter Laslett and Richard Wall, 103–124. Cambridge: Cambridge University Press.

Goucher, Candice. 1999. "African-Caribbean Metal Technology: Forging Cultural Survivals in the Atlantic World." In *African Sites Archaeology in the Caribbean*, edited by Jay B. Haviser, 143–156. Princeton, NJ: Markus Wiener.

Goveia, Elsa. 1993. "The West Indian Slave Laws of the Eighteenth Century." In *Caribbean Slave Society and Economy: A Student Reader*, edited by Hilary Beckles and Verene Shepherd, 346–362. New York: The New Press.

Gravette, Andrew. 2000. *Architectural Heritage of the Caribbean: An A–Z of Historic Buildings*. Kingston: Ian Randle.

Haagensen, Reimert. 1994. "Beskrivelse over Eylandet St. Croix I America I Vest-Indien: Description of the Island of St. Croix." [1758]. In *The Kamina Folk: Slavery and slave life in the Danish West Indies*, edited by George F. Tyson and Arnold R. Highfield, 20–46. Charlotte Amalie, USVI: Virgin Islands Humanities Council.

Hall, Neville A. T. 1992. *Slave Society in the Danish West Indies: St. Thomas, St. John, and St. Croix*. Baltimore, MD: John Hopkins University Press.

Handler, Jerome S. 1984. "Freedmen and Slaves in the Barbados Militia." *Journal of Caribbean History* 19: 1–25.

———. 2002. "Plantation Slave Settlements in Barbados, 1650s to 1834." In *In the Shadow of the Plantation: Caribbean History and Legacy*, edited by Alvin Thompson, 121–158. Kingston: Ian Randle.

Handler, Jerome S., and Stephanie Bergman. 2009. "Vernacular Houses and Domestic Material Culture on Barbadian Sugar Plantations, 1640–1838." *Journal of Caribbean History* 43(1): 1–36.

Handler, Jerome S., and Fredrick W. Lange. 1978. *Plantation Slavery in Barbados: An Archaeological and Historical Investigation*. Cambridge, MA: Harvard University Press.

Handler, Jerome S., and Diane Wallman. 2014. "Production Activities in the Household Economies of Plantation Slaves: Barbados and Martinique, Mid-1600s to Mid-1800s." *International Journal of Historical Archaeology* 18(3): 441–466.

Hanks, William F. 1990. *Referential Practice: Language and Lived Space among the Maya*. Chicago: University of Chicago Press.

Hardy, Meredith D. 2011. *Christiansted National Historic Site: Archaeological Overview and Assessment*. St. Croix, USVI: National Park Service.

Hart, Richard. 1994. "Good Hope, Jamaica: 1744–1994." Unpublished manuscript on file at National Library of Jamaica.

Hartnett, Alexandra, and Shannon Lee Dawdy. 2013. "The Archaeology of Illegal and Illicit Economies." *Annual Review of Anthropology* 42: 37–51.

Hauser, Mark W. 2007. "Between Rural and Urban: The Archaeology of Slavery and Informal Markets in Eighteenth Century Jamaica." In *Archaeology of Atlantic Africa and the African Diaspora*, edited by Akin Ogundiran and Toyin Falola, 292–310. Bloomington: Indiana University Press.

———. 2008. *An Archaeology of Black Markets: Local Ceramics and Economies in Eighteenth-Century Jamaica*. Gainesville: University Press of Florida.

———. 2009. "Scale Locality and the Caribbean Historical Archaeology." *International Journal of Historical Archaeology* 13: 3–11.

———. 2011. "Uneven Topographies: Archaeology of Plantations and Caribbean Slave

Economies." In *The Archaeology of Capitalism in Colonial Contexts*, edited by Sarah K. Croucher and Lindsay Weiss, 121–142. New York: Springer.

———. 2015a. "Objects without History: Substance and Portability in New West Indian Plantations." Paper presented at the annual meeting of the American Anthropological Association, Denver.

———. 2015b. "The Infrastructure of Nature's Island: Settlements, Networks and Economy of Two Plantations in Colonial Dominica." *International Journal of Historical Archaeology* 19(3): 601–622.

———. 2017. "A Political Ecology of Water and Enslavement: Water Ways in Eighteenth-Century Caribbean Plantations." *Current Anthropology* 58(2): 227–256.

Hauser, Mark W., and Dan Hicks. 2007. "Colonialism and Landscape: Power, Materiality and Scales of Analysis in Caribbean Historical Archaeology." In *Envisioning Landscape: Situations and Standpoints in Archaeology and Heritage*, edited by Dan Hicks, Laura McAtackney, and Graham Fairclough, 251–274. Walnut Creek, CA: Left Coast Press.

Haviser, Jay B., ed. 1999. "Social Repercussions of Slavery as Evident in African-Curaçaoan *Kunuku* Houses." In *Proceedings of the Seventeenth Congress of the International Association for Caribbean Archaeology*, edited by J. Winter, 358–375. Rockville Center, NY: Molloy College.

———. 2010. "The 'Old Netherlands Style' and Seventeenth-Century Dutch Fortifications of the Caribbean." In *First Forts: Essays on the Archaeology of Proto-Colonial Fortifications*, edited by Eric Klingelhofer, 167–187. Boston: Brill.

Hayden, Bryan, and Aubrey Cannon. 1983. "Where the Garbage Goes: Refuse Disposal in the Maya Highlands." *Journal of Anthropological Archaeology* 2(2): 117–163.

Headlam, Cecil, ed. (1910) 1964. *Calendar of State Papers, 1701. Colonial Series, America and West Indies*. Vaduz: Krauss Reprint LTD.

Heath, Barbara J., and Amber Bennett. 2000. "'The little spots allow'd them': African-American Yards." *Historical Archaeology* 34(2): 38–55.

Hendon, Julia A. 2006. "The Engendered Household." In *Handbook of Gender in Archaeology*, edited by Sarah M. Nelson, 171–198. Lanham, MD: Alta Mira Press.

———. 2008. "Living and Working at Home: The Social Archaeology of Household Production and Social Relations." In *Companion to Social Archaeology*, edited by Lynn Meskell and Robert W. Preucel, 272–286. New York: Wiley & Blackwell.

Hendon, Julia A., Rosemary A. Joyce, and Russell Sheptak. 2009. "Heterarchy as Complexity: Archaeology in Yoro, Honduras." Paper presented at the annual meeting of the Society for American Archaeology, St. Louis.

Henry, Yann, Frank Bigot, Isabelle Gabriel, Sandrine Grouard, and Noémie Tomadini. 2009. *Macaille: Rue des Pommes Canelles, Anse Bertrand, Guadeloupe*. Basse Terre: Société Hadès.

Herman, Bernard L. 2005. *Town House: Architecture and Material Life in the Early American City, 1780–1830*. Chapel Hill: University of North Carolina Press.

Heuman, Gad J. 1994. *The Killing Time: The Morant Bay Rebellion in Jamaica*. Knoxville: University of Tennessee Press.

Hicks, Dan. 2007a. "'Material improvements': The Archaeology of Estate Landscapes in the British Leeward Islands, 1713–1838." In *Estate Landscapes: Design, Improvement and Power in the Post-Medieval Landscape*, edited by Jonathan Finch and Kate Giles, 205–227. Rochester, NY: Boydell and Brewer.

———. 2007b. *"The garden of the world": An Historical Archaeology of Sugar Landscapes in the Eastern Caribbean*. Oxford: British Archaeological Reports Ltd.

Higham, Charles. 1921. *The Development of the Leeward Islands under the Restoration, 1660–1688*. Cambridge: Cambridge University Press.

Highfield, Arnold. 2009. *Time Longa' Dan Twine: Notes of the Culture, History, and People of the US Virgin Islands*. Cristiansted, VI: Antilles Press.

———. 2012. *Sea Grapes and Kennips: The Story of Christiansted Town and Its People*. St. Croix, USVI: Antilles Press.

———. 2018. *The Cultural History of the American Virgin Islands and the Danish West Indies: A Companion Guide*. Christiansted, VI: Antilles Press.

Higman, Barry W. 1974. "A Report on Excavations at Montpelier and Roehampton." *Jamaica Journal* 8(1–2): 40–45.

———. 1978. "African and Creole Slave Family Patterns in Trinidad." *Journal of Family History* 3(2): 163–178.

———. 1987. "The Spatial Economy of Jamaican Sugar Plantations: Cartographic Evidence from the Eighteenth and Nineteenth Centuries." *Journal of Historical Geography* 13(1): 17–19.

———. 1995. *Slave Population and Economy in Jamaica, 1807–1834*. Kingston: University of the West Indies Press.

———. 1998. *Montpelier, Jamaica: A Plantation Community in Slavery and Freedom, 1739–1912*. Kingston: University of the West Indies Press.

———. 2000. "The Sugar Revolution." *Economic History Review* 2: 213–236.

———. 2001. *Jamaica Surveyed: Plantation Maps and Plans of the Eighteenth and Nineteenth Centuries*. Kingston: University of the West Indies Press.

Hildebrand, Matthieu. 2016. *Parking du sentier de Loyola. Rapport de diagnostic archéologique*. INRAP.

Hilton, John. 1675. "Relation of the First Settlement of St. Christopher's and Nevis, by John Hilton, Storekeeper and Chief Gunner of Nevis." In *Colonising Expeditions to the West Indies and Guiana, 1623–1667*, edited by Vincent T. Harlow, 1–53. London: Hakluyt Society.

Hirth, Kenneth. 1993. "The Household as an Analytical Unit: Problems in Method and Theory." In *Prehispanic Domestic Units in Western Mesoamerica: Studies of the Household, Compound, and Residence*, edited by Robert Santley and Kenneth Hirth, 21–36. Boca Raton, FL: CRC Press.

Hobson, Daphne Louise. 2007. "The Domestic Architecture of the Earliest British Colonies in the American Tropics: A Study of the Houses of the Caribbean 'Leeward' Islands of St. Christopher, Nevis, Antigua, and Montserrat,1624–1726." PhD diss., Georgia Institute of Technology.

Hochschild, Adam. 2005. *Bury the Chains: Prophets and Rebels in the Fight to Free an Empire's Slaves*. New York: Mariner.

Hodder, Ian. 2012. *Entangled: An Archaeology of the Relationships between Humans and Things*. Oxford: Wiley and Blackwell.

Hofman, Corinne, and Menno Hoogland. 2015. "Beautiful Tropical Islands in the Caribbean Sea: Human Responses to Floods and Droughts and the Indigenous Archaeological Heritage of the Caribbean." In *Water and Heritage: Material, Conceptual, and Spiritual Connections*, edited by Willem Willems and Henk van Schaik, 99–119. Leiden: Sidestone Press.

Honychurch, Lennox. 2013. *Dominica's Cabrits and Prince Rupert's Bay*. Dominica: Island Heritage Initiatives Ltd.

Hood, J. Edward. 1996. "Social Relations and the Cultural Landscape." In *Landscape Archaeology: Reading and Interpreting the American Historical Landscape*, edited by Rebecca Yamin and Karen Metheny, 121–146. Knoxville: University of Tennessee Press.

Iles, John Alexander Burke. 1871. *An Account Descriptive of the Island of Nevis, West Indies*. Norwich: Fletcher and Son.

Ingold, Tim. 1993. "The Temporality of the Landscape." *World Archaeology* 25(2): 152–174.

International Stock Exchange of the United Kingdom. 1990. *Register of Defunct Companies*. London: Macmillan.

Jasanoff, Maya. 2011. *Liberty's Exiles: American Loyalists in the Revolutionary World*. New York: Vintage.

Jensen, Niklas T. 2012. *For the Health of the Enslaved: Enslaved Africans, Medicine and Power in the Danish West Indies, 1803–1848*. Copenhagen: Museum Tusculanum Press.

Johnson, Howard. 1996. *The Bahamas from Slavery to Servitude, 1783–1933*. Gainesville: University Press of Florida.

Johnson, Whittington B. 1996. "The Amelioration Acts in the Bahamas, 1823–1833: A Middle Ground between Freedom and Antebellum Slave Codes." *Journal of the Bahamas Historical Society* 18: 21–32.

Jolivet, Marie-José. 1982. *La question créole: Essai de sociologie sur la Guyane Française*. Paris: Éditions de l'Office de la Recherche Scientifique et Technique Outre-Mer.

Kelly, Kenneth G. 1989. "Historic Archaeology of Jamaican Tenant-Manager Relations: Case Study from Drax Hall and Seville Estates, St. Ann, Jamaica." PhD diss., College of William and Mary.

———. 2002. "African Diaspora Archaeology in Guadeloupe, French West Indies." *Antiquity* 76: 333–334.

———. 2008a. "Creole Cultures of the Caribbean: Historical Archaeology in the French West Indies." *International Journal of Historical Archaeology* 12(4): 388–402.

———. 2008b. "Plantation Archaeology in the French West Indies." *Rêves d'Amériques: Regard sur l'archéologie de la Nouvelle-France / Dreams of the Americas: Overview of New France Archaeology, Archéologiques* Hors série 2: 55–69.

———. 2011a. Kelly, Kenneth G., Mark W. Hauser, and Douglas V. Armstrong. "Identity and Opportunity in Post-Slavery Jamaica." In *Out of Many, One People: Historical Archaeology of Colonial Jamaica*, edited by James A. Delle, Mark W. Hauser, and Douglas V. Armstrong, 243–357. Tuscaloosa: University of Alabama Press.

——. 2011b. "*La vie quotidienne*: Historical Archaeological Approaches to the Plantation Era in Guadeloupe, French West Indies." In *French Colonial Archaeology in the Southeast and Caribbean*, edited by Kenneth G. Kelly and Meredith D. Hardy, 189–205. Gainesville: University Press of Florida.

——. 2014a. "Les 'rues cases nègres': Archéologie de la vie des esclaves dans les Antilles françaises." In *Archéologie de l'esclavage colonial*, edited by André Delpuech and Jean-Paul Jacob, 199–213. Paris: La Découverte.

——. 2014b. "The Context of Plantation Archaeology in the Lesser Antilles: Multi-Disciplinary, Multi-Cultural, Pluri-National." In *Bitasion: Archéologie des habitations-plantations des Petites Antilles / Lesser Antilles Plantation Archaeology*, edited by Kenneth G. Kelly and Benoît Bérard, 165–174. Leiden: Sidestone Press.

——. 2014c. "Archaeology, Plantations, and Slavery in the French West Indies." In *Bitasion: Archéologie des habitations-plantations des Petites Antilles / Lesser Antilles plantation archaeology*, edited by Kenneth G. Kelly and Benoît Bérard, 17–31. Leiden: Sidestone Press.

Kent, Nathaniel. 1776. *Hints to Gentlemen of Landed Property*. London: J. Dodsley.

Kidd, Robert S. 2006. "An Archaeological Examination of Slave Life in the Danish West Indies: Analysis of the Material Culture of a Caribbean Slave Village Illustrating Economic Provisioning and Acquisition Preferences." MA thesis, Florida State University.

Klingelhofer, Eric. 1987. "Aspects of Early Afro-American Material Culture: Artifacts from the Slave Quarters at Garrison Plantation, Maryland." *Historical Archaeology* 21(2): 112–119.

——. 1999. "Proto-Colonial Archaeology: The Case of Elizabethan Ireland." In *Historical Archaeology: Back from the Edge*, edited by Pedro Paulo A. Funari, Martin Hall, and Sian Jones, 164–179. London: Routledge.

——. 2005. "Facts, Fiction, and Fable: The Fate of Jamestown on Nevis." Paper presented at the annual meeting of the Society for Post-Medieval Archaeology, Nevis, West Indies.

Knapp, A. Bernard, and Wendy Ashmore. 1999. "Archaeological Landscapes: Constructed, Conceptualized, Ideational." In *Archaeologies of Landscape: Contemporary Perspectives*, edited by Wendy Ashmore and A. Bernard Knapp, 2–30. Oxford: Blackwell Publishing.

Kosiba, Steve, and R. Alexander Hunter. 2017. "Fields of Conflict: A Political Ecology Approach to Land and Social Transformation in the Colonial Andes (Cuzco, Peru)." *Journal of Archaeological Science* 84: 40–53.

Lamendin, Christian. 2010. *Vestiges coloniaux du chemin du roi et du chemin de l'habitation la Gabrielle sur la commune de Roura (Guyane française)*. Cayenne: Service régional de l'archéologie Guyane.

——. 2014. *L'histoire du girofle en Guyane*. Cayenne: Service régional de l'archéologie Guyane.

——. 2015. *l'Habitation Grand-Marée dans le quartier de Roura*. Cayenne: Service régional de l'archéologie Guyane.

Lane, Paul. 2011. "Possibilities for a Postcolonial Archaeology in Sub-Saharan Africa: Indigenous and Usable Pasts." *World Archaeology* 43(1): 7–25.

Lange, Frederick W., and Jerome S. Handler. 1985. "The Ethnohistorical Approach to Slavery." In *The Archaeology of Slavery and Plantation Life*, edited by Theresa A. Singleton, 15–32. Orlando, FL: Academic Press.

Lawaetz, Erick. 1991. *St. Croix: 500 Years Pre-Columbus to 1990*. Herning, Denmark: Poul Kristensen.

Lawson, Charles, William Cissel, David Anderson, John Cornelison, and Meredith Hardy. 2004. *A Geophysical Survey of the Courtyard of the Old Danish West India and Guinea Company Warehouse and the Grounds Surrounding the Customs House*. St. Croix, USVI: National Park Service.

Le Roux, Yannick. 1994. "L'habitation guyanaise sous l'Ancien Régime: Etude de la culture materielle." PhD diss., Ecole des Hautes Etudes en Sciences Sociales.

Leech, Roger. 2005. "Impermanent Architecture in the English Colonies of the Eastern Caribbean: New Contexts for Architectural Innovation in the Modern Atlantic World." In *Perspectives in Vernacular Architecture*, edited by Kenneth A. Breisch and Alison K. Hoagland, 153–168. Knoxville: University of Tennessee Press.

———. 2008. "'In what manner did they divide the land': The Early Colonial Estate Landscape of Nevis and St. Kitts. In *Estate Landscapes: Design, Improvement and Power in the Post-Medieval Landscape*, edited by Jonathan Finch and Kate Giles, 191–198. London: Boydell and Brewer.

———. 2010. "'Within musquett shott of black rock': Johnson's Fort and the Early Defenses of Nevis, West Indies." In *First Forts: Essays on the Archaeology of Proto-Colonial Fortifications*, edited by Eric Klingelhofer, 127–138. Boston: Brill.

Lefebvre, Henri. 1991. *The Production of Space*. Translated by Donald Nicholson-Smith. Cambridge: Blackwell Publishing.

Lewisohn, Florence. 1970. *St. Croix under Seven Flags*. Hollywood: Dukane Press.

Logan, Amanda L. 2016. "'Why can't people feed themselves?': Archaeology as Alternative Archive of Food Security in Banda, Ghana." *American Anthropologist* 118(3): 508–524.

Lowenthal, David. 1952. "Colonial Experiments in French Guiana, 1760–1800." *Hispanic American Historical Review* 32(1): 22–43.

———. 1972. *West Indian Societies*. New York: Oxford University Press.

Mam Lam Fouck, Serge. 1986. "Apogée, déclin et disparition du système esclavagiste (première moitié du XIXè siècle)." In *Deux siècles d'esclavage en Guyane Française, 1652–1848*, edited by Anne-Marie Bruleaux, Régine Calmont, and Serge Mam Lam Fouck, 141–288. Paris: l'Harmattan.

———. 1996. *L'Histoire général de la Guyane française*. Matoury: Ibis Rouge.

———. 2013. *Nouvelle histoire de la Guyane: Des souverainetés amérindiennes aux mutations de la société contemporaine*. Matoury: Ibis Rouge.

Marshall, Lydia Wilson, ed. 2014. *The Archaeology of Slavery: A Comparative Approach to Captivity and Coercion*. Carbondale: Center for Archaeological Investigations, Southern Illinois University Press.

Martens, Vibe Maria. 2010. "Belonging to His Majesty the King." MA thesis, University of Copenhagen, Denmark.

———. 2016. "Royal Slaves in the Danish-Norwegian West Indies 1792–1848: Living in Autonomy." *Scandinavian Journal of History* 41(4–5): 516–540.

Martin, Samuel. 1785. *An Essay upon Plantership*. 7th ed. Antigua: Robert Mearns.

Matthews, Gelien. 2006. *Caribbean Slave Revolts and the British Abolitionist Movement*. Baton Rouge: Louisiana State University Press.

Mattingly, David. 2008. "Comparative Advantages: Roman Slavery and Imperialism." *Archaeological Dialogues* 15(2): 135–139.

Maudlin, Daniel. 2010. "Habitations of the Labourer: Improvement, Reform and the Neoclassical Cottage in Eighteenth-Century Britain." *Journal of Design History* 23(1): 7–20.

McInnis, Maurie D. 2005. *The Politics of Taste in Antebellum Charleston*. Chapel Hill: University of North Carolina Press.

McKee, Larry. 1992. "The Ideals and Realities behind the Design and Use of Nineteenth-Century Virginia Slave Cabins. In *The Art and Mystery of Historical Archaeology: Essays in Honor of James Deetz*, edited by Anne E. Yentsch and Mary C. Beaudry, 195–213. Boca Raton: CRC Press.

McKinnen, Daniel. 1804. *A Tour through the British West Indies, in the Years 1802 and 1803, Giving a Particular Account of the Bahama Islands*. London: B. Taylor.

Meniketti, Marco. 2006. "Sugar-Mills, Technology, and Environmental Change: A Case Study of Colonial Agro-Industrial Development in the Caribbean." *Journal of the Society for Industrial Archaeology* 32(1): 53–80.

———. 2015. *Sugar Cane Capitalism and Environmental Transformation: An Historical Archaeology of Nevis, West Indies*. Tuscaloosa: University of Alabama Press.

———. 2016. "Dimensions of Space and Identity in an Emancipation-Era Village." In *Archaeologies of Slavery and Freedom in the Caribbean: Exploring the Spaces in Between*, edited by Lynsey A. Bates, John M. Chenoweth, and James A. Delle, 183–206. Gainesville: University Press of Florida.

Merrill, Gordon. 1958. *The Historical Geography of St. Kitts and Nevis, The West Indies*. Mexico City: Instituto Panamericano de Geographia e Historia.

Meskell, Lynn, and Robert W Preucel, eds. 2008. *Companion to Social Archaeology*. New York: Wiley & Blackwell.

Meyers, Allan D. 2015. "Historical Landscapes of Golden Grove and Newfield Plantations, Cat Island." *Journal of the Bahamas Historical Society* 37: 42–51.

Miller, George. 1980. "Classification and Economic Scaling of 19th Century Ceramics." *Historical Archaeology* 14: 1–40.

———. 1991. "A Revised Set of CC Index Values for Classification and Economic Scaling of English Ceramics from 1787 to 1880." *Historical Archaeology* 25(1): 1–15.

Miller, John. 1789. *The Country Gentleman's Architect*. London: J. Taylor.

Miller, Joseph C. 2003. "A Theme in Variations: A Historical Schema of Slaving in the Atlantic and Indian Ocean Regions." *Slavery and Abolition* 24(2): 169–194.

———. 2012. *The Problem of Slavery as History: A Global Approach*. New Haven, CT: Yale University Press.

Ministre Secrétaire d'Etat de la Marine et des Colonies. 1844. *Exposé général des résultats du patronage des esclaves dans les colonies françaises.* Paris: Imprimerie Royale.

Mintz, Sidney W. 1960. "The House and the Yard among Three Caribbean Peasantries." In *Actes VIè Congrès Intérnational des sciences anthropologiques et ethnologiques, 30 July–August 6, 1960.* Book 2, Vol. 1, edited by André Leroi-Gourhan, Pierre Champion, and Monique de Fontanès, 591–596. Paris: Musée de l'Homme.

———. 1961. "The Question of Caribbean Peasantries: A Comment." *Caribbean Studies* 1(3): 31–34.

———. 1974. *Caribbean Transformations.* Baltimore, MD: Johns Hopkins University Press.

———. 1978. "Was the Plantation Slave a Proletarian?" *Review (Fernand Braudel Center)* 2(1): 81–98.

———. 1984. *From Plantations to Peasantries in the Caribbean.* Washington, DC: Woodrow Wilson International Center for Scholars.

Mintz, Sidney W., and Douglas Hall. 1960. *The Origins of the Jamaican Internal Marketing System.* Yale University Publications in Anthropology no. 57. New Haven, CT: Human Relations Area Files Press.

Mintz, Sidney W., and Richard Price. 1992. *The Birth of African-American Culture: An Anthropological Perspective.* Boston: Beacon.

Moore, Sue Mullins. 1985. "Social and Economic Status on the Coastal Plantation: An Archaeological Perspective." In *The Archaeology of Slavery and Plantation Life,* edited by Theresa A. Singleton, 141–160. Orlando, FL: Academic Press.

Morgan, Philip D. 1982. "Work and Culture: The Task System and the World of Lowcountry Blacks, 1700–1880." *William and Mary Quarterly* 39: 563–599.

Morris, Elaine L., Robert Read, S. Elizabeth James, Tess Machling, David F. Williams, and Brent Wilson. 1999. " . . . the old stone fort at Newcastle": The Redoubt, Nevis, Eastern Caribbean." *Post-Medieval Archaeology* 33(1): 194–221.

Nash, Donna J. 2009. "Household Archaeology in the Andes." *Journal of Archaeological Research* 17: 205–261.

National Park Service. 2014. *Southeast Region Foundation Document Recommendation.* USVI: St. Croix.

Neiman, Fraser D. 2008. "The Lost World of Monticello: An Evolutionary Perspective." *Journal of Anthropological Research* 64(2): 161–193.

Neiman, Fraser D., Karen Y. Smith, and Sara Bon-Harper. 2014. "Inequality within a Slave Settlement at Monticello in the Late Eighteenth Century." Poster presented at the annual meeting of the Society for American Archaeology, Austin.

Nelson, Louis P. 2011. "The Architectures of Black Identity." *Winterthur Portfolio* 45 (2–3): 177–194.

———. 2016. *Architecture and Empire in Jamaica.* New Haven, CT: Yale University Press.

Nelson, Louis P., Edward A. Chappell, Brian Cofrancesco, and Emilie Johnson, eds. 2014. *Falmouth, Jamaica: Architecture as History.* Kingston: University of the West Indies Press.

Ng, Mee Kam, Wing Shing Tang, Joanna Lee, and Darwin Leung. 2013. "Spatial Practice,

Conceived Space and Lived Space: Hong Kong's 'Piers Saga' through the Lefebvrian Lens." *Planning Perspectives* 25(4): 411–431.

Nissen, Johan Peter. 1838. *Reminiscences of a 46 Years' Residence in the Island of St. Thomas in the West Indies*. Nazareth, PA: Senseman and Co.

Odewale, Alicia. 2016. "Living among Presidents and Kings: Enslaved Africans Coping with Risk in Service to the Elite." PhD diss., University of Tulsa.

Odewale, Alicia, H. Thomas Foster, and Joshua M. Torres. 2017. "In Service to a Danish King: Comparing the Material Culture of Royal Enslaved Afro-Caribbeans and Danish Soldiers at the Christiansted National Historic Site." *Journal of African Diaspora Archaeology and Heritage* 6(1): 19–54.

Oliver, Vere Langford, ed. 1919. *Caribbeana, Being Miscellaneous Papers Relating to the History, Genealogy, Topography, and Antiquities of the British West Indies*. Vol. 6. London: Mitchell Hughes and Clarke.

Olsen, Herbert. 1960. *Historic Structures Report*. Part 1, *Fort Christiansvaern*. Christiansted, St. Croix, USVI: National Park Service.

Olsen, Poul Erik. 1988. *Toldvæsenet i Dansk Vestindien 1672-1917*. Kbh.: Toldhistorisk Selskab.

Olwig, Karen Fog. 1993. "Defining the National in the Transnational: Cultural Identity in the Afro-Caribbean Diaspora." *Ethnos Journal of Anthropology* 58 (3–4): 361–376.

———. 1995. "Cultural Complexity after Freedom: Nevis and Beyond." In *Small Islands, Big Questions*, edited by Karen F. Olwig, 100–120. London: Frank Cass.

Opitz, Rachel S., Krysta Ryzewski, John F. Cherry, and Brenna Maloney. 2015. "Using Airbone LiDAR Survey to Explore Historic-Era Archaeological Landscapes of Montserrat in the Eastern Caribbean." *Journal of Field Archaeology* 40(5): 523–541.

Orser, Charles E. 1988. "Toward a Theory of Power for Historical Archaeology: Plantations and Space." In *The Recovery of Meaning: Historical Archaeology in the Eastern United States*, edited by Mark Leone and Parker Potter, 313–343. Washington, DC: Smithsonian Institution Press.

———. 1990. "Archaeological Approaches to New World Plantation Slavery." In *Archaeological Method and Theory* 2: 111–154.

Orser, Charles E., Jr., and Pedro Funari. 2001. "Archaeology and Slave Resistance and Rebellion." *World Archaeology* 33(1): 61–72.

O'Shaughnessy, Andrew. 1996. "Redcoats and Slaves in the British Caribbean." In *The Lesser Antilles in the Age of European Expansion*, edited by Robert L. Paquette and Stanley L. Engerman, 105–127. Gainesville: University Press of Florida.

Paiewonsky, Isidor. 1989. *Eyewitness Accounts of Slavery in the Danish West Indies. Also Graphic Tales of Other Slave Happenings on Ships and Plantations*. New York: Fordham University Press.

Pares, Richard. 1950. *A West India Fortune*. London: Longmans, Green and Co.

Patterson, Orlando. 1982. *Slavery and Social Death*. Cambridge, MA: Harvard University Press.

Perry, Jeffrey. 2011. *Hubert Harrison: The Voice of Harlem Radicalism, 1883-1918*. New York: Columbia University Press.

Plaw, John. 1796. *Ferme ornée; or Rural Improvements*. London: J. Taylor.

Pluckhahn, Thomas J. 2010. "Household Archaeology in the Southeastern United States: History, Trends, and Challenges." *Journal of Archaeological Research* 18: 331–385.

Polderman, Marie. 2004. *La Guyane française 1676–1763: Mise en place et évolution de la société colonial, tension et métissage.* Matoury: Ibis Rouge.

Pope, Pauline H. 1969. "Cruzan Slavery: An Ethnohistorical Study of Differential Responses to Slavery in the Danish West Indies." PhD diss., University of California, Davis.

Pruneau, Leigh Ann. 1997. "All the Time Is Work Time: Gender and the Task System on Lowcountry Rice Plantations." PhD diss., The University of Arizona.

Pulsipher, Lydia. 1994. "The Landscapes and Ideational Roles of Caribbean Slave Gardens." In *The Archaeology of Garden and Field*, edited by Naomi F. Miller and Kathryn L. Gleason, 202–222. Philadelphia: University of Pennsylvania Press.

Pulsipher, Lydia M., and Conrad M. Goodwin. 1982. "Galways: An Irish Sugar Plantation in Montserrat, West Indies." *Post-Medieval Archaeology* 16: 21–27.

———. 1999. "Here Where the Old Time People Be: Reconstructing the Landscapes of the Slavery and Post-Slavery Era in Montserrat, West Indies." In *African Sites Archaeology in the Caribbean*, edited by Jay B. Haviser, 9–37. Princeton, NJ: Markus Wiener.

———. 2001. "'Getting the essence of it': Galways Plantation, Montserrat, West Indies." In *Island Lives: Historical Archaeologies of the Caribbean*, edited by Paul Farnsworth, 165–203. Tuscaloosa: University of Alabama Press.

Ramsay, James. 1784. *An Essay on the Treatment and Conversion of African Slaves in the British Sugar Colonies.* London: James Phillips.

Redfield, Peter. 2000. *Space in the Tropics: From Convicts to Rockets in French Guiana.* Berkeley: University of California Press.

Rees, John U. 2002. "'As many fireplaces as you have tents . . .': Earthen camp kitchens." Accessed July 3, 2016. http://revwar75.com/library/rees/kitchen.htm.

Reeves, Matthew. 1997. "'By their own labor': Enslaved Africans' Survival Strategies on Two Jamaican Plantations." PhD diss., Syracuse University.

———. 2010. "A Community of Households: Early 19th-Century Enslaved Landscapes at James Madison's Montpelier." *African Diaspora Archaeology Newsletter* 13(4): 1–26.

———. 2011. "Household Market Activities among Early Nineteenth-Century Jamaican Slaves: An Archaeological Case Study from Two Slave Settlements." In *Out of Many, One People: The Historical Archaeology of Colonial Jamaica*, edited by James A. Delle, Mark W. Hauser, and Douglas V. Armstrong, 183–210. Tuscaloosa: University of Alabama Press.

———. 2015. "Scalar Analysis of Early Nineteenth-Century Household Assemblages: Focus on Communities of the African Atlantic." In *Beyond the Walls: New Perspectives on the Archaeology of Historical Households*, edited by Kevin R. Fogle, James A. Nyman, and Mary C. Beaudry, 22–46. Gainesville: University Press of Florida.

Régent, Frédéric. 2004. *Esclavage, métissage, liberté: La révolution française en Guadeloupe, 1789–1802.* Paris: Bernard Grasset.

———. 2012. *La France et ses esclaves: de la colonization aux abolitions (1620–1848).* Paris: Pluriel.

Renouard, M. Félix. 1822. *Statistique de la Martinique*. Paris: Chaumerot, Libraire, Palais-Royal.

Richardson, Bonham. 1983. *Caribbean Migrants: Environment and Human Survival on St. Kitts and Nevis*. Knoxville: University of Tennessee Press.

Riley, Sandra. 1980. "W. E. Armbrister's Loyalist Heritage." *Journal of the Bahamas Historical Society* 2: 3–10.

Roberts, Justin. 2013. *Slavery and the Enlightenment in the British Atlantic, 1750–1807*. Cambridge: Cambridge University Press.

Robin, Cynthia. 2013. *Everyday Life Matters: Maya Farmers at Chan*. Gainesville: University Press of Florida.

Robin, Cynthia, and Nan A. Rothschild. 2002. "Archaeological Ethnographies: Social Dynamics of Outdoor Space." *Journal of Social Archaeology* 2: 159–172.

Rodman, Margaret C. 1992. "Empowering Place: Multilocality and Multivocality." *American Anthropologist* 94(3): 640–656.

Rogozinski, Jan. 1992. *A Brief History of the Caribbean: From the Arawak and the Carib to the Present*. New York: Facts On File.

Rostain, Stéphen. 2014. *Islands in the Rainforest: Landscape Management in Pre-Columbian Amazonia*. New York: Routledge.

Rothschild, Nan A. 1991. "Incorporating the Outdoors as Living Space." *Expedition* 33: 24–32.

Royal Gardens, Kew. 1887. "XII.—Annatto (*Bixa Orellana*, L.)." In *Bulletin of Miscellaneous Information: 1887*, 1–8. London: Eyre and Spottiswood.

Rubertone, Patricia. 1989. "Landscape as Artifact: Comments on 'The Archaeological Use of Landscape Treatment in Social, Economic, and Ideological Analysis.'" *Historical Archaeology* 23(1): 50–54.

Sainsbury, Noel W., ed. 1893. *Calendar of State Papers, Colonial, America and West Indies*. Vol. 9, *1675–1676*. London: Her Majesty's Stationery Office.

Salih, Sara, ed. 2000. *The History of Mary Prince: A West Indian Slave. Related to Herself*. London: Penguin Books.

Samford, Patricia. 2007. *Subfloor Pits and the Archaeology of Slavery in Colonial Virginia*. Tuscaloosa: The University of Alabama Press.

Samford, Patricia, Gregory J. Brown, and Ann Morgan Smart. 1986. *Williamsburg Lodge Tazewell Wing Archaeological Report, Block 44–1 Building 3K*. Colonial Williamsburg Foundation Library Research Report Series 1301. Williamsburg, VA: Colonial Williamsburg Foundation Library.

Samson, Alice V. M. 2010. *Renewing the House: Trajectories of Social Life in the Yucayeque (Community) of El Cabo, Higuey, Domincan Republic, AD 800 to 1504*. Leiden: Sidestone Press.

Sarge, Kristen. 2002. *Les* établissements *coloniaux* à *la confluence de l'Oyak, de la Comté et de l'Orapu (XVIIè-XXè siècles), commune de Roura (Guyane)*. Cayenne: Service regional de l'archéologie Guyane.

———. 2006. "Michel Favard, délégué et directeur de l'intérieur de la Guyane (1797–1863). Amorce d'un chantier d'histoire sociale et économique." In *L'Histoire de la*

Guyane depuis les civilizations amérindiennes, edited by Serge Mam Lam Fouck, 555–579. Matoury: Ibis Rouge.

Schroeder, Hannes, Jay B. Haviser, and T. Douglas Price. 2014. "The Zoutsteeg Three: Three New Cases of African Types of Dental Modification from Saint Martin, Dutch Caribbean." *International Journal of Osteoarchaeology* 24(6): 688–696.

Schroedl, Gerald F., and Todd M. Ahlman. 2002. "The Maintenance of Cultural and Personal Identities of Enslaved Africans and British Soldiers at the Brimstone Hill Fortress, St. Kitts, West Indies." *Historical Archaeology* 36(4): 38–49.

Schwalm, Leslie. 1997. *A Hard Fight for We: Women's Transition from Slavery to Freedom in South Carolina*. Urbana: University of Illinois Press.

Schwartz, Stuart. 2015. *Sea of Storms: A History of Hurricanes in the Greater Caribbean from Columbus to Katrina*. Princeton, NJ: Princeton University Press.

Singleton, Theresa A. 1980. "The Archaeology of Afro-American Slavery in Coastal Georgia: A Regional Perception of Slave Household and Community Patterns." PhD diss., University of Florida.

———. 1985a. "Archaeological Implications for Changing Labor Conditions." In *The Archaeology of Slavery and Plantation Life*, edited by Theresa A. Singleton, 291–307. Orlando, FL: Academic Press.

———, ed. 1985b. *The Archaeology of Slavery and Plantation Life*. Orlando: Academic Press.

———, ed. 1999. *"I, too, am America": Archaeological Studies of African-American Life*. Charlottesville: University Press of Virginia.

———. 2001. "Slavery and Spatial Dialectics on Cuban Coffee Plantations." *World Archaeology* 33(1): 98–114.

———. 2014. "La vie à l'intérieur d'une enceinte de murailles: Archéologie d'une communauté d'esclaves de Cuba." In *Archéologie de l'esclavage colonial*, edited by André Delpuech and Jean-Paul Jacob, 183–197. Paris: La Découverte.

———. 2015. *Slavery behind the Wall: An Archaeology of a Cuban Coffee Plantation*. Gainesville: University Press of Florida.

Sloane, Hans. 1707. *A Voyage to the Islands of Madera, Barbados, Nieves, St. Christopher's and Jamaica with the Natural History of the Herbs and Trees, Four-Footed Beasts, Fishes, Birds, Insects, Reptiles, Etc. of the Last of Those Islands*. Vol. 1. London: B. M. for the author.

Small, David, and Christine Eickelmann. 2007. "Bush Hill Estate, St. John Figtree. A Preliminary Assessment of the Documentary Evidence." Report to the Hoffman family. On file at Montpelier Plantation Inn, St. John, Nevis.

Smith, Frederick. 2008. *The Archaeology of Alcohol and Drinking*. Gainesville: University Press of Florida.

Smith, Frederick H., and Hayden F. Bassett. 2016. "The Role of Caves and Gullies in Escape, Mobility, and the Creation of Community Networks among Enslaved Peoples of Barbados." In *Archaeologies of Slavery and Freedom in the Caribbean: Exploring the Spaces in Between*, edited by Lynsey A. Bates John M. Chenoweth, and James A. Delle, 31–48. Gainesville: University Press of Florida.

Smith, William. 1745. *A Natural History of Nevis, and the Rest of the English Leeward*

Charibbee Islands in America. With Many Other Observations on Nature and Art. Cambridge: J. Bentham.

Société d'Études pour la Colonisation de la Guyane Française. 1843. *Notice statistique sur la Guyane Française.* Publications de la Société d'Études no. 2. Paris: Typographie de Firmin Didot.

South, Stanley. 1977. *Method and Theory in Historical Archaeology.* New York: Academic Press.

Spencer-Wood, Suzanne M. 2010. "A Feminist Framework for Analyzing Powered Cultural Landscapes in Historical Archaeology." *International Journal of Historical Archaeology* 14(4): 498–526.

Stelton, Ruud. 2015. "Heritage Management of an 18th-Century Slave Village at Schotsenhoek Plantation, St, Eustatius." In *Managing Our Past into the Future: Archaeological Heritage Management in the Dutch Caribbean,* edited by Corinne L. Hofman and Jay B. Haviser, 291–303. Leiden: Sidestone Press.

Stewart, John. 1823. *A View of the Past and Present State of the Island of Jamaica.* Edinburgh: Oliver & Boyd.

Tardy, Christophe. 1998. "Paléoincendies naturels, feux anthropiques et environnements forestiers de Guyane française du tardiglaciaire à l'Holocène récent: approches chronologique et anthracologique." PhD diss., Université de Montpellier.

Taylor, Timothy F. 2005. "Ambushed by a Grotesque: Archaeology, Slavery and the Third Paradigm." In *Warfare, Violence and Slavery in Prehistory,* edited by M. Parker Pearson and I. J. N. Thorpe, 225–233. BAR International Series 1374. Oxford: Archaeopress.

Thomas, Brian W. 1998. "Power and Community: The Archaeology of Slavery at the Hermitage Plantation." *American Antiquity* 63(4): 531–551.

Tocney, Emilie. 2009. *Kawka—les éclats du silence.* Rémire-Montjoly: MKT Editions.

Tomich, Dale W. 2004. *Through the Prism of Slavery: Labor, Capital, and World Economy.* New York: Rowman & Littlefield.

———. 2005. "Material Process and Industrial Architecture: Innovation on the Cuban Sugar Frontier, 1818–1857." *Research in Rural Sociology and Development* 10: 287–307.

Townsend, Andrew. 2002. "Mountravers: The 2002 Excavations." In *Nevis Heritage Project interim report 2002,* edited by Elaine Morris, Roger Leech, Andrew Crosby, Tessa Machling, Bruce Williams, and Jen Heathcote, 42–49. Southampton: The Nevis Heritage Project, University of Southampton.

Trouillot, Michel-Rolph. 1982. "Motion in the System: Coffee, Color, and Slavery in Eighteenth-Century Saint-Domingue." *Review (Fernand Braudel Center)* 5(3): 331–388.

———. 1996. "Beyond and Below the Merivale Paradigm: Dominica's First 100 Days of Freedom." In *The Lesser Antilles in the Age of European Expansion,* edited by Robert L. Paquette and Stanley L. Engerman, 305–323. Gainesville: University Press of Florida.

———. 2002. "North Atlantic Universals: Analytical Fictions, 1492–1945." *South Atlantic Quarterly* 101 (4): 839–858.

Troxler, Carole W. 1996. "Henry Williams." In *Dictionary of North Carolina Biography,* vol. 6, edited by William S. Powell, 200–201. Chapel Hill: University of North Carolina Press.

Turner, Grace R. 1992. "An Archaeological Record of Plantation Life in the Bahamas." *Journal of the Bahamas Historical Society* 14(1): 30–40.

Turner, Mary. 1982. *Slaves and Missionaries: The Disintegration of Jamaican Slave Society, 1787–1834*. Kingston: University of the West Indies Press.

Turner, Michael. 1984. *Enclosures in Britain, 1750–1830*. London: Macmillan.

Tyson, George, ed. 1996. *Bondmen and Freedmen in the Danish West Indies: Scholarly Perspectives*. St. Thomas, USVI: Virgin Islands Humanities Council.

———. 2010. "Getting It Straight: The Contributions of Africans to the Establishment of Christiansted, 1735–1755. *Crucian Trader*, May 1–7.

Tyson, George F., and Arnold R. Highfield, eds. 1994. *The Kamina Folk: Slavery and Slave Life in the Danish West Indies*. Charlotte Amalie, USVI: Virgin Islands Humanities Council.

Upton, Dell. 1984. "White and Black Landscapes in Eighteenth-Century Virginia." *Places* 2(2): 59–72.

Vinson, Ben, III, and Stewart King. 2004. "Introducing the 'New' African Diasporic Military History in Latin America." *Journal of Colonialism and Colonial History* 5(2): 1–23.

Vlach, John Michael. 1993. *Back of the Big House: The Architecture of Plantation Slavery*. Chapel Hill: University of North Carolina Press.

———. 1995. "'Snug li'l house with flue and oven': Nineteenth-Century Reforms in Plantation Slave Housing." *Perspectives in Vernacular Housing* 5: 118–129.

Voelz, Peter M. 1993. *Slave and Soldier: The Military Impact of Blacks in the Colonial Americas*. New York: Garland Publishing, Inc.

Wallman, Diane. 2014. "Negotiating the Plantation Structure: An Archaeological Investigation of Slavery, Subsistence and Daily Practice at Habitation Crève Cœur, Martinique, ca. 1760–1890." PhD diss., University of South Carolina.

Wandsnider, LuAnn. 1996. "Describing and Comparing Archaeological Spatial Structures." *Journal of Archaeological Method and Theory* 3(4): 319–384.

Watlington, Roy A., and Shirley H. Lincoln. 1997. *Disaster and Disruption in 1867: Hurricane, Earthquake, and Tsunami in the Danish West Indies*. [St. Thomas, USVI]: Eastern Caribbean Center, University of the Virgin Islands.

Watson, Mark R., and Robert B. Potter. 1993. "Housing and Housing Policy in Barbados: The Relevance of the Chattel House." *Third World Planning Review* 15(4): 373–395.

Watters, David R. 1994. "Mortuary Patterns at the Harney Site Slave Cemetery, Montserrat, in Caribbean Perspective." *Historical Archaeology* 28(3): 56–73.

Watts, David. 1994. *The West Indies: Patterns of Development, Culture, and Environmental Change since 1492*. Cambridge: Cambridge University Press.

Webster, Jane. 2008. "Less Beloved: Roman Archaeology, Slavery and the Failure to Compare." *Archaeological Dialogues* 15(2): 103–23.

Weik, Terrance. 2012. *The Archaeology of Antislavery Resistance*. Gainesville: University Press of Florida.

Wesler, Kit W. 2013. "A Spatial Perspective on Artifact Assemblages at the Edward Moulton-Barrett House, Falmouth, Jamaica." *Journal of Caribbean Archaeology* 13: 1–26.

Westergaard, Waldemar Christian. 1917. *The Danish West Indies under Company Rule (1671–1754): With a Supplementary Chapter, 1755–1917*. New York: Macmillan Company.

———. 1996. "The Slave and the Planter." [1917]. In *Bondmen and Freedmen in the Danish West Indies: Scholarly Perspectives*, edited by George Tyson, 54–65. St. Thomas, USVI: Virgin Islands Humanities Council.

Wilk, Richard R., and Robert McC. Netting. 1984. "Households: Changing Forms and Function." In *Households: Comparative and Historical Studies of the Domestic Group*, edited by Robert McC. Netting, Richard R. Wilk, and Eric J. Arnould, 1–28. Berkeley: University of California Press.

Wilk, Richard R., and William L. Rathje. 1982. "Household Archaeology." *American Behavioral Scientist* 25(6): 617–39.

Wilkie, Laurie A. 2000. *Creating Freedom: Material Culture and African-American Identity at Oakley Plantation, Louisiana, 1845–1950*. Baton Rouge: Louisiana State University Press.

Wilkie, Laurie A., and Paul Farnsworth. 1999. "Trade and the Construction of Bahamian Identity: A Multi-Scalar Exploration." *International Journal of Historical Archaeology* 3(4): 283–320.

———. 2005. *Sampling Many Pots: An Archaeology of Memory and Tradition at a Bahamian Plantation*. Gainesville: University Press of Florida.

Williams, Eric. 1944. *Capitalism and Slavery*. Chapel Hill: University of North Carolina Press.

Williams, James. 1834. *A Narrative of Events, since the First of August, 1834, by James Williams, an Apprenticed Labourer in Jamaica*. Durham, NC: Duke University Press.

Williamson, Tom. 2002. *The Transformation of Rural England: Farming and the Landscape, 1700–1870*. Exeter: University of Exeter Press.

Wood, John. 1806. *A Series of Plans for Cottages or Habitations of the Labourer, Either in Husbandry, or the Mechanic Arts, Adapted as Well to Towns as to the Country*. London: J. Taylor.

Wylly, William. 1789. *A Short Account of the Bahama Islands*. London: William Wylly.

Yaeger, Jason, and Marcello A. Canuto. 2000. "Introducing an Archaeology of Communities." In *The Archaeology of Communities: A New World Perspective*, edited by Jason Yaeger and Marcello A. Canuto, 1–15. New York: Routledge.

Zierden, Martha, and Bernard L. Herman. 1996. "Charleston Townhouses: Archaeology, Architecture, and the Urban Landscape, 1750–1850." In *Landscape Archaeology: Reading and Interpreting the American Historical Landscape*, edited by Rebecca Yamin and Karen Metheny, 193–227. Knoxville: University of Tennessee Press.

Contributors

Todd M. Ahlman is director of the Center for Archaeological Studies at Texas State University.

Hayden F. Bassett is an archaeologist for the U.S. Department of the Navy.

Zachary J. M. Beier is lecturer in the department of history and archaeology at the University of the West Indies Mona.

Elizabeth C. Clay is a PhD candidate in the department of anthropology at the University of Pennsylvania.

James A. Delle is associate provost at Millersville University.

Kristen R. Fellows is assistant professor of anthropology at North Dakota State University.

Meredith D. Hardy is acting cultural resources program manager for Christiansted National Historic Site and an archaeologist and coordinator for interpretation and education at the Southeast Archeological Center of the National Park Service.

Mark W. Hauser is associate professor of anthropology at Northwestern University.

Kenneth G. Kelly is professor of anthropology at the University of South Carolina.

Marco Meniketti is professor of anthropology at San Jose State University and is the founder and director of the Institute for Interdisciplinary Caribbean Studies.

Allan D. Meyers is professor of anthropology at Eckerd College in St. Petersburg, Florida.

Alicia Odewale is assistant professor of anthropology at the University of Tulsa.

Index

Page numbers in *italics* indicate illustrations.

Afro-Caribbean ware, 30, 34, 36, 39, 199; Nevis, 61

Afro-Crucian ware, 199, 207, 214

Animal pens: stone construction, 46, 58, 60, 124; wood construction, 124

Annatto, 166, 169–72, 175, 187; European market for, 172; production of, 172, 175, 177

Antislavery activism, 17, 145, 163, 184. *See also* Slavery: reform movement

Apprenticeship system, 122, 150, 155

Architectural features: cellars, 32, 34, 40; chimneys, 53, 59, 134, 138, 152, 164; doors, 155, 161; fireplaces, 152–53, 155, 158, 161, 164; porches, 134, 138, 144, 177; windows, 32, 50, 52, 59, 144, 153, 155, 162, 236

Bahamas, 4, 21, 36, 142–43, 147–48; emancipation, 147; Loyalist era, 164; model cottages, 144–45, 160–61, 163

Beckford, William, 23

Brimstone Hill Fortress, 24–25, 29

Building materials: boards, 23, 81, 125; bricks, 24, 49, 126, 182, 198, 229–30, 232–33; cane, 22–23, 26, 37, 126; clay, 197–98; coral, 22, 196–97, 229; fire-resistant, 196; flooring, 126; grass, 30; hardware, 100, 207, 229; insect-resistant, 131; limestone, 21, 37, 100, 103, 132, 230; marl, 126; mortar, 21, 62, 131, 146, 197–98, 212, 229–30; nails, 32, 38, 59, 81, 125, 134, 207, 230, 233, 235; plaster, 22, 37, 59, 125, 131, 153, 158, 197; posts, 23, 26, 32, 100, 134, 233; roofing tiles, 230, 232–33,

235; shell, 197–98, 207, 212, 215; shingles, 26, 53, 125, 134; stone, 62–63, 125, 164, 197, 226, 228; storm-resistant, 196, 198; thatch, 22–23, 30, 52–53, 99, 126, 160, 175; wattle and daub, 21–22, 26, 29, 37, 52, 125, 233, 235; window glass, 110, 229; wood, 21–22, 49, 81, 125, 182, 197; wooden shutters, 197

Bush Hill, 55–56, 59–60, 63

Cabrits Garrison, 217, 221; engineers' yard, 226, 228, 236; forge, 226; laborers' village, 218–19, 229; oven feature, 235

Cacao, 166, 169

Cafetal Santa Ana de Biajacas, 69–70

Cat Island, 143, 147–48, 150, 160

Cat Island Heritage Project, 150, 164

Cayenne, 168, 170, 183; port of, 167

Chattel houses, 26, 29, 36–39

Christiansted: auction yards, 188; building code, 196–98; city of, 189–90, 198; housing, 196

Christiansted Harbor, 191, 197, 200, 206

Christiansted National Historic Site, 189–91, 207, 212–15

Cinnamon, 170–71, 175

Clarke Estate, 50, 54, 61

Clifton Plantation, 21

Clove: Dominica, 170–71; European markets for, 170; production of, 169–73, 175–76, 179

Coffee, 118–19, 166, 169, 175; European markets for, 117–20; Jamaica, 118, 120; plantations, 69, 117–18; production of, 117, 131, 173; St. Domingue, 117

Collins, David, 145–46, 155

Colonoware. *See* Afro-Caribbean ware
Construction techniques: African, 48, 52, 125; air circulation, 37, 62, 158; boundary walls, 106, 108, 130, 134; choice in, 110, 112–15, 215; doorways, 59, 79, 144, 152, 155, 158, 161, 178, 182, 232; drainage, 60, 180, 226, 228, 233; European, 52, 161; interior walls, 146, 153, 155, 177; Jamaica, 124–27; kaz en gaulettes, 70, 75, 79; on pilings, 75, 79–83; platforms, 32, 34, 55, 75, 78, 80–81, 232; postholes, 233, 235; post-in-ground, 21–23, 26, 30, 32, 34, 36–37, 40, 70, 77; retaining walls, 78, 176; sills, 37, 81; on slopes, 62, 78, 83; Spanish wall, 99, 125, 131, 134; stone foundations, 22, 30, 36, 60, 68, 97, 100, 103, 134, 175–76; terracing, 38, 46, 56–58, 60, 226, 228, 232; walls, 59, 125, 144, 152, 155, 182; wattle and daub, 22, 24, 29, 36, 40, 70–71, 75, 77, 99, 125; wood frame, 29, 38, 40–41, 81, 175, 180, 185
Cotton, 166, 169–70, 191, 205; plantations, 30

Danish West India and Guinea Company (DWIGC), 188–89, 194
Danish West Indies, 189–90, 195, 213; natural disasters, 201
Dominica. *See* Housing: Dominica
Drax Hall, 100, 123–24, 126–27, 138, 236
Droughts, 198, 201, 203
DWIGC. *See* Danish West India and Guinea Company
DWIGC warehouse, 191, 197, 199, 215

Earl of Balcarres, 116, 118–20
Edwards, Bryan, 54, 87, 102, 109, 145
Emancipation: Bahamas, 150; Nevis, 47, 55; St. Kitts, 21, 41
Enslaved labor: coffee plantations, 122; domestic service, 91–92, 97, 107–9, 146, 149, 162, 188; field, 149, 175, 179; French Guiana, 173; military, 217, 220, 223, 236; Nevis, 46; task-based, 173; tradesmen, 11, 92, 100, 103, 109, 138, 162, 182; wharves, 117, 194, 198, 204, 206

Falmouth, 88, 91, 107; Bend-Down Market, 104
Falmouth Heritage Renewal, 92

Favard, Michel, 178–79
Fencing, stone, 124, 137–38, 150, 153, 158
Flooring: clay, 224, 235; earthen, 40, 126, 178, 180, 182; elevated, 32, 34, 37, 158, 235; plastered, 22, 126, 131, 134, 138, 153, 158, 160–61; shell, 215; stone, 49, 59, 214–15; wooden, 34, 40, 81, 100, 125–26, 196, 230
Forest clearing, 44–46, 131
Fort Christiansvaern, 189, 191, 206
Fort Shirley, 224, 230
French Guiana: annatto production, 171–72; building materials, 176; clove production, 171; ecology, 168, 170, 182; enslaved labor, 168–69, 173; internal markets, 183–84; Kourou, 167; plantations, 166, 183, 186; re-establishment of slavery, 17, 67, 175, 184; Roura, 174–75; water-based travel, 179, 183–84
French Revolution, 74, 85, 117, 174; abolition of slavery, 67, 84

Galways Plantation, 22; village, 22–23
Gambier Bluff, 153, 155, 158, 160–61, 164
Gardelin Code. *See* Slavery: slave codes
Gardens, house-yard, 20, 54, 57, 89, 99, 106–7, 130, 144, 183. *See also* Yards
Garrison Plantation, Maryland, 211
Good Hope Archaeological Project, 92, 97
Good Hope Estate, 88, 106, 108; burial ground, 97; enslaved population, 89, 91; great house, 92; house sizes, 100; village, 89, 93
Guadeloupe, 66–67, 186; architectural shifts, 68, 174; British occupation of, 67; first abolition of slavery, 67; reestablishment of slavery, 67, 71; slave uprisings, 67–68
Guiana Shield, 167, 187
Guyane Française. *See* French Guiana

Habitation Coquenda, 73
Habitation Crève Coeur, 74–75, 77
Habitation Grande Pointe, 68, 70, 73, 75
Habitation Guyonneau, 73–75, 77
Habitation la Caroline, 174–75, 178–80; enslaved population, 179
Habitation la Grande Marée, 174–76, 184–86; enslaved population, 175
Habitation la Mahaudière, 68, 70–71, 73, 75

Haitian Revolution, 67, 69, 117, 169, 174
Hamilton, Alexander, 190
Hilton, John, 44–45
Housing: Bahamas, 4, 21, 143; Barbados, 21, 36, 49; barracks-style, 4, 77, 112; board, 125, 134; cartographic depictions of, 24, 54, 191, 194, 226, 232; contemporary descriptions of, 23–25, 29, 123, 191; domestic servants, 107, 110, 112; Dominica, 80–83; field houses, 129; French Guiana, 184; hall-and-parlor, 143–44, 153, 155, 160, 162, 164; "improved," 75, 142–43, 146, 160, 163; Jamaica, 23, 102, 124; Martinique, 75; masonry, 49, 71, 73, 75, 77, 79, 142, 150, 160, 164; moveable structures, 63, 82–83; Nevis, 23, 48, 55; photographic representations of, 25–26, 63, 82, 127; postemancipation, 29, 40, 55, 60, 63, 77, 85; row houses, 146, 160, 164; shifts in construction, 17, 29, 37, 73–74, 174; shingle, 40, 125, 134; single-room, 50, 143, 160; on slopes, 78, 84; St. Eustatius, 22; St. John, 22; St. Kitts, 20, 25, 40; stone, 62, 125, 128, 146, 196; two-room, 24, 177
Hurricanes, 49, 182, 189, 191, 196–98, 201–3, 235, 248

Jamaica, 47, 52; coffee production, 117, 119; contemporary depictions of housing, 87–88; early plantation archaeology, 124; enslaved labor, 106, 118; house forms, 4, 54–55, 99; internal markets, 139
Jessups Estate, 52

Kaz en gaulettes. See Construction techniques: kaz en gaulettes

Labor. See Enslaved labor; Postemancipation: labor
Labor, indentured, 44–45
Limestone. See Building materials: limestone
Lindsay, Alexander, 116, 118. See also Earl of Balcarres
Lindsay, James, 116, 120. See also Earl of Balcarres

Manioc, 175, 179
Markets. See Slavery: internal markets

Marshall's Pen, 10, 99, 106, 116–20, 122–23, 138–39; building materials, 131; landscape changes, 131; Negro House Hill, 130–31
Martinique, 66–67, 186; British occupation of, 67, 174; slave uprisings, 67
Martin's Hill, 119–20, 123
Masonry. See Housing: masonry
Model cottages. See Bahamas: model cottages
Montpelier Estate, 99, 106, 113, 124–27
Montserrat, housing, 23
Morant Bay Rebellion, 239
Morgan's Village, 50, 55–56, 58, 60
Morne Patate, 79–80

Napoleonic Wars, 118
Natural disasters, 196–97, 201–3, 214
Nevis: building materials, 45; ecology, 45; enslaved population, 44, 52; indentured servitude, 44; traditional potters, 61
Newfield estate, 143, 148, 150, 155; enslaved population, 148; octagonal house, 153, 158–59
New Green, 120, 123, 129
Nutmeg, 170–71, 175

Plantations, infrastructure, 42, 44, 117. See also Coffee: plantations; Cotton: plantations; Sugar plantations
Plaster. See Building materials: plaster; Flooring: plastered; Walls: plastered
Port cities, 45, 91–92, 107, 188, 216
Postemancipation: labor, 47, 64, 117; Nevis, 47; St. Kitts, 41
Postemancipation housing: Bahamas, 36; St. Kitts, 25. See also Housing: postemancipation
Prince Rupert's Bay, 221, 223
Provision grounds, 20, 48, 52, 54, 58, 107, 113, 122, 130, 239

Ramsay, James, 23, 142
Roofing: clay tile, 49; gabled, 59, 62, 65; hipped, 153; shingled, 21, 32, 49, 81, 126, 182; thatch, 22, 24–25, 30, 36, 50, 52, 81, 99, 126
Roucou. See Annatto
Roucouerie. See Annatto: production of
Royal African Company, 46

Sécheries. *See* Clove: production of
Seven Years' War, 67
Seville, 10, 100, 104, 106, 124, 126–28
Shingles. *See* Building materials: shingles;
     Housing: shingle; Roofing: shingled
Sixth West India Regiment, 236
Slave narratives, 205
Slave Registration Act, Bahamas, 150
Slavery: demographics, 93, 144, 147–49, 163,
     175, 179, 190; health and disease, 44, 198,
     200, 202–6, 213–14, 223; internal markets,
     37, 40–41, 104, 107, 113, 130, 139, 183–84,
     203, 214; military service, 220; movement
     of people, 92, 107; reform movement,
     70–71, 195; slave codes, 20, 71, 142, 202,
     204, 213, 239; social differentiation, 22,
     34, 38, 40, 88, 138–39, 159, 162, 221; social
     relations, 39, 99, 106, 239; uprisings, 67,
     69–70, 190, 201, 204, 226. *See also* Village
     organization; Villages
Slave trade: Danish, 194, 213; transatlantic,
     17, 46, 117–18, 139, 142, 145, 174, 184,
     194–95
Smith, John, 45
Spanish wall. *See* Construction techniques:
     Spanish wall
St. Christopher. *See* St. Kitts
St. Croix: building materials, 197; natural di-
     sasters, 202–3; water management, 198–99
St. Domingue, abolition of slavery, 67
St. Eustatius, 21–22, 46
St. John, 22, 189; slave uprisings, 201
St. Kitts, 19
Storage, 42, 62, 83, 144, 150, 200, 215, 232,
     236
Storehouses, 30, 45, 179, 194, 211, 226
St. Thomas, 189, 197, 202
Sugar: European markets for, 116–17, 169, 213
Sugarcane. *See* Building materials: cane;
     Walls: caned
Sugar Loaf, 79–80
Sugar plantations: French Guiana, 172; Gua-
     deloupe, 68; Nevis, 42, 45; St. Kitts, 19, 30
Sugar production, 4, 117, 169–70, 194, 213;
     Cuba, 4; French Guiana, 166, 169; French
     West Indies, 67; Jamaica, 88, 92, 117;

Nevis, 42, 48; St. Domingue, 117, 169; St.
     Kitts, 19
Surinam (Dutch colony), 187

Terracing. *See* Construction techniques:
     terracing
Tharp, John, 88–89, 92, 108
Tharp House, 92, 97, 107–8
Tharp Wharf, 91–92
Thatch. *See* Building materials: thatch; Roof-
     ing: thatch
Troup, Jonathan, 223–24, 233

Urban slavery, 97, 107–8, 189, 194, 204, 213;
     housing, 97, 198

Vaughn's Village, 50, 55, 58, 60
Vernacular architecture, 22, 60–61, 228, 238;
     Nevis, 43, 48, 58, 60–62, 64–65; St. Kitts,
     29, 40
Village organization, 20, 49–50, 52–53, 55, 58,
     60, 78; Bahamas, 21; compounds, 32, 50, 75,
     93, 110–11, 113, 124, 129–32, 137–39; linear,
     29, 50, 68, 73, 171, 174, 176, 180, 184, 191;
     privacy, 39, 43, 124; St. Kitts, 39; surveil-
     lance, 55, 60, 70, 73, 116, 127, 129, 138, 163,
     174; walls, 68–70, 93, 97
Villages: cartographic depictions of, 24–25,
     29, 50, 73, 77, 93; French West Indies, 75;
     relocation of, 73

Walls: caned, 23–24, 26, 29, 37, 40; plastered,
     21–22, 37, 59, 125, 146; stone, 146, 153, 155;
     wattle and daub, 26, 29–30, 32, 34, 36, 81,
     125, 146, 233, 235. *See also* Construction
     techniques; Village organization: walls
Water: acquisition of, 198–200, 203, 214; stor-
     age of, 198–200, 214
Wattle and daub. *See* Building materials: wattle
     and daub; Construction techniques: wattle
     and daub
West India Regiments, 217
Williams, Henry, 147
Williams, Henry M., 143, 147–48, 150, 152, 162
Wood, John, 141–43, 145, 160–61, 164; design
     principles, 141, 143–44, 146, 155, 162

Yards, 11, 39, 54, 104; burials, 11, 104, 137; communal, 95, 104, 110, 213; Drax Hall, 104; French Guiana, 182, 185; Good Hope Estate, 104; Marshall's Pen, 130; Nevis, 50, 53; Seville, 104; St. Kitts, 38. *See also* Gardens: house-yard

Yard sweeping, 11, 26, 93, 97, 99, 103, 108, 110; archaeological signature, 103–4

RIPLEY P. BULLEN SERIES

Florida Museum of Natural History

Tacachale: Essays on the Indians of Florida and Southeastern Georgia during the Historic Period, edited by Jerald T. Milanich and Samuel Proctor (1978)

Aboriginal Subsistence Technology on the Southeastern Coastal Plain during the Late Prehistoric Period, by Lewis H. Larson (1980)

Cemochechobee: Archaeology of a Mississippian Ceremonial Center on the Chattahoochee River, by Frank T. Schnell, Vernon J. Knight Jr., and Gail S. Schnell (1981)

Fort Center: An Archaeological Site in the Lake Okeechobee Basin, by William H. Sears, with contributions by Elsie O'R. Sears and Karl T. Steinen (1982)

Perspectives on Gulf Coast Prehistory, edited by Dave D. Davis (1984)

Archaeology of Aboriginal Culture Change in the Interior Southeast: Depopulation during the Early Historic Period, by Marvin T. Smith (1987)

Apalachee: The Land between the Rivers, by John H. Hann (1988)

Key Marco's Buried Treasure: Archaeology and Adventure in the Nineteenth Century, by Marion Spjut Gilliland (1989)

First Encounters: Spanish Explorations in the Caribbean and the United States, 1492–1570, edited by Jerald T. Milanich and Susan Milbrath (1989)

Missions to the Calusa, edited and translated by John H. Hann, with an introduction by William H. Marquardt (1991)

Excavations on the Franciscan Frontier: Archaeology at the Fig Springs Mission, by Brent Richards Weisman (1992)

The People Who Discovered Columbus: The Prehistory of the Bahamas, by William F. Keegan (1992)

Hernando de Soto and the Indians of Florida, by Jerald T. Milanich and Charles Hudson (1992)

Foraging and Farming in the Eastern Woodlands, edited by C. Margaret Scarry (1993)

Puerto Real: The Archaeology of a Sixteenth-Century Spanish Town in Hispaniola, edited by Kathleen Deagan (1995)

Political Structure and Change in the Prehistoric Southeastern United States, edited by John F. Scarry (1996)

Bioarchaeology of Native American Adaptation in the Spanish Borderlands, edited by Brenda J. Baker and Lisa Kealhofer (1996)

A History of the Timucua Indians and Missions, by John H. Hann (1996)

Archaeology of the Mid-Holocene Southeast, edited by Kenneth E. Sassaman and David G. Anderson (1996)

The Indigenous People of the Caribbean, edited by Samuel M. Wilson (1997; first paperback edition, 1999)

Hernando de Soto among the Apalachee: The Archaeology of the First Winter Encampment, by Charles R. Ewen and John H. Hann (1998)

The Timucuan Chiefdoms of Spanish Florida, by John E. Worth: vol. 1, *Assimilation*; vol. 2, *Resistance and Destruction* (1998; first paperback edition, 2020)

Ancient Earthen Enclosures of the Eastern Woodlands, edited by Robert C. Mainfort Jr. and Lynne P. Sullivan (1998)

An Environmental History of Northeast Florida, by James J. Miller (1998)

Precolumbian Architecture in Eastern North America, by William N. Morgan (1999)

Archaeology of Colonial Pensacola, edited by Judith A. Bense (1999)

Grit-Tempered: Early Women Archaeologists in the Southeastern United States, edited by Nancy Marie White, Lynne P. Sullivan, and Rochelle A. Marrinan (1999; first paperback edition, 2001)

Coosa: The Rise and Fall of a Southeastern Mississippian Chiefdom, by Marvin T. Smith (2000)

Religion, Power, and Politics in Colonial St. Augustine, by Robert L. Kapitzke (2001)

Bioarchaeology of Spanish Florida: The Impact of Colonialism, edited by Clark Spencer Larsen (2001)

Archaeological Studies of Gender in the Southeastern United States, edited by Jane M. Eastman and Christopher B. Rodning (2001)

The Archaeology of Traditions: Agency and History Before and After Columbus, edited by Timothy R. Pauketat (2001)

Foraging, Farming, and Coastal Biocultural Adaptation in Late Prehistoric North Carolina, by Dale L. Hutchinson (2002)

Windover: Multidisciplinary Investigations of an Early Archaic Florida Cemetery, edited by Glen H. Doran (2002)

Archaeology of the Everglades, by John W. Griffin (2002; first paperback edition, 2017)

Pioneer in Space and Time: John Mann Goggin and the Development of Florida Archaeology, by Brent Richards Weisman (2002)

Indians of Central and South Florida, 1513–1763, by John H. Hann (2003)

Presidio Santa María de Galve: A Struggle for Survival in Colonial Spanish Pensacola, edited by Judith A. Bense (2003)

Bioarchaeology of the Florida Gulf Coast: Adaptation, Conflict, and Change, by Dale L. Hutchinson (2004; first paperback edition, 2020)

The Myth of Syphilis: The Natural History of Treponematosis in North America, edited by Mary Lucas Powell and Della Collins Cook (2005)

The Florida Journals of Frank Hamilton Cushing, edited by Phyllis E. Kolianos and Brent R. Weisman (2005)

The Lost Florida Manuscript of Frank Hamilton Cushing, edited by Phyllis E. Kolianos and Brent R. Weisman (2005)

The Native American World Beyond Apalachee: West Florida and the Chattahoochee Valley, by John H. Hann (2006)

Tatham Mound and the Bioarchaeology of European Contact: Disease and Depopulation in Central Gulf Coast Florida, by Dale L. Hutchinson (2007)

Taíno Indian Myth and Practice: The Arrival of the Stranger King, by William F. Keegan (2007; first paperback edition, 2022)

An Archaeology of Black Markets: Local Ceramics and Economies in Eighteenth-Century Jamaica, by Mark W. Hauser (2008; first paperback edition, 2013)

Mississippian Mortuary Practices: Beyond Hierarchy and the Representationist Perspective, edited by Lynne P. Sullivan and Robert C. Mainfort Jr. (2010; first paperback edition, 2012)

Bioarchaeology of Ethnogenesis in the Colonial Southeast, by Christopher M. Stojanowski (2010; first paperback edition, 2013)

French Colonial Archaeology in the Southeast and Caribbean, edited by Kenneth G. Kelly and Meredith D. Hardy (2011; first paperback edition, 2015)

Late Prehistoric Florida: Archaeology at the Edge of the Mississippian World, edited by Keith Ashley and Nancy Marie White (2012; first paperback edition, 2015)

Early and Middle Woodland Landscapes of the Southeast, edited by Alice P. Wright and Edward R. Henry (2013; first paperback edition, 2019)

Trends and Traditions in Southeastern Zooarchaeology, edited by Tanya M. Peres (2014)

New Histories of Pre-Columbian Florida, edited by Neill J. Wallis and Asa R. Randall (2014; first paperback edition, 2016)

Discovering Florida: First-Contact Narratives from Spanish Expeditions along the Lower Gulf Coast, edited and translated by John E. Worth (2014; first paperback edition, 2016)

Constructing Histories: Archaic Freshwater Shell Mounds and Social Landscapes of the St. Johns River, Florida, by Asa R. Randall (2015)

Archaeology of Early Colonial Interaction at El Chorro de Maíta, Cuba, by Roberto Valcárcel Rojas (2016)

Fort San Juan and the Limits of Empire: Colonialism and Household Practice at the Berry Site, edited by Robin A. Beck, Christopher B. Rodning, and David G. Moore (2016)

Rethinking Moundville and Its Hinterland, edited by Vincas P. Steponaitis and C. Margaret Scarry (2016; first paperback edition, 2019)

Gathering at Silver Glen: Community and History in Late Archaic Florida, by Zackary I. Gilmore (2016)

Paleoindian Societies of the Coastal Southeast, by James S. Dunbar (2016; first paperback edition, 2019)

Cuban Archaeology in the Caribbean, edited by Ivan Roksandic (2016)

Handbook of Ceramic Animal Symbols in the Ancient Lesser Antilles, by Lawrence Waldron (2016)

Archaeologies of Slavery and Freedom in the Caribbean: Exploring the Spaces in Between, edited by Lynsey A. Bates, John M. Chenoweth, and James A. Delle (2016; first paperback edition, 2018)

Setting the Table: Ceramics, Dining, and Cultural Exchange in Andalucía and La Florida, by Kathryn L. Ness (2017)

Simplicity, Equality, and Slavery: An Archaeology of Quakerism in the British Virgin Islands, 1740–1780, by John M. Chenoweth (2017)

Fit for War: Sustenance and Order in the Mid-Eighteenth-Century Catawba Nation, by Mary Elizabeth Fitts (2017)

Water from Stone: Archaeology and Conservation at Florida's Springs, by Jason O'Donoughue (2017)

Mississippian Beginnings, edited by Gregory D. Wilson (2017; first paperback edition, 2019)

Harney Flats: A Florida Paleoindian Site, by I. Randolph Daniel Jr. and Michael Wisenbaker (2017)

Honoring Ancestors in Sacred Space: The Archaeology of an Eighteenth-Century African-Bahamian Cemetery, by Grace Turner (2017)

Investigating the Ordinary: Everyday Matters in Southeast Archaeology, edited by Sarah E. Price and Philip J. Carr (2018)

New Histories of Village Life at Crystal River, by Thomas J. Pluckhahn and Victor D. Thompson (2018)

Early Human Life on the Southeastern Coastal Plain, edited by Albert C. Goodyear and Christopher R. Moore (2018; first paperback edition, 2021)

The Archaeology of Villages in Eastern North America, edited by Jennifer Birch and Victor D. Thompson (2018)

The Cumberland River Archaic of Middle Tennessee, edited by Tanya M. Peres and Aaron Deter-Wolf (2019)

Pre-Columbian Art of the Caribbean, by Lawrence Waldron (2019)

Iconography and Wetsite Archaeology of Florida's Watery Realms, edited by Ryan Wheeler and Joanna Ostapkowicz (2019)

New Directions in the Search for the First Floridians, edited by David K. Thulman and Ervan G. Garrison (2019)

Archaeology of Domestic Landscapes of the Enslaved in the Caribbean, edited by James A. Delle and Elizabeth C. Clay (2019; first paperback edition, 2022)

Cahokia in Context: Hegemony and Diaspora, edited by Charles H. McNutt and Ryan M. Parish (2020)

Bears: Archaeological and Ethnohistorical Perspectives in Native Eastern North America, edited by Heather A. Lapham and Gregory A. Waselkov (2020)

Contact, Colonialism, and Native Communities in the Southeastern United States, edited by Edmond A. Boudreaux III, Maureen Meyers, and Jay K. Johnson (2020)

An Archaeology and History of a Caribbean Sugar Plantation on Antigua, edited by Georgia L. Fox (2020)

Modeling Entradas: Sixteenth-Century Assemblages in North America, edited by Clay Mathers (2020)

Archaeology in Dominica: Everyday Ecologies and Economies at Morne Patate, edited by Mark W. Hauser and Diane Wallman (2020)

The Making of Mississippian Tradition, by Christina M. Friberg (2020)

The Historical Turn in Southeastern Archaeology, edited by Robbie Ethridge and Eric E. Bowne (2020)

Falls of the Ohio Archaeology: Archaeology of Native American Settlement, edited by David Pollack, Anne Tobbe Bader, and Justin N. Carlson (2021)

A History of Platform Mound Ceremonialism: Finding Meaning in Elevated Ground, by Megan C. Kassabaum (2021)

New Methods and Theories for Analyzing Mississippian Imagery, edited by Bretton T. Giles and Shawn P. Lambert (2021)

Methods, Mounds, and Missions: New Contributions to Florida Archaeology, edited by Ann S. Cordell and Jeffrey M. Mitchem (2021)

Unearthing the Missions of Spanish Florida, edited by Tanya M. Peres and Rochelle A. Marrinan (2021)

Presidios of Spanish West Florida, by Judith A. Bense (2022)

www.ingramcontent.com/pod-product-compliance
Lightning Source LLC
Chambersburg PA
CBHW071015280326
41935CB00011B/1365